TOWARDS A
LIBERTARIAN SOCIALISM

Reflections on the British Labour
Party and European Working-
Class Movements

G.D.H. COLE

TOWARDS A
LIBERTARIAN SOCIALISM

Reflections on the British Labour Party and European Working-Class Movements

G.D.H. COLE

Edited by David Goodway

ISBN: 978-1-84935-389-2
E-ISBN: 978-1-84935-390-8
Library of Congress Control Number: 2020933547

AK Press   AK Press
370 Ryan Ave. #100   33 Tower St.
Chico, CA 95973   Edinburgh EH6 7BN
United States   Scotland
www.akpress.org   www.akuk.com
akpress@akpress.org   ak@akedin.demon.co.uk

The above addresses would be delighted to provide you with the latest AK Press distribution
catalog, which features books, pamphlets, zines, and stylish apparel published and/or distributed by AK Press. Alternatively, visit our websites for the complete catalog, latest news, and
secure ordering.

Printed in the United States on acid-free paper

Cover design by Morgan Buck
Interior design by Margaret Killjoy, www.birdsbeforethestorm.net

CONTENTS

For Peter and Denise Hirschmann,
friends indeed

G.D.H. COLE: A LIBERTARIAN TRAPPED IN THE LABOUR PARTY

From the 1920s until his death in 1959, G.D.H. Cole was the pre-eminent Labour intellectual, surpassing Harold Laski and R.H. Tawney in the proliferation of his publications and general omnipresence. His *History of the Labour Party from 1914* (1948) was, for many years, the standard text.[1]

Yet Colin Ward was to comment in *Anarchy* that he had been

> amazed as I read the tributes in the newspapers from people like Hugh Gaitskell and Harold Wilson alleging that *their* socialism had been learned from him...for it had always seemed to me that *his* socialism was of an entirely different character from that of the politicians of the Labour Party. Among his obituarists, it was left to a dissident Jugoslav communist, Vladimir

---

1 Peter Ackers concurs, describing Cole as '*the* central intellectual figure of the interwar British left.' Peter Ackers, 'An Industrial Relations Perspective on Employee Participation', in Adrian Wilkinson, Paul J. Gollan, Mick Marchington, and David Lewin (eds), *The Oxford Handbook of Participation in Organizations* (Oxford: Oxford University Press, 2010), 59. The emphasis is Ackers's.

Dedijer, to point what the difference was; remarking on his discovery that Cole 'rejected the idea of the continued supremacy of the State' and believed that 'it was destined to disappear'.[2]

Ward appreciated that Cole was a socialist pluralist. Indeed his major intellectual and organizational effort had been to Guild Socialism.

***

The origins of Guild Socialism are customarily traced to 1906 and the publication by Arthur J. Penty of *The Restoration of the Gild System*. Penty's advocacy of a return to a handicraft economy and the control of production by trade guilds looks back, beyond William Morris, to—as he cheerfully indicates—John Ruskin. He had been a member of the West Yorkshire avant-garde responsible for the foundation of Leeds Arts Club, in which the dominant personality was A.R. Orage, who himself moved to London, taking over (with Holbrook Jackson, another Leeds man) the weekly *New Age* in 1907. Orage had a very considerable input in the emergence of Guild Socialism in the *New Age*'s columns. He published a series of articles in 1912–13 by S.G. Hobson, an Ulsterman then managing a banana plantation in British Honduras, and when Orage collected these as *National Guilds* he located the kernel of Hobson's ideas in Penty's work and also an article of his own (Orage had certainly collaborated with Penty in the development of *The Restoration of the Gild System*), yet these attributions were to be forcefully denied by Hobson, himself.[3]

In contrast to Penty, Hobson envisaged the trade unions converting themselves into enormous National Guilds which would take over the running of modern productive industry as well as distribution and exchange. An anonymous article in the *Syndicalist*, written presumably by the editor Guy Bowman, complained:

> Middle-class of the middle-class, with all the shortcomings…of the middle-classes writ large across it, 'Guild Socialism' stands forth as the latest lucubration of the middle-class mind. It is a

2 Colin Ward, 'The State and Society', *Anarchy* 14 (April 1962), 115. This was the text of a lecture given to the Cole Society (Oxford University's then Sociology Society). Ward emphasized the pluralism of G.D.H. Cole [hereafter GDHC], *Scope and Method in Social and Political Theory: An Inaugural Lecture: Delivered before the University of Oxford on 9 November 1945* (Oxford: Clarendon Press, 1945), 14–16. Cole's inaugural is reprinted in GDHC, *Essays in Social Theory* (London: Macmillan, 1950).

3 David Goodway, *Anarchist Seeds Beneath the Snow: Left-Libertarian Thought and British Writers from William Morris to Colin Ward* (Oakland, CA: PM Press, 2nd edn., 2012), 27–28.

'cool steal' of the leading ideas of Syndicalism and a deliberate perversion of them. We do not so much object to the term 'guild' as applied to the various autonomous industries, linked together for the service of the common weal, such as advocated by Syndicalism. But we do protest against the 'state' idea which is associated with it in Guild Socialism.[4]

As Hobson/Orage explained, alongside and independent of the 'Guild Congress' the State would remain 'with its Government, its Parliament, and its civil and military machinery....Certainly independent; probably even supreme.'[5] There was considerable justice in the *Syndicalist*'s much-quoted indictment of what was undeniably a very middle-class form of socialism, yet Guild Socialism was theoretically more important than it could allow, as it was to become more original and also non-statist. While Hobson seems to have been responsible for initiating the primary features of Guild Socialism, its principal British thinker, pushing far beyond his and Orage's conception, was Cole, a very young Oxford don before the war and research officer to the Amalgamated Society of Engineers during it. (I use the qualification 'British' with deliberation since Cole's rival in originality was Ramiro de Maeztu, a Spaniard working in London as a newspaper correspondent between 1905 and 1919. The articles he contributed to the *New Age* in 1915 and 1916 were collected as *Authority, Liberty and Function in the Light of the War* [1916][6].)

***

George Douglas Howard Cole was born in 1889 in Cambridge, the son of George Cole, a pawnbroker, and his wife Jessie (née Knowles), whose father kept a high-class bootshop in Bond Street. The Coles soon moved to Ealing, west London, where George Cole was able to acquire a flourishing estate agents.[7] Douglas (as he was always known) was educated at St Paul's School,

---

4 *Syndicalist*, February 1914.

5 A.R. Orage (ed.), *National Guilds: An Inquiry into the Wage System and the Way Out* (London: G. Bell, 1914), 263.

6 For Maeztu, see: Wallace Martin, '*The New Age*' under Orage: Chapters in English Cultural History* (Manchester: Manchester University Press, 1967), 225–34; Rowland Kenney, *Westering: An Autobiography* (London: J.M. Dent, 1939), 202–04; Donald L. Shaw, *The Generation of 1898 in Spain* (London: Ernest Benn, 1975), chap. 4.

7 Unless otherwise stated, details of Cole's life are taken from the biography by his wife, Margaret Cole [hereafter MC], *The Life of G.D.H. Cole* (London: Macmillan, 1971). There have been only two full-length studies of his work: L.P. Carpenter, *G.D.H. Cole: An Intellectual Biography* (Cambridge: Cambridge University Press, 1973), and A.W. Wright,

Hammersmith; and it was, he recalled in 1951, while a schoolboy that he became a socialist:

> I was converted, quite simply, by reading William Morris's *News from Nowhere*, which made me feel, suddenly and irrecoverably, that there was nothing except a Socialist that it was possible for me to be. I did not at once join any Socialist body. I was only sixteen....My Socialism, at that stage, had very little to do with parliamentary politics, my instinctive aversion from which has never left me—and never will. Converted by reading Morris's utopia, I became a Utopian Socialist, and I suppose that is what I have been all my life since. I became a Socialist... on grounds of morals and decency and aesthetic sensibility. I wanted to do the decent thing by my fellow-men: I could not see why every human being should not have as good a chance in life as I; and I hated the ugliness of both of poverty and of the money-grubbing way of life that I saw around me as its complement. I still think these are three excellent reasons for being a Socialist: indeed, I know no others as good. They have nothing to do with any particular economic theory, or theory of history: they are not based on any worship of efficiency, or of the superior virtue or the historic mission of the working class. They have nothing to do with Marxism, or Fabianism, or even Labourism—although all these have no doubt a good deal to do with them. They are simple affirmations about the root principles of comely and decent human relations, leading irresistibly to a Socialist conclusion.[8]

He joined the Ealing branch of the Independent Labour Party (ILP) shortly before leaving school and then, a few months later, 'I celebrated my first week in Oxford by joining the University Fabian Society and its parent body in London...'[9]

G.D.H. Cole and Socialist Democracy (Oxford: Clarendon Press, 1979). Wright provides the most useful bibliography since it includes a partial listing of Cole's immense output of articles (283–96). The G.D.H. Cole Papers, Nuffield College, Oxford, are as confusing as they are voluminous, and need to be supplemented by supernumerary boxes and bound volumes of pamphlets and off-prints. (I am indebted to Clare Kavanagh for assistance in locating specific items.)

8 GDHC, *British Labour Movement—Retrospect and Prospect*, Fabian Special 8 (London: Fabian Publications and Victor Gollancz, 1951), 3–4.

9 Ibid, 4.

From 1908 he read Mods and Greats (Classics) at Balliol, graduating in 1912. He accepted a lectureship in philosophy at Armstrong College, Newcastle-upon-Tyne, which oddly he loathed, but was almost immediately rescued by being elected to a seven-year Prize Fellowship at Magdalen College, Oxford. His first book, *The World of Labour: A Discussion of the Present and Future of Trade Unionism*, an admired and influential study of developments in the USA, France, Germany, Sweden, and Italy as well as Britain, was published as early as 1913. What impressed him was the way in which contemporary syndicalist tendencies believed it possible to progress to workers' control of industry without reference to parliamentary institutions. In *The World of Labour* he is also found discovering Guild Socialism from the pages of the *New Age*. Raymond Postgate, his future brother-in-law, recollected that

> A schoolboy friend lent me *The World of Labour*, taking it away when I had read it through, and forcing me to buy my own copy—which I was glad enough to do, for it had in fact opened a completely new world to me. The education which I, and every other middle-class boy, had received, had not referred to one single thing mentioned in the book.[10]

Cole's intellectual and political commitment to the trade-union movement deepened in 1915 when he was appointed as an unpaid research officer to the Amalgamated Society of Engineers (ASE), the first university graduate to be engaged by a British union. His conscientious objection to conscription was allowed as long as he undertook this work of 'national importance'.[11] Cole, an astonishingly prolific author throughout his life, was particularly fecund between 1917 and 1920 when he published four books on Guild Socialism— *Self-Government in Industry*, *Social Theory*, *Chaos and Order in Industry* and, the most systematic exposition, *Guild Socialism Re-stated*—another four with major Guild Socialist bearings, together with several pamphlets and many articles on the subject.[12] He developed a highly original theory of functional democracy, rejecting democratic representative government in favour of a pluralistic society in which representation would be functional—that is, derived from all the functional groups of which the individual is a member (the most

---

10 Written for MC, *Life*, 59. Cf C.E.M. Joad, *The Book of Joad: A Belligerent Autobiography* (1932; London: Faber and Faber, 1943 edn), 12–13.

11 For Beatrice Webb's entertaining take on Cole's appointment, see *The Diary of Beatrice Webb*, ed. Norman MacKenzie and Jeanne MacKenzie (London: Virago and London School of Economics and Political Science, 4 vols, 1982–85), III, 247–48.

12 See the selective bibliography for articles and pamphlets, 1914–24, in Wright, *G.D.H. Cole*, 286–88.

important are named as political, vocational, appetitive, religious, provident, philanthropic, sociable and theoretic), final decisions having to emerge as a consensus between the different groups, not as the fiats of a sovereign authority:

> There must be...as many separately elected groups of represen-
> tatives as there are distinct essential groups of functions to be
> performed. Smith cannot represent Brown, Jones and Robinson
> as human beings; for a human being, as an individual, is funda-
> mentally incapable of being represented. He can only represent
> the common point of view which Brown, Jones and Robinson
> hold in relation to some definite social purpose, or group of
> connected purposes. Brown, Jones and Robinson must there-
> fore have, not one vote each, but as many different functional
> votes as there are different questions calling for associative ac-
> tion in which they are interested.[13]

Much of Cole's conception of a fully participatory society had its origins in Rousseau, whose *Social Contract* and *The Discourses* he translated for the Everyman's Library edition of 1913, though Morris, whom he described as 'of the same blood as National Guildsmen', was, as has been seen, the major lifelong influence on Cole.[14] The Anglican theologian, John Neville Figgis, and the legal historian F.W. Maitland need also to be mentioned since the Guild Socialists in general were much impressed by their pluralism. It was Maitland's partial translation of part of the great German jurist Otto von Gierke's monu-mental *Das Deutsche Genossenschaftsrecht* as *Political Theories of the Middle Ages* in 1900 which introduced into English the notion of the 'real personality' of groups and the appreciation that churches, trade unions, or whatever were not necessarily the subordinates of but co-existed with the State.[15]

---

13 GDHC, *Guild Socialism Re-Stated* (London: Leonard Parsons, 1920), 33. GDHC, *Social Theory* (London: Methuen, 3rd edn, 1923), 66–72, classifies the range of functional associations.

14 GDHC, *Self-Government in Industry* (London: G. Bell, 1917), 121. For Morris, see also ibid., 119–22, 280, 302. For the debt to Rousseau, see GDHC, 'Conflicting Social Obligations', *Proceedings of the Aristotelian Society*, XV (1915), an important paper in the evolution of Cole's ideas; and GDHC, *Essays*, chap. 8.

15 For Figgis and Maitland: Ernest Barker, *Political Thought in England, 1848 to 1914* (2nd edn., 1928; Westport, CT: Greenwood Press, 1980), 15–16, 175–83; David Nicholls, *The Pluralist State: The Political Ideas of J.N. Figgis and His Contemporaries* (Basingstoke: Macmillan and St Antony's College, Oxford, 2nd edn., 1994); Paul Q. Hirst (ed.), *The Pluralist Theory of the State: Selected Writings of G.D.H. Cole, J.N. Figgis, and H.J. Laski* (London: Routledge, 1989). For appreciations of Cole's contribution to political theory, see—in addition to

The National Guilds League had been set up belatedly in 1915, and from 1916 published the *Guildsman* (initially from Clydeside, significantly). R.H. Tawney joined the National Guilds League and one of his most impressive works, *The Acquisitive Society* (1921), bears the imprint of the Guild Socialist emphasis on function. By the end of the war, the mental landscape of much of the labour movement had been, although only temporarily, transformed. Tawney commented in 1920:

> It is a commonplace that during the past six years the discussion of industrial and social problems has shifted its centre. Prior to the war students and reformers were principally occupied with questions of poverty. Today their main interest appears to be the government of industry. An increasing number of trade unionists regard poverty as a symptom of a more deeply rooted malady which they would describe as industrial autocracy and demand 'control'.[16]

But the traditional moderation of British trade unions was soon to reassert itself; the first phase of the interwar depression arrived during the second half of 1920, overwhelming the chances of success for militant action; and the Labour Party's electoral advances, above all the breakthrough in the election of 1922, went far to restore faith in parliamentarianism and to set the British working class, after the decade-long dalliance of some of its sections with libertarian alternatives, firmly on the parliamentary road to socialism. Cole and his wife

---

Wright, *G.D.H. Cole*, and Carpenter—C.E.M. Joad, *Introduction to Modern Political Theory* (Oxford: Clarendon Press, 1924), 74–86; Carole Pateman, *Participation and Democratic Theory* (Cambridge: Cambridge University Press, 1970), 35–42; Darrow Schecter, *Radical Theories: Paths Beyond Marxism and Social Democracy* (Manchester: Manchester University Press, 1994), 111–24, 182–86; Geoffrey Ostergaard, *The Tradition of Workers' Control: Selected Writings*, ed. Brian Bamford (London: Freedom Press, 1997), 55–80; Marc Stears, *Progressives, Pluralists, and the Problems of the State: Ideologies of Reform in the United States and Britain, 1909–1926* (2002; Oxford: Oxford University Press, paperback edn, 2006), esp. chaps. 3, 5, 6. (Ostergaard had been a doctoral student of Cole's in the early 1950s.) For Cole's self-assessment: GDHC, *The Development of Socialism During the Past Fifty Years* (London: Athlone Press, 1952), 15–17; GDHC, *A History of Socialist Thought* (London: Macmillan, 5 vols, 1953–60), III, Part 1, 242–48. For an excellent evaluation of Guild Socialism—and Cole's place within it—there is Anthony W. Wright, 'Guild Socialism Revisited', *Journal of Contemporary History* IX, 1 (January 1974), 165–80 (reprinted in Tony Wright, *Doing Politics* [London: Backbite, 2012]).

16 R.H. Tawney, 'Foreword' to Carter L. Goodrich, *The Frontier of Control: A Study in British Workshop Politics* (New York: Harcourt, Brace & Howe, 1920), vii.

Margaret—they had married in 1918—had, from 1919, edited for the National Guilds League the *Guildsman*, which they kept going as the *Guild Socialist* until 1923, and then brought out their own *New Standards*. The twelve issues of the monthly *New Standards* melded Guild Socialism with working-class adult education of which, particularly the Workers' Educational Association (WEA), Cole was also a fervent and lifelong proponent.[17] That Arthur Penty and G.K. Chesterton were among the contributors is indicative of the eclectic sources of Guild Socialism. The Coles were obliged to admit defeat in 1924 with the termination of *New Standards*, overwhelmed by the statism of both the Labour and the Communist Parties. Although many of his fellow Guild Socialists—together they had converted the Fabian Research Department into the Labour Research Department—had become Communists, Cole himself reluctantly transferred his allegiance to the Labour Party, resigning from the Labour Research Department in 1924 when the Communists took complete control.[18]

Beatrice Webb was, according to Margaret Cole, 'fond of describing herself and her husband as belonging to "the B's of the world", who, she explained were "bourgeois, bureaucratic, and benevolent", in contrast to the "A's"—as for example Bertrand Russell, G.D.H. Cole, and a good many others, who were "aristocratic, anarchist, and artistic"'.[19] It was in 1922 that Orage, although by then obsessed by Social Credit and his spiritual self-development, abandoned the *New Age*, to counter whose youthful and provincial 'anarchism' the Webbs had launched in 1913 the aptly titled *New Statesman*; and it was the latter's metropolitan 'bureaucracy' which was to flourish in the coming decades. Paradoxically, Cole was a major contributor of political journalism to the *New Statesman* from 1918 until his death (and under Kingsley Martin's editorship he became an influential advisor after 1930). Significant decentralizing tendencies in Labour's policies were to be extinguished by the economic and political crisis of 1931 and the adherence to planning.

Back in 1908 Cole had joined first the ILP and then the Fabian Society, membership of either conferring membership of the Labour Party (which was not possible to join directly until 1918). He considered in 1951:

17 For Cole and workers' education, see Lawrence Goldman, *Dons and Workers: Oxford and Adult Education Since 1850* (Oxford: Clarendon Press, 1995), 147–51, 180–83; Carpenter, 115–19.

18 For marriage and Guild Socialism, Cole's *Life* may be supplemented by Margaret Cole's attractive autobiography: MC, *Growing Up into Revolution* (London: Longmans, Green, 1949). See too MC, 'Guild Socialism and the Labour Research Department', in Asa Briggs and John Saville (eds.), *Essays in Labour History, 1886–1923* (London: Macmillan, 1971). There is also a biography of MC: Betty D. Vernon, *Margaret Cole, 1893–1980: A Political Biography* (London: Croom Helm, 1986).

19 MC, *Beatrice Webb* (London: Longmans, Green, 1945), 65–66. See also GDHC, 'What Next? Anarchists or Bureaucrats?', *Fabian Journal*, no. 12 (April 1954), 30–31.

I do not think I ever, though I became a Fabian, contemplated a gradual evolution into Socialism by a cumulative process of social reforms. My notion of the advent of Socialism was always catastrophic, whether it should come late or soon.

Also in 1951, in his Webb Memorial Lecture, he remarked: 'The Communists are entirely correct in holding that Socialism, as a way of life, cannot be established except by revolution...' Further, in 1908, he had 'no love for the Labour Party':

I was never in the very least a 'Lib-Lab'; and the last thought that could ever have entered my head would have been to look hopefully on the Labour Party as the heir to the Liberal tradition....The Labour Party of the years between 1906 and 1914 was much too 'Lib-Lab' for me.[20]

This attitude persisted and, as Asa Briggs observed, 'Cole was bound to be a peripheral figure in Britain rather than at the centre', because 'the "Lib-Lab" approach to politics has been the foundation of Labour's effective power or share of power in twentieth-century British society...'[21] The ILP appointed Cole (who was without an academic post between 1919 and 1922) to the writing staff of its *Labour Leader* in January 1921, incorporating the following year the Guild Socialist programme of industrial democracy based on workers' control into its new constitution.[22]

***

During the 1920s, on the rebound from the failure of Guild Socialism as a movement, he cosied up to political Labour, becoming especially close to his old friend Clifford Allen, chairman of the ILP (1923–26). Cole was, however, sceptical about the ILP's campaign for 'Socialism in Our Time' in 1925–26,

---

20 GDHC, *British Labour Movement*, 5; GDHC, *Development*, 30.

21 Asa Briggs, 'The Intellectuals and the Labour Movement: G.D.H. Cole', *Listener*, 20 October 1960. For Briggs's overall assessment of Cole, see also John McIlroy, 'Asa Briggs and the Emergence of Labour History in Post-War Britain', *Labour History Review* LXXVII (2012), 218–19. In 1953, Cole was unconvincingly asserting that the Labour Party was ideologically Fabian (GDHC, 'The Socialism of British Labour', *Review of International Affairs*, nos. 10 and 11 [16 May, 1 June 1953]).

22 Robert E. Dowse, *Left in the Centre: The Independent Labour Party, 1893–1940* (London: Longmans, 1966), 65–69, 209–11; GDHC, *A History of the Labour Party from 1914* (London: Routledge and Kegan Paul, 1948), 149–50.

considering its central demand for a living wage economically fraudulent. L.P. Carpenter concludes: 'The deficiencies of the left virtually forced Cole to turn to parliamentary reformism'. Indeed, in 1930, he was adopted as Labour parliamentary candidate for Birmingham King's Norton, although he was able to rescue himself from this temperamental misjudgement the following year when his diabetes was diagnosed and the candidacy abandoned. He had rejoined the Fabian Society in 1928, having resigned in 1915, and presumably remained a member of the ILP until its disaffiliation from the Labour Party in 1932. It has not proved possible to ascertain whether he ever took out direct membership of the Labour Party.[23]

Cole's newly pragmatic outlook was signified in 1929 by *The Next Ten Years in British Economic and Social Policy*, a very substantial work intended to provide guidelines for a future Labour government, and in which he accepted state planning and limited state socialism with the nationalization of some industries. As will be seen in greater detail later, he was always at pains to speak of 'socialization', only one form of which was nationalization. Socialization, he explained in 1929, would

> certainly involve the transference of a large number of enterprises now in private hands to various forms of public ownership and administration; but it does not involve either universal public ownership, or any one form of control or management in industry. As Socialism develops, the forms of 'socialization' are likely to be very diverse; and their diversity will be a source of strength.[24]

In *The Next Ten Years* Cole went so far as to advocate a voluntary National Labour Corps for the unemployed from which they might be expelled for failing to do satisfactory work: 'The directors of the corps would thus retain the power of preventing its efficiency and morale from being lowered by the presence of slackers or unemployables', yet 'the unemployed man, on his side, would be subject to no sort of coercion beyond the necessary measure of discipline which he had voluntarily accepted in agreeing to join the corps'. He was rewarded in 1930 with membership, alongside Keynes, of MacDonald's Economic Advisory Council.[25]

---

23 MC, *Life*, 161–63; Carpenter, 130–32. For 'Socialism in Our Time', see GDHC, *History of the Labour Party*, esp. 197–200. The circumstances of Cole's resignation from the Fabian Society are recounted in *Diary of Beatrice Webb*, III, 229–30.

24 GDHC, *The Next Ten Years in British Economic and Social Policy* (London: Macmillan, 1929), 131.

25 Ibid., 52; MC, *Life*, 167–68; Carpenter, 145–46.

L.R. Phelps, Provost of Oriel, chair of the Oxford Board of Guardians and a Liberal, contended that Cole 'has changed his position amazingly: everything is now to be controlled not worked by the State [sic]—such is the sum of his book on *The Next Ten Years*.'[26] Beatrice Webb had rejoiced in her diary in 1928:

> G.D.H. Cole and wife....have dropped Guild Socialism and any other form of 'proletarianism'....change will come in the main through controlled capitalism and intermediate forms of government and...the Expert and the advance of science will dominate the situation—in fact the pure word of Webbian Fabianism....He is writing a book on *The Next Ten Years*—really a text-book for Labour Party administration, local and national. From his account this policy does not differ substantially from what we should advocate....For the rest, Cole has matured alike in intellect and character...'[27]

Phelps and Webb, however, both saw recantation where it did not exist. Cole began *The Next Ten Years* by explaining:

> I set about writing this book because, whether I liked it or not, I had been compelled by the movement of events to think out afresh my social and political creed. I do not mean by this that my fundamental views had changed; and certainly I have no dramatic act of conversion to offer my readers. But I did feel the need to start thinking again as near as I could to fundamentals; and I felt this none the less for being fairly certain that the result would not be a recantation, but only a restatement of old conclusions.

In the chapter on 'Workers' Control' he repudiated not 'the Guild Socialist view as a whole' but only 'the later excesses of Guild Socialist system-making'— the ultra-democracy of electing 'masses of committees to perform all manner of representative functions'—and 'for which I accept my full share of the blame'. What, he asserted, remained 'sound and alive in the Guild idea is, above all, its insistence that the worker, as a worker, must be treated as a human being, and not as a mere factory hand'. He was confident that Guild Socialism had

---

26 Letter of 3 April 1930, cited by R.C. Whiting, *The View from Cowley: The Impact of Industrialization upon Oxford, 1918–1939* (Oxford: Clarendon Press, 1983), 141.

27 Quoted by MC, *Life*, 161–62. This diary entry for 12 September 1928 is omitted from the MacKenzies' edition of *The Diary of Beatrice Webb*—as also, surprisingly, from *Beatrice Webb's Diaries, 1924–1932*, ed. MC (London: Longmans, Green, 1956).

killed dead...the old Collectivism which thought of the mechanism of nationalization as a mere extension of the political government of the State, and proposed to hand over the running of industries to Civil Service departments under political heads. That notion is safely buried; and every Socialist who is not merely antediluvian now recognizes that the growth of socialization involves the development of a totally new technique of public industrial administration and control. Guild Socialists went wrong in desiring to base this new technique wholly on the representative principle; but they were thoroughly right in insisting on its necessity. The new socialization, based on expert boards or commissions of full-time administrators, checked and guided by largely representative workers' bodies from below, conserves all that was valuable in the Guild Socialist plans for the reorganization of industries under public control. It concedes the essential principle of industrial self-government.[28]

Cole's extraordinary assurance concerning the form nationalization would take was based on no more than his confidence in the preceding chapter that 'actual socialization...will turn out a very different thing from the idea of "nationalization"', collectivist and bureaucratic, 'as it was conceived in the minds of Fabians and other propagandists a generation ago'.[29]

***

Beatrice Webb had noted in 1914 that Cole was 'the ablest newcomer' to the Fabian Society since H.G. Wells, but

> he is intolerant, impatient and not, at present, very practical. I am not certain whether the present rebel mood is in good faith or whether it is just experimental, seeing how it will go down.

Two months later she commented that 'Cole is a really able man, with much concentrated energy'. She approved that, unlike Wells, he and his Guild Socialist

---

28 GDHC, *Next Ten Years*, vii, 161, 172. In contrast, there is a very forceful statement: GDHC, 'Workers' Control', ts, 16 February 1934 (Cole Papers, Box 9, A1/52/9). Marc Stears, 'Cole, George Douglas Howard', *Oxford Dictionary of National Biography*, also exaggerates the revisionism of *The Next Ten Years*. See too Stears, *Progressives*, 268–69. Carpenter, on the other hand, provides a balanced discussion (137–44). See also GDHC, *A Plan for Britain* (London: Clarion Press [1932]).

29 GDHC, *Next Ten Years*, 133–34.

comrades 'do not tamper with sex conventions—they seem to dislike women':
'But all other conventions they break or ignore'. The following year she admitted:

> I often speculate about G.D.H. Cole's future. He interests me
> because he shows remarkable intensity of purpose. Is he as per-
> sistent as intense? He has a clear-cutting and somewhat subtle
> intellect. But he lacks humour and the *bonhomie* which springs
> from it, and he has an absurd habit of ruling out everybody and
> everything that he does not happen to like or find convenient.
> Since the outbreak of war he has modified this attitude, and is
> now willing to work with the Labour Party in order to get into
> closer touch with the trade unions....he resents anyone who is
> not a follower and has a contempt for all leaders other than
> himself. With his keen intelligence and aristocratic tempera-
> ment it is hard to believe that he will remain enamoured with
> the cruder forms of democracy embodied in the Guild Socialist
> idealization of the manual working class.

Webb continued to be nonplussed by this last in 1926:

> Why he remains so genuinely attached to the working class, so
> determined to help forward their organization, puzzles me. The
> desire *to raise the underdog and abuse the boss* is a religion with
> him, a deep-rooted emotion more than a conviction. Will it
> endure? It certainly has survived many disappointments. And
> yet he is essentially an aristocrat of the sophisticated, ascetic,
> priestly type, aloof from the common passions and low plea-
> sures of the average social man…

Yet her diagnosis two years before was probably correct:

> Politically he is a lost soul....His best escape from [his] mental
> isolation would be to retire into an academic career, at any rate
> for a time. He is too much of the aristocrat and the anarchist...
> to succeed with an Anglo-Saxon democracy.[30]

Cole's briefly interrupted academic career had resumed in 1922 when he
was appointed as Director of Tutorial Classes, University of London; but three
years later he moved back to Oxford as University Reader in Economics with
a Fellowship at University College.

---

30 *Diary of Beatrice Webb*, III, 202, 204, 222–23; IV, 27, 98.

Throughout his adult life, Cole was a Guild Socialist and libertarian. On reading the autobiography of his Guild Socialist comrade, Maurice Reckitt, Margaret Cole commented:

> I'd like to suggest something which I think you've missed. This is [Douglas's] almost morbid dislike of *any* sort of coercion (not merely physical force), & of authority in any form. Right deep down, he is neither Fabian nor Bolshevik, but an anarchist. An anarchist is a perfectly possible thing to be; but it doesn't square happily with institution-making & I think part of the sterility... of some of his political writing is due to this fact. It isn't *really* political work; it's playing games, because he won't admit the need for authority or the government of men.[31]

Cole wasn't, of course, an anarchist and it is surprising how often he found it necessary to say so (was this a consequence of Beatrice Webb's sustained critique?) as in the typographically arresting

> Nor are people who know what they like popular with Governments; for most Governments want most people to behave as much like sheep as possible, in order to simplify the task of governing them...the people who have strong tastes and wills to match are simply an intolerable nuisance.
> If there were more of them, they would make the art of government, as we know it, impossible; and how dreadful that would be—for the business of Governments we are told is to govern.
> I AM NO ANARCHIST,
> and I believe as much as you do, reader, in the necessity for government—even strong government. But I also believe with all my strength in vigorous personal tastes among as many people as possible. For the stronger the Government needs to be, in face of the complex problems of the modern world, the stronger we individual men and women need to be if we are to stand up to it successfully, and keep secure possession of our own souls.[32]

---

31 Letter from MC to Reckitt, 7 July 1941, quoted in John S. Peart-Binns, *Maurice Reckitt: A Life* (Basingstoke: Bowerdean Press and Marshall Pickering, 1988), 18. The emphases are MC's.

32 GDHC, 'The Case for Going One's Own Way', *Kensington News*, 8 September 1933 (Cole Papers, Box 6, A1/36/4). Cf GDHC, 'For Democracy', *Rotary Service*, August 1941, 1.

On the other hand, how close Cole was to anarchism is manifest in 'The Inner Life of Socialism', an article of 1930:

> In one sense...all Socialists are Anarchists in their ideal; for they regard coercion as an evil, and the presence of coercion in the organization of Society as a sign of its essential imperfection.... The Socialist ideal seems to me to involve the substitution of the rule of consent for the value of coercion. Perfect consent I do not expect ever to be realized; but it remains the ideal. And it is a possible ideal because the fundamental fact of man's sociality is there to build upon. There is a consciousness of consent; and in a healthy and well-ordered Society, the area of this consciousness will tend steadily to grow.[33]

He could write in 1941 in 'The Essentials of Democracy':

> One man cannot really represent another—that's flat. The odd thing is that anyone should have supposed he could.

Similarly he believed that 'every good democrat is a bit of an anarchist when he's scratched'.[34]

***

With the foundation of Nuffield College at Oxford he became a 'Faculty Fellow' and then, in 1941, its first Sub-Warden, the University sitting uneasily on Lord Nuffield's gift of one million pounds. Cole was just completing a Manpower Survey for Beveridge at the Ministry of Labour and suggested transferring the teams of local investigators to a Social Reconstruction Survey. The College Committee approved as, assuaging its guilt, did the University, and the Treasury contributed handsomely (£5,000 in 1941–42, the remaining £8,000 being found from Nuffield's endowment). Cole's workload on the resultant Nuffield Reconstruction Survey was immense, leading to serious illness; but within three years the Treasury had declined to renew its grant, there was criticism within the University about the quality of the research, and Cole had resigned from not only the Survey but the College also.[35]

---

33 'Silver Jubilee Reprints: II', *Aryan Path*, March 1955 (Cole Papers, Box 10, A1/62/1).

34 GDHC, *Essays*, 98, 100.

35 For the Nuffield Survey, in addition to MC, *Life*, chap. 23, see Carpenter, 196–202, and G.D.N. Worswick, 'Cole and Oxford, 1938–1958', in Asa Briggs and John Saville (eds), *Essays in Labour History: In Memory of G.D.H. Cole, 25 September 1889–14 January 1959*

Cole stood as the Labour candidate for the University of Oxford constituency in the 1945 general election, declaring in his address that 'my Socialism is, and has always been, of a strong libertarian brand':

> In my political faith I put foremost recognition of the value of tolerance, kindness of man to man, variety of social experiment, and encouragement of voluntary as well as statutory activity over the wide field of social service. I believe that the public ownership of key industries and services can be so arranged as to admit of wide variety, to exclude bureaucracy, and to enlarge instead of limiting freedom, alike for the manager, the technician, and the manual worker.[36]

During his final two decades Cole's libertarianism increasingly asserted itself. Margaret Cole emphasizes the significance of the débâcle of the Nuffield Reconstruction Survey on her husband's general outlook:

> He had no quarrel with Sir Henry Clay [the new Warden of Nuffield]...and with the University at large, except for a few individuals, his anger did not last long....Against the civil servants resentment endured much longer—in fact, I am not quite sure that he ever fully forgave them. This is quite intelligible, because it was in part a return to his Guild Socialist hatred of bureaucracy, which deepened steadily to the end of his life and caused him to suspect instinctively all institutions (such as the London County Council [on whose Education Committee Margaret Cole was co-opted, later being elected an alderman]) which had a large corps of administrators. Administrators were not his kin...teachers were, and he was prepared to forgive them for the weakness (or wickedness) which had led some of them to be misled by the administrators in the University—whom he regarded as *sans phrase* the villains of the piece. Some of this resentment rubbed off on the leaders of the Labour Party, whom he felt ought to have supported him more strongly against the bureaucrats; this, again, revived earlier attitudes towards the parliamentary machine.[37]

Cole agonized about the increase in size of the social unit, criticized the

---

(London: Macmillan, 1967 edn), 27–34.

36 'G.D.H. Cole's Election Address', Cole Papers, Box 41, D2/7/6.

37 MC, *Life*, 252.

decline of democratic participation and growth of bureaucracy in the trade-union and co-operative movements, and lamented the flawed programme of nationalization of the Labour governments of 1945–51.

Shortly after the Second World War had ended Cole was visited by the French political theorist, Bertrand de Jouvenel, who found him preoccupied with the problem of 'Democracy Face to Face with Hugeness', as he had entitled an important paper of 1941. For Cole 'the democratic spirit...finds its truest expression in small communities and small groups', but social solidarity was 'disrupted by success and the growth of the group':

> Democracy exists to the extent that the individual has a hand in what is done. And Cole finds...a trace of such participation wherever there is some personal link between the representative and the represented, as when the representative is personally known, himself, his habits, his parents, his wife—everything in short which is known about a man in a village and is not known about him in a city. Nothing of this is known any more when votes are cast not for a familiar face but for a stranger—a stranger who is...the representative of a party which gives him his title deeds.

De Jouvenel reported that for Cole it was 'an urgent matter to re-discover in this vast framework of organized society small human cells where men help each other, feel for each other, decide in common and do in common the things they think important: communities of neighbours, communities of work-mates'.[38] In 1941, Cole had observed that men had 'built up Trade Unions, Co-operative Societies, Friendly Societies, and a host of voluntary associations of every sort and kind; and in these the true spirit of democracy had flourished':

> But this associative life had...to contend with difficulties arising out of the rapidly changing material basis of social life. The associations had to become larger and to unify organization over larger and larger fields...Therewith they became less completely democratic, threatening in their turn to develop the same atomistic perversion of democracy which was its ruin in the State.

Cole considered the problem formidable yet simple to state:

---

38 Bertrand de Jouvenel, *Problems of Socialist England* (London: Batchworth Press, 1949), 131–32.

It is to find democratic ways of living for little men in big societies. For men are little, and their capacity cannot transcend
their experience, or grow except by continuous building upon
their historic past. They can control great affairs only by acting
together in control of small affairs, and finding, through the experience of neighbourhood, men whom they can entrust with
larger decisions than they can take rationally for themselves.
Democracy can work in the great States... only if each State is
made up of a host of little democracies, and rests finally, not on
isolated individuals, but on groups small enough to express the
spirit of neighbourhood and personal acquaintance.[39]

When, in 1947, he published his impressive *Local and Regional Government*
in an attempt to influence the Local Government Boundary Commission, he
urged 'the need for preserving and for recreating really small-scale agencies
for...purposes closely related to the everyday lives of the people': the retention
of the parish councils and the introduction of other 'small "neighbourhood"
Local Authorities'.[40]

He advocated 'a new kind of Trade Unionism, in which many more of
the rank and file members will be required to play an active part', believing
that since 1939 'the Trade Unions have become much too centralized, and
that Trade Unionists have come to expect everything to be done for them by
their officials and national executives instead of doing things for themselves'.[41]
Similarly Cole, author in 1945 of *A Century of Co-operation*, the centennial
history of the co-operative movement, regretted the rise of bureaucracy in the
large co-operative societies, wholesale or retail, and that the apathy of most
members had allowed the emergence of a cadre of 'professional laymen' who
exerted disproportionate influence.[42]

In 1949, Cole announced himself 'an inveterate and unrepentant Guild
Socialist, believing in the democratic self-government of industry as a necessary
part of any real democracy and a goal towards which our society should seek to

39 'Democracy Face to Face with Hugeness', in GDHC, *Essays*, 93–95. A typescript of the essay, written for the *Christian News-Letter*, is to be found in the Cole Papers, Box 6, A1/35/2.

40 GDHC, *Local and Regional Government* (London: Cassell, 1947), xv, 256.

41 GDHC, 'The Trade Union Outlook', *Fusion* VI, no. 4 (July–August 1952), 3–4. See also
   GDHC, *What Is Wrong with the Trade Unions?*, Fabian Tract 301 (London: Fabian Society,
   1956), esp. 7–9, 24–27, and GDHC, 'The Labour Party and the Trade Unions', *Political
   Quarterly* XXIV (1953), 26.

42 GDHC, *Co-operation, Labour and Socialism* (n.p.: Co-operative Co-partnership Propaganda
   Committee, 1946), 11; GDHC, *The British Co-operative Movement in a Socialist Society*
   (London: George Allen & Unwin, 1951), 21–23.

advance as speedily as it can'.[43] In contrast, each of the industries nationalized in 1945–51 was run by a public corporation, with the appropriate minister appointing its members, largely from private industry and with none nominated directly by the unions. The model was the Central Electricity Board and BBC (both of 1926) and the London Passenger Transport Board (of 1933). The latter originated under Herbert Morrison, while Minister of Transport, 1929–31; and it was Morrison (who had written a book, *Socialization and Transport* (1933), developing his views), who imposed this template of common ownership upon the Labour Party.[44] Cole's conception of socialization— for example, as expressed in 1929 in *The Next Ten Years in British Economic and Social Policy*—was very different; and he proceeded to criticize Labour's nationalization accordingly, continuing to advocate workers' control while opposing 'trade union control of industry':

> If Public Boards are to be retained at all, they will have to be reconstructed on much more democratic lines, and so as to give a real say to the workers concerned, as well as to the consumers....Industrial democracy means much more than mere 'joint consultation', which is at most only a useful first step. If the workers are expected to labour harder, more cooperatively, and more intelligently in the service of society, and if they are to acquire the habit of thinking of the management as 'us' and not as 'them', power, real power, and responsibility will have to be given over into their hands, both through some sort of central representation on the authorities responsible for public supervision of the nationalized services and at every other level—regional, local, establishment, and actual working group.[45]

What is unexpected—and extremely attractive—is that Cole, a left-wing, 'fundamentalist' socialist, did not equate socialism with nationalization or

---

43 GDHC, 'New Conceptions of Industrial Relations', galley-proof marked in hand 'BFMP— Annual Convention' and '1949' (bound in 'G.D.H. Cole, Articles 1943–52', Nuffield College). See also GDHC, *The Case for Industrial Partnership* (London: Macmillan, 1957).

44 See GDHC, 'Liberty in Retrospect and Prospect', *Rationalist Annual* (1950), 37.

45 GDHC, *Labour's Second Term*, Fabian Tract 273 (London: Fabian Publications and Victor Gollancz, 1949), 10. See also GDHC, 'Workers and Management in the Nationalized Industries', *Co-operative Year Book* (1951), 16–17; GDHC, *Is This Socialism?* (London: New Statesman & Nation and Fabian Society, 1954), 7, 20, 26, 29–30; J.M. Chalmers, Ian Mikardo and GDHC, *Consultation or Joint Management? A Contribution to the Discussion of Industrial Democracy*, Fabian Tract 277 (London: Fabian Society, 1949), 26.

even public ownership, explaining that he had 'no wish to nationalize any more industries than must be nationalized in order to ensure their being conducted in accordance with the public interest'. It was unnecessary 'to nationalize everything—heaven forbid!' The 'public sector' should be highly diversified:

> I count not only municipal but also Co-operative conduct of industry as fully compatible with Socialism; nor have I any objection to leaving many small-scale industries and services in private hands, provided that their conduct is made subject to public regulation in order to prevent either the exploitation of labour or the pursuance of monopolistic practices at the expense of the consumers' welfare. Socialism is not nationalization, and by no means involves the omnipotent and omnipresent State. It is a way of living on terms of social equality, and of organizing the essential services for the common benefit and under conditions of the utmost personal freedom. Above all, Socialism is not bureaucracy, or consistent with it; for bureaucracy implies centralization of power, whereas democratic Socialism aims at its diffusion among all the people.[46]

Stuart Hall, the first editor of the *New Left Review* and previously one of the editors of the *Universities and Left Review*, which came out of Oxford, has highlighted the importance of Cole, 'an austere and courageous veteran of the independent left, who was...still teaching politics at Oxford', to the New Left:

---

46 GDHC, 'What Socialism Means to Me', *Labour Forum*, I, 5 (October-December 1947), 20; GDHC, *Socialist Economics* (London: Victor Gollancz, 1950), 53. See also GDHC, *A Guide to the Essentials of Socialism* (London: Labour Party, 1947); GDHC, 'New Conceptions of Industrial Relations'; GDHC, 'Socialism and the Welfare State', *New Statesman*, 23 July 1955. That Cole was not advocating a 'mixed economy' is made clear in GDHC, 'Twentieth-Century Socialism?', *New Statesman*, 7 July 1956. Stears, 'Cole', states that Cole 'refused to welcome the social policy reforms of the Attlee administration as warmly as might have been expected, demanding instead that the government take more seriously the need to involve welfare recipients, workers, and consumers directly in decision making at a local level'. I regret that I have found no indication of a concern with the democratic rights of claimants. He displayed, in general, minimal interest in the Welfare State (although there is GDHC, *Beveridge Explained: What the Beveridge Report on Social Security Means* (London: New Statesman and Nation, 1942); and see also GDHC, 'British Labour's Achievement after 1945: An Assessment', *Review of International Affairs* (Belgrade), no. 12 (16 June 1953).

Although he was a distinguished historian of European socialism and a student of Marxism, Cole's socialism was rooted
in the co-operative and 'workers' control' traditions of Guild
Socialism. His critique of bureaucratic 'Morrisonian'-style nationalization was enormously influential in shaping the attitude
of many socialists of my generation towards statist socialism.[47]

In a *New Statesman* pamphlet of 1954, Cole maintained that socialism
meant 'something radically different from the managerial Welfare State'.[48] He
also returned to the division of political temperaments between 'anarchists'
and 'bureaucrats', explaining that the Webbs had been fond of using it at the
time when he had joined the Fabian Society back in 1908. He acknowledged
the bureaucratic achievements of—the list is revealing—'the advance towards
the Welfare State...the promotion of state enterprise...the attack on anti-social
vested interests...pressing for the assurance of a national minimum standard of
life...devising schemes of redistributive taxation, and...attacking private monopolies with proposals for unification under public ownership'. The problem,
though, was whether the B's 'are the right people to discover how to make the
new social order they have partly succeeded in setting up *work* when it has
been established?' It was now necessary to pass 'beyond the Welfare State, in
which people get given things to the kind of society in which they find satisfaction in doing things for themselves and one for another.' This need to progress
from provision to democratic participation was 'precisely what the "B's" are
temperamentally unfitted to do by themselves: only the "A's", held in check by
the "B's", can do it in any effective way'.[49]

***

Cole had been rescued from the irascible resignation from Nuffield by his
fortuitous election in 1944 to the newly established Chichele Professorship
of Social and Political Theory, which carried with it a fellowship at All Souls.
He was, though, shortly to make his peace with Nuffield by becoming a
professorial fellow and selling to the college the bulk of his immense library.

---

47 Stuart Hall, 'Life and Times of the First New Left', *New Left Review*, 2nd series, no. 61
(January–February 2010), 178. See also Stuart Hall, 'The "First" New Left: Life and Times',
in Robin Archer and Oxford University Socialist Discussion Group (eds.), *Out of Apathy:
Voices of the New Left Thirty Years On* (London: Verso, 1989), 15. Cole contributed an arti-
cle, 'What Is Happening to British Capitalism?', to the first number of *Universities and Left
Review* in 1957.

48 GDHC, *Is This Socialism?*, 3.

49 GDHC, 'What Next?', 30–32. The emphasis is Cole's.

Tenure of the Chichele chair, which he held until his retirement in 1957, gave him considerable satisfaction and allowed him to produce his last and largest work, *A History of Socialist Thought*, appearing in five volumes (and with the third and fourth both split into two) between 1953 and 1960. Few, if any, can have read it in its entirety, most (like myself) using it as an invaluable work of reference.

Writing *A History of Socialist Thought* enabled Cole to engage in rich reflection on the libertarian or anarchist current of socialism and its relationship to utopian socialism, Marxism, and social democracy—with particular reference to his bugbears of hugeness, centralization, and bureaucracy. Centralization, he believed, is 'always the foe of democracy, and should be the foe of Socialism':

> But, alas, many who call themselves Socialists are actually strong supporters of centralization and even look to Socialists to carry it further still. This was always a characteristic of German Social Democracy with its Marxist tendency to identify the trend towards Socialism with its increasing unification of the control of the means of production and its intense dislike of the libertarian Socialism of Proudhon and Bakunin, of Kropotkin and of William Morris, and of that considerable Belgian theorist, César de Paepe.[50]

De Paepe was a prominent participant in the controversies within the First International. While, in Cole's words, 'never completely an Anarchist', he was much nearer to the Bakuninists than the Marxists and, when the split between them finally came, he initially supported the anarchists in the anti-authoritarian Saint-Imier International.[51]

Cole approved of Kropotkin and Gandhi in contrast to theorists, 'whether of the Communist or of the Social Democratic varieties [who] have alike accepted the assumption that the most advanced techniques—and accordingly those most appropriate to Socialism—involve not only a continued increase in the scale of production, but also workplaces employing ever larger aggregations of routine workers':

> The most notable writers who have stood out against the acceptance of this trend have not been Socialists, but Anarchists such as Kropotkin and original thinkers such as Gandhi. To Kropotkin, writing before automation had become technically

---

50 GDHC, 'Socialism and Social Democracy', f. 8 (typescript, n.d., Cole Papers, Box 10, A1/62/11).

51 GDHC, *History*, II, 340. For de Paepe in general, see ibid, esp. chaps. 6, 8.

possible, it appeared that the spread of electric power would give a new opportunity to the small workshop and could bring about the decentralization of industry; while Gandhi envisaged the economic development of India largely in terms of relatively small production units resting on village production. These, I know, are unpopular authorities to quote to present-day Socialists; but may they not prove to have been prophetic?[52]

Tony Wright, Cole's most penetrating analyst, considers:

Cole's *History of Socialist Thought* may (and perhaps should) be read as a long essay in retrieval: the retrieval of a valuable and neglected tradition of 'federalistic' socialist pluralism. His rehabilitation of Fourier, his defence of Proudhon against Marx, his account of Bakunin and the First International, his embrace of Kropotkin, his attack on the rigid centralism of German Social Democracy, his rescue of William Morris: all this, and more, formed part of his retrieval of a motley historical tradition. It was a tradition, moreover, to which Guild Socialism...could be readily assigned'.[53]

The 'large ambitions' of Guild Socialism, Cole recalled, were for 'the creation of a libertarian Socialist society...'[54] In 'Socialism, Centralist or Libertarian?', he reflected that 'there have always been two fundamental cleavages in Socialist thought—the cleavage between revolutionaries and reformists, and the cleavage between centralizers and federalists'.[55] The first cleavage had monopolized attention at the expense of the second, Cole's own tradition of libertarian, decentralist socialism. The latter stood outside the conflict between Bolshevism and parliamentary social democracy, both of which 'regarded increasing centralization of power as an unmistakable characteristic of progress, and regarded themselves as the destined heirs of capitalist concentration and of the centralized power of the modern State'.[56]

---

52 GDHC, 'How Far Must We Centralize?', f. 7 (typescript, c. 1958, Cole Papers, Box 10, A1/62/5).

53 Wright, *GDHC*, 137. See also GDHC, 'What is Socialism?, I', *Political Studies* I, 1 (February 1953), esp. 21–8; and GDHC, 'What is Socialism?, II', *Political Studies*, I, 2 (June 1953).

54 GDHC, 'Education and Politics: A Socialist View', *Year Book of Education* (1952), 52.

55 GDHC, 'socialism, Centralist or Libertarian? I', *ISSS Information*, no. 7 (September 1959), 5 (Margaret Cole Papers, Box 39, H1/5, Nuffield College, Oxford).

56 GDHC, *History*, III, Part 2, 970. See also ibid., IV, Part 1, 26.

Two or three months before his death in January 1959 he explicated the difficulty of his position in the years following the First World War:

> ...I was a left-wing Socialist who was never at all tempted... to go over to Communism, because I entirely disagreed with its fundamental approach—as I did indeed with the Labour Party's. For the basis of my Socialism was a deep belief in the value and free will of the individual...I was against centralism whether it manifested itself in the dictatorship of a class—or of a party supposed to represent a class—or in an overweening advocacy of the claims of the State as representing the whole body of citizens. I believed that democracy had to be small, or broken up into small groups, in order to be real, and that it had to be functional for this to be possible...To this conception of democracy I have adhered all my life...[57]

At the same time he fittingly concluded *A History of Socialist Thought* with the forthright statement, albeit astonishing for an esteemed member of the Labour Party:

> I am neither a Communist nor a Social Democrat, because I regard both as creeds of centralization and bureaucracy, whereas I feel sure that a Socialist society that is to be true to its equalitarian principles of human brotherhood must rest on the widest possible diffusion of power and responsibility, so as to enlist the active participation of as many as possible of its citizens in the tasks of democratic self-government.[58]

As he had previously explained in 1957, 'I was—and I remain—a Guild Socialist—neither a Communist nor a Social Democrat in the ordinary sense,

---

57 GDHC, 'Foreword', to Branko Pribićević, *The Shop Stewards' Movement and Workers' Control, 1910–1922* (Oxford: Basil Blackwell, 1959), vi–vii.

58 GDHC, *History*, V, 337. In his review of this volume, a former member of the *Universities and Left Review* group quotes Cole's declaration, observing: 'The New Left has often been tempted to claim him a patron, but perhaps it would be more accurate to say that we have caught up with him, about fifty years late'. (Peter Sedgwick, 'Liquidating the Thirties', *New Left Review*, no. 7 (January/February 1961), 67.) See also Peter Sedgwick, 'Varieties of Socialist Thought', in Bernard Crick and William A. Robson (eds.), *Protest and Discontent* (Harmondsworth: Penguin Books, 1970), 37, where Cole is characterized as 'a maverick thinker' of 'high personal integrity'.

but something, not betwixt and between these two, but essentially different from both'.[59]

There is a perhaps unexpected convergence in the thought of the louche and hedonistic revisionist, Tony Crosland, and the asexual and ascetic fundamentalist, Cole. In *The Future of Socialism*, Crosland asserted that in the blood of socialists 'there should always run a trace of the anarchist and the libertarian, and not too much of the prig and prude'. He himself had been raised as a Fabian, but 'a reaction against the Webb tradition' was necessary. He admitted that the Webbs were 'no doubt right to stress the solid virtues of hard work, self-discipline, efficiency, research and abstinence: to sacrifice private pleasure to public duty, and expect that others should do the same: to put Blue Books before culture, and immunity from physical weakness above all other virtues', because they were reacting against 'an unpractical, Utopian, sentimental, romantic, almost anarchist tradition on the Left...' This alternative stream of socialist thought, which he was now advocating, he identified as 'stemming from William Morris'.[60] This was Cole's tradition also. He had been converted to socialism as a schoolboy by reading *News from Nowhere*. Morris's socialism was close to anarchism although—unsurprisingly in the era of the bomb-throwers—he opposed anarchism vehemently. Cole understood this. His socialism was also close to anarchism, which he too rejected but with considerably more sympathy than Morris had.[61] In a posthumously published lecture, delivered to the newly established William Morris Society, he reasserted his debt, explaining that in Morris's oeuvre, visual as well as literary, he had found a 'quality that strongly appealed to me and gave me a deeper devotion to Morris as a person than I have ever felt for any other whom I have not met face to face'.[62]

A Note on the Contents

Cole wrote 'Socialism, Centralist or Libertarian?', the final item included in this volume, as the foreword to an Italian selection of his uncollected articles

---

59 Ibid., IV, Part 1, 10. See also ibid., IV, Part 1, 7.

60 C. A. R. Crosland, *The Future of Socialism* (London: Jonathan Cape, 1956), 522–23. For Cole and Crosland, see Carpenter, 207–10, 228.

61 GDHC, *William Morris as a Socialist: A Lecture Given on 16th January 1957 to the William Morris Society at the Art Workers' Guild* (London: William Morris Society, 1960), 12–14; Goodway, *Anarchist Seeds*, 20–24; Ruth Kinna, 'Anarchism, Individualism and Communism: William Morris's Critique of Anarcho-communism', in Alex Prichard, Ruth Kinna, Saku Pinta, and David Berry (eds.), *Libertarian Socialism; Politics in Black and Red* (Basingstoke: Palgrave Macmillan, 2012), esp. 49–53.

62 GDHC, *William Morris*, 1, 17. See also GDHC, 'Introduction' to *William Morris: Stories in Prose, Stories in Verse, Shorter Poems, Lectures and Essays*, ed. GDHC (London: Nonesuch Press, 1934).

and lectures, *Studi sul Socialismo* (*Studies in Socialism*), announced for publication by La Nuova Italia in Florence in 1959, the year of his death—he died on 14 January—but which never appeared. This was being edited by Carlo Doglio, a young Italian anarchist, working as a journalist in London in the 1950s (and actually living in Vernon Richards's house at 33 Ellerby Street, Fulham, also shared by Colin Ward, one of whose pseudonyms in *Anarchy* was 'John Ellerby'). Doglio's son, Daniele, informs me that the preferred title had been *Towards a Libertarian Socialism*.

I am grateful to Daniele Doglio and Stefania Proli for providing me with copies of the relevant correspondence from Doglio's papers, held by the Biblioteca Libertaria Armando Borghi, Castel Bolognese, including the proposed contents of *Studi* (no indication of which is to be found in the Cole Papers, Nuffield College, Oxford), undoubtedly drawn up by Cole himself.

Doglio had also been interested in publishing some other innovative English-language social and political thinkers in Italian, including R.H. Tawney, Margaret Mead, A.S. Neill, the child psychiatrist and therapist Margaret Lowenfeld, and Wilhelm Reich, as well as, rather surprisingly, Harold Wilson. Yet it was at just this point that there was a major change in his life with his return to Italy in 1959 to work with Danilo Dolci in Sicily. The prospective publisher of *Studi sul Socialismo*, Tristano Codignola, required an extensive introduction made even more necessary by Cole's death; and Doglio did not now have the time to write it. He was later to become a respected specialist on urbanism and planning, on much the same lines, I am told, as Lewis Mumford.

'Socialism, Centralist or Libertarian?' appeared in two issues of *ISSS Information* in 1959, preparatory to the intended publication of *Studi*. The full essay in both Cole's virtually illegible longhand and a typescript in which his indefatigable typist, Rosamund Broadley, was obliged to leave some words blank, can also be found in the Cole Papers. (*ISSS Information* was the organ of the International Society for Socialist Studies, founded by Cole and of which Doglio became chairman.)

The following items are specified in the contents proposed by Cole:

'What Socialism Means to Me'; 'Liberty in Retrospect and Prospect'; *The British Labour Movement—Retrospect and Prospect*; 'What is Socialism?'; *The Development of Socialism during the Past Fifty Years*; 'Education and Politics: A Socialist View'; 'The Socialism of British Labour'; 'British Labour's Achievement after 1945'; *Is This Socialism?*; 'Socialism and the Welfare State'; 'Reflections on Democratic Centralism'; *William Morris as a Socialist*.

On the other hand, the following have, for various reasons (of contemporary relevance, accessibility, or length) been excluded:

'The Future of Socialism' (1955); 'Marxism'; 'What Is Happening to Capitalism?'; 'Socialism and Democracy' (*Espirit*); 'As a Socialist Sees It' [The War in Korea]; 'Reflections on Hungary'; 'The Idea of Progress'.

In compensation, the current editor has added the following: 'Conflicting Social Obligations' (an essential early article, which has inexplicably never previously been reprinted); 'Loyalties' in which Cole developed the line of thought in 'Conflicting Social Obligations'; 'For Democracy'; 'G.D.H. Cole's Election Address'; 'The Trade Union Outlook'; 'What Next? Anarchists or Bureaucrats?'; 'Socialism and Social Democracy'; 'How Far Must We Centralize?'; 'Socialism, Centralist or Libertarian?'

Cole had also wanted the inclusion of 'Socialist Philosophies and Present Problems', his Laski memorial address delivered at Hampstead Town Hall on 3 July 1951. It is greatly regretted that it has not been possible to satisfy this wish as no complete text has been found. The manuscript, located in the Cole Papers, is fragmentary, and that shown in the 1970s to Tony Wright by Margaret Cole, has disappeared—it is not to be found in the Margaret Cole Papers, now also at Nuffield.[63]

A final note: Cole uses language here and there that is now regarded as sexist, but which was prevalent at the time. It has been left in without comment though that should not suggest agreement.

63 Wright, *G.D.H. Cole*, 231n.

CONFLICTING SOCIAL
OBLIGATIONS

'The body politic is a moral being possessed of a will; and this general will, which tends always to the preservation and welfare of the whole and of every part, and is the source of the laws, constitutes for all the members of the State, in their relation to one another and to it, the rule of what is just or unjust.'

'Every political society is composed of other smaller societies of different kinds, each of which has its interests and its rules of conduct; but those societies which everyone perceives, because they have an external and authorized form, are not the only ones that actually exist in the State; all individuals who are united by a common interest compose as many others, either temporary or permanent, whose influence is none the less real because it is less apparent, and the proper observance of whose various relations is the true knowledge of public morals and manners. The influence of all these tacit or formal associations causes, by the influence of their will, as many different modifications of the public will. The will of these particular societies has always two relations; for the members of the association it is a general will; for the great society it is a particular will, and it is often right with regard to the first object, and wrong as to the second. An individual

may be a devout priest, a brave soldier, or a zealous senator, and
yet a bad citizen. A particular resolution may be advantageous
to the smaller community, but pernicious to the greater. It is
true that, particular societies being always subordinate to the
general society in preference to others, the duty of a citizen takes
precedence of that of a senator, and a man's duty of that of a
citizen; but unhappily personal interest is always found in inverse
ratio to duty, and increases in proportion as the association grows
narrower and the engagement less sacred ; which irrefragably
proves that the most general will is always the most just also, and
that the voice of the people is in fact the voice of God.'
—Rousseau, *Political Economy*.

I HAVE SET THESE TWO PASSAGES AT THE HEAD OF THIS PAPER BECAUSE I BELIEVE
that, both where they are right and where they are wrong, they afford the most
valuable guidance in approaching the problem of conflicting social obligations.[1] This problem, we have no difficulty in seeing today, is closely bound up
with the whole question of the place of particular associations in Society—a
question which becomes increasingly urgent as the opposing forces of philosophers and practical men meet in a conflict which is at once theoretical and
practical. During the nineteenth century the theory of State Sovereignty won
an almost universal triumph in abstract political theory; it now seems likely
that, under pressure from religious and industrial theorists, it will suffer during
the twentieth century a defeat no less decisive. It is the bearing of this controversy upon the problem of social obligation that I propose to examine.

Rousseau's theory of the General Will is, in its profoundest aspect, the expression of the truth that all social machinery is the organization of human
will. Social organization can be studied only as a branch of conduct: it is neither more nor less than the instrument of co-operative action, in whatever
guise it may manifest itself. Wherever two or three are gathered together, a
common will different from their individual wills may emerge: wherever two
or three form a coalition or association, of whatever sort, a new corporate will
comes into being.

The effect of this theory on philosophy is twofold: it both breaks down a
distinction and creates one. It breaks down the hard and fast distinction between ethics and politics which comes of treating the one as an interpretation
of human will and the other not as philosophy, but as science, mechanism.
It creates a distinction, not between governmental acts on the one side and

1 *Proceedings of the Aristotelian Society*, 1915.

private acts on the other, but between all social or corporate acts and all individual acts—a distinction between will acting directly, without intervening mechanism, and will that acts only through such a mechanism.

How comes it, then, that philosophers, who have set out since Rousseau from a conception of both ethics and politics in terms of will, have still treated private associative acts as rather of the individual than of the social type? It is, I believe, this mistake that lies at the root of our failure to provide any satisfactory answer to the problem of conflicting obligations.

In *The Social Contract* Rousseau was discussing the general will only in one of its manifestations—in the City-State. In the passages I have quoted he is treating the subject universally, so that corporate will in general becomes evident as the basis of his whole theory. Every particular association within the State, he assures us, has a general will of its own, and so far resembles the body politic, in which the pre-eminently general will is supposed to reside. But, he continues, while the will of any association is general in relation to its members, it is purely individual in relation to the State. And elsewhere, especially in the first book of the original draft of *The Social Contract* (published in the edition of M. Dreyfus-Brisac) he expressly declares that, in relation to a world-federation, the body politic itself would be purely individual.

Rousseau, in his City-State, decided, if possible, to banish associations altogether, on the ground that they would inevitably prove conspiracies against the public. He admitted, however, that there must be one important exception to this rule, since the people must appoint a government, and this government will inevitably use its corporate will in order to usurp Sovereignty, which belongs to the people. This is, in Rousseau's phrase, the inevitable tendency of the body politic to deteriorate.

Beginning, then, with an identification of the body politic with the ultimate sovereign people, Rousseau goes on to reduce to a minimum the number of conflicting wills within Society, and only admits the intrusion of any will other than those of the body politic and of the individuals composing it as a necessary imperfection of human societies. Similarly, the whole tendency of nineteenth-century philosophy was to regard the association as, at the most, a necessary imperfection, to be tolerated rather than recognized, with no rights beyond those of expediency, and no powers beyond those conferred expressly by statute. From this point of view we are now struggling slowly back to a saner doctrine; but we have done this so far more on grounds of practical necessity than on grounds of philosophic theory. We are still too apt to take a view resembling Rousseau's as our basis, and to admit exceptions only as they arise.

What, then, was the fundamental error in Rousseau's presentation of the problem? We can best understand it by trying to envisage the types of particular association he conceived. As soon as we make this attempt, Rousseau's statement of the case cannot help appearing unnatural in view of the problems our century has to face. Rousseau states the difference between the body politic and the particular association as if it were simply a question of size, extent, membership. Just as the government consists of a select body, all of whom are also members of the sovereign people, so he seems to think of every association as consisting simply of so many persons who are also citizens. General wills within general wills, from the smallest possible association to the widest possible 'confederation of the world', he envisages and fears: the division of one corporate will from another by function is a division he never seems to face, and one which he sweeps away merely by implication.

The corporate will of the government, or executive, is clearly a subordinate will of the kind of which Rousseau is thinking, and where the will of the government conflicts with that of the Sovereign, it will be universally admitted that the former should, in the end, give way. But, if we ask ourselves why this is so, we shall not, I think, reply with Rousseau that it is merely because it is smaller, but because it is both smaller and of the same kind.

Rousseau, in fact, as we can see most clearly in the famous chapter in which he dismisses particular associations, always thinks of them in terms of cliques, parties, conspiracies against the public. He does not distinguish between political and non-political associations, probably because he feels that every non-political association, from the Church to the city-guild, inevitably becomes political in defence of its vested interests and privileges. With a pessimism which the experience of France in the eighteenth century almost justified, he therefore declared in theory against every form of particular association.

When Rousseau's principle was put into practice by the *loi Chapelier* of 1791, there was, then, considerable reason, on grounds of mere expediency, for the general abolition of associations. But, as all students of French history know, the prohibition was never in effect complete, and it was not long before associations of various kinds, and especially workmen's societies, began to fight their way back to toleration and, at a later date, to recognition by the State. In practice, the revolutionary principle of the law of Chapelier broke down, and there came into existence new associations which were not conspiracies against the public, but natural human groupings with a specific function of their own.

If, then, the distinguishing feature of eighteenth-century associations was privilege, passing easily into conspiracy against the public, the feature of nineteenth-century association is speciality of function, which, though it may sometimes lead to controversy and prejudice the common good, is in no sense based on a conspiracy against the public. If it is privileged, it holds its privileges from the public on the ground that they are in the public interest: it is not privileged in the bad sense of constituting a vested interest irrespective of the common good.

What, we must now ask, is the relation between these particular associations and the State? Let me begin by defining my terms a little more exactly.

By State I mean the governmental machine, national and local, with its various dependencies; by Association I mean any body which, whether or not it stands in a defined relation to the State, does not form part of the governmental machine; by Society I mean, for the time being, the whole complex of organized bodies within the national area, including both the State, national and local, and every organized association, of whatever kind; by Community I mean something wider still, the whole mass of desires, opinions, traditions, and possibilities which are, for the moment, incarnated in the citizens.

The State is thus itself a complex of institutions of a more or less uniform type, which, whatever else they may take into account, generally resemble one another in being based on geographical grouping. Society is a wider complex of institutions, which resemble one another throughout only as being one and all expressions of man's associative will. The Community, as I have used the word, is the sum total of social values, organized or unorganized, capable or incapable of organisation, within the national area.

I say 'the national area', not because there is necessarily a magic in it, and still less because national grouping invariably determines the extent of associative grouping, but simply and solely in order to simplify the problem. The fact that some non-governmental groupings cover an area far larger than that of a single State is of the greatest practical importance, since it may immensely strengthen them in their conflicts with any State: it is none the less irrelevant to the discussion of the respective rights of governmental and non-governmental associations; and I am discussing, not expediency, but rights. I shall, therefore, assume an isolated national area, completely covered by a Nation-State and its various local governmental bodies, and including many functional associations of varying extent. What is the relation between these bodies, and, in the event of a conflict of principle between them, how ought the individual to determine his allegiance?

Philosophical writers on the general question (as distinguished from its particular applications) have answered in one of three ways. Either they have tried to define, absolutely and inclusively, the sphere of State action, or they have imposed certain theoretical limitations upon the otherwise universal Sovereignty of the State, or, thirdly, they have accepted the theory that the State is absolutely and universally sovereign.

In the first case, which has been as a rule the earliest in point of time, the State is regarded as an *ad hoc*, or at any rate an ad *haec*, authority, sovereign in certain defined spheres of action peculiarly its own, but elsewhere an interloper, wholly without right of intervention. This, roughly speaking, was the view of John Locke and of Herbert Spencer, much as they differed in many respects: it is the view which treats the State as primarily the upholder of something, whether it be property, law and order, liberty, religion, or morality, and not as the expression of any positive common will. Such a theory, in its old form, can have only an exceptional survival in face of modern social conditions. Those who hold it today are not philosophers, but practical men who wish to safeguard or to destroy some special interest. It still finds expression in the pamphlets of the Liberty and Property Defence League and in the pages of the *Spectator*: it also persists among Anarchists and Syndicalists, who still regard the State solely as the protector of property.

The second view, which became popular as the State, in the hands of opportunists, extended its sphere of activity, reverses the process of the argument: instead of defining inclusively what the State is and can do, it tries to define it by the exclusion of what it is not and cannot do. Its advocates often begin with a 'bill of rights', a 'declaration of the rights of humanity and citizenship', which lays down certain inalienable natural rights. The exclusion may be more or less comprehensive, and may even confine itself to excluding one special type of action from the jurisdiction of the State. It may attempt, as Mill attempted, to set up some general principle of division between actions with which the State is concerned, and actions with which it is not concerned. In any case, it accepts the view that the State is sovereign except where it is specially indicated not to be: it does not attempt an inclusive definition, and it excludes only by limitation. The further this theory removes itself from the *ad hoc* theory of the State, the nearer it comes to the acceptance of universal State Sovereignty, into which indeed most of its adherents have been forced by the breakdown of their attempted distinctions.

Just as the aesthetic philosopher goes in search of the ultimate principle of beauty, just as the moral philosopher tries to define the ultimate nature of moral obligation, so social philosophers are inevitably driven to seek out the ultimate principle of social obligation. Their failure lies, not in this attempt, but in the answer they have been induced to accept. For, driven from the two positions we have just defined, the philosophers have almost invariably accepted, as if it were the only alternative, a theory of complete State Sovereignty. They have been Austinian enough to shut their eyes to any Sovereign that might run the risk of being indeterminate, and Hobbesist enough to accept the heroic simplification which merges all conflict of obligations into a single all-embracing State obligation.

Agreement on the theory of State Sovereignty has not led, indeed, to agreement on questions of practical policy, and herein lies the chief hope that this theoretical conversion is not final. The 'limitation' theory was advocated by men who wished to save something they prized from the desecrating grip of the State. It may have been a communal value they were trying to conserve; but they were called, all the same, 'individualists'. Sooner or later a case would be bound to arise in which the common interest was clearly prejudiced by some action of the particular type which they had excluded from the jurisdiction of the State—at all events, they could never be sure that such a case might not arise. In such a case, they would be asked, should State interference be allowed? They might answer in the negative, and so save their consistency and nothing else; for they could offer no reason. Or they might throw up the sponge, and become, theoretically, advocates of State Sovereignty.

Thus we have, on the one hand, the author of *The Philosophical Theory of the State* (or should it be 'of the Charity Organization Society'?) coupling with a theory that amounts to State Sovereignty a note of solemn warning to the State not to presume too much upon its rights; and, on the other hand, we have Mr. Ramsay MacDonald and his like practically claiming the doctrine of State Sovereignty as a justification of Socialism, with which it has nothing to do.

If we ask what has led men who differ so in practice to agree upon their theoretical basis, if we ask, that is, why men accept the theory of State Sovereignty, even while they dislike and distrust the State, we shall find the answer if we understand the problem they were trying to face. Modern social theory was born in the period of political revolution, and is throughout both a reflection of existing political conditions and an attempt to justify various political opinions. When men studied in the eighteenth century the basis of human societies, what primarily interested them was not associative action as such, but State action: they were seeking, not so much the basis of human association, as the justification or refutation of the democratic argument. Rousseau's *Social Contract* appealed to his contemporaries, and even to himself, rather as a justification of democratic State Sovereignty than as an account of the fundamental nature of supra-individual will. The current political controversies turned social philosophy into political philosophy: thinking always of the State, philosophers sought, not the principle of social obligation, but the principle of political obligation.

This attitude has indeed persisted all through the nineteenth century, and up to our own times. That mid-Victorian Rousseau, T. H. Green, is infected, in an even greater degree than his predecessor, with a purely political bias. If anything besides the State creeps in, it is regarded as a form of association essentially different from the State, and in no sense the depository of ultimate social obligation.

We have seen that all modern social philosophy goes back to Rousseau, and that Rousseau's distinctive contribution lies in the recognition that social life, no less than individual life, is the expression of organized will. Rousseau set out to find the universal principle on which human society is based; almost as a by-product he created the theory of the modern democratic State. We have only to read the *Political Economy* as well as *The Social Contract* to be quite sure that he was seeking, fundamentally, not a theory of the political State, but a statement of the life of the community as expressed in terms of will, individual and general, or rather individual, corporate, and general. But as a result of the political preoccupations of the time, instead of creating a philosophical theory of Society, Rousseau and his successors created a philosophical theory of the State, in which other associations found a position only on sufferance, if at all.

The main reasons which led to the triumph of the theory of State Sovereignty were three—two theoretical and one practical. Thinkers of every shade of opinion felt the need for some ultimate sovereign authority; their failure to regard associations as distinguished primarily by function led them to regard all association as a potential conspiracy against the public, and therefore to support the 'democratic' State against the 'privileged' association; and, thirdly, the immense political upheavals of the eighteenth and nineteenth centuries, by fixing men's eyes on the State, have tended to make all theories of social action chiefly theories of State action.

Today, when most of us, however firmly we may retain our belief in political democracy, have at least lost the illusion of an inevitable democratic political progress, we may reasonably hope to reach a more inclusive conception of social action, and a better idea of the relation of particular associations to the State. The key to Rousseau's whole social theory is to be found in his conception of the General Will. Nay more: the key to any rational social theory must be found in some conception of a General Will. Social science is the study, and social philosophy the interpretation, of the phenomena of collective personality. What right, then, has the State to claim a monopoly of such personality? Is not the very existence of particular associations a sufficient proof that the State cannot fully express the associative will of man? And is not the fact that these associations are the work of human volition a sufficient reason for crediting them with all the attributes of collective personality? Finally, if all these questions are answered in the affirmative, what superior claim has the State to the allegiance of the individual as against some particular association to which he belongs?

The General Will has been called an abstraction, and has been rejected as a guiding principle precisely by those who have felt this inadequacy on the part of the State to serve as collective 'will of all work' to man's social consciousness. They have rejected the General Will because they have been always in search of a 'determinate human superior', and the General Will has not seemed to form a natural attribute of any such superior. In fact, like Rousseau, they have conceived of the General Will as belonging only to the body politic, or State, and in such a connection the whole idea has seemed, as indeed it is, fantastic and abstract.

Yet what theory, in the freshness of youth, has not claimed too much for itself? The discoverers of the democratic State felt that in it they had found a method of expressing the whole civic consciousness of the individual, that political democracy was not only infallible, but omnipotent. Their ardent faith in democracy led them to an absolute trust in an absolutely generalized democratic machine, which, they believed, would equally express the common will whatever the matter in hand might be. At its best, this doctrine led to the repudiation by the State of all knowledge of distinctions of class; at its worst, it led to such absurdities as a State religion. Yet we must not forget that, fundamentally, Rousseau's general principles were nearly always far more true than his ways of applying them. It makes no difference that the General Will cannot find complete expression through any single piece of social machinery. It is indeed precisely that universal will which all social machinery only partially expresses. The degree in which the General Will finds expression at all through organized machinery, governmental or non-governmental, the relative share borne in such expression by the State and by particular associations, and the actual intensity of the will itself, may vary from nation to nation and from generation to generation; but always and everywhere, all social machinery, alike in its agreements and in its conflicts, is a partial and more or less successful expression of a General Will which every community possesses.

The ultimate obligation of the individual is clearly not to any piece of mechanism, but to this General Will itself. How, then, is he to decide between conflicting claims to his allegiance, and how is he to answer the claim of the State to be served with a loyalty surpassing, and different in kind from, other loyalties? The State is the national geographical grouping, and as such can claim to represent those elements in the common life which are best represented on a geographical basis, that is, by a general vote of all the persons resident in the national area, split up into such territorial subdivisions as may seem desirable.

This conception of the State as an essentially geographical grouping is, no doubt, a modern conception, and is perfectly true only of the purely democratic State. In so far as any privileged order retains special governmental rights or functions, the State is not purely geographical in its basis. But though perhaps no purely geographical State exists, the typical modern State is in the main a geographical grouping, and such rights as it possesses in a social system resting on popular Sovereignty must be founded on this geographical basis.

If we assume that a larger homogeneous group has always the ultimate right to override a smaller group *of the same kind*, it seems clear that geographical representation will serve to express those purposes which are distributed with some approximation to equality among all the citizens. If we assume that a national interest should, in the last resort, override a local interest, the supremacy of the National State over local governmental bodies follows. But this does nothing to mark out the proper sphere of action of either national or local government.

The State, national and local, should be the expression of those common purposes which affect all the citizens, roughly speaking, equally and in the same way. In those spheres of action in which a man's interest is determined by the fact that he lives and makes his home in a particular country or district, the geographical group can best express the desires which he shares with his fellows. Here, therefore, the State is sovereign.

The case is altogether different when we come to those spheres of action which affect men unequally, or in different ways. The power of the State adequately to represent the common will on such questions, so far from being demonstrated by experiment, becomes with every attempt more doubtful. The incursions of the State into the realm of organized religion have been invariably unhappy, and the attempts of State departments to run industry, while there is no evidence that they have been on the whole inefficient in the commercial sense, have wholly failed to satisfy the demand of the workers engaged in them for freedom and self-government at their work.

The reason for this failure is not far to seek. Religion is a disease which takes people in different ways, or not at all. It neither affects all men equally, nor affects them in the same way. It is therefore pre-eminently unfit to be governed by a body which has no principle of selection other than the geographical, and in which the irreligious man has an equal say with the religious, and men of different religions in the government of one another's churches. Similarly, industry affects different men in different ways, and would do so even in a community in which every man had his place in industry. Each industry has its special interests, and industry as a whole has an interest and an outlook of its own which no geographical group can adequately represent. In both cases, a broad functional difference is manifest which justifies the constitution of special associations to control the spheres of religion and industry, no doubt in relation to, but not under the domination of, the geographical group.

There is a further consideration which lends additional weight to this repudiation of universal State Sovereignty. Not only cannot an electorate gathered together on a geographical basis alone be fitted to deal with special questions which do not affect them all, or all alike, but also the persons whom they elect cannot possess this fitness. If we have learnt to distrust our politicians, is it not largely because we have allowed them to do things for which a geographical electorate is unfit to select the right representatives?

Strong as these arguments may seem, they will fall on deaf ears unless those who urge them do something to disprove the charge of individualism. Men have fallen into the theory of State Sovereignty, not because they like it, but because it has seemed the easiest, if not the only, way out of the slough of individualism. Half a hundred principles of social obligation, each binding us to a different social unit, cannot take the place of the unifying principle we set out to find. If this principle indeed proves not simple, but complex, its complexity, can only be that of diversity in identity. The withdrawal, therefore, of some class of actions from the sphere of the State must not carry with it any denial of their social character, or even of their ultimate commensurability with social actions of another class. It must be simply a denial that the State is the right mechanism for the execution of certain types of social purpose. If we can keep this social element recognized in actions outside the sphere of the State, we may hope to avoid the theory of State Sovereignty.

It is, of course, universally admitted that individual acts have, as a rule, a social element. The tendency of social theory has been to treat the social element in associative acts as similar to the social element in individual acts, and to set both in contrast to State action, which is supposed to be wholly social. It is my whole point, not that associative acts are wholly social, but that State acts are not. The associative act has two relations: it is, as Rousseau says, general in relation to the association which performs it; but it is particular in relation to the Society of which the association forms a part. It may be general in the second case, in the sense that it may be directed to the good of the community as a whole; but it is still the act of an individual in relation to that Society. The State, I contend, even if it includes everybody, is still only an association among others, because it cannot include the whole of everybody.

The object, then, of my argument is not to generalize the association, but to particularize the State. Rousseau, thinking, as we saw, always in terms of local, and not of functional, association, always conceived the body politic as the great association, claiming a loyalty before which all other loyalties faded. But as soon as we make a clear distinction between the State and the community, and still more as soon as we make one between the State and Society, the body politic loses its omnipotence, and becomes at the most *primus inter pares*.

Let us here meet one difficulty which may make against the adoption of this idea. The historical fact that the State has, in modern times, secured a monopoly of law-making, and has kept in its hands the power to recognize or outlaw all other associations, proves nothing; for it may well, under the instigation of democratic or autocratic partisans of State Sovereignty, or from the mere pressure of events, have usurped a power to which it has no rightful title. We may repeat in this connection one of Rousseau's wisest sayings in dealing with social theory: *Écartons tous les faits!*

Even, however, if it is recognized that history is irrelevant to a discussion of right, it is not so easy to brush away the 'tidy' logician, who does at least find in the universal Sovereignty of the State a theoretically ultimate resolution of all conflicts of obligation. Where, in effect, if we destroy State Sovereignty, is our ultimate Sovereign to be found? Is it not fair to answer that a dearth of good men is no reason for making a bad man king: it is rather a reason for a republic? There remains, however, the question whether this republic of obligations would not be in effect so loosely federal as to amount to anarchy. Would not obligations ceaselessly conflict, and would not the possibility of deciding such conflicts have been beyond remedy destroyed?

There are here in reality two questions. How far will functional devolution reduce the possibility of conflict to a minimum? And how far will there be any way of resolving such conflicts between two functional authorities, when they arise?

It is surely evident that the greater number of the conflicts of obligation which arise in the Society of today are due to an imperfect demarcation of spheres. The Ulster question was the result of fear concerning the religious effects of a political change. The most glaring failure of modern politics is in the sphere of industrial legislation. Inhumanity, arising from a lack of understanding, is the mark of the State in its dealings with man in his religious aspect, and in his capacity as worker. A division of spheres would obviate many of the conflicts of today, but, as both religion and, still more, industry, have their relations to men in their geographical groups, the possibility of conflict can never be altogether avoided.

We come back, then, to our second question. Where, in our view, does the ultimate Sovereignty lie? Clearly it cannot lie in any one piece of machinery: either it is not embodied in any machinery at all, or else it exists only as the resultant of a system including many pieces of machinery of varying kinds.

All machinery is necessarily imperfect, because all machinery tends to standardize what is, in its real nature, infinitely various. The individual who wills purely wills in and for the individual situation in which he is acting: as soon as he makes for his guidance a general rule, he detracts from the perfection and purity of his willing, because he tries to classify the essentially unique. Yet the individual must, in most cases, make such general rules, because he is not strong enough to trust his judgment of each situation as it arises. He can only aim at making his rules as little crude and machine-made as may be.

All associative will, save the unruly judgments of a mob, must act through general rules, and all associative will is therefore necessarily imperfect. But if in this case the necessity for some imperfection is absolute, the degree of imperfection is none the less relative. The General Will of the community must suffer some leakage as soon as the attempt is made to confine it: at once it becomes something less perfect, the General Will of Society, including only that part of the will of the community which the least imperfect rules and formulae can cover. This General Will in its turn consists of a number of lesser wills, differentiated by function, all of which are essential to its fullest possible expression.

On this showing, ultimate Sovereignty clearly lies with the fullest possible organized type of will. The quest for a true 'ultimate' is, no doubt, in some sense a wild goose chase, since behind all organizations lurks always the final voice of the community. We are, however, dealing with this last court of appeal only in so far as it expresses itself in a mechanism or mechanisms, and we may therefore pass by, with this tribute, the General Will of the community.

With Society, the complex of organized associations, rests the final more or less determinate Sovereignty. We cannot carry Sovereignty lower without handing it over to a body of which the function is partial instead of general.

We must, therefore, reject the three theories of State Sovereignty, Theocracy, and Syndicalism, the theories of political, religious, and industrial dominance. All these mistake the part for the whole; our difficulty seems to be the making of a whole out of their parts.

The task of the social philosopher is to define the nature of social obligation; the task of the practical man is to make a Society to fit the philosopher's definition. It is mainly the philosopher's fault that the order of precedence has been so often reversed in the past. It remains, none the less, the philosopher's task to say where Sovereignty should lie, and the business of the practical man to find the requisite machinery. If, then, objection is taken to the Sovereignty of Society on the ground that it is, at best, only 'more or less determinate', the philosopher's answer is clear. The determinateness is none of his business: it is for the practical man to make the Sovereign determinate. It is true that in the communities of today, which are permeated by the idea of State Sovereignty, the last determinate authority is the State. But, as man has made the State, man can destroy it; and as man has made it great, man can again restrict it. Moreover, as man has made the State, man can make something greater, something more fitted to exercise a final Sovereignty, or at least to provide a final court of appeal.

The demand, then, for functional devolution is not a demand for the recognition of associations by the State, but a demand that the State itself should be regarded only as an association—elder brother, if you will, but certainly in no sense father of the rest. This, I take it, has been the real motive behind the demand for equality between Church and State—or, as I would rather say, religion and politics. This is certainly behind the new demand for an industrial democracy outside politics which has been put forward in the National Guild System of the *New Age*. It undoubtedly seems to complicate matters very considerably; but our philosophy should have taught us not to be afraid of necessary complications. We are too fond of counting heads to save the trouble, not of breaking, but of convincing them. We are too fond of patching up our quarrels without settling the principle that is at stake. Yet we know well that, though we may compose, we cannot settle a controversy between religion and politics or industry and politics merely by making one or other of them supreme. Attempts to avoid conflict by establishing the dictatorship of one of the contestants inevitably provoke, if not active conflict, at least passive discontent. Yet this is the 'State Sovereignty' solution of the problem. A well-organized Society will admit the ultimate possibility of conflict, but will try to reduce the need for conflict to a minimum. Attempts to avoid conflict altogether merely end by making it inevitable.

We are left, then, with, at the strongest, a merely federal body including representatives both of the State and of the chief functional associations as the sole mechanism able to speak in the name of our Sovereign. When, therefore, differences arise between one great functional group and another, when, say, the individual finds himself torn between his loyalty to the State and his loyalty to the industrial body of which he is a member, how is he to make his choice? Simply, as Rousseau said, by means of the General Will that is in him, if he tries to choose either what is in the interest of his Church or his Trade Union or his State or municipality, he is 'putting himself the wrong question', to use once again a phrase used by Rousseau. What he has to consider, and what, in a case of corporate action, his association has to consider, is none of these things, but the good of the community as a whole, which is neither the State, nor the Church, nor the Trade Union, nor even quite the complex I have called Society, but something greater than all these. He has to decide, in fact, by falling back upon his judgment of the individual situation, guided, but not finally determined, by general precepts.

But if he has to make his choice, he has also to stand the racket. If a machine representing the will of Society can be devised to harmonize the occasional conflicts between the various functional authorities, that is no doubt all to the good. But the devising of such machinery is not philosophy, but science. Whether or no such a body can exist, Sovereignty remains with Society, and the State has no right to mount the throne, which, even if no determinate person or persons sit in it, is full of a presence which is none the less active for being indeterminate in an Austinian sense.

A last word, and I have done. Much that has gone before has been an attack on a theory which has animated political democrats; but none of it has been an attack upon democracy. Democrats have too often confused the ultimate equality, not of men's powers, but of their rights, with the sacredness of a mass vote on a purely geographical basis. Functional devolution involves, not the abandonment of democracy, but the substitution, for an omnipotent political democracy, of a functional democracy. The unit of self-government should be a functional unit: whatever a mass vote may be, a representative system on a geographical basis is certainly not the last word of democracy.

Note: by Bernard Bosanquet[2]

I think that written notes by people who are not going to be present at the discussion can only be admitted on sufferance; but I shall be glad if I am permitted to make a brief contribution, as I am much interested in Mr. Cole's paper, and I cannot possibly come up to the meeting.

I will go at once to the point which, I think, is the centre of Mr. Cole's interest, and I will attach to this point any slight criticisms I may desire to make. But my main object is to be more in agreement with Mr. Cole than I think he desires to let me be.

---

2   Editor's note: Bernard Bosanquet (1848–1923) was the foremost British idealist, Hegelian philosopher, author of *The Philosophical Theory of the State*.

His interest is—is it not?—in the question whether the State would not be better treated as a particular association, and the elder brother of other associations, than as the father of the rest (p. 43). On this plan you would get at the strongest a loose federation, including representatives of the State and of the 'functional associations' (p. 43). The State may be now the ultimate determinate authority but man might make something greater, or at least more fitted to be a final court of appeal (p. 43); or, perhaps, you might do better with nothing at all but the individual's General Will, to decide in case of conflict (p. 44). It is the risk of conflict, mainly between the functional associations, that is the difficulty to be met. I note a pregnant expression on p. 40—'in relation to, but not under the domination of' (the State). Does not our whole problem turn on this 'in relation to', and the shape which it must assume? At the point of contact, if not between the State and other associations, then between other associations themselves, the necessary 'in relation to', does there, of course, grow up a State, or a something greater, or is there nothing at all beyond a free contact?

Now I want to approach this question on its merits; but, of course, I desire to show how, as I think, this has largely been done on my view, and how this view admits of easy extension and adaptation. As a transition, one word of something like criticism. I hold Mr. Cole quite right in attaching great importance to Rousseau as construing social organization in terms of will. But I do not think he lets it appear how fundamentally Hegel and the philosophy founded on him contradicted Rousseau on this question of the particular associations. Rousseau's view, shared with the statesmen of ancient Greece, is very natural to anyone contemplating small States, governed by mass meetings. Such States and meetings might be 'captured'; and often were so.

Now Mr. Cole, desiring to correct Rousseau, corrects him very much in Rousseau's own manner. He does not, indeed, suspect the functional associations and subject them to the State, but he does, in their own interest, eject them from the State. And this solution rests on a view of the State which is limited in much the same way as Rousseau's, that is, regarding it as the expression of society which can be got through a general vote of individuals occupying a certain geographical area, and therefore as, in Mr. Cole's view, a partial association compared with society and the community (pp. 34–35, 39, 44). This follows for Rousseau from the well-known defect of his formulation of the General Will.

On this fundamental point Hegel, and all philosophy that descends from him, is diametrically opposed to Rousseau. To identify the State either with the governmental machine, or with what is ordered by a plebiscite over a certain area (which has hitherto usually been the instrument of despotism), is, we all think, I believe, to support the error which Rousseau pointed out in speaking of the will of all, and also himself made in formulating the expression of the

General Will. For Hegel the State is what is sovereign; the defining term is sovereignty, and this is by definition the 'ideality' of all parts of the community, trade and religious corporations being expressly intended. 'Ideality' = the tendency of any thing to pass beyond itself and seek completion in a greater thing. This is what I tried to express (*The Philosophical Theory of the State*, p. 185) by saying the State is Society as a unit, so far as exercising control over its members, and sovereignty is the working of a complex of institutions (e.g., *The Philosophical Theory of the State*, p. 150). Thus belonging to the State is plainly a matter of degree, and this is very plain in Hegel's analysis of Society. The Corporations, etc., are the very stuff of which the State is made.

Well, then, this is our answer to Mr. Cole's question. It is very like something he suggests (I am not sure if he negatives it) on p. 42: '(Sovereignty) is the resultant, etc.'

What then do we say arises at the point of 'the relation to' (p. 40) or as, or in place of, the 'federal body' (p. 43). Mr. Cole's answer and suggestions we have seen: a federal bond or something greater than the State, or just the individual's best decision. I do not despise any of these; but I am bold to think our answer worth hearing. We say what arises is a 'constitution' and that no inhabitants of an area form a State without that. And we think that Rousseau in his best mind (in his remarks on the legislator) is with us. By a constitution we mean a whole of parts and organs, all functional (as Hegel of course perpetually insisted) and all bearing on one another in very various relations and degrees of intimacy. It lies, we think, in habits, traditions, recognitions. No plebiscite can express it; but it is the nearest thing to an expression of the community's will. (A will in principle unexpressed, goes near to enjoy the *otium cum dignitate* of the thing in itself.) And it acts as the State, in so far as it solves conflicts by authority, though in a civilized society this is never by bare authority, but always by reason speaking with authority.

A constitution is primarily a way of co-living and co-operating. It might come to be a very loose bond, as in many ways our English constitution is; and if it became very loose, the question whether it was a State or no might become verbal. But I think that the ideality of all organizations and corporations will always remain a truth, i.e., they will always, at the points where they bear on each other, need to pass beyond themselves into something greater; perhaps, as Mr. Cole says, some Court of Appeal. And I believe that the collective force of the whole, when evoked by emergency, either internal or external, will continue to be very great, and capable of drastic operation; though the occasion for its display may become, we will hope, rarer and rarer.

The history of Letchworth by Mr. Purdom is an interesting example of the way in which the administration of an area raises all problems, and how, I think, the wise administrator brings them all into beneficial bearing on each other, showing separate treatment to be impracticable.

LOYALTIES

'I hate half-hearted friends. Loyalty comes before everything'.

'Ye-es; but loyalties cut up against each other sometimes, you know'.

—Galsworthy

A GOOD MANY YEARS AGO, I READ TO THE SOCIETY A PAPER UNDER THE TITLE 'Conflicting Social Obligations'.[1] This paper is essentially an attempt to develop the line of thought which I then sketched out. In most of the books that I read on Political Theory, the starting point and the centre of the study seemed to me to be wrongly conceived. Most writers, despite their disclaimers of the abstract contrast, seemed to me too much dominated by the problem of 'the State' and the 'individual', too much concerned with the search for an ultimate principle of 'the individual's' obligation to 'the State', and too much inclined, in seeking an answer to this problem, to simplify the study of sociality in such a way as to make it valueless as a guide to the practical questions of politics and social organization.

This artificial simplification of the problem, I felt, beset the 'metaphysicians' fully as much as the 'individualists'. The latter, indeed, presented the contrast in a cruder fashion, treating the State as an artificial mechanism devised for the furtherance of individual aims, and therefore lacking any capacity for natural

---

1 *Proceedings of the Aristotelian Society*, 1925–26.

or teleological growth. But the 'metaphysicians', as Professor Hobhouse has called them, were equally the victims of this error. They had seized, from Rousseau and Hegel, the vital truth that 'the State' is natural and that its life consists in the development, in some sort, of a common or general will. But they had assigned these real attributes of sociality to a 'state' still conceived far too nearly in accordance with individualist conceptions of structure and practical function. That which belongs properly to the 'state' of Hegel they were disposed to assign to the 'state' of Locke and Bentham. The metaphysical theory of sociality became in their hands a most dangerous and misleading metaphysic of political government.

In my first expression of my reaction from this point of view, there was a good deal of crudity. I came face to face with 'the State' as I found it, in the form of a practical political instrument; but I could find no correspondence between its working and the metaphysical theory which I had been taught. One might, of course, have become aware of this contrast—as many do—without discarding the metaphysical doctrine. But I wanted a practical guide. An ultimate principle of obligation and a teleological view of 'the State' did not help me unless I could find some relation between them and the practical problems in which I was concerned. I perceived that, in the past, theories of politics had borne a close practical relationship to political affairs. From Plato to Aquinas, from Grotius to Bentham and Rousseau, not one of the great political thinkers was a mere academician. T. H. Green himself was as much an interpreter of Victorian Liberalism as Locke was of the English Revolution. But the contemporary theorists on whom I was brought up seemed to me mere academicians both in their own thinking and in their interpretation of the great thinkers of the past. The search for the principle of political obligation had become a refuge from the attempt to answer the practical problems of social organization.

With a keen sense of this sterility, I looked at the world of social thought. Such liveliness as I found there seemed to come from writers concerned less with Political Theory than with a number of distinct practical causes and movements. In Figgis, in Sorel, and in Thorstein Veblen, in the Marxists and in such sociologists as Gumplowicz and Ratzenhofer, I found far more lively and useful political ideas than in the contemporary philosophic writers.

There was, indeed, in these latter one vital goodness. They had learnt from Rousseau and Hegel to make the naturalness of the social will their fundamental doctrine. But they had tended to narrow the conception of this will so as to find the expression of it solely in a 'State' of whose nature they have given only a metaphysical account, and no working analysis. A doctrine which in the hands of Rousseau and Hegel had been a shearing sword of politics had become, in theirs, a merely pious sentiment.

I went back to Rousseau. And I found, in his *Political Economy*, a passage which seemed to me to illuminate the whole doctrine of his *Social Contract*.

That passage I set at the head of my previous paper, and I need not quote it here. The essence of it was the statement of Rousseau's doctrine of the *moi commun* or 'common will', as applying not only to 'the State', but also to every form of association and recognized common interest, whether it takes shape in any formal organization or not.

This passage set me to the study of social obligation in a new way. I recognized that, as Dr. Bosanquet said in his pointed 'Note' to my previous Paper, 'the State' in Hegel is not merely a piece of political machinery, or identified with the government, but a totality of social relationships. But 'the State', as government, easily came to be, if not identified, at least treated as the representative of this totality, and no one will deny that both Hegel and the Hegelians were concerned to stress rather the unity or universality of 'the State' than the diversity in which this unity was found. Dr. Bosanquet contrasted Hegel with Rousseau by setting Hegel's 'State' as a totality of relationships in contrast to Rousseau's 'State' as either a machine of government or the expression of a plebiscitary vote. Herein he was right enough, if the *Social Contract* is to be treated as by itself the quintessential and complete outline of Rousseau's doctrine. But it was Rousseau's *Political Economy* and, incidentally, the first unfinished draft of his larger *Social Contract* scheme, that helped me to a different, and I think, a more vital, way of interpreting his thought. Of course, I do not suggest for a moment that Rousseau was either a systematic or an entirely consistent thinker. Such systematization as he attempts in the *Social Contract* tends to spoil his idea. It is more vital in these earlier expressions of it.

Rousseau, then, helped me to see the same underlying basis of common will as the sustaining force, not only of 'the State', but of all associations and of all informal human groupings. And he led me to just what I wanted—a principle which would guide me in the study of the parts as well as the whole, and would set again in place the broken links in the chain of which ethical and political theory are, in separation, disconnected fragments. For when once we see that man's sociality is φύσει (that is, in becoming if not wholly in being, in intention if not thoroughly in fact), a matter of a natural will which is not purely individual, we see at once man's relation to 'the State' as only one aspect, not different in kind from the other aspects, of his relation to his fellow-men, as it finds expression in his countless social contacts, memberships, associations and loyalties.

Loyalties. In that word I more and more found my clue to the problem of sociality. I called my previous paper 'Conflicting Social Obligations'. Today, I speak not of obligations but of loyalties—in terms not of the Kantian imperative, but of that common sentiment of us all which is the whole basis of our capacity to live and work together. 'What others give as duties', said Whitman, 'I give as living impulses. Shall I give the heart's action as a duty?' It is in the living impulse, rather than in the obligation, that the secret of sociality—of the naturalness of human societies—is to be found.

Graham Wallas helped me here enormously. His distrust of what he calls 'Professionalism' has grown with him, in these days, to an obsession. But, in *Human Nature in Politics*, he did make just that approach to the study of sociality that I needed. MacDougall and the so-called Social Psychologists I had found exceedingly unhelpful. The more I read them, the more they seemed merely to revive the older abstractions of 'Faculty Psychology' in new forms. Their classifications of instincts led me nowhere. But Wallas did set out, though he never quite reached his goal, to look at human behaviour, and especially social behaviour, with the eyes of a keen observer, attempting a real measurement of social phenomena as the starting point for a practical valuation. From his conclusions I often dissented; but his method I saw was right.

I began then, from the standpoint of a practical interest, to attempt a survey of such social facts as came specially within the range of my observation. And more and more the problem stood out in my mind as a problem of loyalties, but no longer mainly of conflicting loyalties. It is true that the conflict of loyalties is apt to occupy a very large place in the discussion of the problem; but this is not because it is the heart of the problem, but because it sticks out. In just the same way psychologists are apt to concern themselves largely with abnormal behaviour, and with the diseases of personality, because these things obtrude themselves on the observation, whereas normality normally does not. It is, however, just as dangerous in social theory as in psychology to mistake the abnormal for the normal, or to state the problem in terms of the abnormal, because the abnormal instances have received the closest study.

No society, from a bridge club to a nation, could hold together unless a considerable proportion of its members felt a considerable degree of loyalty towards it. So much is, of course, commonplace. It does not exclude either the subjection of one body of men to another by force (of which the history of States affords abundant examples), or the survival, in a condition of suspended animation, of atrophied organizations maintained by their officials (of which a survey of the list of organizations in, say, *Whitaker's Almanac* will provide an overflowing crop). But these latter bodies, if they have lived at all, have at one time lived by the loyalty of their members, while the most oppressive States have been held together by the loyalty of their oppressing classes. Nothing is done without loyalty. Loyalty is the root of the tree of good and evil conduct.

Obviously, as Galsworthy says, these loyalties 'cut up against each other sometimes', as they did in the play from which this quotation comes. But this conflict, while it is to some extent inevitable, is not of their essence. And Rousseau, when he made his momentous discovery of the *moi commun* as the basis of all sociality, misunderstood (doubtless largely for historical reasons) the nature of the loyalties which exist in smaller or 'particular' societies, and their relationship to the greater loyalty which he called the 'General Will'. The following sentence gives the gist of his mistake. 'The will of these particular societies has always two relations; for the members of the association it is a general will; for the great society it is a particular will, and it is often right with regard to the first object, and wrong as to the second'.

This sentence obviously embodies a truth. Each particular association, or clique, or group may have a will and interest of its own, which is unrelated to, or in conflict with, the will and interest both of other groups and of the community as a whole. It is indifferent to the whole community whether my bridge club plays 'auction' or 'contract', or whether, in my church, the service is conducted in a cassock or a frockcoat. It is not indifferent if the bridge-players privately mark the cards and then invite strangers to play, or if my church demands the right compulsorily to instruct other people's children in its own ethics and cosmogony; and on these points the common will of the bridge-players or the Church members may be a will not merely particular in relation to the larger will of the community, but positively hostile.

So far Rousseau is obviously right. But because the common will of a group may conflict with other wills, individual and social, and may fall foul of the 'General Will' of the community, it does not at all follow that this common will is to be regarded, in relation to the whole, as merely particular. This view of it really makes nonsense of the whole doctrine; for it involves treating the 'particular' associations as just what they are not, bodies artificial and unnatural, essentially unlike the greater body in which the 'General Will' is supposed to appear.

This does not square with Rousseau's essential doctrines; for elsewhere (in the first sketch of *The Social Contract*) he recognizes that 'the State' itself is, in relation to the world of States, a particular association, and its will, in this relation, a particular will. It is, of course, in this regard a particular will; but it cannot be a particular will alone. For it cannot, by entering into relation with other wills, divest itself of its own essential character. And this character, Rousseau makes quite plain, is that of generality, not merely in the sense that it is a will of all, but in the far deeper sense that it is a will in individuals who are willing universally. It is, as I insisted in my Introduction to Rousseau's *Social Contract*, 'above all a universal and, in the Kantian sense, a "rational" will'. But, if this is its fundamental character, it cannot put this nature off, or become merely particular into whatever relations it may be caught up. It is at bottom the will of individuals taking a universal form.

We come back then, to the individual as the source of will. But if the individual can will universally in his relation to 'the State', which in the world of States is only a 'particular association', so also can he will universally in those other groups, formal or unorganized, into which he enters as a social being. He may, it is true, will in his action inside such groups his own private interest or the interest of his friends or of the group instead of willing the interest of the whole. But so may he do any of these things when he is willing as a member of 'the State' or of any wider body. It may be, or it may not, that the danger of his willing in a 'particular' or an anti-social way is greater in the smaller than in the more inclusive groups. But this does not follow logically; it requires demonstration or disproof. And, if he may will 'particularly' or anti-socially as a member of either 'the State' or any other group or association, so may he in either case will universally or generally, striving to make his particular group or association a means in its measure to the good of the whole.

The realisation of this truth seems to me important. It connects itself directly with those doctrines which recognize groups and associations, not as *personae fictae* or mere creatures of 'the State' or the law, but as natural expressions of social personality—with Gierke and Maitland for example. And it is also fully consistent, as Dr. Bosanquet pointed out, with Hegel's doctrine of 'the State', and with any view which identifies 'the State' with a natural totality of social relationships. The doctrines, however, which concentrate on totality, fail to bring out the practical bearing of the truth. For the rational totality of the Hegelian 'State' is not being but becoming, and the vital question is how it is to become.

Social thinking has, of course, greatly changed during the eleven years since I read my previous paper. Since then, doctrines of political pluralism have come greatly to the front. The metaphysico-legal doctrine of 'State Sovereignty' has gone markedly out of fashion. Following the march of practical affairs, social theorists have given the 'particular associations' a place in their systems. But even if one can take this new attitude as securely established, there is still a great deal of thinking to be done. In especial, the tendency has been so far to study the problem mainly on its institutional side, so as to admit in the particular association a natural capacity for growth and the assumption of fresh functions and purposes, and in 'the State' a nearer approach to a federative and pluralistic character. My own view of 'the State' as a particular association like and among others has by no means found general acceptance; the tendency has been rather to widen the structural form and constitution of 'the State' so as to bring other associations within it. But I think my view has also gained ground; for it is clear that most plans for widening the 'State' as an instrument of government, or for giving it more a federal structure, leave outside a vast network of groupings and associations in which also the principle of natural sociality and growth must be entirely admitted.

This way of looking at the problem from the standpoint of institutions is valuable and necessary. But the time has come, I think, to look at it more closely from the standpoint of the individual himself. I insisted on this point in my previous paper, and it is to some extent stressed in Professor MacIver's *Community*. But it has not, directly at least, received nearly enough attention. I stated the point before chiefly in terms of the possible conflicts of social obligations. As soon as the plurality of loyalties or obligations is admitted, and various groups and associations are seen as the points of focus for these various loyalties, it becomes plain that the individual will or conscience, guided by the consideration of right, is the sole rational arbitrator of such conflicts. There is not an automatic or overriding loyalty of right to 'the State' or to any group or association; there is a principle of universality in the mind of man, and in this lies the final standard of obligation.

So far, so good. But this way of stating the problem is really unsatisfactory. For it stresses the possible conflict, instead of the positive contributions which all these different loyalties can make to the common good. The best community is that which, in a positive fashion, establishes the closest harmony among its members in working towards a common good. This harmony is fully as much the harmony of associative and group life as of the individual life in a narrower sense. The making of 'the State', in Hegel's sense, is then the eliciting of the good will in us all, so that it penetrates every aspect of our life, and so that our private and associative actions tend, in the greatest degree, to take shape as contributions to the common good.

The idea from which we have to escape is that, because this good is a common good, and has about it a final unity and universality, it is therefore to be sought mainly along a single road. We have to get away from the error (historically natural in Rousseau and the Benthamites, but most unnatural and perverse in Professor Wallas[2]) that particular associations are primarily conspirators or that the will of the individual in 'the State' is different in kind or content, or naturally superior, to his will as a member of any social group to which he may belong. We have come rather to the positive idea of the social will as finding its fullest expression where the will of individuals find their fullest and most diversified expression through a rich variety of free associative life.

But this associative life and will, I have agreed, is, like the wills of the individuals who make it up, potent for evil as well as good. It is, therefore, a vital question whether 'particular' associations tend to encourage rather social or anti-social motives. Professor Wallas appears to tend more and more to the latter view; but is this opinion finally reconcilable with any save an anarchist conception of sociality? For why should men in their particular associations be more anti-social than they are either in their private lives on the one hand or in their relations to 'the State' on the other? As for 'the State', no one accepts Rousseau's statement that the General Will is automatically realized by the cancelling-out of particular wills; but, unless this statement is accepted, there is no *prima facie* or *a priori* reason for expecting men to act more socially in the affairs of 'the State' than in any other sphere. Nor is there any reason for drawing such

---

2   In what I say here of Professor Wallas I am thinking of *Our Social Heritage*—that is, of his latter-day views. I have the greatest admiration for his earlier work.

a distinction between their private and their associative actions, save in a sense which makes equally against 'the State' and particular associations.

There is, indeed, a very real and important sense in which all forms of organization, since they involve some degree both of mechanization and of abstraction, involve in some degree a distortion of the wills of the individuals who enter into them. Co-operation always involves sacrifices as well as gains. But, unless we take the anarchist view that the sacrifices necessarily outweigh the gains, the recognition of this fact has no bearing on our present problem. It applies to all organized group life, and perhaps in greatest measure of all to 'the State', as the largest and most complex kind of continuous association.

Men's motives are mixed, both in their private acts and in their 'State' acts, and in those acts which they perform as members of any group or association. Some groupings are, of course, far more important than others, and have far greater power to contribute a value or a disvalue to the common life, in proportion to the strength of the loyalty which they excite in their members. And if, in our fear of anti-social loyalties, we frown on this associative life, we dismember community, and deny to it essential means of social self-realization. Nothing is potent for good, without being potent for evil also.

We recognize that both men and 'States' may be, on balance, good or bad. But those of us who are not anarchists work for the self-realization of man through some form of 'State' action, though we know the 'state' may turn out wrong as well as right. We believe that, on the whole, sociality makes for good, and tends towards unity of us one with another in pursuit of the common good. If this view holds good in relation to 'the State', it holds good also of particular associations, which have also their vital contribution to make to the common life.

What, then, are the causes which make for this interworking of private, associative and 'State' life in the common good? The condition clearly is harmony. In order that there may be a common good to which all can know how to contribute, there must be at least the broad conception of a common plan. The association, like the individual, must have some knowledge of his 'place' if it is to set up for itself any satisfactory standard of social behaviour. In other words, the interworking of the associative life must be consciously and purposefully promoted. The doctrine of 'function', Plato's master-concept in politics, is vital for the association as well as for the individual.

The harmony has, indeed, its seat in the minds of the individuals. But it will be constantly thwarted in its expression, and anti-social motives will receive constant stimulus at the expense of social motives, if, for any reason, the institutional life of the community fails to correspond to its vital needs, or if the 'State', for any reason, is more concerned to thwart than to develop the associative life. For in this case the loyalties as well as the institutions get into conflict, and men, without losing their sense of the social totality altogether, set up in their minds steep barriers between their group and their 'State' loyal-ties. This both tends to a stressing of the particularism of the groups, and sets up a destructive moral conflict in the mind of the individual.

The political philosophers of nineteenth-century England, with all their sharp differences, tended from opposite extremes to this vice. The Benthamites in their hostility to particular associations exalted not 'the State', but a mysti-cal and immanent harmony to be realized by *laissez-faire* methods. They did their work of destruction, and produced for a brief space, in mid-Victorian England, the illusion of a lasting harmony. But they left out power of asso-ciation, and were therefore incapable of facing the new problems which took the place of the old. Their harmony dissolved in a welter of Imperialist and Socialist doctrines.

The Hegelians, on their side, with all their grip of the need for organizing sociality, and for all their master's grip of Society as a being rather than a be-coming, so whelmed the individual in the universal as to negate in practice the doctrine which they affirmed in theory. Refining the real will into the rational and universal, they lost hold of men as they are and flew away into the clouds. In their Cloud-Cuckoo-town, sociality could be fully expressed through a perfect scheme of universal Statehood in which all loyalties could find a coordinated meaning. But this doctrine, when it was brought down again to the actual world, tended to an exaltation of the actual 'State', and to a demand that everyone should treat it as the representative of the ideal 'State', and should subordinate all his purposes to it. In this form, it became an argu-ment for tyranny, and an invariable justification of things as they are. While it recognized associative life as part of the 'State' life, it tended in practice to regard all associations with suspicion, unless they were prepared to subordinate themselves utterly and unconditionally to the actual 'State'. In this way again, a destructive mutual conflict is aroused.

I am not suggesting that this was all the philosophers' fault. For philoso-phers, like other men, are creatures of their times. Nor am I suggesting that there is any way of setting up a perfect or automatic harmony of the personal and associative life. For circumstances change, and necessitate readjustments in social and political relations. And associations, being natural and not purely mechanistic groupings, have an inherent capacity for growth and change. If a harmony is possible, it cannot be a static harmony. There is no such place as Utopia.

There is, however, a possibility of greater or less harmony in the working of the social principle. And the securing of greater harmony depends, not merely on the avoidance of conflicts and clashes of loyalties in men's minds or between rival groups or associations, but still more on the positive evocation of many different loyalties in the common service. For, if we suppress the grouping in which some particular loyalty finds its expression, we cannot rely on being able to transfer that loyalty to 'the State' or to some other grouping which we regard as more appropriate and beneficial. Loyalty is essentially a question of will, and the voluntary principle is therefore vital to it. Certain groups, such as 'the State' itself, must doubtless, from the nature of their functions, possess in a considerable degree a compulsory character. But a wide opportunity for purely voluntary grouping, and for the constant making and adapting of associations as new common purposes develop, is essential to the positive realization of the common good.

Loyalty, I have just said, is a question of will. This is fundamental to my argument; but is it true? I can see some psychologists disputing it, and pointing to the large irrational element that is present in most of our group and associative loyalties. We are born into this group, and flung into that association, by force of contacts, rather than by any clear or conscious assumption of its purposes as our own. Few even of the most loyal members of most groups or associations have fully thought out their intellectual positions in regard to them, or completely rationalized the relationship. Indeed, there is a sense in which one cannot be quite so loyal with reason as without it. For the reasoner may see conflicts of loyalty which are not apparent on the surface.

All this is true enough; but it does not touch what I have been saying. For I am not assuming that loyalties are purely rational, any more than the Kantian assumes that men in fact obey only their 'real' or rational will. Loyalties, as we find them, are a mass of instincts, prejudices, customary ideas and assumptions caught up at secondhand, selfish and unselfish purposes, ethical strivings and corporate egoisms, all mixed up together. But so, of course, is man, and all that the psychologists have told us of the irrational in man, and all the sociologists have contributed to our knowledge of the growth of man as a social animal, do not affect the fundamental issue. For they apply whatever course we shape, and they do not affect our aim of so arranging the world as to encourage men to act as rationally as possible, and in doing so to make their irrational subserve their rational purposes and pursuits.

At least, this is so, unless we throw up the sponge altogether. There is, of course, a statecraft (and still more a rhetoric) that appeals deliberately to the irrational and either dislikes or despairs of the rational in man. And there is not one among us who does not often attempt to heighten his appeal to the rational by what he regards as a legitimate attempt to get the irrational as well on his side. All rhetoric, and still more all controversial journalism, embodies such an appeal. Nor can anyone regard it as in itself illegitimate; for what is right for the individual is right for the propagandist also. In our own lives, success depends largely on enlisting our irrational in the service of our rational being; and this is what we ought to do. So must the politician, and so, in a less degree, must the philosopher.

This process becomes illegitimate only when we use the irrational to falsify or obscure the rational, instead of using it to heighten the appeal of the rational. The line is, of course, hard to draw; but so are all lines that are worth drawing. It is, however, plainly passed when, instead of trying to promote a rational harmony of loyalties in the service of the whole, a leader or a class attempts to substitute for such a harmony a single loyalty in which the irrational element is consciously made to preponderate. The commonest example of this is the beating of the war-drum as the means of diverting men's attention from their rational wills to an unquestioning acceptance of the will of 'the State'. Napoleon I was an adept at this, and he has had many less successful imitators.

It is, however, obvious that Napoleon did manage to attach to himself a great deal of loyalty, and to catch up to his own person a great many loyalties that he had really pilfered from other sources. If he made hay of the old 'States' of Europe, he also made hay of French revolutionary doctrines. I suppose it is facts of this order that make many people sceptical of doctrines which place loyalty at the heart of sociality. Loyalties, they say, are irrational; only obligations or duties have the rational element clearly in a position of dominance.

This is true, but unhelpful; for men are moved by obligations only in so far as they find expression in loyalties. And that community has the best chance of being proof against Napoleonic perversions which can develop the most free and full and harmonious associative life. The French Revolution unwittingly prepared the way for Napoleon by declaring war on particular associations within 'the State'. Affirming one over-riding loyalty, it opened the way to the men who learned best how to exploit that loyalty. There is safety in numbers of loyalties, not because they must engender conflict, but because they compel comparison, choice, judgment. That community is likely to have the most rational citizens which has the fullest associative life.

And yet it may easily appear on the surface the most irrational. For it is easiest to get the best of an argument by banging all one's adversaries firmly over the head. The 'State' which forcibly suppresses, or keeps under, the expression and organization of other loyalties, both presents, if it is successful, an extraordinary appearance of that unity which is easily mistaken for rationality, and does often actually succeed in evoking towards itself a fierce nationalistic loyalty. Napoleon's France and Bismarck's Germany both achieved this; even Mussolini's Italy has achieved something of it. But such unity is in fact highly irrational, as readily appears in the external relations of the 'States' which rely upon it.' A good 'State' ought to be a good member of the comity of nations; but such 'States' most emphatically are not.

The free burgeoning of associative life is, however, by no means an automatic method of securing the good health of the body politic. It is essential to good health; but 'the State' may suffer from other diseases. In particular, we have seen that harmony among the various expressions of the associative life is a vital need. What is this harmony? It depends, first of all, on a basis of common ideas and assumptions broad enough to sustain the citizens in their common life, and finding substance in a set of social institutions which most people regard as, in essence, fair and reasonable. If this condition is not realized (and it is not over a large part of the world today), the basis for the harmonious working of the associative life is knocked away, and men group themselves into rival factions, and develop essentially conflicting loyalties, based upon their rival conceptions of social justice.

When this situation arises, society is in peril until either one of the rival conceptions triumphs, and compels a reconstruction of the social order, or a new synthesis is reached. But to put the matter in this way is to ignore the vital character of such conflicts as I have been discussing. For divisions so vital do not develop without good practical warrant. They arise, as Marx made clear once and for all, from changes in the problem itself—that is, from changes in the material environment of man and in his command over that environment. Save under the impulsion of forces from outside, they do not arise in communities which are relatively static in their material life. But, when the material basis of life changes swiftly, or when the character of social organization is changed by conquest from without, the harmony of institutions is upset, and the conflict of loyalties and obligations develops apace.

Let us ignore the case of external conquest as immaterial to our present purpose. When the disturbing material forces arise within the community, there is always the theoretical possibility of adapting by common consent the old institutions to meet the new needs. But, if the changes are far-reaching, they will almost inevitably give rise to strong rivalries and conflicts, because they will menace vested interests which are strongly entrenched and cause the rise of new interests which see their chance in the new conditions. Vested interests and established associations tend to perpetuate themselves beyond the needs they arose to serve; new groups, with a sense that material forces are on their side, claim a right to ride roughshod over others. Of such stuff are the great Revolutions of human history.

In such times, it is hard for men to distribute their loyalties. They have to make choice of their course and to cleave to it, backing their faith through right and wrong alike. This is not irrational of them; for the triumph of a cause is the only way to the re-establishment of a rational harmony. But it is an evil, though it is a necessary evil when once the point of disharmony which is its starting-point has been reached. At all times, men to some extent back their loyalties against their judgment on each particular case. The greater the disharmony of institutions, the more insistently they are led to do this. But their aim is the re-establishment of a harmony which will remove the need for such distortions of conduct.

Loyalties, then, can find free and rational expression only within a harmony which is twofold—a harmony of men and institutions one with another, on a basis of sufficient agreement about fundamental ideas; and a harmony of institutions with the underlying conditions of life, so that the institutions of society are consistent with, and help forward, the best use of men's material resources in accordance with their power over nature. Until these major conditions are fairly well satisfied, it is of no use to expect men to behave in accordance with the general will. For there is no general will which can find expression in their associative life. Loyalties therefore tend, in such circumstances, to present themselves in the superficial form, not of contributions to the common good, but of conspiracies against the 'public'. But this is because there is no 'public' whose interests the associative life can find satisfaction in serving.

The mistake, in such times, is to denounce the particular loyalties on account of the perversions to which they are subject, and to urge their submergence in a unifying loyalty to the whole. Such an insistence is usually ineffective; for loyalties cannot be easily transferred. But it is also disastrous if it succeeds. For the loyalty which is concentrated on the general by the suppression of the particular is an irrational loyalty, liable to achieve expression in disastrous forms, fatal alike to liberty at home and to fellowship abroad. Rational loyalty to the whole is what we want; but that is to be achieved only through a harmony of diversified loyalties to the parts. The freedom of voluntary association is the life-breath of its being.

FOR DEMOCRACY

WE PROCLAIM THAT IN THIS WAR WE ARE FIGHTING FOR DEMOCRACY AGAINST dictatorship.[1] Well, what do we mean by 'democracy'? I think I know what I mean by it, and I believe my definition of it will appeal to a very large body of my fellow-countrymen. But it is not what everybody means by 'democracy'; for each man interprets the word in accordance with his own scale of ultimate human values.

Those who know anything of my writings know that I have for very many years called myself a Socialist, and maintained that Socialism, involving the common ownership of the basic instruments of production, is the only foundation on which real democracy can be built under the conditions of twentieth-century industrial society. In this sense, I am a Socialist; but I am and have always been a Socialist *because* I believe profoundly in the ultimate value of the individual human spirit. I have been a Socialist *because* I have seen modern, large-scale industrialism and finance steadily establishing a centralized, irresponsible power which denies to the individual, or rather to the vast majority of individuals, the means of living a satisfactory life, and oppresses men with the hugeness of an organization altogether past their capacity to control. Knowing that it is impossible to get away from this hugeness, which is the direct outcome of man's advance in scientific achievement, I have seen in

_____

1 *Rotary Service*, August 1941.

61

the control of it by the democratically organized people the means to make it less oppressive to the spirit of man and more amenable to liberating influences deliberately imposed upon it for the individual's sake.

I am a Socialist politically *because* I am an individualist in my scale of ultimate human values. I call myself a democratic Socialist; and by 'democracy' I mean that, within the environing conditions of present-day society, which I must accept as the basis for any practicable social system, I want each individual man and woman to count, and to have a chance of living a satisfactory life of their own. Valuing individuality, I necessarily value difference, in which it finds expression. The very last thing I want, in working for Socialism, is to impose on society a flat uniformity of organization or opinion. I want a social system which, taking as its basis the inescapable hugeness of modern productive technique, will nevertheless find room and opportunity for individuals to express themselves, and to serve the community, in many and diverse ways.

Now there is, I believe, another conception of 'democracy' which is radically opposed to this attitude. 'Democracy', on this showing, is neither more nor less than the prevalence of the will of a majority over that of a minority, with the corollary that the minority is to submit itself to the majority's will. Let me say at once that I agree that, where a sharp decision has to be made between two opposing views and one acted upon as against the other, the will of the majority ought to prevail. This is an essential part of the democratic creed; but it is, in my opinion, only a small part of it. For in the vast majority of decisions, it is not essential that the will of the minority shall be merely effaced. The majority can get the vital substance of what it wants, and still leave room for the minority to go its own way to a sufficient extent to satisfy its basic needs. Majority and minority can both be, if not satisfied, at all events left with a sense that life is still worth living, and the road to creative satisfaction can be kept open to men of diverse aspirations and values. The so-called 'democracy' which allows the majority to ride rough-shod over all minorities is a perversion of real democracy, because it denies the basic democratic principle that each individual is to count. The democratic slogan, 'Each to count as one, and none as more than one', does not mean, though it is often so interpreted, that each is to count as a cypher.

Let us try to apply the democratic principle, as I have defined it, to the problems of social organization in our own day and country. The position, as I see it, is that for a long time past the organization of business has been growing more and more undemocratic in two distinct though related ways. The huge capitalist structures which increasingly dominate both industry and finance are undemocratic in two separate respects. They pursue policies which are contrary to the common interest of the community—for example, when bankers take fright and cause widespread unemployment and distress by a restriction of credit, or when great trusts deliberately restrict production in order to exact monopoly profits. And they also deny reasonable opportunities to the small-scale producer, the inventor, and the man of unorthodox initiative, often regardless of their capacity to serve the public, and quite ruthlessly in respect of the suffering imposed upon those who are crushed out by their giant power.

Now, the State, with its nearly universal electorate and its theoretically unlimited power to make the common will prevail, ought, one would suppose, to be in a position to prevent these abuses. But everyone knows that it has not hitherto shown itself able in practice to achieve this. I believe the reason for the State's impotence—in what is called 'trust-busting', for example—is due to the very same hugeness as creates the trusts as the engines of capitalist monopoly. The electors are so many, and have so little and so loose contact one with another, that it is impossible for them to count, or really to influence the main course of events. They are swamped by their own unorganized numbers, and become a prey to demagogues, who lead them hither or thither with but scant attention to their fundamental needs and desires.

This happens because political 'democracy' has been organized chiefly on the perverted notion of democracy to which I have already referred. It has been organized as a mere counting of heads, with the unavoidable consequence that, the more numerous the heads become, the less each head is able to count for in the other sense of the word; and this though the increasing complexity of social problems requires that each head ought to count for more, by exercising greater social intelligence and making a greater individual contribution towards the common good.

But, it will be objected, the numerousness of modern societies cannot be helped. It is bound, in fact, to be intensified, as men and things have, for technical reasons of efficiency (and also for the preservation of peace), to be governed and administered in larger and larger aggregations. True, all this cannot be helped: it is the problem, set to our generation and to those who will come after us, which we can by no means evade. We can, however, avoid adding to its difficulty by applying a narrow conception of democracy which stands in the way of even seeking a solution of it. Surely, the evident truth, consistent with everything we know about human nature and its potentialities, is that men can act together humanely, decently, and democratically in big things and in big groups only in proportion as they are accustomed to acting together humanely, decently, and democratically in groups small enough to give each man a sense that his contribution counts, and about things near enough to the life of each man for him to feel that his judgment about them has value and relevance.

If this view of man's nature is correct, it follows that democracy can flourish in the great State only if it is based on a general diffusion of democratic practice throughout the smaller units of which the great Society is made up. Nay more, it follows that the great State must encourage by every means in its power the creative, autonomous working of these smaller units, its function in relation to them being to ensure their democratic character and to keep the road open to a wide diversity among them.

My main concern in this essay is with the economic implications of this view. But I cannot make my economic conclusions clear without pursuing a little further the political conclusions to which my argument leads. Despite the hugeness of cities, the greater hugeness of States, the still greater hugeness of the new political structures which we must build for ourselves if the world is to live in peace, we must get back, as the indispensable nucleus of real democracy, to the neighbourhood group—to a group small enough for every individual in it to be linked to all the others by a continuous chain of personal acquaintance, like that which binds together all the people of a village or a very small town. We must give these little groups, within our towns of all sizes as well as in our villages, some real governing authority over the matters that concern them closely as neighbours; and we must build up from these democratic neighbourhood groups to the larger groups which must assume the tasks of administration and government in larger affairs. Only so can we make a democratic great society: only so can we give to every individual a chance to count as more than a cypher.

Now let us try to apply this same principle to our economic affairs. It is common knowledge that there are many men who would sooner be 'on their own', at the cost of having smaller incomes, than be caught up into the vast, regimented structure of one of the great trusts. There are many workmen, including not a few of the best, who would sooner work, for less money, in a small workshop where they can find a spirit of comradeship than in a vast factory. There are many 'intellectuals', like myself, who would find it sheerly intolerable to work inside a great intellectual machine—unless, indeed, they could find one, so broken up, like my own University of Oxford, into small self-governing groups of fellow-workers as to make its bigness consistent with the needs of individual self-expression and freedom.

I could not call 'democratic' any society which denied to men of this type the opportunity of working for society in their own way. I do not mean that anyone has the right absolutely to be maintained in business as a small employer, or to be guaranteed a job in a small workshop, or the chance of working as a 'freelance intellectual', merely because he prefers it. He has no such right, unless he can serve the community better in that way than by accepting absorption into the large units which are characteristic of modern business. But the larger the typical unit grows, the more needful it becomes, for society to ensure opportunity to those able and willing men who will give the best service if they are allowed to go their own way, and will be miserable and thwarted if they are compelled all their lives to accept a large-scale discipline for which they are by nature entirely unfit.

Such men, mind you, are a minority—a small minority today, though they will, I think, be more in a society based on truly democratic principles of organization. They will stand no chance at all in a society based on the powerful 'democracy' of mere majority rule. They will be crushed out, to humanity's dire loss. For they are an important creative element in the community, though by no means the only creative element. There are other men, probably much more numerous in this age of vast machines, whose creative impulses can find satisfaction by working inside large organizations—from skilled tool-setters who find a joy in the smooth running of a team of well-ordered machines to foremen, managers, and administrators of every sort and kind whose creation takes the form of organizing men and things within the discipline of a great, complicated social structure. I am not undervaluing these men, or denying their key place in modern society. I am only saying that it takes both sorts to make a real democracy.

What is the moral? I, as a Socialist, think that we ought to bring under public ownership all those parts of industry, and of the services which need, for reasons of technical efficiency, to be organized and managed on the great scale. I hold this, because private ownership in such cases leads straight both to the exploitation of the common mass of men by monopolists seeking maximum profit and power, and to the crushing out in the lines of business concerned of those men who would give better service to the community as the heads of small, independent workshops or factories or shops or farms or offices, or as workers in these small concerns, free from the impersonal discipline of the great establishment.

Beyond this point, I have no desire at all, as a Socialist, to nationalize or municipalize, or otherwise communize, any productive or service undertaking. I want the small man to be free to go his own way, wherever he can do his job efficiently by small-scale methods, and wherever the technical conditions of production and marketing do not lead straight into monopoly. Consequently, save in a few cases, I want to apply public ownership not to the whole industries, but to establishments. I do not want the State to become a monopolist, save where monopoly is indispensable for reasons of technical efficiency and the elimination of waste. I want public ownership only where private ownership has ceased to be a means to personal freedom and self-expression, and has become an instrument of tyranny over the common man.

On this point, I venture to believe that most Socialists would agree with me, if they could be brought to look at the problem from the human angle. After all, Socialists stand for common ownership not as an end in itself, but as a means of preventing exploitation. If the public owns the banks and the other great centralized financial services, those basic industries which can, for technical reasons, be carried on efficiently only by vast enterprises, and such individual establishments in other industries as have grown so huge as to rob their 'privateness' of all real meaning, what more need the Socialist ask? Unless he is at bottom a totalitarian enemy of mankind, a believer in the perverted democracy which reduces all ordinary men to cyphers, he cannot want more. He must want to leave room for diversity, because he must recognize the diversity of the human spirit as the ultimate governing factor in social organization.

But—and it is a big 'but'—will not the common ownership even of the industries and services to which I have pointed mean in practice the substitution of one form of tyrannical hugeness for another, and even of a more for a less dangerous form, because of a form more powerful and complete? Yes, it will, unless we can infuse into our politics the real spirit of democracy. The economic case for public ownership of the great monopolies is clear and clamant, because these monopolies damp down production in the interests of profit and thereby cause unnecessary poverty and unemployment. Public ownership and control would make an end of this restrictiveness, because the general desire of men for more goods would impel Governments, even under a perverted democracy, to expand production, as soon as the responsibility for it was placed plainly in the Government's hands. But it would be fully possible for the State, while expanding production, to proceed remorselessly with the crushing out of freedom. This is what Hilaire Belloc feared long ago, when he wrote *The Servile State*; and nothing that has happened since has made his fears less worthy of being taken into account.

Men will argue endlessly for and against socialization, according as they set greater store by the higher output which it would make possible, or by their fear of the uniformity which it might impose. I do not propose to argue upon this plane, because I am convinced that modern society is being impelled towards socialization by irresistible, technical forces, which it is futile to oppose. The increasing restrictiveness of capitalist monopoly, its growing panic at the limitation of markets, its flight from self-reliance to clamour for State-protection of its interests, are alike omens of its impending dissolution. It is doomed because, unlike the more competitive capitalisms of which it is the degenerate heir, it is unable to deliver the goods.

What concerns me is what is to take its place. Heaven forbid, say I, that we should, in an orgy of perverted democracy (totalitarianism), merely replace private by public monopoly! It is open to us, if we will, to comply fully with the technical need for hugeness, and to give to everyone who can express himself, best by working within the discipline of a large organization, the opportunity to serve the community in his own way, without therewith making victims and martyrs of those whose best service can be rendered by other methods. We can socialize what needs socializing, and no more. We can afford, in full consistency with the technical needs of our age, the opportunity for diverse initiative and small-scale enterprise to all those who can really serve best by working on their own, or in small, democratic groups. But we can do all this only on one condition—that we democratize our politics as well as our economics, by making for ourselves a political structure so designed that the ordinary man is given in it a real opportunity to count—not merely as a voter among millions, but as a participant in democratic processes near enough to his daily life for him to have first-hand views about how they ought to be run.

Without this basic social democracy, we shall be victims of totalitarianism, whoever wins the war. Hitlerism is, in essence, an exaggerated form of the perversion of democracy which pervades every vast modern society in which minorities are merely swept aside, and individuality and idiosyncracy are merely ignored. Our historic boast in Great Britain is that, man for man, we have wills and tempers of our own, and a traditional faith in freedom. Let us show these characteristics now, not by a futile resistance to ways of organization which are made imperative by the advance of science, but by adapting our institutions, economic and political alike, to the needs of the twentieth century, without therewith throwing away our individualism, which is at the root of freedom. Let us create for ourselves a democratic way of life in which diversity has room to flourish within a structure whose vastness is inescapable and, rightly directed, a means to greater health, wealth, and happiness for us all.

G. D. H. COLE'S
ELECTION ADDRESS

(for the University of Oxford constituency, 1945)

ALTHOUGH I HAVE BEEN ACTIVELY ASSOCIATED WITH THE LABOUR PARTY SINCE 1908, this is the first parliamentary contest that I have fought; nor should I have accepted nomination now except for my own University and under conditions which would allow me to continue to carry out in full my duties as a Professor. I have no personal ambition to sit in Parliament, and I should be most unwilling to be regarded primarily as a politician. My essential vocations are those of teaching and writing; and these they will remain if I am elected. This would not be possible if I were contesting an ordinary seat; but I believe it is and should be possible in a University Member. Indeed, I can see no possible justification for the existence of University constituencies, and of the plural voting which they involve, unless they do, as they have happily done of late in more than one instance, return to Parliament men who are not simply politicians.

It follows that, if I were elected, I should hold myself both specially concerned to safeguard the interests of higher education, which I have much at heart, and also authorized to exercise a wider right of personal judgment than is commonly allowed (or perhaps than can commonly be allowed) to Members returned under the auspices of a party. I was tempted to allow myself to be put forward as an Independent; but I came to the conclusion that there would be some inconsistency in doing so, as my Socialist convictions are tolerably well known and I have certainly no desire to cover them up. I believe that I shall be able in practice to exercise, as a member of the Labour Party, an independence of judgment, based on some expert knowledge, which entitles me to appeal for support to progressive electors generally, and not only to fellow Socialists.

I believe this the more, because my Socialism is, and has always been, of a strong libertarian brand. In my political faith I put foremost recognition of the value of tolerance, kindness of man to man, variety of social experiment, and encouragement of voluntary as well as statutory activity over the wide field of social service. I believe that public ownership of key industries and services can be so arranged as to admit of wide variety, to exclude bureaucracy, and to enlarge instead of limiting freedom, alike for the manager, the technician, and the manual worker. I believe in wide freedom for local government, and in the utmost freedom of voluntary association and expression of opinion as essential ingredients in the making of a real democracy.

There is no need for me to recite here the details of the programme on which I am appealing for support. My platform is that of the Labour Party—public ownership of a limited number of key industries and services, planning for full employment, including an improved distribution of industries so as to avoid over-employment and congestion in some areas and distress in others, a thoroughgoing policy of town and country planning, with social control over the use of land, a determined execution of a programme of public house-building that will as speedily as possible end slums and provide all families with decent houses at rents which they can afford to pay, and a real national Health Service, with wide opportunities for Health Centres based on group practice, and with much greater choice of doctor than most people enjoy today. I stand also for the maintenance and development of such controls, but only of such controls, as are necessary to ensure the success of full employment policy, to secure a fair distribution of available supplies as long as shortages exist, and to prevent the exploitation of the public by monopolistic influences.

In the international field, I stand for stern treatment of war criminals and total disarmament of Germany, for promoting close collaboration among the peoples of the world on democratic foundations in the common development of their means of living, and for friendship between Great Britain and the Soviet Union. Germany must be disarmed, but not destroyed; and the way must be left open for the re-entry of a German democracy into the comity of a peaceful and united Europe. I stand for recognizing the right of independence for India, while hoping that the Indian peoples will settle down in friendship as part of the British Commonwealth of democratic nations. I stand for large measures of economic and social development in the Colonies, with a view to their self-government and final independence, I hope, within the Commonwealth.

Finally, may I say something more of my views on educational development? I hold that the most important tasks for educational reformers are (1) to make an end of the waste of human ability which is involved in present methods of selecting pupils for the higher stages of education, and (2) to break down the barriers which have disastrously separated what is called 'cultural' from technical education. I believe that we must, for reasons of sheer self-preservation as well as of necessary adaptation to the conditions of the modern world, put much more weight on technical (including higher technical and applied scientific) education than we have done hitherto. But I believe that this can be done, not merely without sacrificing the culture that we have inherited from the past, but in such a way as to deepen and enlarge it and to penetrate culture with the spirit of science and science with the best achievements of that older culture. If there is one particular thing that I shall hope to do if I am returned to Parliament, it is to talk sound and practical sense about education, from the stand-point of a scholar who, not being a scientist, yet seeks to understand the scientific basis of the age we live in.

As for myself, I have worked in Oxford continuously for the past twenty years, and have previously held positions in two other Universities. I am Chairman of the Fabian Society, and play an active part in its work. My age is 55, and I am married and have three children.

WHAT SOCIALISM MEANS TO ME

SOCIALISM MEANS TO ME, MORE THAN ANYTHING ELSE, A SOCIETY WITHOUT classes, and without the mass-structures of rich and poor to which a capitalist system gives rise.[1] It means, therefore, the opportunity to maximize personal liberty, within a general social structure based on public ownership and control of the vital instruments of production.

Personal Liberty?

There is a manifest danger of the need for mass-organization of the poor to overthrow class-tyranny leading, in the course of the struggle, to an emphasis on mass-solidarity and to a mood of under-rating personal liberty, and even treating insistence on it as a bourgeois prejudice. However necessary it may be to stress solidarity in the actual struggle, we must never lose sight of the point that the Socialism at which we are aiming requires the mind of every man and woman to be filled with the sense of freedom, as much as their bodies to be assured of food. The purpose of Socialism is to end not only poverty, but also slavery, including enslavement of the individual mind. Accordingly, we must

---

1   *Labour Forum*, October–December 1947.

never forget the danger that, if we lay too much stress on the need for solidarity in the struggle, we may lose sight of an essential part of our objective—the release of the individual from bondage of all sorts—from bondage to the mass as well as from bondage to the rich.

Socialism, as I see it, is a means of releasing individual initiative and energy in the common service. It involves democracy, not merely in a formal sense and not merely in the form of centralized popular control, but also diffused through every part of the social structure, so as to give everyone who is so disposed the fullest possible opportunity of really sharing in the work of government. I am thinking not only of democratic local self-government, and of the need to preserve small units of self-government in order to meet the capacities of ordinary men and women, but also of *functional* self-government—that is, of the self-government of men and women in relation to particular to spheres of social action. For example, I do not regard a system of industrial control as satisfactorily socialist or democratic unless, in addition to providing for national ownership and final authority in the hands of representatives of the whole people, it also encourages the fullest practicable participation in control by the actual workers by hand and brain, at every level from the individual workshop up to the general controlling body for the entire industry.

In other words, I am still a Guild Socialist and, as such, equally critical of the purely political brand of Social Democracy and of the no less political type of revolutionary Communism. I believe in a Socialism that includes democracy everywhere where it can be made to work—and as far as possible includes *direct* democracy in the hands of small groups of people co-operating on a particular task within the general framework of a common plan.

Scientific Socialism

I do not at all accept the view that in Great Britain, now that we have made some real advances towards social security for the poor and towards the reduction of real economic inequalities, we can afford to throw away the old crusading spirit of Keir Hardie and treat Socialism mainly as a matter of scientific organization of the forces of Society. Scientific organization of the use of our resources is no doubt highly necessary; but the more scientific productive processes become the greater the danger of forgetting that they are made for men, and not men for them. Somebody has to be in a position to tell the enthusiastic scientist that what he recommends, even if it might increase production, would make the tasks of labour more irksome and devoid of interest, and would produce worse people.

Of course, I do not mean that all or most scientific improvements are open to this charge—only that the scientific technician, in pursuit of higher output, is apt to be merely unaware of the effects of his plans on the happiness of his human tools. The more industry comes to be scientifically organized and managed, the more necessary will it be for the actual workers to have the last word and to be in a position to insist on managers and technicians accommodating their projects to the convenience and happiness of the men at the bench or on the assembly line.

Enlisting Co-operation

It would be a bad day for Socialism on which men came to think of it merely as a superior kind of Rationalization or Scientific Management, to be judged solely by its efficacy in turning out more goods. We can, indeed, by no means ignore the need for higher production; but, if we are Socialists, we must seek to get this by means which will satisfy, and enlist the co-operation of the ordinary workers—by leading them, and not by driving them with a whip that is none the less a whip because its use has been authorized by Act of Parliament.

I have always objected strongly to the phrase 'Scientific Socialism'. I object to it on more grounds than I have space here even to name. Here are a few. First, I object to it because it implies that the advent of Socialism is to be regarded as an inevitable outcome of the evolution of economic forces. What these forces render inevitable is not Socialism, but large-scale organization and planning of economic processes, which are fully as consistent with totalitarian autocracy as with democratic Socialism. Whether we get democratic Socialism or totalitarian autocracy depends, not on the impersonal march of economic forces, but on our own skill and right-mindedness in controlling them. It is a matter not of scientific certainty or predictability, but of human capacity and commonsense and enlightened goodwill.

Secondly, I object to talk of 'Scientific Socialism' because it obscures the point that Socialism is, at bottom, essentially ethical. Why should we want Socialism at all except because Socialism is the best means of advancing 'the greatest happiness of the greatest number' and of making the way clear for people to live a 'good life'. Even if Socialism inevitable, that would be no reason for wanting it or working for it. The point is that, for our day and generation and for as far ahead as we can see Socialism is *good*, and we *ought* to work for it because it is good.

Science as a Tool

Thirdly, I object to calling Socialism 'scientific' because I deeply mistrust the 'scientists', and not only the 'natural scientists' but fully as much the 'economic scientists' and the 'social scientists' and all the tribes of professors who attempt to wear the mantle of science. Science is a useful tool, but it can tell us nothing about what our ends had better be, beyond salutarily warning us of difficulties and actually warning us off the pursuit of impracticable designs. The choice of ends, among those which are practicable, is a matter not of science, but of the *art of living*, which can never be reduced to scientific terms.

All true Socialists are and must be idealists, in pursuit of social ideals which they think worthwhile. To the extent to which we succeed in eliminating sheer poverty and in making the conditions of living less unequal in a material sense, we shall only be getting nearer to the real problem of Socialism, which is the improvement of the quality of human life. Watching the rich should have taught us that escape from poverty does not prevent people from living wretchedly ignoble and illiberal lives; and we should be well enough aware, from the example of America, that a nation with a high average income per head and a considerable diffusion of material prosperity among the working classes may nevertheless miss most of the decent human values and give itself over to gadgets instead of building up good fellowship between man and man. This spirit of fellowship is indispensable if the establishment of Socialist institutions is not to end up in miserable fiasco. Under Capitalism, the workers have worked hard largely because, if they did not, they risked the loss of their jobs and a fall into destitution for their dependants as well as for themselves. As we begin to build Socialist institutions, to plan for full employment, and to guarantee a minimum standard of social security for all, this compulsion to work hard necessarily loses force, simply because fear of the sack can no longer play its traditional role as a driving force.

New Incentives

I have been arguing for at least thirty-five years against the error of those who expect the mere change to public ownership and to a system under which production is broadly planned to serve the general interest, to provide a sufficient substitute for the emasculated incentive of fear. Public control, exercised nationally through Parliament, is far too remote to give the ordinary worker a sense of personal responsibility for doing his job as well as it can be done; and a Public Board, appointed by a Minister responsible to Parliament, is nearly as much 'they', instead of 'we', to the rank-and-file miner or transport worker on whose effort the success of socialized industry depends. Nor is the establishment of machinery for joint 'consultation' a sufficient remedy, as long as the power of decision rests with an authority which the worker does not mentally identify with himself.

No doubt, the Russians have for the time being partly solved this problem of incentives under Socialism; but how? Partly by developing still further the piece-work inducements which existed under Capitalism side by side with the incentive of fear; but also partly by keeping constantly alive in the workers' minds the belief that the country and the revolution are in danger from foreign capitalist aggression—so that they have been able to enlist on the side of high production the extraordinary incentives which usually apply only in time of war. This atmosphere of 'war emergency' has also made possible the continuance of drastic restrictions on personal liberty, without provoking serious resentment. But, clearly, no appeal of this type can last for more than a limited time. The essence of an 'emergency' is that it is not permanent; and sooner or later the Russians will have to face the same problem of incentives as we are facing today. What they have done gives us no answer to our difficulty, except as showing that piecework inducements are in no wise inconsistent with Socialism.

Freedom to Withhold

The point is that such inducements cannot be enough, and that we have also to find some effective substitute for the capitalist incentive of fear. As Socialists, we believe—or at any rate I think we should believe—that this substitute is a feeling of responsibility to and for the public—a feeling not just held individually by each worker, but also acting upon each worker as a sense of what his fellows expect of him and are ready to help him to achieve. Such a feeling diffused by the art of leadership through each group of workers co-operating upon a common task, is the accompaniment of the spirit of fellowship on which Socialism rests. But—and this is the vital point—it can be aroused only when the workers are really conscious that they are free to give or to withhold their service, and that the responsibility for giving good measure lies with them.

No one, I think, pretends that this sentiment can be diffused in sufficient strength all at once, as soon as the capitalist incentives lose their force. That is why the transition to a Socialist Society is necessarily difficult, most of all when it is made by constitutional means, so as not to give rise to the mass-sentiment that develops in face of war. I am not suggesting that it is practicable to pass straight over, in the situation in which we are placed today, from the capitalist incentives to those which are needful for the effective working of a fully Socialist system. I am, however, saying that we cannot begin the real building of Socialism unless we at least begin constructing the new system of incentives by transferring a substantial amount of positive responsibility for production to the workers in mine and factory and dock and field and office; and when I say this I do not mean by it merely giving Trade Union leaders seats on national or regional Boards of Control, but delegating responsibility to the actual groups of workers engaged in the various productive tasks.

Some Will Rise...

My conception of a Socialist Society is that of a Society in which everyone is given a real opportunity of participating in the control of social processes, and as many as can be induced to respond to this opportunity to participate in practice. Nothing short of this is democracy, or is consistent with the Socialist aim of giving every person the fullest chance of developing his or her capacity for service and for responsible behaviour. Of course, some will rise to the opportunity much more than others, and there will no doubt be some who will not rise to it at all. But I believe those who fail to rise at all will be few, if the natural leaders who exist at every level and in every social group are given good encouragement to influence their fellows and to make their own weight felt. The task of Socialist education lies largely in helping to equip these natural leaders among men, and in sowing in the minds of all the spirit that will guide them to a right response to good leadership that sets out to guide, and not to drive.

Enlarging Liberty

Finally, it needs to be understood that planning is no threat to liberty, but is rather the means to enlarging it, provided that it is not unduly centralized, but is conceived essentially as a two-way process, with plans being made in small units and sent up to the centre, as well as being made at the centre and sent down for amendment and adaptation at the points where they have to be carried into detailed execution. Large-scale planning constitutes a danger to human freedom only when the attempt is made to devise detailed plans at the centre and to enforce their performance rigidly, in terms of the central planners' conceptions of what is needed, without due regard to the reactions and concrete experience of the men and women whose activities are being planned. Given the elasticity of plans through the participation of local and factory groups in the making and modification of detailed plans, planning can become a framework for the liberty of the people, within which self-government and responsibility, can be widely diffused without jeopardy to the general interest.

I have stated my conception of Socialism in terms of a single Society; but of course the establishment of Socialism in any one country is only part of the process of establishing it as a worldwide system, not on a basis of strict uniformity, but with many national variations to meet the differences of national tradition and economic and social development. We are setting out, as Socialists, to construct a system of international relations based on fair dealing between peoples and on the development of the sense of worldwide interdependence. I have left myself no space to follow up this theme, but I should not like to be supposed to have left it out of account.

Avoiding Bureaucracy

It follows from what I have written that I do not think of Socialism primarily in terms of nationalization of industry. I have no wish to nationalize any more industries than must be nationalized in order to ensure their being conducted in accordance with the public interest. I count not only municipal but also Co-operative conduct of industry as fully compatible with Socialism; nor have I any objection to leaving many small-scale industries and services in private hands, provided that their conduct is made subject to public regulation in order to prevent either the exploitation of labour or the pursuance of monopolistic practices at the expense of the consumers' welfare. Socialism is not nationalization, and by no means involves the omnipotent and omnipresent State. It is a way of living on terms of social equality, and of organizing the essential services for the common benefit and under conditions of the utmost personal freedom. Above all, Socialism is not bureaucracy, or consistent with it; for bureaucracy implies centralization of power, whereas democratic Socialism aims at its diffusion among all the people.

LIBERTY IN RETROSPECT AND PROSPECT

It is altogether a curious situation that today sets political reactionaries singing the praises of liberty and Communists crying it down as a *petit bourgeois* prejudice, while Social Democrats try to hold a middle position and are shot at from both sides.[1] Through most of history, love of liberty has been a characteristic doctrine of the 'Left', and love of order of the political 'Right'. And yet, when one comes to reflect on it, the change of attitudes is not so surprising. Historically, the 'party of order', under whatever name it has passed, has been almost universally the defender of minority privilege: it has demanded 'order', if not exclusively at any rate largely, with the object of keeping the unprivileged classes in check. There have been exceptions, as when the merchant classes have allied themselves with the kings in order to put down a turbulent and exacting nobility and to assert the 'rule of law'. But much more often the 'party of order' has been the party of the privileged and of their supporters, whereas the slogan of 'liberty' has been that of their opponents.

This simple confrontation of 'order' and 'liberty' could not survive the development of political democracy. As soon as the idea—very old in itself—that power belongs of right to the people has become embodied in actual

---

1 *Rationalist Annual*, 1950.

constitutions which allow the whole people, or most of them, voting rights, there comes to exist at any rate the possibility of a state of affairs in which the unprivileged majority will capture the government, at least formally, and the privileged minority will find itself defending its privileges in the name of liberty. In the extreme case, where a thoroughgoing revolution has occurred, there may be few or none of the old privileges left to defend; but all the more, in such a situation, will there be *émigrés* and refugees calling for the overthrow of the 'despotisms' that have dispossessed them, and sympathizers with such refugees calling down imprecations on the 'tyranny' of the new revolutionary States. Where there has been no social revolution, but only a constitutional and perhaps temporary conquest of parliamentary power by the leaders of the unprivileged classes, the privileged will have still a great deal to defend, and will cry out no less loudly against the 'servile State' which even the most moderate Socialist government will be accused of endeavouring to introduce.

Accordingly, in the eyes of the upholders of traditional privilege, Communists and Social Democrats alike will appear as enemies of liberty; and attempts will be made to induce the lower classes to believe that their liberty is being attacked, even when the liberties actually being restricted are such as only a minority of the people has ever enjoyed. For example, in England today, you can hear petrol-rationing, or even food-rationing, denounced in middle- or upper-class circles as gross infringement of the 'liberty of the subject', and equated with the control of labour engagements as if the attempt to guide labour into the jobs where it is most needed were quite on all fours with the attempt to check wasteful expenditure on food in time of scarcity, or pleasure-motoring which uses up precious dollars that could be spent on food or essential materials. Even more can you hear, in the United States, every measure in Roosevelt's New Deal attacked as a monstrous invasion of personal liberty, even if it was evidently necessary to prevent the spread of mass-unemployment both in America and, by its repercussions, through most of the civilized world. The truth is that, in the more advanced capitalist countries, it needed world war to bring home to the richer classes that the laws (except those dealing with recognized crimes) applied to them as well as to the poor. As soon as war-enforced and war-prolonged restrictions hit the wealthy as well as the poor, the wealthy began talking loudly about the sacredness of liberty, and ceased for the time to be eloquent about an 'order' which was no longer devoted chiefly to protecting their exclusive interests.

There is a further, and closely connected, reason for the new-found enthusiasm of the privileged classes for the slogan of liberty. In every advanced economic society, a greatly increased amount of State intervention in economic and social affairs is being sheerly forced on governments, whatever their political principles may be. Even the United States, where the gospel of Individualism is most widely preached, is honeycombed with public bodies administering this, subsidizing that, or organizing some form of collective service. Compulsory social insurance in various forms has increased enormously, under governments of every possible variety of complexion. State regulation of industry and of finance has made a no less startling advance. Even nationalization has been practised nearly as much by opponents as by advocates of Socialism. In Great Britain, the Conservatives set up the BBC, the Electricity Grid, and the London Passenger Transport Board, besides greatly extending the scope of social insurance on a compulsory footing. Such things get done, not only because certain parties wish to do them, but also because even parties which dislike them are forced to do them by sheer pressure of facts. But the increase of State intervention, though all parties have to bow to its necessity, is associated in the minds of the privileged classes with progressive—often called 'confiscatory'—taxation and with an attack on the 'rights of property'. Even if Conservative governments have to resort to such measures, they are not estopped from denouncing them when they are introduced by their opponents, or from appealing to the electors as the defenders of a 'liberty' which, if they win power, they will find themselves forced to curtail.

Meanwhile, Social Democrats—to use the word in a very broad sense—favour extended public control and intervention on principle, but defend this extension as the means to an increase of liberty for the unprivileged majority—arguing, for example, that full employment and social security bring with them a greatly enhanced liberty for the main body of the people, and that the measures needed to ensure them are therefore liberty-creating and not liberty-destroying on balance. At the same time these Social Democrats regard with abhorrence the destruction of liberty in the totalitarian States of the Communist world, whereas the Communists hold that the real liberty of the people consists, not in freedom of speech or writing or organization, but in freedom from exploitation by a privileged owning and ruling class, and deny that liberty can rest on any foundation other than the 'dictatorship of the proletariat', exercised through a privileged and monopolistic party which is the guardian of revolutionary truth. Within this philosophy, personal liberty is hardly mentioned, except as something to be enjoyed as the reward, soon or late, of revolutionary mass freedom from the tyranny of the Capitalist State.

The fundamental difference here lies in the distinction between individual and group liberty. Historically, though here and there from Socrates onwards certain great men, and certain 'mute, inglorious Miltons', have put up a fight for personal liberty, usually religious or intellectual or aesthetic, the big battles for the enlargement of liberty have been fought mainly by groups on a collective basis, and have been, in effect, either claims to share in the privileges of the existing privileged classes, or assertions of new claims to privileges which would not extend to everybody, but only or chiefly to themselves. In Great Britain, and indeed in most Western countries, the struggle for liberty has been, historically, in the main a struggle for the extension of privileges to wider groups, until it has come, in our own day, to take on the form of a claim to privileges for all. Such a claim is differentiated from the claim for the sweeping away of privileges root and branch by its willingness to tolerate the retention, at any rate up to a point, of minority privileges that are felt not to stand seriously in the way of the realization of the privileges claimed for all. As against this, where there has been no historical process of extending privileges step by step to more and more, the demand of the unprivileged—or on their behalf— is for a clean sweep of the old privileges such as can be achieved only by social revolution in an extreme form.

When such a revolution has taken place—and it may be the only way of advance where other roads are barred by force—the prospects for personal liberty are bound to be poor until the revolution has either been utterly defeated or has fully consolidated its position. A root-and-branch attack on traditional privileges is bound to leave so much ill-blood behind as to enforce on the leaders of the revolution a policy of violent suppression of potential as well as actual opponents, and therewith a rigid discipline of the groups favourable to the revolution or capable of being regimented under its banner. Thus personal liberty, except in forms favourable to the revolution, tends to disappear, and the whole emphasis shifts to an assertion of a collective liberty defined in purely negative terms—as freedom *from*, not freedom *to*.

Freedom *to* is of its very nature a much more personal thing than freedom *from*. It can take, of course, collective forms—for example, the freedom to form dissenting Churches or conventicles, to organize opposition parties, or trade unions, or artistic cults, or to establish connections with institutions which transcend national frontiers, such as the Labour or Communist Internationals, or the Catholic Church. But all these collective freedoms can have a marked personal quality, in that they all involve recognition of individual rights to deviate from current norms of social behaviour: besides, most of them involve, as one of their aspects, an appeal to the individual conscience as a guide to conduct. This appeal is, of course, precisely what neither reactionary nor revolutionary regimes can easily stomach, because both rest on dogmatic conceptions of what is 'right' for society, and therefore to be required of all its members. Personal liberty is an outgrowth, at its best, of a recognition that differences are positively valuable as outlets for varying types of valuable personality and as means to the discovery of new values, or, on a lower plane, of that tired tolerance which emerges when rivals have failed to stamp one another out and have come to value peace and quietness above the zest of conflict. In the higher of these forms, personal liberty is essentially a faith of enlightenment, demanding a considerable degree of rationalistic objectivity in its votaries, and not capable of being either really understood or believed in by most people, even in the most advanced societies. Tom Paine believed in it ardently: most of the readers of *Rights of Man* were no more capable of understanding it than those who persecuted the salesmen of so subversive a book.

Personal liberty, then, always needs the support of the tolerators as well as of those who believe in it on principle. But tolerance is the characteristic of a society that is either weary of indecisive conflict or confident enough of the stability of its structure not to be afraid of rebel teachers. In a world such as we live in today, tolerance makes few new converts: its power depends on the strength of the tradition behind it, and especially on the extent to which this tradition is diffused among all sections of the people. Great Britain is a very tolerant country, by any comparative standard, mainly because the diffusion of privilege has been for a long time past a continuous process affecting more and more people, so that the notion of tolerance has filtered down to all classes, except perhaps the very lowest. Such a tradition can be bent by circumstances but not easily broken. It has given us the sort of government we have, with one foot in Socialism and the other in longstanding political tradition, and with its determination to tolerate even Fascism, despite Hitler, as well as Communism, despite the Cominform.

This tradition, however, which is the principal safeguard of personal liberty in a situation which calls for more and more public regulation of affairs, is inevitably precarious, because it is understood only by a minority and practised without understanding, or at any rate without principle, by the majority of those who abide by it. Its survival depends on nothing occurring to break off the continuous tradition of democratic betterment, in both an economic and an educational sense. A crisis serious enough to confront the leaders of the people on either side with an unavoidable choice between destroying their opponents' power and facing irreversible defeat themselves could rapidly transform the mere tolerators into suppressors, leaving only the intellectual believers in liberty to fight a lost cause without mass following.

In many European countries the weakening of democratic Socialism and the strengthening of both reactionary and Communist extremes are signs of the effects of difficult contemporary conditions in the absence of any continuous tradition of what I can only call the democratization of privilege. In Great Britain this tradition of the past hundred years was the outcome of a happy combination of circumstances—of the adaptability of the parliamentary regime to transformation by instalments, and of the leadership of British industry in the march of technical progress, which afforded a continual surplus of productivity for passing on first to the skilled and later to the less skilled workers. These twin developments blunted class conflict; and the effect was reinforced by the strength of religious Dissent, which had won some degree of tolerance through exhaustion as a sequel to the struggles of the seventeenth century. All these factors combined to make an evolutionary creed in politics acceptable to the leaders of the working as well as of the middle classes, and not at all intolerable even to the old governing classes, which merged more and more with the most successful sections of the middle class. No other major country in the world has had such an evolutionary experience; and in no other, accordingly, does personal liberty rest on the same foundations. It is, however, necessary to bear in mind that these foundations, which until 1914 seemed so firmly based, have been seriously undermined economically by the erosion of two world wars.

But surely, it may be answered, the United States has built, even more fundamentally than Great Britain, on a set of social values in which personal liberty is given a high place? Yes, and no. Yes, because in America traditional and hereditary privilege have counted for much less, so that a sort of social equality has counted rather as a starting-point than as a goal to be reached. But also no, because the United States has been faced for a century or more with a gigantic problem of assimilation—not of Negroes, who, despite the Civil War, have been left as an alien community within the frontiers, but of the hordes of voluntary immigrants from Europe whom the ruling powers have wished to convert into one hundred per cent believers in the 'American way of life'. This assimilation has involved both mass indoctrination with American ideas and a habit of thinking in masses, or averages, rather than individuals. The 'average man' is not an individual, but a unit in a mass, as much so as a proletarian in Eastern Europe who is treated as a unit in the class group which it is his business to serve. American constitutional theory remains highly individualistic, as a hangover from the Declaration of Independence and the original federal Constitution. American practice diverges from the theory—which is perhaps one reason why American political theory has been, ever since Jefferson and *The Federalist*, so intellectually poor a product of a nation by no means lacking in intellectual capacity.

In particular, for the Americans, liberty is not an exportable commodity. They have no instinct, in international policy, to support the side of liberty, except in a sense which restricts the notion of liberty to that of competitive capitalist enterprise. The Americans are addicted to 'trust-busting' at home, but have no objection to pushing the interests of American capitalist pressure groups abroad; nor do they recoil, even at home, from even the most ridiculous baiting of intellectual nonconformity. Their instincts, as far as the louder voices of opinion express them, are totalitarian rather than libertarian, despite their distrust of government. They use social, even more than governmental, pressure as a means of enforcing conformity with 'the American outlook'. They may grow out of this; but the strength of the existing pressure is made plain by the habitual defeatism of the American intellectuals—even in their hours of triumph.

We on the other hand, and in varying degrees the countries of the old British Commonwealth and of Western Europe, have a much more personal attitude to both political and social affairs, and therewith a greater readiness to insist on personal liberty. This has its bad as well as its good side. For example, in France, and to a smaller extent in Great Britain, it leads certain sections of the middle classes to shape their politics as a sheer reaction to personal comforts and discomforts, with no attempt to think or to act reasonably in the light of either principles or long-run interests. French defeatism in 1940 and some English middle-class reactions to rationing since 1945 are clear instances of this tendency—though the French nation has been much more deeply infected than the British so far. Insistence on personal liberties is, indeed, consistent with national well-being only when it rests on foundations of principle and not of sheer egoism. A privileged class that believes in itself as a good leader of the nation may at the same time act with gross selfishness towards the classes below it; but it is to some extent redeemed, and able to lead the nation, as long as it can continue to believe in its mission and not only in its right to consume the people's substance. When any privileged class becomes simply selfish, the nation that continues to be led by it is in sight of disaster.

But even a privileged class that does believe in its mission may have little use for personal liberty—even its own, if it fears that its dominance is seriously threatened. And a country which, as a sequel to social revolution, throws up a new disciplined elite is in continual danger of the conversion of this elite into a new privileged class which, not valuing personal liberty for itself, can hardly be expected to value it for others. In a world dominated as to one-third by Americanism, with its 'hundred-per-cent' tendencies based on the need for national assimilation, and as to another third or more by still unconsolidated revolutionary Communism, the prospects of personal liberty are poor for some time to come, unless the countries which are still, in spirit, apart from both groups can act together in defence of the libertarian principle, and can maintain the alliance between those who believe in liberty and those who merely assent to tolerance. I fail to see how this can happen except on the basis of a broadly common policy in both economic and political affairs; nor, in face of the measures needed to maintain full employment and the standard of life, can I see any basis for such a policy except democratic Socialism, at least as an accepted tendency if not as a positively expressed politico-economic creed. I know this is a hard saying in face of the setbacks democratic Socialism has suffered since 1945 in a number of 'Western' countries. But the revised *laissez-faire* Liberalism that is being preached up by many middle-class thinkers, and practised by many middle-of-the-road politicians as far as they dare, seems to me quite hopeless as a foundation for the closely knit unity that is needful to preserve Western civilisation—and therewith personal liberty—from being crushed to death between the rival embraces of the great mass-powers of America and the Soviet Union. For the European West it is for the moment above all a matter of holding out; for the hope for the future lies in avoiding war and in the development of mutual tolerance between the two great rivals, when each sees that it had better make up its mind to live side by side with the other in the world. With such a development of mutual live-and-let-live, I dare to hope that there will come in both societies internal tolerance as well. At present, there are many more signs of this in the United States than in the Soviet Union, which has recently been moving fast in the opposite direction under the influence of fear. But such tendencies are not irreversible; indeed, in such a development as I have described lies the world's sole hope of not tearing itself to pieces in a war that could leave little personal liberty alive anywhere at all.

THE BRITISH LABOUR MOVEMENT: RETROSPECT AND PROSPECT

Prefatory Note

THIS PAMPHLET IS A REPRINT OF A LECTURE WHICH I GAVE AT HALIFAX IN April, 1951, at the request of the Ralph Fox Memorial Committee.[1] It was the first of a series of annual lectures, to be given in memory of a citizen of Halifax, well known to the Socialist movement and as a writer, who died fighting for his faith in the Spanish Civil War.

Ralph Fox was born in Halifax on March 30, 1900. From his twentieth year he was actively associated with the Labour Movement and the Communist Party. He was best known as an historian for his biography of Gengis Khan; as a literary critic for his association with *Left Review*, the *Daily Review* and *New Writing*, to which papers he contributed articles, political journalism and short stories. On the outbreak of the Spanish Civil War he volunteered for the International Brigade and served as political officer to the British Battalion. He was killed in action before Cordoba on June 2, 1937. It seemed to me fitting to honour his memory by surveying, over the period covered by my own knowledge, the changing phases of Labour development, and trying to see what tendencies are at work in the movement today. After the lecture, it was suggested that a printed version might serve as a basis for discussion groups in some of

---

1   Ralph Fox Memorial Lecture, April 1951.

the considerable number of Labour Party, Trade Union, and other organizations represented in the audience. I readily agreed; and the Fabian Society is publishing my lecture with this purpose, as well as its own members, in view.

***

My own recollections of the British Labour movement go back over forty-five years. I became a Socialist as a schoolboy a year or so before the General Election of 1906, which first put the Labour Party firmly on the parliamentary map. Till then it was only the Labour Representation Committee, with no more MPs than could be counted on the fingers of one hand. In 1906 it rose suddenly to a party of thirty members—still a mere handful besides the 400 Liberals and not much more than a third as many as the Irish Nationalists. Nevertheless, Labour became a party, and from 1906 there was no longer any doubt that it was destined to become a major force in British parliamentary affairs—though it was then impossible to foresee the speedy break-up of the Liberal Party, which seemed at the very height of its powers, or the great accession to the strength of the Labour movement during the First World War.

Why I Became a Socialist

My conversion to Socialism had very little to do with parliamentary politics, which were at the time of it mainly occupied with the struggle over Free Trade and Tariff Reform, with the issues of Irish Home Rule and Women's Suffrage ranking next in current estimation, and that of Trade Union rights, challenged by the Taff Vale Judgment, a poor fourth, outside a few industrial areas. I was converted, quite simply, by reading William Morris's *News from Nowhere*, which made me feel, suddenly and irrevocably, that there was nothing except a Socialist that it was possible for me to be. I did not at once join any Socialist body. I was only sixteen, and had the best part of three years more school in front of me before going up to Oxford, which was already my planned destination. I do not remember even taking a great deal of interest in the General Election of 1906 until it was over—when I shared in the common excitement and wonder about what would happen next. My Socialism, at that stage, had very little to do with parliamentary politics, my instinctive aversion from which has never left me—and never will.

Converted by reading Morris's utopia, I became an Utopian Socialist, and I suppose that is what I have been all my life since. I became a Socialist, as many others did in those days, on grounds of morals and decency and aesthetic sensibility. I wanted to do the decent thing by my fellow-men: I could not see why every human being should not have as good a chance in life as I; and I hated the ugliness both of poverty and of the money-grubbing way of life that I saw around me as its complement. I still think these are three excellent grounds for being a Socialist: indeed, I know no others as good. They have nothing to do with any particular economic theory, or theory of history: they are not based on any worship of efficiency, or of the superior virtue or the historic mission of the working class. They have nothing to do with Marxism, or Fabianism, or even Labourism—though all these have no doubt a good deal to do with them. They are simple affirmations about the root principles of comely and decent human relations, leading irresistibly to a Socialist conclusion. If I were talking today to persons who had grown up in the same mental climate as I did, I should hardly need to add that before long my favourite weekly reading was the *New Age*. I was, of course, an 'intellectual' of the middle class: had I been a worker it would probably have been the *Clarion,* to which I took a little later, after overcoming an initial distaste for its jollity and its liking for getting people to go about in droves. Judged by any standard, the *Clarion* was well past its prime when I first met with it; but it was still a considerable force in the industrial centres.

I did not join up with any Socialist body until 1908. Then, shortly before leaving school, I discovered a small branch of the Independent Labour Party in my home town, and joined it, but found it rather depressing. A few months later, I celebrated my first week in Oxford by joining the University Fabian Society and its parent body in London, and my second week by starting, with one friend I had made a few days before, a new paper, called the *Oxford Socialist.* I remember waylaying R. H. Tawney in the quadrangle at Balliol and getting him to write me an article. That was our first meeting: he was then the leading figure in the small band of University Tutorial Class Tutors connected with the Workers' Educational Association.

Socialist Prospects Forty Years Ago

As I look back and try to discover what were my expectations in those days about the future of Socialism and of the Labour movement, I find it difficult to be sure what I felt or expected. I think I felt sure that Socialism was the cause of the future, and that some day there would be a Socialist society from which poverty would have been banished—and therewith the unpleasant necessity of worrying one's head about economic or social problems, as against the many more attractive things one wanted to do instead. I was then reading and writing poetry at a great rate, and much more interested in literature than in economics, of which I knew nothing. I did not want to be a politician, or to concern myself with such matters as economics except in the hope of pushing them away by getting their problems solved on Socialist lines. Socialism presented itself to me, not as an economic or political doctrine, but as a complete alternative way of living—as I still regard it. In this guise, it offered itself as something which seemed at one moment very near, and at another a long way off. When it seemed very near, I was feeling revolutionary, and dreaming of a day when, how I hardly knew, the masses would rise up and overthrow capitalism and create on the morrow a complete Socialist society. But at other moments capitalism looked to me very well entrenched; and I envisaged a long process of Socialist education and propaganda culminating in its destruction at some distant date in the future. I do not think I ever, though I became a Fabian, contemplated a gradual evolution into Socialism by a cumulative process of social reforms. My notion of the advent of Socialism was always catastrophic, whether it should come late or soon. I was never in the very least a 'Lib-Lab'; and the last thought that could have entered my head would have been to look hopefully on the Labour Party as the heir to the Liberal tradition.

Indeed, in those days I had no love for the Labour Party, though as a member of the ILP as well as of the Fabian Society I belonged to it. The Labour Party of the years between 1906 and 1914 was much too 'Lib-Lab' for me. I was well aware that nearly all the Labour victors of 1906 owed their seats in Parliament to Liberal support, and that not a few of them were ex-Liberals who at the behest of their trade unions had changed their party but not their opinions. Year by year after 1906, and even more after the elections of 1910, which left the Liberal Government more dependent on Labour support, I could not help seeing more and more plainly the ties in which the Labour Party was held by its support of the Government, the bargaining with the Liberals over seats and electoral alliances, and the wide gap between the Labour right wing and the left. A left, may I remind you, that was becoming stronger and more vocal as the cost of living rose, and as the claims of the workers were postponed to the exigencies of party politics or side-tracked—as I saw it—by Lloyd George's Bismarckian social insurance measures—denounced by Hilaire Belloc as leading to the 'Servile State'.

British Socialism before 1914

Two things impress me above all others as I look back on the feelings of those years. One is the insularity not only of my own outlook, but of that of most of my contemporaries—if 'insularity' is the right word. The other is the sense of squeezability of the capitalist orange. By our 'insularity' I mean, not that we were unaware of foreign countries or of a community between our problems and theirs, or that we ignored ideas from abroad, but that, despite our awareness and our openness to other peoples' ideas, we thought of ourselves as fighting the battle for Socialism as a national battle, side by side with similar battles that were being fought elsewhere, and had no notion of our particular struggle being altered in its nature or seriously deflected by the course of international affairs. We were simply not considering world war as a factor, or social revolution as a world event. We were, in effect, most of the time assuming that capitalism would continue developing but not essentially changing, until we were ready to supersede it, and that it could afford, out of its surplus earnings, to make large concessions to working-class claims without losing its potency to 'deliver the goods'. We were very far from the mood in which Marx and Engels had confidently expected a rapid intensification of the 'contradictions' of capitalism, to be manifested in recurrent and increasingly severe crises, each of which might prove to be the last—the death-throe of capitalist exploitation, the birth-pang of Socialism. We expected capitalism to last our time, unless we roused the workers to overthrow it; and this, I feel sure as I look back, gave us confidence to preach left-wing doctrines, because we were not afraid that labour revolt might paralyze or slow down capitalist production without putting any alternative system in its place.

Syndicalism and the Labour Unrest

I am of course speaking now, not of the Labour leaders of my youth, but of my contemporaries of the Socialist left and of their analogues in the trade unions. The political conditions which confined the Labour Party of the years before 1914 to playing a secondary role as the ally of Liberalism helped to breed in the young a spirit of antagonism to the compromises of politics and to prepare a welcome for the industrialist theories of working-class action which were influencing many workers in France and in the United States. The great 'Labour Unrest' of the years immediately before the First World War was not in any sense a product of French Syndicalist or of American Industrial Unionist theory. These became influential in Great Britain as a *result* of the unrest and as attempts to give it a clear meaning: they were rationalizations rather than causes. The causes were rather the freeing of trade unionism from the chains of the Taff Vale Judgment by the Trade Disputes Act of 1906 and the rising prices which parliamentary action seemed able to do nothing about, *plus* a sense of power which the advent of the Labour Party had first stimulated and then flouted. The rise of the militant suffrage movement also had a little to do with it; and it is undeniable that there was in the air a feeling of impatience of old restraints which affected not only Bergsonian philosophers but also the man in the street. The victory of 1906 had seemed at the time to promise so much: within a very few years it seemed to contemporaries to have achieved so little—infinitely less than, looking back on it now, we can see that it had actually brought to birth.

The wave of 'Labour Unrest', with militant Syndicalist and Industrial Unionist ideas carried on its crest, struck Great Britain in the middle of my university career. It struck me, and my student contemporaries. We watched the strikes of 1910, 1911, and 1912 with fascinated attention, attracted above all in them by anything that involved an assertion of the worker's claim to equality of human rights with his 'betters'. Strikes against tyrannical employers or foremen, strikes for the right to a share in determining industrial policy, strikes for the right of workmen to do as they pleased in their hours of freedom from labour, strikes for trade union 'recognition', sympathetic strikes in which workers asserted their right to refuse to handle 'tainted goods'—all these possessed a human appeal which seemed to us, in comparison with the familiar processes of collective bargaining about wages and hours, to involve an assertion of higher status—a revolt against the 'undemocracy' of capitalist enterprise and of the bureaucratic State.

Guild Socialism

Yet most of us were very moderate revolutionaries after all—trade unionists and young intellectuals alike. Most of us did not swallow whole the Syndicalist gospel of 'Direct Action', or throw overboard the parliamentary method of advance towards social equality, or even accept in full the Marxist doctrine that the State was to be regarded as simply an instrument of the capitalist class, and would have to be overthrown and replaced by a new proletarian State made in the imagine of the governing class of the coming revolutionary era. We tried to construct a theory of Socialism that would embody and reconcile what was good in the conflicting theories of Fabians and Syndicalists, of the Labour Party—as far as it then had a theory—and of the Industrial Workers of the World. For the group with which I was associated, this attempt was embodied in Guild Socialism, which for a time, though sponsored mainly by a small body of Socialist intellectuals, exerted a widespread influence on the trade union leaders—especially on those younger leaders who were in search of a halfway house between old-style trade unionism, with its limited objectives, and the full-blooded revolutionism of Tom Mann and the Industrial Unionists.

I am not suggesting that Guild Socialism ever bit deeply into the consciousness of the Labour movement. I think it was too intellectual a creed ever to do that, and too little capable of being simplified down to such emotive slogans as gave Marxism, despite its intellectual complexity, its mass-appeal. But an idea closely associated with Guild Socialism, with Syndicalism, and with Industrial Unionism did get across to large numbers of the younger workers. This was the idea of the 'control of industry'—of 'workers' control'. This idea, however, in its Syndicalist and Industrial Unionist forms, came sharply up against the traditional Socialist advocacy of nationalization, as it had been preached by the stalwarts of both the Independent Labour Party and the Social Democratic Federation. It was therefore unacceptable to most Socialists; whereas Guild Socialism, which retained the demand for national ownership of the means of production, while advocating that the administration should be entrusted to 'Guilds' representing all the workers 'by hand and brain' organized on an industrial basis, enabled Socialists to take over the libertarian drive behind the Syndicalist movement without breaking with Socialism as they had understood it in the past. Even the Webbs, in their *Constitution for the Socialist Commonwealth of Great Britain,* went some way towards compromise with the Guild idea; and most of the younger working-class Socialists of the ILP went a good deal further, though most of the older leaders did not. Philip Snowden, in particular, fought Guild Socialism and 'workers' control' as forms of anarchy quite as implacably as he had fought Lloyd George's Insurance Act as an attempt to introduce the 'slave State'. The old collectivist Socialism, he kept saying, was good enough for him. Ramsay MacDonald, too, disliked the new ideas, but characteristically temporized, and tried to capture the slogans of the Guild Socialists without changing his meaning.

The battle of ideas continued to be fought out during the First World War. The many and quick changes in the factories called for by war needs—the dilution of labour, the suspension of cherished craft union practices, the questions about who should be called up for the armed forces and who left in the workshops—gave a strong impetus to the demand for 'workers' control'. But, as the war dragged on, the emphasis shifted more and more from matters of workshop organization to matters of the 'call-up'; and anti-war feeling grew stronger when all who were willing to go to the forces had gone and it came to be a question of prising more and more reluctant workers out of their jobs. Moreover, the workers became more and more uncertain what the war was about, and more inclined to call for a negotiated peace as against the entire victory required by Lloyd George and his government colleagues, who by that time included the leaders of the parliamentary Labour Party.

The Russian Revolution

Into this cauldron of conflict was thrown the Russian Revolution of 1917. I think nearly all of us recognized this as the earthshattering event it was; but we held differing views about its nature, and these differences grew steadily wider after the Bolshevik seizure of power. As long as the war lasted, the growing numbers who wanted peace rather than absolute victory were held together, support for the Stockholm Conference which the Russians tried to convene acting for some time as a bond of union. But even during the war the Russian Revolution caused the shop stewards' movement to take a more militant turn, which foreshadowed the coming of the Communist Party. There was a growing cleavage between those who regarded 'workers' control' as a form of industrial self-government, to serve as the complement to parliamentary democracy, and those for whom 'workers' control' meant the social revolution and the dictatorship of the proletariat. The one group insisted on the internal democratization of each industry, through the strengthening of the trade unions and the development of 'encroaching control' by means of an extension of collective workshop bargaining: the other insisted that the workers could win no real control until they had made themselves masters of the State, and that the true democratic control was control by the whole working class, organized as the masters of a new revolutionary State. I am of course here over-simplifying; for there were many intermediate attitudes, and most active Socialists did not formulate the issues clearly in their own minds. But the shop stewards' movement did break up into revolutionary and 'constitutional' factions, and then went to pieces as soon as the wartime scarcity of man-power disappeared; and the Guild Socialists were riven into three fractions, one of which was speedily in full cry against the authoritarian tendencies of Bolshevism, while a second was in process of going over to the Communist side, leaving a centre, to which I belonged, supporting the Russian Revolution but standing out strongly against any attempt to apply its 'democratic centralism' or its method of dictatorship to the half-democracies of the West.

The New Labour Party of 1918

This struggle was only beginning when Arthur Henderson, driven out of the War Cabinet because of his support of the Stockholm Conference, set about reorganizing the Labour Party on a wider basis as a claimant to political power. It needs to be remembered that up to 1918 the Labour Party had never had any pretensions to be so regarded. It had contested only a small number of seats, mostly in alliance with the Liberals; and it owed a high proportion of its election successes to the existence of two-member constituencies in which the Liberals could be persuaded to concede it one of the seats in return for a common front against the Conservatives. But after 1916 the Liberal Party was rent into two; and Henderson saw the chance of making the Labour Party the heir to its historic position. Where there had been only a few constituency Labour Parties and a scatter of small ILP branches, he set about the huge task of organizing a party machine capable of fighting nearly every seat at the first post-war election; and in order to achieve this he converted what had been a loose federation of trade unions and small Socialist societies into a nationwide party aiming at mass individual membership. The ILP, who had been from 1914 an anti-war opposition within the Labour Party—an opposition which Henderson resisted all attempts to drive outside its ranks—did not at all like the new plan, because it threatened to deprive the ILP of its key position of influence as the chief propagandist agency and policy-maker for the party as a whole. But, weakened by their differences with the trade union leaders over the war, they were in no position to resist; and MacDonald, their foremost leader, was already preparing to shift his main allegiance from the ILP to the Labour

Party as soon as the war was over. Henderson, aided by Sidney Webb, was able to carry his plans through the Party Conference with only a scattered opposition from a few ILPers on the left and a few trade union leaders, who wanted a purely working-class party without the intellectuals, on the right. The reorganized Labour Party was heavily defeated by the Lloyd George Coalition in the election of 1918; but the new machine had been made, and its chance was soon to come.

The Acceptance of Gradualism

Looking back, it is easy to see—much easier than it was at the time—the immense significance of the Labour Party reorganization of 1918. In terms of declared policy, there was a sharp move to the left. Up to 1918, the Labour Party had never formally adopted a Socialist creed: it had been an exponent of immediate working-class demands and of a vague social idealism which trade union divisions forbade it to formulate into a Socialist definition of its aims. Webb and Henderson and MacDonald, in drafting and getting accepted the new declaration of policy embodied in *Labour and the New Social Order,* committed it to Socialism, but also committed it equally to seek Socialism exclusively by constitutional and gradualist means. At the same time, by enlarging the basis of membership and making a general appeal to men and women of goodwill to join, they replaced the ILP as the principal local organizing and propagandist agency of the movement by a network of local Labour Parties concerned much more with electioneering than with preaching Socialism, and therefore disposed to keep off militant tactics that were liable to estrange the marginal electors. The effect was not that the Labour Party became less Socialist than it had previously been: that could hardly have happened. It was that it became more completely committed to a middle way.

This indeed was involved in the whole conception of making it the heir of Liberalism and aiming at the speedy attainment of office. An outright Socialist Party could not, in 1918 or for long afterwards—could not, indeed, today—hope to be more than a minority group in Parliament. There were neither enough Socialists nor good enough prospects of making them to wrest the position of His Majesty's Opposition from the Liberals without making Socialism appear to be a moderate creed, which could win the support of citizens who were by no means ready to welcome a revolutionary transformation of their way of life. The main body of the British people did not want revolution: the most it could be hopefully asked to vote for was social reform, with a dash of Socialism by way of seasoning. But the seasoning had to be just hot enough to keep the main body of believing Socialists willing to remain in the Party, and to campaign for it, rather than desert it and join up with the small revolutionary wing, which was beginning to take on a Communist shape.

The Non-Communist Left

Between the constitutional Social Democracy of the new Labour Party and the militant Communism of the new extreme left, the middle groups, to which the Guild Socialists mostly belonged, could find no place to stand, when once the post-war slump had set in, and the militant movement in the workshops had been destroyed by the advent of large-scale unemployment. They became a permanent minority invoking vainly the spirits of the pioneers—of Keir Hardie, of Blatchford, and of William Morris—while the leaders of the party, with the support of most of the rank and file, got on with the 'real business' of winning parliamentary power. It was obviously impracticable—as the ILP discovered after 1931—to establish a new party of the left in opposition to both the Labour Party and the Communists; and attempts to work inside the Labour Party could be effective only on condition that they did not endanger its electoral success. There was always in the local Labour Parties a considerable amount of left-wing sentiment, which was able to find expression at particular moments, but never to establish any lasting ascendency. After the depression of the early 1920s this sentiment at first expressed itself chiefly in industrial action. Disappointment with the minority Labour Government of 1924 combined with anger at the policies of its Conservative successor to provoke the movement which culminated in the General Strike of 1926. During this period *Lansbury's Labour Weekly* became the principal organ of non-Communist leftwing sentiment; but the collapse of the General Strike and the defeat of the miners brought the phase of industrial militancy to an abrupt end and shifted trade union policy sharply to the right.

Mond-Turnerism and MacDonaldism

Then followed the Mond-Turner negotiations for industrial peace and the second minority Labour Government under MacDonald, which lasted from 1929 to 1931. There is no need for me to retell the calamitous story of those years. The second Labour Government doubtless had bad luck in being faced by the earlier phases of the great world slump; but this cannot excuse either its sheer failure to cope with the growing problem of unemployment or its evident lack of understanding of the forces with which it had to contend. It was made all too clear that MacDonald had abandoned his Socialist beliefs, that Philip Snowden was an orthodox capitalist financier and Free Trader much more than a Socialist, and that most of the Cabinet were merely bewildered by the crisis and had no notion of the right ways of meeting it. The one excuse that can be made for MacDonald is that he became exasperated at the futility of his Cabinet; but it is a poor excuse, for he was quite as futile as the rest.

The Labour Party after 1931

The defection of MacDonald, Snowden and J. H. Thomas, and the crushing defeat which the Labour Party sustained in 1931, had a momentary effect of strengthening the Labour left and causing the Party Conference to adopt a stronger Socialist programme. But even in 1932 it was apparent that the leadership was nervous about the new line. The test issue that year was the proposal to include in the party programme nationalization not only of the Bank of England but also of the joint stock banks. This was carried, against the platform and against Ernest Bevin's strong opposition; but it soon became plain that the party leadership did not intend to act on the decision. They were willing to include in the short-term programme considerable measures of nationalization of industry and the taking over of the Bank of England; but taking over the joint stock banks they regarded as bad electioneering, because it would offend the middle classes, and they managed to persuade themselves that the conditions necessary for Socialist planning could be secured without it. Moreover, in the nationalization plans that were worked out by a series of committees after 1931 the model adopted was that of the Public Corporation, taken over from the Conservatives who had used it for the Central Electricity Board as well as for the BBC; and on the question of 'workers' control', which was advocated by some of the trade unions but opposed by others, the Labour Party leaders showed themselves strongly hostile. Their plans of nationalization were substantial and challenging to some great capitalist interests, especially in the cases of coal and steel; but they were plans which could be carried out without interfering seriously with the main structure of capitalist ownership and control.

As against this, the Labour Party of the 1930s stood for a great development of the social services and of redistributive taxation of incomes—but not of property. Except for a prolonged hesitation over family allowances, about which the trade unions were sharply divided, the Party came to stand for a far-reaching programme of social welfare, as well as for a substantial amount of public ownership (with full compensation) and a not very clearly defined measure of national economic planning. In its proposals for dealing with unemployment it was deeply influenced by Keynes: indeed, it came to put almost entire faith in the Keynesian mechanisms for maintaining full employment under capitalism. Apart from its advocacy of nationalization, it was coming to be more and more plainly the inheritor of the traditions of progressive Liberalism, and less and less tolerant of the more aggressive Socialists who remained within its ranks.

Foreign Policy in the 1930s

While these policies were being worked out in relation to home affairs, the international situation was becoming continually more menacing as the belligerent intentions of the Nazis grew more and more evident. But the Labour Party found great difficulty in adapting its foreign policy to the new conditions. It had been in the 1920s the party of peace and disarmament and of fair treatment of Germany; and it was not easy for it to change its line in face of Nazi aggression. George Lansbury, its best-loved leader, was a pacifist; and, even when the danger from Germany had become plain, many Socialists hesitated to support rearmament under Conservative rule, fearing that the strength thus acquired would be used in the wrong way. Even after the Party had declared for rearmament and Lansbury had resigned from the leadership, fear of world war kept the Party from advocating effective help to the Spanish Government in the Civil War and induced it to take its stand by the policy of 'non-intervention'.

This hesitancy was responsible for the revival of left-wing activity in the years before Munich. There were movements, in which some Liberals and even a few Tories joined, for a 'Popular Front' or an 'United Front' against Fascism, in the hope of rallying sufficient support to turn out the Government. But the Labour Party leadership set its face firmly against all such movements, partly because it was suspicious of Liberal help, but mainly because it would have nothing to do with the Communists, who threw their entire energy into the anti-Fascist campaign and contrived to get a great deal of its organization into their hands.

By this time, the feelings of the Labour Party leaders towards the Communists had become much too embittered for any sort of collaboration to be accepted. This is hardly to be wondered at, in view of the continual vilification to which they had been subjected and of the struggle that had been going on in the trade unions ever since the turn towards industrial pacifism that had followed the defeat of the General Strike. The trade union leaders regarded the Communists as intolerable trouble-makers at home; and much of the friendly feeling towards the Soviet Union had evaporated in face of the increasing totalitarianism of the Stalinist regime. In Great Britain the Communist Party was small but active; and it saw in the condition of international affairs in the middle 1930s its chance to establish a leadership of the left against the existing leaderships of the Labour Party and the trade unions. The non-Communist left thus found itself in a very difficult position. If it joined hands with the Communists in the anti-Fascist crusade, it ran the risk of being driven out of the Labour Party and of becoming their captive. But if it refused to act with the Communists against Fascism, it was powerless to bring any effective pressure to bear on the official Labour leadership. This was the dilemma that led Sir Stafford Cripps and Aneurin Bevan into courses which resulted in their expulsion from the Labour Party and the dissolution of the left-wing, non-Communist movement they had set up.

The Second World War

The Second World War, and the Nazi-Soviet Pact which heralded it, reunited the Party, and for the time threw the Communists into deep discredit and unpopularity. But the Nazi invasion of the Soviet Union presently rehabilitated them, and enabled them to play a leading part in the workshop movements for high production. Their influence in the trade unions increased, and remains considerable in some unions even now; but there was no parallel movement in the political sphere. The Labour Party remained as determinedly hostile to the Communists as ever; and a good deal of the non-Communist left returned to it, while others found a temporary outlet during the suspension of parliamentary contests under the Churchill Coalition in Sir Richard Acland's Common Wealth movement. As soon as the Coalition broke up, most of these latter joined the Labour Party, and the election of 1945 was fought by a reunited movement which had temporarily buried its dissensions. The programme on which the Labour Party fought the election, though vague about international affairs, was in other respects strong enough to satisfy the left: the victory sent a wave of enthusiasm through the movement. During the five years that followed, the programme was carried into effect with remarkable completeness and fidelity. Yet, even by 1950, a great deal of the enthusiasm had died away. We must ask why.

1945 and After

Part of the answer is obvious enough. The enthusiasts of 1945 had not taken account of Great Britain's changed economic position in the post-war world, so as to expect a continuance of shortages and a stop on wage-movements in face of mounting profits and conditions of full employment. Nor had the workers in the industries due for nationalization realized how little difference the establishment of Public Corporations would make to their actual status and conditions of work. Nationalization had been a dream: the reality brought disillusion. Nor, again, had the main body of active Labour workers visualized in advance a state of affairs under a majority Labour Government at all like that which they found to exist. There had been vague anticipations of a changed way of life and of a putting down of the mighty from their seats. But, after five years, the upper and middle classes remained, grumbling but unsubdued, and the class structure still seemed to be much as before. Perhaps good Socialists ought not to have been disappointed at this; but they were. Perhaps they ought not to have felt uneasy when so many of the key positions in the new Corporations and in other branches of public life were given to anti-Socialists, and when Labour Honours Lists—except for a sprinkling of trade union and co-operative ennoblements—looked very like those of previous Governments. Perhaps they ought to have been satisfied with the great advance made in the social services, with the practical disappearance of destitution and really grinding poverty, and with the undoubted improvement in social security and in the standards of living of a large part of the people, and ought not to have expected a long-established and well-entrenched class system to be greatly altered overnight. The fact remains that the limitations of what had been achieved were evident, whereas the improvements were no sooner made than they came to be taken almost for granted. It is always easy to absorb an addition to real income; and gratitude for past favours is seldom a powerful political sentiment.

World Affairs since 1945

A second factor making for disillusionment among Socialists has been the steady worsening of the international situation, both from a specifically Socialist and from a more general point of view. In 1945 I think most British Socialists expected democratic Socialism to emerge as the dominant force over most of Europe—in France and Italy, in Belgium and Holland, in Czechoslovakia, and in Germany, as well as in Scandinavia. They felt that the British Labour Government, especially in Germany, could have done much more than it actually did to forward the Socialist cause and to strengthen the Socialists' hold on society: it seemed that, in the name of democracy, the Government was following a neutral policy which in practice played into its opponents' hands. They felt that little attempt was being made to establish a common front of European Socialism against the capitalist parties, or even to prevent a revival of Fascist tendencies. They were encouraged by the statesmanlike handling of the problems of India and Burma and by a forward policy in most of the Colonies; but they could not make out what Mr Bevin was playing at in Palestine and the Middle East, and they were acutely disturbed by what was going on in Greece. I think most of them also disliked the increasing subservience of Great Britain to America, but did not see how to avoid it. They were not prepared as a body to face the serious deprivations that would have resulted from a withdrawal of American help, even before that help had got tangled up with the cold war between the Soviet Union and the West.

Disquietude about international affairs became much deeper and more pervasive as, step by step, Great Britain became more deeply committed to an alliance under American leadership against the Soviet Union, and as, on the American side, the alliance turned more and more into an anti-Communist crusade in which Western values came to be identified with those of capitalist (called 'free') enterprise and Socialism came to be confused with Communism in an indiscriminate warfare against the left all over the world. I cannot by any means exempt the Soviet leaders from a share in the blame for this unhappy state of affairs. Their fears of American 'imperialism' and ideological belief in the inevitability of a world conflict between capitalism and Communism, with the non-Communist Socialists counted as part of the capitalist *bloc* and denounced as the betrayers of the revolution, destroyed the possibilities of pan-European economic co-operation; and their liquidation of the non-Communist democratic regimes in Czechoslovakia and Poland, together with their destruction of Social Democracy in Eastern Germany, helped to force West European Socialists to the acceptance of the American alliance as the only course left open. But I think most of us felt that a more Socialist foreign policy in 1945 could have prevented the disastrous series of developments which began in 1947 and reached their height in the Korean crisis and the threat of war against China in 1950–51.

Gradualism at Home and Abroad

Indeed, it was all too evident throughout the period after 1945 that British Socialism had no international policy of its own and was in no way minded to put itself at the head of an international Socialist movement distinct both from Communism and from American conceptions of the 'free world' order. I am sure this disastrous lack of an international policy was not due merely to Mr. Bevin's presence at the Foreign Office or to Mr. Attlee's dislike of the left to which he once belonged. Its roots went much deeper: it was an outcome of the tendency to model foreign policy on the conditions prevalent at home. In home affairs, the Labour Party stood entirely committed to gradualist constitutionalism: it was the declared enemy of all revolutionary notions. What its leaders could not see was that, even if this was the correct policy under British or Scandinavian conditions, its transference to other parts of the world might rest on a fundamental misunderstanding of the facts. What was the use of telling peoples who had no experience of parliamentary democracy and had come through the searing experience of social war between the classes that they must do everything by strictly constitutional and parliamentary methods? Where the first necessity was to overthrow a still feudal aristocracy and to build up swiftly a new political regime to replace a ruling class tainted by collaboration with the Nazis, what was the sense in urging that the first need was to have free elections and that the displacement of the landlords and capitalists should be deferred until it could be done in due order under the auspices of a democratically chosen Parliament? Such precepts made nonsense, and were an invitation to the defeats which they have helped to bring about. But Labour leaders who knew little about international affairs and had been accustomed to thinking politically in terms of purely national problems could not see an inch beyond their British noses; and it is not altogether surprising that the acutely suspicious leaders of the Soviet Union mistook their parochialism for subservience to capitalist and imperialist designs.

Whether there is now any way back from the mistakes made in international policy since 1945 I do not profess to know. Certainly there is no present possibility of establishing that democratic Socialist 'Third Force' which could, I feel sure, have become predominant in Western Europe if the task had been rightly tackled in the first instance. Had that been done, such a Third Force, joining hands with India and Indonesia and Burma, could have prevented the division of the world into two hostile *blocs,* the one under Russian Communist and the other under American capitalist domination. The danger of world war, which now overshadows everything, would have been much less; and democratic Socialism would have been, not third man out, but a great world influence in its own right. This chance has been cast away, I repeat, not because Ernest Bevin was a bad Foreign Secretary, but because almost the entire leadership of British Labour has shown itself incapable of putting itself in the place of peoples who have not grown up in the British parliamentary tradition.

The Future: At Home and Abroad

What then of the future? It is none too promising, even if we concentrate our attention for the moment wholly on home affairs. For the time being, the Labour Party has done most of what it can afford to do towards the establishment of the 'Welfare State'—fully as much as it can afford if we are to be burdened for years to come with an immense expenditure on armaments out of resources which are scanty enough without such claims upon them. As for nationalization, the gilt is off the gingerbread; and, apart from that, the election programme of 1950 made it clear that the Labour Party did not know what it wanted to nationalize next and was quite unprepared with any further ambitious plans for the supersession of capitalist enterprise. What is left with which to appeal to the electorate, or even to its own stalwarts, if neither social services nor nationalization can play the major part? Very little, except 'Down with the Tories', and that will serve only when the Tories have had a spell of power, and have given the poor something fresh to hate them for.

On the international plane, the prospects are even worse—yet they could be more hopeful if the Government would take a firmer stand against American and Communist hysteria and would, even now, constitute itself, with India and the majority of the peoples of Western Europe, the champion of peace. There is no doubt at all that most of its supporters want peace, and would like to see their Government mediating between intransigent Americans and intransigent Russians, rather than lined up on one side of a divided world in company with Syngman Rhee and Chiang Kai-shek and General Franco and all the reactionaries from pole to pole. I say this, not out of any love for Communism, or any will to see Great Britain lined up on the other side. I say it as a democratic Socialist, wishing to save the world from domination by either capitalism or Communism, and, above all, from war. But I almost despair of our Government, at the eleventh hour, giving such a lead.

The Pioneers and Ourselves

These are not comfortable words. I have, alas, no comfortable words to give you: I cannot even offer you the usual consolation prize of a peroration about the spirit of Keir Hardie and Robert Blatchford and William Morris. For these pioneers of the modern Labour movement were products of a situation which it is impossible to recall. They were moved to strong indignation by the sight, everywhere they looked around them, of unmerited and unnecessary human suffering, among men and women and children whom they recognized as like unto themselves and as members of the same social family. They were men who had grown up in a social atmosphere that was at one and the same time moral and hard; and they inherited its moral tendency while they revolted against its hardness. Growing up in the great days of British capitalist expansion, they saw lying ready the wealth that could be used to relieve distress; and they hated the system which in the name of individual self-reliance denied this use of it. They became Socialists because they regarded capitalism and human suffering as inseparable partners, and saw no way save Socialism of making an end of both.

But today, though poverty is still widespread, the sheer misery the pioneers saw around them has been either done away with or tidied away out of sight. There is very much less in the sights and contacts of everyday life to stir the sentiments of compassion and moral indignation; and misery afar off, which we do not see with our own eyes, has a great deal less power to move us than misery that directly affronts our senses. Nor are most of us as sure about our morals as the Socialists were sixty or seventy years ago. Two World Wars and the threat of more have dulled our sensibilities to other people's troubles, and have made the road to Utopia look much rougher and stonier than it used to look. We trust our feelings less, and have much less confidence that everything will be brought to rights if we only do our duty by our fellow-men. The political realist and the logical positivist are abroad, to reinforce Communist jibes at Socialist sentimentalism. After all, we can say, most people are not so badly off nowadays: the great threat to human happiness is no longer capitalism, but war and the totalitarian spirit which it encourages. Can we not afford to relax our efforts for Socialism, having already achieved so many reforms? Is it even worthwhile to try really hard, when at any time a few atom bombs may sweep away all the fruits of our labours—not to mention ourselves?

What We Need Now

I find this attitude fully understandable among those for whom politics and social affairs have never been more than a minor interest. I find it partly understandable even among the more convinced Socialists, in face of the deep disappointments of the past few years. It is not, however, my attitude, or I hope yours. What I do recognize is that the British Labour movement has, over the past six years, exhausted the impetus that has driven it on since the 1880s and stands in need of a new interpretation of the Socialist gospel. There is a great deal still to be done in developing the social services—education above all—as means of advance towards the classless society; but, even were the economic circumstances less restrictive, the gospel of human compassion could no longer have the same compelling power as it did. There is an immense task still ahead in devising new forms of social ownership and control to replace capitalist enterprise; but few hearts will be lifted up by the prospect of more nationalization on the model of the existing schemes. There is a keen desire for a world organized on a basis of friendly co-operation among the peoples to lift the poorer countries out of their primitive poverty; but how can we enlist that desire on the side of Socialism while we are showing ourselves the friends of reaction and the foes of revolution in countries which need revolution, even if we do not?

I do not know how far Ralph Fox would have agreed with what I have said in this lecture, had he been alive today. I do know that he was a fighter for the ideals and values which I have been trying to put before you, and that he died faithful to them. I pay tribute to his memory.

THE DEVELOPMENT OF SOCIALISM DURING THE PAST FIFTY YEARS

I HAVE BEEN ASKED TO SPEAK ABOUT THE DEVELOPMENT OF SOCIALISM DURING the past fifty years.[1] I shall begin with 1900, because two events of that year make a good starting-point. In 1900 an International Socialist Congress, held in Paris, set up the International Socialist Bureau, and thus formally inaugurated the 'Second International' as successor to Marx's First International of 1864. Earlier in the same year delegates from the British Socialist bodies and from a number of Trade Unions, convened by the Trades Union Congress, set up the Labour Representation Committee, which adopted the name 'Labour Party' six years later. Let us begin by asking how the Socialist cause stood, internationally and in Great Britain, at the time of these events.

The Paris International Socialist Congress was one of a series which had started in 1889, but only at Paris was the 'Second International' given a regular constitution. At the earlier meetings there had been continual conflicts between Social Democrats and Anarchists, with the question of parliamentary action as the principal issue. But by 1900 the Anarchists had been driven

1   Webb Memorial Lecture, October 1951.

out, leaving the parliamentary parties in control. By this time well-established political parties, mostly accepting Marxism as the basis of their doctrine, existed in a number of European countries; and the German Social Democratic Party held the highest prestige among them and had largely influenced their structure and policy. The German Socialists' Erfurt Programme of 1891, together with Karl Kautsky's commentary on it, was widely regarded as the most authoritative exposition of Socialist doctrine. The Swiss, the Austrians, the Scandinavians, the Dutch, the Belgians, and also large sections in France, Italy, and Spain, had accepted German Social Democracy as their model; and in Great Britain this was true of the Social Democratic Federation. The Russian Social Democrats, not yet divided into Bolsheviks and Mensheviks, and the Polish Socialists were also largely under German influence. The German Social Democratic Party carried the prestige of Marx's name: it had not long emerged from the repression of Bismarck's Anti-Socialist Laws, and it was still regarded as belonging to the Socialist left, though, side by side with its revolutionary professions of principle it had already formulated an immediate programme of reforms to be worked for by parliamentary means before the anticipated overthrow of capitalist society.

German Marxism, however, did not have matters all its own way among continental Socialists, even after the Anarchists had been driven into isolation. In France Jules Guesde's *Parti Ouvrier*, which was based on the German model, was only one among five Socialist parties competing for the favour of the French workers. The others were the Blanquists—faithful to their master's insurrectionary doctrine—the Possibilists, or Broussists—followers of Proudhon rather than of Marx, and particularly active in local government—the Allemanists—a left-wing split from the Broussists—and the Independents, led by Jean Jaurès, who were the group most nearly analogous to the British Fabians, with an undogmatic approach and an appetite for well-documented research. The Independents, however, unlike the Fabians, were primarily a group of parliamentarians. In France, moreover, the Trade Unions were already adopting the anti-political line of revolutionary Syndicalism. In Italy and in Spain there were strong Anarchist and Anarchist-Communist movements hostile to the Marxists, with substantial Trade Union followings. In Russia the Social Revolutionaries, heirs to the Narodniks and exponents of a Slav peasant Socialism based on hostility to industrialism and to western ideas, were arrayed against the Social Democrats—the 'westernizers' among the Slav peoples. In Great Britain, Keir Hardie's Independent Labour Party, aided by the Fabians, had wrested from the Social Democratic Federation the main influence in the 'New Unions' of 1889; and the Socialism of the ILP was essentially ethical and humanitarian. Keir Hardie was militant; but his roots were in Christian ethics and not in historical determinism. His pamphlet, *Can a Man Be a Christian on £1 a week?*, rather than the *Communist Manifesto*, embodied the essence of the

ILP's popular appeal. In practice, moreover, the ILP concentrated largely on such issues as the eight hours day, the legal minimum wage, and the 'right to work'. Its ally, the Fabian Society, was even less Marxist. The whole approach of *Fabian Essays* was from an angle of evolutionary gradualism, assuming a progressive conversion of sensible men to socialistic notions, and adopting a policy of 'permeation' which rested on a belief that Socialism would develop as a product much less of class-warfare than of a growing acceptance of social control and planning as the necessary completion of representative democracy. The Fabians built much more on Mill and Jevons than on Marx, or on any Socialist thinker: for them non-revolutionary Socialism was the logical outcome of the utilitarian philosophy—the means, in the modern world, of achieving the greatest happiness of the greatest number.

Not only did Marxian Social Democracy have to meet these challenges from Fabians, Proudhonists, Anarchist-Communists, and Christian Radicals: it was also divided against itself. In Germany Eduard Bernstein had just put the cat among the pigeons by publishing his book *Die Vorausetzungen des Sozialismus* (1899; translated as *Evolutionary Socialism*) in which he called for a fundamental revision of Marx's doctrine in the light of the later developments of capitalism and of political democracy. Bernstein questioned the entire revolutionary basis of Marxism, denying Marx's doctrines of 'increasing misery' and of capitalist concentration, and arguing that experience had shown the possibility not only of using the capitalist State, with the aid of a democratic franchise, to secure reforms that bettered the position of the workers, but also of transforming it gradually, without revolution, into a fully democratic instrument of Socialist policy. Bernstein's views gave rise to a tremendous controversy throughout the Socialist world. In Germany, where Kautsky took the leadership on the orthodox side, the 'Revisionists' were voted down; but their views fitted in with powerful trends both in Great Britain, from which Bernstein had largely derived them, and also in France, in Scandinavia, in Belgium, and in Austria. Indeed the German party, though it rejected Revisionism in theory, came more and more to accept it in practice, and to concentrate its efforts on the demand for social reforms and for the gradual democratization of the still largely feudal state machines of Prussia and of the German *Reich*.

In France, meanwhile, a related issue had stirred up a no less vigorous controversy among the Socialists. In 1899 Alexandre Millerand, a leading member of the Independent Socialist group led by Jaurès, had entered the Radical Government of Waldeck Rousseau, formed chiefly for the defence of republican institutions amid the ferment caused by the *affaire Dreyfus*. Millerand defended his action as justified by the need to stand by the Republic in its hour of danger; but nearly all Socialists regarded with horrified disapproval participation by a professing Socialist in a non-Socialist government—even in a government of the left pledged to measures of social reform. They could the more easily take this line because in most countries there was still no likelihood of their being invited to enter a government. John Burns, who took office in the British Liberal Cabinet of 1906, had ceased some time before to be connected with the Socialist movement. The controversy which followed Millerand's action served to impel the European Socialist parties to close their ranks and to smother discussion of their other differences. It helped to consolidate the International Socialist Bureau under German leadership and to bring about, under the Bureau's influence, the amalgamation of the rival French Socialist parties into a single party, of which Jaurès became the leader.

From 1900 onwards the Second International was primarily a federation of national parties acting, wherever the conditions allowed, on parliamentary lines and putting forward, side by side with declarations of their Socialist objectives, immediate programmes of reform designed to appeal to popular electorates. But it had been the practice to summon to the Socialist Congresses held before 1900 the Trade Union movements of the various countries as well as the Socialist parties; and this practice was continued after the establishment of the Bureau, without any attempt to exact from the Unions a formal profession of Socialist faith. The Trade Unions, it was argued, were practising the class-struggle even if they did not profess it; and they, as the representatives of the main body of the workers, were the indispensable allies of the Socialist political parties. The immediate programmes of the parties were designed largely to appeal to the Trade Unionists; and propaganda inside the Trade Unions and the winning of key positions in them by Socialists were essential means of winning a majority. The Germans, who were the foremost exponents of these opinions, never regarded the Trade Unions as more than valuable auxiliaries of the Socialist parties, to which they assigned the leading role. But in Great Britain the Trade Unions had a long history of successful activity which made Socialism seem something of an upstart; and in France, where the traditions of Proudhonism were strong, Anarchist influences were powerful in the Trade Unions and the division of the Socialists into a number of contending groups had made political allegiance a source not of united working-class action but of divisions which undermined industrial strength. In these circumstances, the attempts of the Guesdists to bring the Trade Unions under party influence failed, and the main body of French Trade Unionism, under Anarchist-Communist influence, repudiated political alliances and went over to the doctrine of revolutionary Syndicalism. Fernand Pelloutier, the leading theorist of the *Confédération Générale du Travail,* formulated the doctrine of Direct Action, advocating the use of the strike weapon as a means not only of improving working-class industrial conditions but also of forcing Parliament to pass laws useful to the workers (*'On peut arracher directement les lois utiles'*). Beyond these fruits of direct action within capitalist society lay the hope of a coming revolutionary general strike, by which the workers would bring about the downfall of capitalism, replacing it by a new social structure resting directly on the local *syndicats* federated into communal groupings endowed with such functions of social administration as would be needed in a classless society.

The French Trade Unions, taking this anti-parliamentary line, would have nothing to do with the Second International, but became the leaders of the militant wing in the International Federation of Trade Unions, which was set up in 1901 as a sequel to the establishment of the International Socialist Bureau and was also largely under German influence. The British Trades Union Congress, on the other hand, continued to send delegates to the International Socialist Congresses and refused to connect itself with the IFTU. This rather anomalous arrangement fitted in well enough with the course of development in Great Britain, where the Labour Representation Committee had been set up *not* as a professedly Socialist party, but on the basis of a federal political alliance between the Socialists and the Trade Unions. The fact that the British Trade Unions were connected with the Second International also smoothed the way for the admission of the Labour Representation Committee, which was accepted, despite its lack of a Socialist basis, on the same ground—that it was waging the class-struggle in practice, even if it omitted to say so.

During the years which followed the establishment of the Second International and the International Federation of Trade Unions both these bodies came to be largely preoccupied by the threat of European war. How, it was asked, should Socialists and Trade Unionists act in order to prevent war, or in the event of war actually breaking out between the States whose working-class movements stood for the principle of international class solidar-ity against capitalist exploitation? The French in particular lost no chance of raising this issue. The French Trade Unions demanded that the IFTU should pronounce in favour of an international general strike against the threat of war; and anti-militarist feeling was strong enough in the French working class to make the French Socialists sympathetic to the idea. The CGT wanted the world Trade Union movement to take its stand without reference to the Socialist parties; but the Trade Union leaders of most of the other countries, including Germany and Great Britain, argued that a general strike against war was essentially a political measure, falling outside the scope of Trade Union action and needing to be considered, if at all, by the Socialist International rather than by the IFTU. The Socialist parties, however, were sharply divid-ed on the question. The Germans for the most part disliked the idea of the general strike, and, fearful of Russia, stressed the justifiability of defending the homeland against an aggressor: the British Socialists were uncertain, but the British Trade Unions were hostile to the general strike and to the revolu-tionary Syndicalists who were its principal advocates. The debates in the ISB and in the Socialist Congresses ended in the compromise resolution carried at the Stuttgart Congress of 1907 and reaffirmed three years later at the Copenhagen Congress.

> If a war threatens to break out, it is the duty of the working class in the countries concerned and of their parliamentary representatives, with the aid of the International Socialist Bureau, to do all in their power to prevent war by all means which seem to them appropriate and which naturally vary according to the sharpness of the class-struggle and the general political situation.
>
> Should war nevertheless break out it is their duty to cooperate to bring it promptly to an end and to utilize the economic and political crisis created by the war to arouse the masses of the people and to precipitate the downfall of capitalist domination.

This resolution had a menacing sound; but it committed the Socialist parties of the various countries to no definite course of action—certainly not to the general strike or even in all circumstances to the refusal of war credits for what a particular party might regard as a 'war of national defence'. Its hollowness was seen in 1914, when it did not prevent the majority of the German Social Democrats from voting war credits or the majority in both France and Britain from giving full support to the war policy of their respective States. The International Socialist Bureau, it was then clearly seen, had no authority over the national parties affiliated to it: the Second International was no more than a great debating ground for the various Socialist parties and fractions, with no power to frame a common policy which all its adherents would be under an obligation to carry out.

This, indeed, was fairly clear—or should have been—from the very beginning. Each national party, in its attempts to win electoral support in the hope of bringing a majority of the voters finally over to its side, was forced to adapt its policy to the national conditions and to the national climate of opinion, and was not prepared to take orders about its behaviour from any international body. The Anarchists and Syndicalists pointed to this as a sign of the necessarily demoralizing effects of parliamentary politics, and put their hopes in revolutionary Trade Unionism. The Russian Bolsheviks drew the different conclusion that the western Social Democrats were betraying Marxism because of their failure to see the need for closely-knit, centralized Socialist parties, committed to work for revolution internationally as well as nationally and to accept a common discipline based on the undiluted Marxism of the *Communist Manifesto* of 1848. Lenin and Rosa Luxemburg were among the participants in the Stuttgart Congress which drew up the resolution I have quoted; and it

was largely through their efforts that the militant second paragraph was insert-
ed. But they could not persuade the Congress to commit itself to any specific
measures or to establish any machinery capable of taking practical steps to put
the terms of the resolution into effect.

From this rapid review of the international Socialist scene of fifty years
ago I must now turn back to look more closely at the state of Socialist affairs
in Great Britain. The Labour Representation Committee of 1900 rested on a
compromise. The Trade Unions which took part in framing it and those which
joined it during the ensuing years up to 1914 committed themselves to the
establishment of an independent group (not until 1906 formally to an independent party)—that is, they accepted a political alliance with the Socialists
and a severance of connections with the Liberal Party, and also agreed to give
the Socialists a place on the executive quite out of proportion to their numerical strength—but they did not in any way commit themselves to Socialism.
Keir Hardie and the other leaders of the ILP refrained from asking for any
such commitment, knowing that, if they had, the Trade Unions would have
drawn back. It seemed to the ILP leaders, Socialists though they were, to be
worthwhile to get the Trade Unions to take part in an independent political
movement, even without any Socialist commitment. They believed that when
an independent political movement had been founded they would be able
before long, with the support of most of the New Unionists, to bring it over
to an acceptance of Socialist objectives, even if it continued for some time to
concentrate its main attention on measures of social reform. They were correct in this opinion, though the conversion took much longer than they had
expected. Only in 1918, as a sequel to the collapse of the Liberal Party during
the First World War, did the Labour Party make a formal profession of faith
in Socialism—a profession embodied in a series of resolutions carried by the
Labour Party Conference in 1918, and translated into popular form in the
new programme, drafted by Sidney Webb under the title *Labour and the New
Social Order*. Moreover, this profession of faith, when it came at last, committed the Labour Party not simply to Socialism, but equally to a gradualist, evolutionary conception of the means by which Socialism was to be attained—to
an extent that would by no means have satisfied either Keir Hardie or most of
his leading colleagues in the Independent Labour Party of 1900.

The compromise on which the Labour Representation Committee of
1900 was based was acceptable to the ILP leaders and to the Fabians; but the
Marxists of the Social Democratic Federation found it altogether too much to
stomach. The SDF sent delegates to the constituent Conference of the LRC,
and these delegates did all they could to persuade the Conference to commit
itself to Socialism and to the class-struggle. When they failed, the SDF with-
drew from the LRC and continued on its way as the exponent of Marxism in
Great Britain; but it had little popular support and was soon torn by internal

dissensions of its own. One group of extremists broke away from it to form the Socialist Party of Great Britain, which developed an unqualified opposition to having any truck with palliatives and proclaimed the need to give revolutionary political education the primary place as against the compromises of parliamentary action. A second group, mainly in Scotland, seceded to form the Socialist Labour Party, largely modelled on Daniel De Leon's American party of the same name, and set out, like De Leon, to bring into being a centralized revolutionary Trade Union movement based on Industrial Unionism. Some compensation for these losses was found in a series of secessions from the ILP, some of whose members were always finding the compromises involved in working with the Trade Unions in the new Labour Party too much to endure. The largest of these secessions resulted in a merger which replaced the SDF by the British Socialist Party—the principal political rallying point for left-wing dissidents during the years of unrest from 1910 to 1914.

The SDF and its successor, the BSP, however, commanded only a small and ineffective following. The LRC, on the other hand, after a shaky start, was greatly stimulated by the reaction of the Trade Unions to the Taff Vale Judgment of 1901. The threat to the right to strike involved in this legal decision brought many Trade Unions into the new body and caused the whole Trade Union movement to bestir itself for the ensuing General Election. At the 'Khaki Election' of 1900, held when the LRC had barely been formed, the Trade Unions attached to it put no more than three candidates in the field, while the ILP had ten. Only Keir Hardie and one Trade Union candidate were elected, and the latter soon seceded and returned to the Liberal fold. But in 1906 the Labour Party, as it then became, and its ally, the Scottish Workers' Representation Committee, fought fifty-six seats and returned to the House of Commons thirty strong; and a high proportion of the successful candidates were Trade Union nominees. The Labour Party had definitely 'arrived' as a political force; electorally, Keir Hardie's policy of the 'Labour Alliance' appeared to have achieved a resounding success—though, of course, still nothing comparable with the electoral record of German Social Democracy.

Yet, in reality, the Labour Party of 1906 was a good deal less independent than it seemed. Only two of its thirty seats were won against official Liberal opposition; ten of them were in constituencies returning two members, where the Labour candidates fought in virtual alliance with the Liberals, each party putting forward only one candidate; fifteen were won in straight fights with Conservatives, largely because of Liberal support. Despite its formal 'independence', the Labour Party fought the election mainly as the ally of the Liberals and shared in the gains of the electoral landslide which carried the Liberals to office with an overwhelming majority behind them.

Moreover, though every Labour Party candidate had to fight formally as an 'independent' and to refrain from open support of the Liberals, not a few of the Trade Unionists who were returned to the House of Commons in 1906 were by conviction still Liberals, and not Socialists, even of the mildest kind. When the Miners, who had previously stood aloof, joined the Labour Party in 1909, the accession of their M.P.s increased the strength of the Lib-Lab contingent. The General Election of 1910, fought on the issues arising out of Lloyd George's 1909 Budget and the ensuing struggle with the House of Lords, deprived the Liberals of their clear majority and rendered the Liberal Government thereafter dependent on Labour support. This could not well be withheld, because both on the House of Lords issue and on that of Irish Home Rule, which subsequently dominated the political situation, the Labour Party was ranged with the Liberals and it could not vote against them on any question without risking their defeat. These conditions made it more and more difficult, right up to 1914, for the Labour Party to take a line of its own; but its compromising policy antagonized a growing number of its supporters, and drove them, not for the most part into the ranks of the Marxist BSP, but into the movements of industrial militancy which swept over the country between 1910 and the outbreak of war.

The growth of Syndicalist and Industrial Unionist movements in France and in the United States during the first quarter of the twentieth century was in part the 'come-back' of the Anarchists after they had been driven out of the Socialist movement by the rising Social Democratic and Labour parties and in part a spontaneous development of Trade Union militancy in face of increasing costs of living. But the French and American movements, though they were often grouped together, were in reality very different. The French Syndicalists were in doctrine Anarchist-Communists, with an intense belief in the independence of the small unit of social organization and a sharp dislike of every kind of centralization and bureaucracy. Faced by a capitalism which was still mainly based on fairly small-scale business, the French saw no need for the State or for any large-scale substitute for it. They were federalists, and the units they wished to federate were local communes based on local workers' associations. The American Industrial Unionists, on the other hand, found their support among the workers in large-scale capitalist industry and, confronted by the much more developed and repressive capitalism of the great American business corporations, thought in terms of a vast, centrally controlled class organization of the workers capable of waging the class-war on a continent-wide scale. Their objective was the 'one big union', subdivided into industrial sections, which was to take the entire control of industry into its hands and was itself to replace the Government when the capitalist system was overthrown. The French Syndicalists were scornful of detailed planning and put their trust in the spontaneity of working-class action under the energizing influence of a 'conscious minority' of militants: the American Industrial Unionists were planners, proclaiming the need for the workers to draw up their own 'blue-prints' for the democratic conduct of production, but they too put their trust in a militant minority ready to exploit every wave of working-class feeling. In practice, the Industrial Unionists were much more militant and violent than the French Syndicalists, largely because they had to meet a much more ruthless and highly organized body of capitalists, who were able and ready to invoke the state power to suppress working-class attempts at combination.

In Great Britain, neither Syndicalism nor out-and-out Industrial Unionism ever obtained a powerful hold. What did appear was a widespread unrest, manifested both in a spread of strikes, great and small, and in a movement to reorganize the Trade Unions on a broader basis, especially by bringing skilled and less skilled workers together in Unions covering whole industries. The British Syndicalists and Industrial Unionists—or rather, those who adopted these labels—did not develop comprehensive theories: most of them did not break away from the existing Unions or even from the Labour Party. Only in Ireland, under the leadership of James Larkin and James Connolly, did a movement closely akin to the American Industrial Workers of the World appear and win a considerable following; and the events of the Dublin strikes of 1913–14 showed how little the leaders even of the more militant British Unions had in common with Larkin's conception of the class-war.

The new Socialist theory that did develop in Great Britain before and during the First World War was Guild Socialism, which was influenced by French Syndicalism but took from it only the ideas of industrial self-government and the primary importance of industrial action, while rejecting its anarchistic repudiation of politics and of the State. The Guild Socialists agreed with the Syndicalists that the 'revolution' would have to be made primarily by economic rather than by parliamentary action. They aimed at a 'blackleg-proof' organization of the workers in great industrial combinations extended to include the non-manual as well as the manual grades. These Unions were then to demand from the State that the control of industry should be taken out of the hands of the capitalists and transferred, under public charter, to National Guilds developed out of the Trade Unions. The State was to own the means of production: the organized workers were to administer them on the public's behalf. Later, the Guild Socialists fell out among themselves about the structure of the coming society—some holding that the State would continue to exist as the democratic organ of the whole people, while others looked forward to its replacement by some sort of federal structure representing the functional organizations of producers and consumers, and also the civic and cultural bodies standing for noneconomic values. But this difference did not much affect the Guild Socialists' immediate policy. Both schools called on the State to nationalize the means of production and to entrust the administration to the Guilds representing the workers by hand and brain.

Guild Socialism remained predominantly a British movement. During and just after the First World War it had a considerable influence on British Trade Union policy, and many Unions—among them the Miners, Railwaymen, and Post Office Workers—embodied demands for industrial self-government and workers' control in their programmes of post-war reconstruction. The movement, however, fell to pieces in the slump which swept the country in 1921. The building workers, who had embarked on an ambitious programme of house-building under public contract on a non-profit basis, found their Guilds driven out of business and into bankruptcy when the Government abruptly suspended the housing scheme under which they had been able to operate largely with public capital. In other industries hopes of nationalization receded, and the Unions, driven on the defensive, lost interest in Guild Socialist projects. The shop stewards' movement in the engineering industries, which had provided the Guild Socialists with much of their support, broke down. Moreover, the Guild Socialists fell to quarrelling among themselves. The Bolshevik Revolution of 1917 had caused sharp divisions, and the Guild Socialist left wing gradually broke away and went over to Communism. A right-wing group took up with the Social Credit doctrines of Major Douglas; and the centre, left alone, dissolved the movement rather than carry on under conditions which offered no prospect of success.

Guild Socialism, as an organized body of opinion, disappeared, leaving only a legacy of 'workers' control' notions to influence the subsequent developments of Socialist doctrine. Before it vanished, however, it had exerted some significant influence abroad as well as at home. The French Trade Union movement, no longer so Syndicalist as before the war, adopted a programme of *nationalisation industrialisée* which had much in common with the Guild Socialist projects of industrial self-government combined with public ownership. There were similar movements among the American railroad workers; the Germans set up Building Guilds, which met the same fate as the British; and in Palestine the Trade Union movement developed forms of workers' control, especially in the building and transport industries, that closely resembled the Guilds proposed by the Guild Socialists.

Guild Socialism was throughout a strongly idealistic movement. It challenged orthodox parliamentary Socialism largely on the ground that a truly democratic Socialist society should rest on the widest possible diffusion of power and responsibility among the working people, and that parliamentary Socialism would in practice result in a bureaucratic system which would leave the workers, even under public ownership, still 'wage-slaves' rather than free men. Freedom, said the Guild Socialists, could not be real unless it rested on the free organization of the economic life of society, through self-government at every level, from the workshop upwards. The nature of men's economic relations, they argued, would in practice determine the character of their political relations: a free society could not coexist with an autocratic system of industrial control. The Guild Socialists were suspicious of the politicians and Trade Union leaders, as not wishing to diffuse power and responsibility, but rather to concentrate it in their own hands.

This insistence on functional self-government, built up from small co-operating work groups to larger economic and social units, put the Guild Socialists into sharp opposition to the Marxists as well as to the orthodox Labourites. For the Marxists too believed in centralization and in authority as descending from the top down wards. In the shop stewards' movement, which after 1917 passed more and more under the control of Communists, there were sharp differences between the Guild Socialists, who insisted on the need for diffused workshop control, and the Marxists, who regarded the stewards in particular establishments as merely agents of a class policy to be worked out on the principle of 'democratic centralism'.

In referring to these conflicts of social philosophy I have been led some way ahead of the general thread of my narrative. I must go back now to the impact of war on the world Socialist movement of 1914. Everywhere in the belligerent countries war, by causing an acute shortage of labour and making continuously high production an indispensable part of the war effort, great-ly added to the power and influence of the organized workers, even where they were subjected to strongly repressive measures. The Trade Unions, in particular, grew rapidly in membership and prestige; and side by side with them there developed powerful unofficial organizations of the shop stew-ard, workers' council type. The working-class political parties, on the other hand, were adversely affected, because in most countries there were sharp divisions on war policy. The German Social Democratic Party broke asunder in 1915, when the anti-war Independents seceded under Kautsky and Haase to form a separate party; and before long a movement considerably further to the left—the *Spartakus bund*—developed as an underground organization in the factories, led by Karl Liebknecht and Rosa Luxemburg. This was the real beginning of German Communism. In France the assassination of Jean Jaurès immediately after the outbreak of war deprived the French Socialists of their outstanding leader and left them at sixes and sevens. The French Socialist Party did not actually split; but there was a running struggle between the pro-war *Majoritaires,* led by Pierre Renaudel and Albert Thomas, and the *Minoritaires* whose chief spokesman was Jean Longuet—Marx's grandson. In Great Britain the Labour Party supported the war, but the ILP opposed it, and, though remaining within the party, acted in effect as a separate body, under MacDonald and Philip Snowden. Only Arthur Henderson's sustained efforts prevented an actual split. The British Socialist Party opposed the war; and Hyndman, who was strongly pro-war, broke away with a small group of faithful followers to form the National Socialist Party, which later resumed the old name, Social Democratic Federation, but exerted no real influence. In Italy

Mussolini, advocating entry into the war, broke with the Socialists and formed his Fascist Party. The Socialist International practically disappeared, only a small Dutch-Scandinavian group holding together in readiness to seize any chance of promoting a negotiated peace. The pro-war Socialists of the allied countries presently formed a joint organization which prepared a statement of war aims and began to lay plans for a new post-war International. The anti-war Socialists held two Conferences, at Zimmerwald and at Kienthal, at which Lenin played a leading part in carrying resolutions in favour of revolutionary action to bring the war to an end by overthrowing the capitalist rulers of the belligerent States. These gestures were not much to the taste of the pacifists who were prominent in some of the anti-war Socialist bodies, such as the ILP, but the deep conflict of attitude between pacifists and anti-war revolutionaries did not appear plainly until after the Russian Revolution.

Meanwhile, in both France and Great Britain, war conditions led to Coalition Governments in which pro-war Socialists took office. In Great Britain, the Labour Party had a tiny representation in the first, Asquith, Coalition and a larger place in the Lloyd George Coalition, which it helped to form. But in 1917 the whole situation was profoundly altered by the revolutions in Russia. After the first Russian Revolution it became clear that the Russians had neither the power nor the will to go on fighting. Henderson, sent to Russia to appraise the situation on behalf of the Lloyd George Government, came back convinced of this, and a supporter of the Russian proposal to call a peace conference at Stockholm to put forward, on behalf of the working classes, terms for a negotiated peace. For taking this line, which he narrowly persuaded a Labour Conference to endorse, Henderson was thrust out of the War Cabinet, and was thus set free to devote himself to the task of reorganizing the Labour Party for the post-war political struggle. The break-up of the Liberal Party in the contest between Asquith and Lloyd George had cleared the way for the Labour Party to turn itself into a nationally organized party making a real claim to power; and in the new party Constitution of 1918 Henderson equipped it with the electoral machine needed to give substance to its claims. At the same time, as we saw, a new policy statement—*Labour and the New Social Order*—drafted mainly by Sidney Webb—at length committed the party to a formal profession of faith in evolutionary Socialism. This profession of faith was an important factor in giving the British Labour Party the leading place in the West European Socialist movement—a place occupied up to 1914 by the German Social Democrats, but falling in 1918 to the one major party which had been able to preserve its unity in face of dissensions arising out of the war and the Russian Revolution.

During the first years of Soviet rule in Russia the sympathy of the main body of Socialists and Trade Unionists throughout Western Europe was keenly on the side of the Russians in their struggle to establish their new society against counter-revolutionary attacks from within and without. The leaders of the Socialist parties and the Trade Unions of the West had no love for Bolshevism, which was already proclaiming the gospel of 'world revolution' and endeavouring to stir up revolutionary movements in the West. Nor were most of the followers of these leaders supporters of Communism; but almost all sections felt an intense sympathy for the new Soviet Socialist Republic which had replaced the most reactionary regime in Europe and had become the target for vehement abuse and attack at all possible points by the reactionary forces in every capitalist country. During the period of industrial and social unrest which everywhere followed immediately on the conclusion of the war, workers who were engaged in a daily struggle in their own countries naturally felt a kinship with the Russian peoples. Already exiled Socialists—Mensheviks and Social Revolutionaries—from the Soviet Union were denouncing the new regime as a totalitarian autocracy which had no right to call itself Socialist; and these exiles found sympathetic hearers among the leaders of western Socialism. But in view of the popular feeling, the western leaders had to take the side of the Russians against western attempts at armed intervention—for example, in the Polish-Russian War of 1920. It took a long time for this popular goodwill towards the Soviet Union to be dissipated, despite the virulence of Soviet attacks on the leaders of the western Socialist and Trade Union movements. Even in Great Britain it has not been entirely dissipated now, though the course of events since 1945 has greatly weakened it.

Great Britain, however, is by no means typical; for there has never been a British Communist movement of any considerable strength. In Germany, France, and Italy, on the other hand, the Communist appeal was powerful enough to split the working-class movements from top to bottom. In Germany the Social Democrats, soon rejoined by most of the Independent Socialists who had broken away during the war, remained numerically superior to the Communists, who were however strong enough so to divide the workers first to enable the capitalist parties to regain their influence and later to open the door to Hitler. In France, the Communists actually won a majority both in the Socialist Party and later in the Trade Unions. The non-Communist Socialists were forced to form a new party, which came more and more to rely on the support of the 'black-coats' rather than of the manual workers; and until the middle thirties the French Trade Union movement was rendered impotent by its division into rival Communist and anti-Communist groups. In Italy the Socialists and the Trade Unions, having taken a half-hearted revolutionary line, were swept aside by Mussolini's march on Rome, and thereafter liquidated by stages, the workers being regimented into corporative associations under the complete control of the Fascist Party. Only in Great Britain and Ireland, in Scandinavia, in Switzerland, and in Austria did Communism fail to gain considerable working-class support.

The Bolsheviks, intent on hastening the world revolution which they regarded as historically necessary and without which they then believed their own Revolution could not be maintained, set out immediately after the war to create a new Communist International, heralded by a new *Communist Manifesto* meant to recall world Socialism to the full-blooded Marxism of 1848. The western Socialists meanwhile set to work to reconstruct the Second International, mainly on the basis of the Allied Manifesto on War Aims drawn up by the French and British parties. There were, however, a number of parties and groups which were not prepared to throw in their lot with either of the rivals; and these, headed by the Austrians and the Swiss, and with the support of the British ILP, maintained for some time a third body which had as its object the formation of a united International including Communists and Social Democrats of every colour. This attempt was doomed to failure from the first; but its protagonists took some time to find this out. There was in reality no possibility of accommodation between the constitutional gradualism of the British Labour Party and the German and Scandinavian Social Democrats and the uncompromising revolutionism of the Communists; and, over and above this, the two contestants had totally different theories of what a Socialist International ought to be. The Communists demanded a powerful centralized International laying down a common policy which all the national sections would be required to obey; whereas the Social Democratic parties wanted only a loose federation which would leave the final policy-making power in their own hands and would enable each party to follow the tactics required by its own electoral situation. The Social Democrats looked to the gradual conquest of power by winning a majority of the electors over to their side: the Communists postulated a revolutionary seizure of power in the name of the proletariat, to be followed by the suppression of all rival parties—or at least of all which would not submit to become the mere instruments of centrally determined Communist policy.

Thus, despite the continued existence of a substantial body of middle opinion, which accepted neither the complete revolutionism of the Communists nor the no less complete constitutional gradualism of the British Labour Party and of the German Social Democrats, the working-class movements of Europe came to be sharply divided between the two extreme views. The Vienna Union, or 'Two-and-a-Half' International, as it came to be called, having failed to bring the two extremes together, threw in its lot with the constitutionalists and joined with them in forming the Labour and Socialist International. The Trade Unionists of the West similarly reformed the International Federation of Trade Unions, and the Communists countered with a Red International of Labour Unions which, completely dominated by the Russians, set to work to create rival points of focus for the Trade Unionists of the western countries. For a time, in the 1930s, the developing menace of Fascism led to temporary alliances between the rival groups in certain countries—for example, France and Spain. But in Great Britain the Labour Party and the Trades Union Congress successfully defeated attempts to form a Popular Front against Fascism.

Throughout the inter-war years the two rival movements—Communist and Social-Democratic Labour—were continually denouncing each other and blaming each other for the disasters which were overtaking the working classes. The Communists attacked the Social Democrats as class-traitors and 'Social Fascists' who were doing the dirty work of capitalist imperialism. The Social Democrats retorted that the Communists, by dividing the workers, had brought on the disaster of the Nazi victory in Germany and were everywhere standing in the way of the advance of Socialism by democratic constitutional methods. The western Social Democrats had, indeed, been from the outset somewhat disconcerted by the advent of Socialism, not as they had expected in the advanced industrial countries but in backward Russia, with its predominantly peasant population and its low standards of living and industrial production. They failed for the most part to see that the programme of the *Communist Manifesto* of 1848, outmoded in the more advanced countries by the growth of political democracy and of the Welfare State, had remained appropriate to the conditions prevailing in Eastern Europe, where there were no foundations on which a parliamentary system could rest and no means of establishing Socialism except by revolution and the institution of some sort of dictatorship by a closely knit proletarian party. As against this the Russians had little understanding of conditions in Western Europe, and refused to recognize the plain fact that, over large areas of the West, the Marxian theories of 'increasing misery' and polarization of economic classes had simply failed to work out in practice. Each side held the other to blame for not behaving as it ought to behave—the Social Democrats denouncing the Communists as betrayers of democracy, and the Communists the Social Democrats as betrayers of the world revolution.

Even while Lenin remained alive, this diametrical opposition of philosophies governed the relations between the rival parties; and the situation was accentuated after Lenin's death. In the ensuing duel between Trotsky and Stalin neither of the protagonists had anything to offer that could have helped to bridge the gulf. Trotsky's theory of the 'permanent revolution' implied the necessity of Communist agitation in the West; and Stalin's doctrine of 'Socialism in one country' meant not a *rapprochement,* but a withdrawal of Russia into itself, for the purpose of consolidating the Soviet power, and thus, even more than Trotsky's attitude, involved an isolation of Russia from contact with and understanding of western ways of thought. The new generation of Communist leaders, headed by Stalin, lacked knowledge of Western Europe and thought in terms of Russian power politics rather than of any sort of real internationalism. For a while in the 1930s, when Hitler seemed likely to attack the Soviet Union with the benevolent neutrality of western governments, there was a change in policy, marked by the new Soviet Constitution of 1936. Litvinov, who did know the West, was brought back into favour and made a real effort to reach an accommodation with the League States. But he met with little encouragement, and after Munich the Russians not merely reverted to their previous line, but went right over to the policy of giving Hitler a free hand in the West, in the hope of diverting him from an attack in the East. At the same time the repression of all dissent within the Soviet Communist Party became much more severe. The series of treason trials of dissident Communists produced strong reactions in the West, and destroyed much of the sympathy that had been felt for the Russians in their titanic struggle.

These developments of Soviet totalitarianism had not reached their height when Sidney and Beatrice Webb published their first-hand study of Soviet Communism—and of course the materials on which their book was based had been collected some time before it appeared. Many western Socialists were astonished and dismayed when the theorists who had been most closely associated with the Fabian Society and with the Labour Party's policy of constitutional 'gradualness' appeared as the ardent defenders of the Soviet Union and as keenly sympathetic with the one-party system which it had developed as the instrument of proletarian dictatorship. The Webbs were no friends to the British Communist Party or to the Comintern: they did not at all regard Soviet Communism as an article suitable for export to their own country. But, looking at the Russian situation, they gave credit for the immense liberation of popular energy which the Revolution had brought about and recognized the key part played by the Communist Party in the running of a vast and heterogeneous society with no experience of democracy or of parliamentary institutions behind it, with a huge peasant population incapable of governing the country or of holding it together except under strong, authoritative leadership, and with enormous arrears of industrial development to make up before there could be any prospect of a tolerable standard of civilized living.

Besides, the Webbs were fundamentally planners, with orderly minds more revolted by inefficiency than by lack of political and personal freedom. They loved the ambitious Five Year Plans, which had much in common economically with their own projects for a planned Socialist society. They loved too the asceticism and the devotion to a cause which they thought they saw as the outstanding qualities of the active members of the Russian Communist Party; and the contempt for peasants which they shared with so many Socialists made them insensitive to the ruthlessness with which the liquidation of the *kulaks* and the collectivization of Soviet agriculture were being carried into effect. They were disposed to regard these measures as necessary for the 'socialization' of the mind and spirit of the peoples of the Soviet Union. In the first edition of their book, there was a question-mark at the end of the title—*Soviet*

Communism: A New Civilization?—but this vanished later on. It seemed as if the Webbs, after looking at the Soviet new order, had forgotten their gradualism and turned into Fabian revolutionaries, with Bernard Shaw, much less surprisingly, cheering them on.

The Webbs, indeed, had understood, as most of their colleagues in the West had not, that the gospel of evolutionary gradualism, with parliamentary democracy as its instrument, had no appeal or relevance to the problems of a large part of the world. They saw that it made nonsense to say that the Russians ought to have set up a parliamentary government on the western model, with freedom to form counter-revolutionary parties, with free elections, and with all the freedoms that had been gradually and painfully developed over a long period in Great Britain. Such methods could not possibly have led in Russia, or indeed in any country without a long tradition of constitutional government, to any sort of Socialism—or indeed to any other result than breakdown and defeat. To tell the Russians to behave as western democrats was to tell them to give up Socialism, to throw away the fruits of the Revolution, and to invite counter-revolution at the hands of the West. The Webbs were convinced that the Soviet new order, despite its evil features, inevitable in view of Russian history, was fundamentally Socialist and that as it became consolidated it would also grow progressively more liberal. Very likely they would have been right had not Nazism conquered Germany and thus transformed the entire shape of the political world. For the Russians under Stalin, drawing from the events in Germany and from their reception in the West the moral that only power counted, moved, after the brief Litvinov episode of wooing the West, sharply in the opposite direction—moved so far that gradually more and more western Socialists were led to deny that the system existing in the Soviet Union was really Socialism at all, and to denounce it in the same breath with Fascism as merely a variant form of totalitarian dictatorship.

Of course, this denial was echoed back from the East. With no less vehemence and with much greater unanimity and vituperation, the Communists denied the name of Socialists to the Labourites and Social Democrats of the West. When the latter attacked the Soviet Union as 'undemocratic', the Communists retorted that democracy and capitalism were by nature incompatible and that the only true democracy was that which rested on the expropriation of the ruling classes and the establishment of proletarian dictatorship as an instrument for the final abolition of class-conflicts. The word 'democracy' was bandied to and fro, the one side identifying it with free elections, freedom of speech and association, freedom of personal movement, and toleration of different opinions, while the other side identified it with freedom from class-oppression and with the recognition that there could be only one 'right' policy for the ruling proletariat and that it was the historic democratic mission of the Communist Party to lay down what the one right policy must be. That this was what Marx had believed I have not the smallest doubt, though I think he, and even Lenin, would have recoiled from some of the glosses appended to the doctrine by his present-day disciples.

Now, from the standpoint of Socialism, the danger inherent in the western interpretation of democracy was that it forbade Democratic Socialists to set about establishing Socialism except on the basis of a mandate from a majority of the people. But was such a mandate at all likely to be secured in elections held under a capitalist system—above all, where, in the name of democracy, a system of proportional representation had been introduced? The experience of the years since 1918 goes to show the extreme difficulty of getting so large a measure of electoral support as to give the Socialists a clear majority, even on an immediate programme falling far short of a mandate to introduce Socialism. Under British electoral conditions, a Labour majority has been shown to be possible on the basis of a programme involving considerable measures of nationalization together with great developments of welfare services. But the programme of 1945 did not ask for a mandate for Socialism—only for an instalment; and the programme of 1950 and 1951 asked for much less. Nor could there be any assurance that a majority, once won, would be maintained long enough to make possible the constitutional establishment of a predominantly Socialist society.

There was, moreover, a further factor. Up to the 1930s, nearly all Socialist propaganda was conducted on the assumptions that unemployment was an ineradicable disease of capitalist societies and that there were narrow limits to the practicable redistribution of incomes and property and to the development of the welfare services, as long as private enterprise remained in control of the main part of the means of production. But in the 1930s, as a sequel to the great world depression, which many Socialists at first regarded as the beginning of the death-pangs of capitalist enterprise, both these assumptions were increasingly challenged. The challenge came, not from Socialists, but in the realm of economic theory from J. M. Keynes and in that of economic practice from President Roosevelt. Keynes declared, and many Socialists believed him, that it was quite possible for a capitalist society to maintain full employment by taking the appropriate budgetary and financial measures. President Roosevelt, in the New Deal, demonstrated that the most capitalistic society in the world could both go some way towards this and bring about a large development of social services without in any way changing the economic basis of production. The British Labour Government, after 1945, further showed that substantial redistribution of incomes and large extensions of the social services could be achieved without taking the greater part of industry out of capitalist hands.

The effect of these developments, in conjunction with the intensified ideological warfare between western and Communist Socialism, was to emphasize the elements of agreement between American and European Labour. The

American Trade Unions—the Congress of Industrial Organizations as well as the American Federation of Labor—were almost untouched by Socialist doctrines, but were—at any rate the CIO—supporters of the 'Welfare State'. British and American Trade Unionists found themselves in close agreement on many issues—on full employment as well as on the social services—and united in denouncing the totalitarian outlook of the Communists. They began to draw more closely together, and in the absence of any effective American Socialist or Labour party, the American Trade Unions also drew closer to the Labour and Socialist parties of Europe, agreeing to differ about Socialism, and to stress the matters on which they were nearly agreed—above all, their hostility to Communism. This *rapprochement* with American Labour had, under the conditions of growing world tension between West and East, a marked diluting influence on West European Socialist doctrines. It disposed the western Socialists to follow Eduard Bernstein's advice, given half a century ago, to think less of Socialism as a system and more of social and economic reforms that could be achieved without uprooting capitalism. Socialism, as a system, retained its place in the philosophy of western Labourism and Social Democracy as an ideal; but it receded into the future, and its claims were postponed to those of the struggle against Communism and for maintenance and further development of the Welfare State.

In describing this evolution of Socialist doctrines and attitudes I have tried so far to keep my own views well in the background. My opinion is that, in the countries of Western Europe, Socialism is dissolving, even as an ideal related to current practice, and is being replaced by a striving towards the Welfare State, in a form which leaves open the indefinite continuance of a 'mixed economy', still largely capitalist, but involving a growing amount of centralized state regulation designed to secure full employment and an improved redistribution of spendable incomes. Obviously, in the relatively advanced countries, including Great Britain, the majority of the electors do not want the upsets involved in overthrowing capitalism and installing a complete Socialist system if they can have full employment, good living conditions, and expanding social services without these upsets. Obviously, most Trade Union and party leaders share this attitude. If the Welfare State can be lastingly sustained and developed without Socialism, Socialism is not coming in the West and not even the Socialist leaders will try to make it come.

About most of this there is, fundamentally, nothing new. The difference is in the clearer recognition of aims. The Labour Party and most of the western Social Democratic parties have been always, or at least for the whole of the past half-century, primarily reformist parties, owing their main electoral support to their immediate proposals for reform rather than to their long-term Socialist aspirations. Even in face of recent changes of attitude, the Labour Party today is much more, and not less, socialistic than it was in 1906, or even in 1918.

The Socialists who really mean that they are bent on establishing Socialism as a way of life have always been a tiny minority: they have owed their voting support to the Trade Unions and to the less wealthy consumers, most of whom do not know whether they are Socialists or not. It is in effect impossible to get even a large minority of the whole people to believe in Socialism (any more than in capitalism, or in any -ism) except by setting it up and then using every available point of vantage for indoctrinating the people with it.

That is, or was, the strength of the Communist case—on the assumption that the people *ought* to want Socialism, whether they do or not. The Communists are entirely correct in holding that Socialism, as a way of life, cannot be established except by revolution and by the occupation of all the key points for controlling opinion by propagandists of Socialism as the only right way of organizing human affairs. Socialist parties which are not prepared to face this fact *may* be able to advance further towards the Welfare State and towards a 'mixed economy': they are most unlikely—and more unlikely now than ever, in view of America's increased influence—to get a mandate for full Socialism as it was conceived by the Socialists of fifty years ago.

This, however, applies only to the advanced countries, which are used to parliamentary government—and perhaps not to all of them. There are many parts of the world in which there is still no basis for advance towards the Welfare State and no prospect, without social revolution, of even mitigating the existing conditions of gross exploitation and irresponsible class rule. This is the position in the Middle East, as it was in China, and probably will be again in Japan. For the peoples of these countries there is no choice between Communism and Democratic Socialism, as there was none in the Russia of 1917. Some sort of Communism is, for these countries—Korea among them—the only practicable kind of Socialism; and I wish more of my fellow Socialists would recognize, as the Webbs did recognize, this unpalatable truth.

It is unpalatable—more so to most of us than it was to the Webbs—because we have seen the later developments of Communism in Russia and in Eastern Europe, and also because, I think, most of us rate personal freedoms more highly. I hate, as much as a man can hate, the developments of Soviet 'centralism' and power-realism which George Orwell satirized in *Animal Farm*. I am accordingly watching with intense interest what is now occurring in Yugoslavia since the break with the Soviet Union; for the Yugoslavs are undoubtedly trying hard to create a form of Communism that is compatible with a wide diffusion of power and responsibility and with some concessions to liberal values. Whether they will succeed, even if war does not sweep their experiment away, I do not profess to know. But what I do know is that nothing except world war, which will sweep our civilization away, whoever wins, can in the long run prevent the backward countries from going Communist, broadly in the Russian sense, unless there can be found a form of revolutionary Socialism that fits their conditions and avoids the excesses of totalitarian amoralism that have gone so far towards undermining the great historic achievement of the Russian Revolution of 1917. For it was a great achievement—fully as momentous as the French Revolution of 1789. And it is as difficult to judge now as the French Revolution was in the 1820s. To regard what has happened in the Soviet Union as having nothing to do with Socialism, as so many western Socialists seem now ready to believe, is I am sure bad thinking; Stalin's misdeeds can no more destroy the essential legacy of 1917 than Napoleon could destroy that of 1789. If today there seem to be in the world two Socialist movements, Western and Eastern, which have in common only one thing— that neither of them is Socialist, or at any rate neither acts Socialist—let us not put out of our minds either that the Soviet Union possesses the basic economic structure of Socialism, even if its rulers lack the will to use this structure in the spirit of Socialist fraternity, or that Western Europe, though parts of it have made large advances towards the Welfare State, lacks this structure and for the most part shows few signs of achieving it. If for a moment, instead of looking back over the past half-century, we try to look forward, are we so sure that, unless the world has to face the unpredictable consequences of atomic total war, the Soviet Union, Communist China, and other countries which have thrown or can throw off the burdens of landlordism, capitalism, and obsolete feudal institutions will not also throw off the totalitarian autocracy which has taken the place of these abuses? I have not lost hope that this may be so, though as heartily as any western 'liberal' can I dislike the monolithic structure of present-day Communism and dissent from the materialistic Marxian philosophy from which it derives its theoretical support. On the other side— our side—of the iron curtain, are we so sure that the colossal power of the Americans will not both erode the Socialist faith and, in pursuance of the policy of deterrence through strength, bolster up all over the world regimes which obstruct the road to social progress and human enlightenment? The fire and the fervour, I feel, are dying out fast from the Socialism of the West, which has a good case against Communism only if it stands fast to the idealism that went to its making. In fact, the problem confronting western Socialism today is simply this—can it meet the challenge of Communism without accepting the philosophy of Americanism as a substitute for its lost ideals? I do not know the answer: I know only that I feel lonely and near despair in a world in which Socialist values as I understand them are being remorselessly crushed out between the two immense grinding-stones of Communist autocratic centralism and hysterical American worship of wealth and hugeness for their own sake and not as means to that human fellowship which lies at the very foundation of the Socialist faith.

EDUCATION AND POLITICS:
A SOCIALIST VIEW

SOCIALIST THEORIES—AND SOCIALIST THEORIES OF EDUCATION AS A PART OF them—have sprung mainly from three sources—the desire for social equality and social justice, the belief in the influence of environment upon character, and the attempt to interpret history in terms of the evolution of what Marx called 'the powers of production'.[1] In Marxian theories, which treat the last of these as of preponderant importance, education, in any formal sense, is relegated to a secondary role. If the development of mankind follows a determined course, set for it by the growth of man's mastery over the forces of nature—of which man is himself a part—no *primary* creative function can be assigned to education in shaping the destiny of human society. According to Marx, the growth of the powers of production gives rise to a series of economic and social systems, each resting on the predominance of a particular class and involving the exploitation of the classes below it: each such system is an advance on its predecessor, because it rests on a higher development of the productive powers; and at last a point is reached at which the proletariat, the only class still subject to exploitation, becomes strong enough, because of the power conferred on it by the increasing 'socialization' of the productive process, to overthrow its

---

1   *Year Book of Education*, 1952.

capitalist masters and to set about the establishment of the 'classless society'. Thereafter, what? Marx tells us no more than that 'prehistory ends, and history begins'. Of the nature of this new history of mankind he has nothing at all to say. Speculations about it he dismissed as 'utopian' until the final class victory had been won. In the meantime, the task of those who were on the side of the proletariat was to hasten the victory. 'The philosophers have only interpreted the world in various ways; the point, however, is to change it.'[2]

Accordingly, in Marx's opinion, education, as a socially creative force, could be only propaganda. The forces of history could be hastened along by man's understanding of them: education would be of help as far as it made proletarians, and sympathizers with the cause of the proletariat, understand the historic role of that class and afford it leadership and inspiration. The general educational system in any society, Marx held, could be only a part of the paraphernalia of class government and of indoctrination in the notions and attitudes required by the ruling class in its subjects in order to make its system of exploitation work smoothly, or mere technical training of the people in the tasks required of them in the processes of social labour. As far as education dealt with ideas, as distinct from mere techniques, the ideas would be derivative from the underlying realities of the economic order. They might be presented as autonomous, or as the teachings of religion or philosophy; but behind this façade would be their real substance as pillars sustaining the prevalent class system. Rebel ideas, where they were allowed to find expression, would be discovered on critical examination to be equally derivative, and to emanate from the needs of the class or classes that were challenging the established economic order as the representatives of alternative arrangements of the powers of production. To regard ideas—and therefore education—in any other way was to be guilty of the sin of 'idealism', or, in Socialists, 'utopianism'. Marx and his followers claimed to have advanced Socialism from its 'utopian' stage to the higher dignity of a science that could predict the future of mankind.

Marxists, accordingly, were not concerned to frame a philosophy of education until they found themselves in certain countries, after 1917, faced with the task of establishing an educational system for Socialist societies in which the social revolution had already taken place. Then, indeed, they were confronted with an immediate need to define their educational objectives; but not in utopian terms. In the backward countries in which alone Socialism, in the Marxian sense, has so far come to power, what the leaders of the new society had to face was the imperative need to build up as rapidly as possible both the technical and the administrative manpower required for the consolidation of victory and a popular indoctrination in the ways of life and thought which were the necessary props of the new economic and social order. Their

---

2   Marx, *Theses on Feuerbach*, xi.

educational arrangements were at one and the same time intensely utilitarian, or pragmatic, in an economic sense, and intensely ideological and, to use their own word, 'monolithic', in the realm of theory. The leaders of the new societies based on social revolution, feeling themselves under constant threat both of dissolution from within and of attack from without, had to treat education in both its technical and its general aspects essentially as an instrument of Socialist defence and construction. In carrying out this policy, they were no doubt moved by the desire to eradicate class inequalities and to give preference to proletarians over 'class enemies'; but even this motive appeared rather as a factor in revolutionary defence and construction than as an 'ideal': indeed, it found acceptance as an ideal by virtue of its correspondence with the practical needs of the new social order.

We must not, then, look to Marxism for any 'philosophy' of education save that which emerges directly from the doctrine of class conflict. A simple example of what I mean can be found in the conflict which has repeatedly rent the movements for adult working-class education in Great Britain—a conflict which was in full swing long before Marx had begun to write. In the 1820s two men—J. C. Robertson and Thomas Hodgskin—were mainly instrumental in setting up the London Mechanics' Institution—the ancestor of Birkbeck College. These two were strong opponents of capitalism and strong believers in the theory of the capitalist exploitation of labour. Hodgskin was an important forerunner of Marx in proclaiming the doctrine of surplus value: he expounded this doctrine in the lectures on *Popular Political Economy* which he gave at the Institution in its early days. There were, however, other advocates of working-class education who were fervent believers in orthodox political economy, and looked to mechanics' institutes to explain to the workers the fundamental harmony of interests between employers and employed, as well as to aid the self-helpful workman to improve his technical and scientific knowledge so as both to contribute more fully to the general well-being and to rise in the economic scale. In the affairs of the London Institution, the adherents of these rival doctrines soon fell out; and the struggle ended in the victory of the latter group, which, helped by the subscriptions of middle-class supporters, drove out the class-warriors and converted the Institution into a mainly technical and scientific place of education offering no challenge to the capitalist order. Renamed after its principal benefactor, George Birkbeck, the once-revolutionary working-class institution became in due course a college of London University, providing mainly for part-time evening students. Probably few of the students who attend Birkbeck College today have any clear notion of how it began.

A century later, a contest, in some respects similar and in some different, was being fought out between two rival agencies of working-class education—the Workers' Educational Association and the National Council of Labour

Colleges. In 1899 two well intentioned Americans, Walter Vrooman and Charles Beard, helped to found a college for working-class students in Oxford and expressed their idealism in naming it after John Ruskin. Within a few years the new college was rent by a dispute about the kind of economics it ought to teach—really part of a wider dispute about its entire curriculum and social purpose. The quarrel culminated in a split: the principal and a considerable body of students broke away, proclaiming the necessity for Marxist teaching, and set up a rival college—the Labour College—out of which presently arose a national movement—the National Council of Labour Colleges—offering Marxian education to the workers as an alternative to the pink impartiality of its rivals. 'I can promise to be candid, but not impartial', the new movement proclaimed; for, in the view of its sponsors, there could be no such thing as impartial education in face of the class war.

Before the split at Ruskin College, Albert Mansbridge, previously active in the Co-operative movement, had founded the Workers' Educational Association and had gone to the universities for help in building up a system of adult education that would meet the needs of intelligent working men and women. Mansbridge was no Marxist: he did not set out to destroy 'bourgeois culture' and to replace it by a new culture emanating from the proletariat as a class. He thought rather in terms of a great cultural heritage from which the workers were for the most part excluded, and wished to find means of opening this heritage to them and, in doing so, of broadening it out to find room for their aspirations. In this spirit he went to the universities—to Oxford first of all—and pleaded for a new kind of University Extension to be controlled in equal partnership by the universities, representing the teachers and the cultural tradition, and by the WEA, as the representative of the students and of their aspirations towards a more democratic culture. Out of this approach has arisen the network of university tutorial classes, summer schools, one-year classes, terminal courses, and WEA branch activities that today constitute a major element in the adult-education movement.

Between the WEA and the Labour Colleges soon arose a bitter dispute. The NCLC accused the WEA of being an agency for indoctrinating the workers with *bourgeois* ideologies, and pointed as evidence to the support given to it by the universities and, presently, by the state—both, according to the Marxian logic, agencies of capitalist domination. The NCLC received no such financial aid: it turned for support mainly to the trade unions, promising them help in the struggle against capitalism. The WEA also appealed to the trade unions, in the name of democracy, urging that the working-class movement should place its strength behind the demand for a more equalitarian and democratic educational system from primary school to university and should also itself aid the higher education of those whom the prevalent class system had excluded from opportunities of making the best of their mental endowments in childhood and adolescence. Trade-union conferences found themselves debating the rival educational policies of the two bodies, and voting now for the one and now for the other—or, sometimes, in view of the divisions in their own ranks, deciding to support neither or to split between the contestants such money—usually not very much—as they were prepared to devote to educational objectives. Long years—and, perhaps even more, the rift among Marxists themselves between Communists and anti-Communists, with the NCLC leaders taking the anti-Communist side—have somewhat softened the earlier animosities; but the fundamental differences remain. Either education is a by-product of class, and each class must build up its own educational philosophy and practice to suit the needs of the class struggle—that is, as long as class divisions persist— or, alternatively, education rests on fundamental values which transcend class differences (though not uninfluenced by them), and stands for a social heritage which is to be developed and transmitted to coming generations rather than uprooted and replaced.

In Great Britain, where Marxism as a social philosophy has never struck deep roots, the Socialist tradition is mainly on the side of the second view. The word 'Socialism' was first used in Great Britain to describe the followers of Robert Owen; and they adopted it as their own. The social doctrines of Owen—who was essentially a 'utopian'—have their roots farther back, notably in the ideas of William Godwin, who in turn developed them out of eighteenth-century rationalist optimism. Godwin saw mankind becoming more and more rational with the growth of knowledge; for he thought that to know the good and to act upon that knowledge were but two inseparable aspects of a single process. Accordingly, his entire philosophy turned upon education as a means of making men more rational and therewith better; and he looked forward to a society from which all coercion, and almost all formal regulation, would have disappeared because everybody would agree and everybody do the right thing without being compelled by any force outside his own mind.

Owen added to this doctrine an immense stress on the importance of the social environment. He agreed with Godwin in assigning a vital function to education in the 'formation of character'; but he also put high emphasis on the evil effects of the competitive system in setting man against man and on the power of a co-operative economic and social order to alter the behaviour of men by appealing to their social, rather than their anti-social, instincts. As a great manufacturer at New Lanark, Owen made the education both of the factory children and of his adult employees, and also of their children long before they reached the age of employment, an integral part of the system which he set up; and when he began to preach his wider social gospel of Co-operative Socialism and to advocate the establishment of 'Villages of Co-operation' as a solution of the social problem, education for both children and adults continued to occupy a central position in his schemes. New Harmony

and Queenwood were hardly less centres of education than of socialistic experiment; and when Owen's model communities had broken down, his disciples
continued to give educational activity a foremost place in their later projects.

Owen's educational ideas have been often misunderstood. They had two
aspects. On the one hand he insisted that education should be regarded as an
instrument for the formation of character from the very outset: on the other
hand he was no less insistent on the need for the teacher to take full account
of the individual nature of each child. By 'character' he meant mainly the
structure of ideals and values in people's minds; and this he believed to depend
almost wholly on environment and upbringing, and therefore to be capable of
being brought under social control. He held that if children were brought up
from the first in co-operative, as against competitive, ways of behaviour, the
whole society could be permeated with the spirit of mutual helpfulness and
fraternal goodwill. He did not, however, make the mistake—which has often
been attributed to him—of supposing that a co-operative kind of education
would turn his citizens out all alike, except to the extent of possessing a largely
common system of moral values. He protested vigorously against the methods
of mass-education advocated by Bell and Lancaster precisely on the ground
that they ignored the important differences of nature between child and child;
and he was most assiduous in urging his teachers to take full account of these
differences and to be at pains to accommodate their ways of approach to the
personal 'nature' and bent of each individual child.

Owen and his followers made strong attacks on established religion, ac-
cusing the churches of preaching a doctrine which made men responsible for
'sins' which were really the product of evil environment. But it was no accident that when, after the collapse of the Owenite movement, the Christian
Socialists came forward with a new gospel of Co-operative Socialism resting on
Christian foundations, many of the old Owenites joined hands with them. For
F. D. Maurice and his friends, no less than Owen, had a deep belief in the central importance of education as a moral and social force; and, reacting against
the 'other-worldliness' that dominated so much of contemporary Christianity,
they set out to make education in good principles of social action a pillar of
the Kingdom of God that they were seeking to establish on earth. Queen's
College, and, still more, the Working Men's College in London were intended
to be, above all else, places of education and culture resting on firm foundations of social morality. It may be said that the Christian Socialism of Maurice
and Kingsley can be called 'Socialism' only in a very extended use of the term;
and it is true enough that its protagonists were not Socialists in the modern
sense. But Socialism, in the modern sense, was then at the very beginning of
its development; and the ideas of these early Christian Socialists had undoubtedly a great influence on later advocates of Christian Socialism, from Stewart
Headlam to Charles Gore and William Temple. On the Continent, the sharp

rift between Socialism and the churches—above all between Socialism and the Catholic church—involved a complete break between the advocates of 'Christian Social' doctrines and the main body of the Socialist movement. In Great Britain there was no such absolute cleavage: only a small section of the modern British Socialist movement has been hostile to religion as a whole, and many of its leaders have been deeply religious in their personal attitudes. Accordingly, Christian Socialist influence has been able to operate, right up to the present day, inside the main structure of British Socialism and has not been driven into antagonism; and this factor has been important in obstructing the development of educational doctrines based on the Marxian conception of class war, just as it has acted as a force on the side of social solidarity and against revolutionism in many other fields.

For the most part, then, British Socialists in modern times have felt able to work without qualms for the democratic development of the existing educational structure, and have not felt impelled to denounce it as, in its very nature, an instrument of indoctrination in capitalist and anti-socialist beliefs and attitudes. They have, of course, often denounced particular parts or aspects of it as having such a tendency, but have done so, as a rule, with the purpose of agitating for reforms rather than of discrediting the entire structure. Revolutionism, in theory as well as in practice, has been weak in Great Britain ever since 1832. Even the Chartists, who had their revolutionary wing, thought for the most part in terms of making the state more democratic rather than of overthrowing it as a tainted agency of the capitalist class; and just as they demanded universal—or at any rate manhood—suffrage, so they demanded universal popular education—though some of them, including William Lovett, had serious fears about state action in the educational field because they were afraid it would carry with it the domination of the schools by the established church. After the decline of Chartism, the main body of the working-class leadership ranged itself behind the advocates of secular education not, in the main, out of any love for secularism as such, but rather as the only way of keeping out one-sided church control and of preventing educational advance from being frustrated by endless controversies between the sects.

After the decline of Owenism, Chartism, and Christian Socialism, which were all in eclipse by the later fifties of the last century, Socialism did not again become a force in Great Britain until the 1880s. Its revival in the Social Democratic Federation, under H. M. Hyndman's leadership, associated it closely with Marxism; and the SDF was too much occupied with the class struggle to make any significant contribution to educational theory or practice. William Morris, who broke away from the SDF in 1884 and founded the Socialist League, had more to say on the matter, but only as a Socialist 'utopian' looking forward to the new society that was to come after the revolution. In his utopia, *News from Nowhere*, the educational problem had simply solved itself. With the parents living in love and friendship in a free society from which all economic difficulties had disappeared, the children were represented by Morris as simply picking up what they needed and wanted to know without any necessity for formal schooling. Their elders would have plenty of free time to help them; and the children would learn one from another and in the process of doing things co-operatively for themselves. This almost-anarchist vision of utopia found, in its educational aspects, few echoes in later British Socialist writing except in the work of Bernard Shaw.

For the most part, the new and wider Socialist movement that grew up in the later eighties and in the nineties, and found expression first in Keir Hardie's Independent Labour Party and then in the Labour Party, made democratic educational advance a plank in its immediate programme of far-reaching social reform, side by side with the minimum wage, the eight hours' day, and the 'right to work'. The new Socialists agitated for free elementary education; for a raising of the school-leaving age; for medical inspection and treatment of school children, and also for school feeding for those who needed it; for public provision of secondary education open effectively to the children of the poor and aided by scholarships and allowances for maintenance; for fuller access to higher education, including the universities, and for the development of greater facilities for adult education; for better school buildings, smaller classes, better pay and more freedom for teachers. On the whole, they had remarkably little to say about the curriculum: they did not, like the Owenites, stress the significance of the school as a place in which the children should be taught the social values appropriate to a Socialist, or even to a fully democratic, society. They were much more concerned with demanding more education and better, in the sense of better-equipped, schooling than with criticizing the positive content of education for any fault except its low level of quality. Of course, they often attacked the exclusive 'public schools' and the older universities as hotbeds of reaction, and often demanded that the 'public schools' should be liquidated and all children go to a common system of schools. But in relation to the elementary schools and to the small but growing number of higher schools conducted under public auspices they put forward no proposals essentially different—except perhaps school feeding—from those which were advocated by other advanced advocates of educational reform.

I am speaking here both of the Socialist and working-class movement as a whole and of the body of academic and middle-class fighters for educational advance who formed the backbone of the Workers' Educational Association. There were, of course, a good many Socialists among the pioneers of new educational methods in 'progressive' schools of various types; but these did not exert any wide influence on the main body of Socialist thought. The main distinctive contribution which did come largely from Socialist sources was the movement for nursery schools, of which Margaret and Rachel McMillan, both active in the Independent Labour Party, were the pioneers. In this field and in that of school feeding the Socialists took a prominent part. Over the rest of the field, they were claiming mainly that the benefits of the superior education open only to the well-to-do should be extended, at least by way of opportunity, to the children of the poor.

At the same time, there was a controversy in which the Socialists were all on one side, and some sincere educational reformers on the other, concerning two conflicting ways of looking at educational advance. The rival conceptions became crystallized in rival metaphors—'ladder' and 'highway'. The Socialists, and some other educational reformers, wanted a system that would open a 'broad highway' of education up to the higher levels, not merely to a chosen few clever children, who would thereby be educated to become members of a superior social class, but either to all or at least to all who were capable of travelling along it. Their aim, as against those who favoured the 'ladder' of promotion, was to raise the whole people by affording to every individual the fullest educational opportunity by which he, or she, was capable of benefiting. They did not want to reduce all to a level: they recognized the need for the training of some in special skills and for the continuance of a group of devotees of the higher learning. But they wanted the basic minimum of education for every citizen to be raised to include higher as well as elementary schooling, and they expressed their main objective in the slogan 'Secondary Education for All', which Professor Tawney took as the title of one of his books written as a contribution to Labour policy. On this foundation of universal secondary education, the Socialists felt that it would be relatively easy to build a sufficiently democratic structure of still higher education in universities, colleges, and adult-education institutes and classes.

Undoubtedly one factor in drawing the attention of British Socialists away from the curriculum and in concentrating it on problems of quantity and quality, rather than of type, was the structure of the new educational system built up during the nineteenth century under the effective control of the local authorities rather than of the central government. Education, as a national issue, usually raised questions of curriculum only when the religious issue persisted in cropping up: in terms both of legislation and of central administration, the main issues had to do chiefly with the numbers and qualities of schools to be provided, and very little with what was to be taught in them. This, however, is by no means a sufficient explanation of the Socialist attitude; for the Socialists were active in local as well as in central government, and indeed made a bigger impact in the earlier stages on the local councils of the bigger towns than on Parliament. Perhaps the most remarkable educational success of the Socialists was scored by Sidney Webb and his fellow Fabians on the London County Council in its early days; and F. W. Jowett at Bradford is another outstanding name among the protagonists of democratic educational policies in local affairs.

Jowett was the pioneer of the movement for school feeding; but in other respects his attitude was not notably different from that of other advanced advocates of democratic educational reform. Equally with Sidney Webb in London, his main aims were to extend the public facilities for higher education and to make them more widely open to the children of working-class parents. On the London County Council, Webb is generally agreed to have done a really remarkable piece of work in the field of higher education; but no one has suggested that what he did involved any sharp break with the past in respect of the content of the curriculum or the ideologies taught in the schools.

Indeed, from the moment when Keir Hardie's Independent Labour Party and the Fabian Society led by Webb and Shaw replaced the Marxian Social Democratic Federation as the principal exponents of British Socialist policy, the entire theoretical basis of British Socialism, except for a small band of heretics of the left, became evolutionary and reformist, even if its real tendencies were sometimes concealed behind phrases of revolutionary tone. Not only the Fabians, who harked back by way of John Stuart Mill to Jeremy Bentham and preached a doctrine of radical utilitarianism as a justification of state action and of Socialism itself, but also the main body of Keir Hardie's working-class followers, were reformers rather than outright revolutionaries. Even when they spoke, as they often did, of the class war or of the class struggle, they thought of it rather as an unpleasant fact of existing society than as the slogan of a revolutionary struggle destined to invert the entire structure of social values. They had in many cases come to Socialism by way of Radicalism and out of disillusionment with the Liberal Party, especially after Joseph Chamberlain's defection; and they had also come to it in large numbers from the Nonconformist chapels and without necessarily breaking away from them—though some found in the Labour churches founded in the 1890s a sufficient sublimation of their previous religious impulses. Trailing these clouds of Radical Liberalism and of democratic religious fellowship along with them, they were not at all minded to throw over all the values of the society which, in its economic aspects, they challenged on grounds of social injustice and denial of human opportunity. They carried with them the traditions of *bourgeois* liberty and religious equality, and wanted these good things to be rapidly extended to more and more of the people and given fuller content by relief from under-nourishment of mind and body, and from the social insecurity of unemployment in a society almost devoid of public-welfare services except the detested Poor Law, with its taint of pauperism and degradation. They were, in effect, demanding not a brand-new social order, but a general diffusion of the advantages enjoyed by the privileged classes; and accordingly it came natural to them, even while they attacked the 'public schools' and the universities as haunts of class privilege, to attempt to remodel the inferior educational opportunities paid for out of public funds largely after the pattern set by the education of the middle class. To out-and-out Marxists, this attitude appeared to be sheer treason to the cause of proletarian revolution; but in Great Britain the out-and-out Marxists were few and uninfluential, and on the Continent the Marxian gospel was undergoing highly significant changes wherever its exponents were able to climb to positions of parliamentary influence or to perceive significant processes of democratic transformation occurring within the existing social order. German and French Social Democracy were alike influenced after 1890 by the British example, as well as by the internal developments of social relations under more advanced and productive techniques of capitalist industrialization. In Germany these forces gave rise to the struggle within the Social Democratic Party between orthodox Marxists and 'Revisionists'—a struggle in which the 'Revisionists', headed by Eduard Bernstein, were formally defeated but in reality won the day. In France the new United Socialist Party, led by Jean Jaurès, relegated the more extreme Marxists to a secondary position—only to be challenged almost at once by the new-old gospel of Revolutionary Syndicalism, which went even beyond Marx in proclaiming the need for a new set of social values and a new way of life emanating directly from the proletariat.

This Syndicalist gospel, reinforced by class-war doctrines developed largely among immigrants on the economic battlefields of the United States, where it took the name of 'Industrial Unionism', had its repercussions in Great Britain during the years of acute industrial unrest just before the First World War. But Revolutionary Syndicalism never came near to capturing the allegiance either of the main body of the British working class or of the leaders of British Socialism. Transmuted here, on the intellectual plane, into Guild Socialism, which was put forward as a reconciliation of Syndicalist and Socialist ideas, it lost its out-and-out revolutionary character, and discarded altogether the characteristic Syndicalist and Industrial Unionist denunciations of the moral code of *bourgeois* society. It became utopian rather than revolutionary, and set out to achieve its large ambitions for the creation of a libertarian Socialist society by building up, rather than uprooting, the libertarian and democratic traditions inherited from the past. Guild Socialism influenced many of the leaders of the trade unions and some of the leaders of the political Socialist movement; but among neither group did it ever come near winning a majority. The Webbs, in common with most of the political leaders while making some concessions to the Guild Socialist claims, held fast to their collectivism as well as to their evolutionary attitude; and after the troubles of the years immediately after 1918 had ended in the temporary defeat of the trade unions, there was an almost complete return to the older policies. Socialism, in practice, came again to mean in Great Britain a policy of social reform and social security complemented and guaranteed by substantial measures of industrial socialization and by stiff progressive taxation levied upon the well-to-do. It carried with it, beyond this, no fundamental challenge to the values of the existing society, and accordingly no imperative to set about building a distinctively Socialist educational programme based on a new proletarian ideology.

To be sure, there were always, from 1910 onwards, groups which challenged this evolutionary attitude; and before long the newly founded Communist Party of Great Britain, under Russian inspiration, provided a rallying-point for some of these groups. But never for all of them; for many of the most ardent 'proletarians' in Great Britain soon found the yoke of Communist discipline too hard to bear and broke away, mostly to return to the Labour Party, and to become within it the advocates of a variety of left-wing doctrines which failed to shake the essential reformism of the main body of leaders and followers alike. Thus, the Socialist educational reformers, despite some skirmishing in the field of adult education by the Marxists of the National Council of Labour Colleges, were able to pursue almost undisturbed their campaigns for a 'broad educational highway' within the potentialities of the existing structure, without formulating any revolutionary notions about the desirable content of the education they were endeavouring to open to the whole people. Even the NCLC, relying as it did on the trade unions for most of its support, soon tempered its Marxism and got rid of its Communists, who proceeded to build up their own system of party education on strict Leninist lines, while they also did their best to infiltrate into other working-class educational agencies, as they were doing in the case of the Labour Party on the political plane.

All this does not mean that the leaders of British Socialist educational opinion have been satisfied with the educational system as it is, or concerned merely to improve it and extend its higher opportunities more widely. It does, however, mean that, except for a limited number of practising Socialist teachers, the tasks of extension and development have seemed to be much more pressing than those of altering the content and the values—which latter have indeed appeared, for the time being, as impossible projects. The Socialist teachers who have been most conscious of the problem of the educational *values* as distinct from the quantity and quality of educational provision, have focused most of their attention on the means to be adopted in eradicating, or at least greatly reducing, class differences in schooling, by attacking the regime of the 'two nations'—the social division between those who get their schooling through the local authorities and those who get it at the private preparatory and at the so-called 'public' schools. They have wished to make an end of class segregation by improving the elementary schools and forcing the private preparatory schools out of business, and to build up the state system of secondary education to a standard high enough to deprive the 'public schools' of their *raison d'être*, and to make the public grammar schools as good an avenue to the universities and the professions as any other. Therewith, in the interests of democratic values, they have advocated the 'comprehensive school' as against the segregation of 'grammar school', technical school, and 'modern school' pupils in separate institutions between which they see insuperable difficulties in bringing about any real 'parity of esteem'. By making the state system comprehensive enough to meet all democratic needs, and at the same time by insisting on 'comprehensiveness', in the second sense, as the alternative to segregation, they have aimed at building up by stages an educational structure which would have the effect of democratizing the access to the universities and to other institutions of higher education; and by these means they have thought they saw their way to the establishment of the 'classless society' in the educational sphere.

Even these forthright reformers, however, have not set out to establish a new ideology, on the basis of a sharp break with the past. They have held rather that the progressive democratization of the access to education and of its institutional structure would carry with it such transformations of social values as are needed for the building of a Socialist society. To the extent to which they have considered questions of curriculum and of social values, they have tended in most cases to stress the need for allowing each child to develop its individual bent and abilities rather than the need, no less emphasized than this by Robert Owen, to make the school a place of training in the collective attitudes and values needed for the successful working of a Socialist society. In this, as in most respects, there is in British Socialism a very strong element of individualist doctrine. There is no wish, as there is in Russia and as there has been in the past in many non-Socialist countries, to 'socialize' the minds of the people by indoctrinating them with a one and only correct social outlook and equipment of moral ideas. Indeed, any such notion would be anathema to such an extent that there is a danger of the very need for a society to possess a broadly common way of life and pattern of values being overlooked. This, no doubt, has mattered the less in practice because the element of common tradition in the British way of living has been so strong, as a result of long continuous development without revolutions, as to stand in little need of reinforcement until quite lately. It is, however, doubtful whether British society can stand the considerable transformations which it has undergone from within, or the heavy impact made upon it in recent years by forces from outside—from America even more than from the Soviet Union—without more necessity than has existed hitherto to carry into its schools some teaching of the requirements of democratic living in the disturbed conditions of the present day.

Needless to say, I am not suggesting that British Socialists are in the least likely to take to totalitarian educational gospels—or that they should. What they are now facing is not the need to indoctrinate every child with a common social gospel, but rather to adapt their educational objectives to the changing structure of British society and to the changing place of Great Britain in the twentieth-century world. The educational programme of British Socialism was built up at a time when practically every industry was under capitalist control and accordingly nearly every road to promotion in industry was in capitalist hands; when the higher professions were for the most part close preserves for the uppermiddle classes; and when there was a gulf fixed between gentlemanly schoolmasters and ladylike schoolmistresses and the ruck of mere 'teachers' in the state schools. Today, the position in all these respects is much more fluid. The universities have become much more widely open (though they are shutting again a little just now); new and less gentlemanly professions have developed side by side with the old, and the class monopoly of the latter has been to some extent invaded; the lines between masters and mistresses and mere teachers have become to some extent blurred; and, most important of all, a number of important industries and services have been socialized, so that appointments to them and promotions within them have become to some extent matters in which considerations of public policy are involved. What remains unclear is whether these changes are to lead to the emergence of a new 'managerial' class, largely hereditary but open to talents from any social stratum, or will in due course of time really undermine class distinctions and bring about conditions of much greater social equality between man and man, irrespective of the nature of their several jobs.

The advocates of the 'comprehensive school' wish to prevent the first of these two things and to further the second. They wish to ensure that parental status, as well as parental income, shall count for little in the choice of a calling or in promotion to a higher post, and that each child shall be given as fully as possible a chance to prove his or her capacity at every stage of the educational process. But even if the comprehensive school could be made a reality at both the primary and the secondary levels, even if private preparatory and socially superior 'public' schools could be liquidated or absorbed into the common system, this would not suffice to achieve what the Socialists have in mind— though it would of course mean a great advance towards the preconditions of a classless society. In order to avert the danger of the emergence of a new managerial class it is necessary to have regard, not only to schools and universities and colleges, but also to the principles to be adopted in providing for promotions for those who have left school or college and entered upon their life's work, to the opportunities afforded for the training of such persons, to the special case of 'late-developers', and to the social composition of the boards and commissions that are put in charge of the various enterprises, and of their leading executants.

It is a notable fact that when the British Labour Party embarked on its programme of extensive nationalization it appears to have given almost no thought in advance to problems of this kind. Only recently has the National Coal Board produced what it has called, somewhat unfortunately, its 'ladder plan'—for the 'ladder' metaphor has for Socialist educationists an unhappy connotation of climbing out of one's class. Yet, in a sense, the 'ladder' is a correct metaphor; for in relation to the jobs to be done, only a few can climb up from the lower to the higher rungs. There must be a few who will occupy the managerial and executive posts, a larger number, but still a minority, who can reach supervisory positions, a considerably larger number who will achieve manual skill or clerical capacity—and yet others who will remain in the ranks of the less skilled. A structure hierarchical in this way is inherent in the very nature of most industrial operations and of many kinds of mass-produced service. The question for Socialists is how such a hierarchy of functions can be made compatible with social equality and, more particularly, with democracy in the educational sphere. Socialist educational thought has hitherto paid little attention to this problem, largely because the Socialists have been thinking mainly about general and very little about technical or specialized education. The rift on this issue goes back a long way. At Robert Owen's settlement of New Harmony, in the 1820s, there was a great dispute about the type of education appropriate to a community setting out to establish a 'New Moral World'. Owen himself laid the main stress on education in the moral principles of co-operative behaviour: some of his lieutenants held that the children could be best educated in the principles of the good life by being taught a trade in such a way as to arouse their creative instincts and give them a sense of its social meaning. But most of the Owenites seem to have set little store by any education that could be called 'vocational'. The disastrous divorce between the exponents of the 'vocational' and the 'cultural' was already beginning.

This divorce, made largely unavoidable by the conditions of the nineteenth century, has done much to hamper the development of a realistic Socialist educational policy. The school has been thought of primarily as a place in which, at the first formal stage, the rudiments of general education would be implanted, and at the higher stages the pupil who stayed at school would proceed beyond the rudiments to the acquisition of 'culture'. Technical education has always been treated as a relatively unimportant part of the public system of education, and has attracted but little attention from the educational idealists. Science was a late-comer to the schools, and edged its way in gradually to parity only at the higher levels. The cultural teachers who played a large part in framing Socialist educational policy were apt to look askance at any attempt to give schooling a vocational bias, because they thought of such attempts as meaning so much subtracted from 'culture' and alienated for the benefit of employers who, they felt, should see to the training of their workers in their own time.

This attitude, not a little of which persists today despite the great expansion of applied science, had in part an anti-capitalist and in part a 'snob' basis, and often united persons who fundamentally held sharply opposing views. It was tenable, as long as the training of skilled labour was carried out largely

by means of apprenticeship on the job, and as long as it was taken for granted that most children would pass into employment very young, with barely
time to master the rudiments of literacy before they left school. But such a
view of education is entirely incompatible either with the establishment of any
real 'secondary education for all' or with the conditions of the modern world,
which requires from nearly all of us both an understanding of the general basis
of modern productive techniques and a 'sense of the machine' which can serve
as a foundation for more specialized training when and if it is needed.

What I am suggesting is that, in a democracy, there needs to be a close
resemblance between the education of those who occupy the leading positions
and of those whom it is their function to lead. If the promising young persons who are 'spotted' for positions of leadership and high technical expertness
are removed from the rest at an early stage and given a segregated education,
nothing can prevent them from developing the characteristics of a 'managerial
class', even if the hereditary element among them can be kept within bounds.
Nor can anything be done in such a situation to prevent the growth of a feeling
of antagonism between those who have been thus selected for higher training
and those who have been left behind. The comprehensive school has at any
rate the advantage, from the Socialist point of view, of postponing the age of
educational segregation; but over and above this there is need for the fullest
opportunity for those who have not been 'spotted' young to equip themselves
later with the knowledge needed for promotion, in such a way that the upper
ranges of management and administration come to be filled with men and
women recruited in a wide variety of ways and through a number of different
channels of promotion.

It will be impracticable to achieve this diversity, unless the higher forms
of specialized education are developed upon common foundations appropriate to the type of industrial society in which we are living. This in turn will
be impracticable as long as 'literary' and 'scientific-technical' education are
allowed to remain, in the lower and middle ranges, as sharply separated as
they are today. We are beginning slowly to realize that there ought to be more
basic science and more basic teaching of practical ways of applying it in our
general school curricula, and more mixture of the scientific and the literary
in our technical schools and in the technical colleges conducted by the local
authorities. Perhaps we should start thinking of getting rid of 'unilateral' colleges as much as of 'unilateral' schools, and of merging the technical colleges
in people's universities at which every range of subjects would be taught—as,
indeed, is half-happening already in a few of the more recent local colleges set
up by certain local authorities.

On matters such as these, however, it can hardly be said that there is as yet
any distinctive Socialist theory. Nor have Socialists yet at all clearly made up
their minds about the problems of education in citizenship. It has come to be

fairly generally understood that it is a part of the business of our schools, at all stages, to teach 'civics', or something of the kind, and to give the pupils some understanding of the manner in which the main political and social institutions of our society actually work. But as we operate under a parliamentary system which involves alternations in power of the main parties, and as these parties differ very greatly about the principles on which our society ought to be conducted, it is necessary for the teachers to do their best to carry on instruction in these subjects 'impartially', and not to give a collective preference to the views of one side. Indeed, as the teachers differ among themselves nearly as much as the rest of the population, there is no possibility of their following a common partisan line except under a compulsion which it would be quite inconsistent with our kind of parliamentary democracy to apply. A totalitarian regime, be it Communist or Fascist or Catholic, can order all its teachers to preach such doctrines about society as the leaders of the regime desire: we in Great Britain can do no such thing—nor would the vast majority of British Socialists wish to, if they had the power.

Yet there is in this something of a real dilemma—which is the dilemma of the whole society and not merely of its educational institutions. The capitalist and the Socialist ways of life are different: they require for their working different sets of values and appeals to different motives. Just as a whole society poised between Socialism and capitalism suffers unavoidably from a divided mind, and is in some danger of getting the worst of both worlds so teachers who are allowed to preach the virtues neither of Socialism nor of capitalism run the risk of giving their pupils no lead at all in the art of good living and of turning them loose without any adequate equipment of assured values. If, over a period, the contest between the two systems in the whole society gets sufficiently resolved to make the one or the other the established norm of social behavior—as capitalism actually was until a little while ago—the teachers will no doubt find themselves adapting their teaching to the tone of the social environment, and either teaching again, as they used to, within the assumptions of a capitalist structure of values or substituting a set of values based on the changed environment of a Socialist society. They will find themselves doing this, even if individuals among them dissent from the victorious doctrine—just as in the past teachers who were Socialists used to adapt themselves to a capitalist environment (and some still do). But in the meantime, with the issue unsettled and capitalist and Socialist parties acting on the assumption of alternating spells of office and opposition, it is impracticable for Socialists who accept this state of affairs as necessary to formulate any clear ideas about the kind of moral and civic education that is needed to serve as a firm basis for a Socialist society. The Socialist society has to be created first, before they can begin, except quite tentatively and purely as a personal matter, to educate the rising generation in its values.

This, of course, is where the Russians have the advantage of us, though we may hold that they abuse their advantage. They can set out without hesitation to plan a school system that fits in with the needs of their monolithic society, assigning whatever place they please to the 'vocational' and to the 'literary', to science and to techniques and to the arts, to education in citizenship and in the uses of leisure. They can set out to make their schools training-grounds for Communists, who will imbibe in them the rudiments of the Marxian gospel and the Marxian way of life, fully as much as the child in a Catholic school in a Catholic country is indoctrinated in a different faith from theirs. To most British Socialists, the way in which the Russians approach this opportunity is abhorrent; for it seems to us to involve a monstrous suppression of dissentient opinions, and even a good deal of straight lying about sheer facts. British democratic Socialists have no hankering after any such form of totalitarian teaching; but at the other extreme I think a good many Socialist educators are aware of the vacuum of social values in which the present situation of Great Britain compels the schools to exist.

For the 'liberal' Socialist, from the days of Robert Owen and of Fourier, the Socialist way of life has meant a co-operative, as against a self-seeking or competitive, social pattern. It has involved an educational system designed to play down the self-seeking and aggressive impulses and to give the fullest possible encouragement to the impulses making for mutual aid. At the same time, the 'liberal' element in non-Marxian Socialism has carried with it a stress on individual development and freedom for each person to grow in his or her own way. These aims have seemed to be compatible; and as means of combining and reconciling them emphasis has been put on self-government in the school, on group activities in and out of school hours, and on friendly, co-operative relations between teachers and taught—and also between teachers and parents. The desire to make the school a place animated by the spirit of mutual help, rather than of relentless competition, has been, in practice, continually at war not only with the need to use competition as a spur to effort, but also with the intense competitiveness of the struggle for access to higher education as a means to material and social advancement. Socialists for the most part strongly disliked the conditions which made entry to a secondary or higher technical school, for most children, dependent on success in a single examination which was not merely 'qualifying', but keenly competitive. They stood, as we have seen, for 'secondary education for all' as a general right; and they were led, by their desire to promote social equality, to insist on the need for 'parity of esteem' between different kinds of secondary school, and beyond this on the need for 'comprehensive schools' open to all normal children whatever their scholastic abilities. But when they came to face the practical issues of educational reform, they could not help knowing that, in the short run, it was impossible to offer to all children, or even to most, a secondary education equal in sheer quality to that offered by the better 'public schools' to the children of the well-to-do. This was only in part a matter of cost—of better buildings and equipment and of higher staffing ratios of teachers to pupils—though considerations of cost were formidable enough. It was also a question of absolute shortage of really able teachers and therewith of rival demands from education, industry, government, and other professions on the limited total supply of high quality in the population. The number of men and women who take to teaching because they love it as a vocation is, and is likely to remain, small in relation to the numbers needed; and for a high proportion of its manpower, education is bound to depend on persons who feel no special calling, but weigh teaching in the balance against other opportunities of earning a livelihood. This means that there is bound to be a scramble for really good teachers, and that any system applicable to all children is bound to put up with a large complement of the second-rate. A general system of comprehensive schools could not in the short run possibly attract, *on the average,* as high a quality of teachers as have been recruited to the limited number of expensive 'public schools' conducted in the interests of the well-to-do. In the long run, this difficulty *might* be overcome, if the numbers of the able and well-educated could be greatly increased. In the short run it cannot.

Accordingly, there is a dilemma, of which Socialists belonging to the 'intellectual classes' are apt to be particularly conscious. Many of these see the need for a Socialist society to train its own elites up to very high levels of capacity and responsibility, and stress the need for forms of higher education which will produce the requisite supply of leaders. Some of these 'intellectuals' are afraid that, if the emphasis is laid heavily on equality, the quality of higher education will fall off as its quantity is rapidly increased, and are disposed to tolerate, for the time being, a continuance of the 'public schools' in a special position, subject to access to them being effectively opened by means of scholarships to a sufficient proportion of poor men's children. Some go even farther and wish to retain a special kind of school for the special purpose of training an elite, while insisting that access to it should be made to depend, as soon as possible, on personal prowess and not on the means or social standing of the parents.

Most Socialists, I think, find this attitude inconsistent with their aspirations towards social equality, and dislike the notion of segregated groups of able children being trained for leadership. It is often pointed out that the middle-class 'public schools' owe not a little of their virtue as places of training for leadership and responsibility to the fact that they are *not* reserved for specially able boys and girls, but include a mixture of the clever, the average, and the fairly stupid, within the limits of the classes from which their pupils are drawn. To turn them into preserves for the very clever, or into places where selected pupils (however selected) would be specially educated for positions of command, would be entirely inconsistent with the Socialist desire to stimulate a spirit of democratic co-operation and a type of leadership based on democratic fellow-ship rather than on authoritarian command.

Socialists cannot, however, by any means afford to accept a lowering of the quality of higher education in the interests of social equality. They must accordingly refrain from destroying what they cannot speedily replace, and must for the time being condone the continuance of class elements in the edu-cational structure, while doing their best to work out a satisfactory adjustment to the requirements of social democracy. This means experimenting with com-prehensive schools of the highest quality, working out new, democratic ways of deciding which pupils are to stay at school past the minimum leaving-age, and which are to go on to a university or to a full-time college education elsewhere; discovering what means can best be used to give a good chance to 'late-devel-opers', including adults who have been following regular trades or professions; and also, at the other end of the scale, doing what can be done to reduce, by special educational methods, the numbers of the 'subnormal', so as to fit them for the tasks of citizenship and make as many as possible able to play a normal part in the life of the community.

Whatever may be done to make the school more a place of training in at-titudes of good citizenship and mutual help, it will, of course, be impossible to extrude from it the consideration of material advancement. However 'cul-tural' education may be, it has to prepare boys and girls to face the work they will need to do when they enter on employment. The schools must not turn out too many clerks and typists and too few who are prepared to enter man-ual employments: nor, at higher vocational levels, must schools and colleges produce supplies of qualified persons irrespective of the demand for different types of service. All organized education, in any society, is bound to be greatly influenced by vocational considerations: indeed, the education we think of as representing 'culture' in its purest form was in origin mainly education for the recognized 'learned professions' of an earlier day.

What has happened now, and what will continue to happen in a Socialist society, is an immense multiplication of higher professions needing special knowledge, and therewith an immense increase in the number of lesser pro-fessions which also call for such knowledge at lower levels. At the same time there has been a considerable shift from the learning of skilled trades by means of apprenticeship 'on the job' to learning them, at least in part, in technical institutions. These developments, together with the decline in the numbers of the unemployed rich and well-to-do-especially among women—have tended to emphasize the vocational character of education and to make its helpfulness towards getting a better job much more present to the minds of both parents and children. Thus, the Socialist cannot set out to eliminate considerations of self-advancement from the educational process—and could not, even if the payments for different kinds of work were to become much less unequal than they now are; for differences of prestige would persist even in face of equality of rewards. The aim cannot be that of taking the 'success' motive wholly out of education: it can be only that of making success more dependent on co-operative, as against merely self-seeking, behaviour. The education that will achieve this will call for very high personal qualities in the teachers.

The nearer a society advances towards Socialism and social equality, the greater the difficulties of establishing a satisfactory educational system appear. The class system has simplified the educational problem by the assumption that higher education should be the monopoly of a limited class, with exceptional chances for a few gifted individuals, or children of gifted individuals, to climb up the ladder from the classes below. Socialism, on the other hand involves the initial assumption that talents and capacities for service ought to be sought out and discovered wherever they exist, and that no valuable talent or capacity should be allowed to run to waste because of parental poverty, ignorance, or neglect. A Socialist school system has therefore to be so designed as to give every child its chance, but at the same time to avoid the creation of a new class structure based on differences of ability. Just as in a family or in an aristocracy the individual members belong to the same class whether they are clever or stupid or merely ordinary, so in a Socialist democracy it is necessary to prevent differences of ability from being converted into differences of social class. This can be done only if there is a foundation of common schooling at the primary stage, followed up by some form of 'comprehensive' secondary schooling in which differences of curriculum and standard in the classroom are combined with equal participation in mixed activities on the playgrounds, in clubs and societies, and in any sort of out-of-school activity.

It cannot, however, be expected that the school should advance towards social equality out of step with other parts of the social system. The educational advance is only one aspect of a development that has to be achieved simultaneously in many different fields. In the last resort, the school system is bound to reflect the general characteristics of the social and economic structure of the society within which it exists. Socialist educational objectives and policies are only an element in the wider policies that are being pursued in the fields of political and economic policy, and can develop in practice only *pari passu* with these. The Socialist educator of today can dream dreams of Utopia, as his predecessors have done from Sir Thomas More to H. G. Wells. The practical realization of his dreams depends on the actual structure of the society in which he works—on the jobs it offers to his pupils, on the degrees of economic inequality it allows and recognizes, and on the extent to which, in its general behaviour, it accords prestige to money-making or to hereditary or acquired social status. There can be no practical Socialist educational policy except in conjunction with a general policy making for social equality in every part of the structure of communal life. That is why Socialist educational ideas are so difficult to disentangle from general Socialist conceptions of human relations in other fields. All education that is not meaningless is education *for some end*; and the ends which schools and colleges must serve are set for them by the general pattern of living in the societies whose purposes and values they exist to serve.

THE TRADE UNION OUTLOOK

It is always dangerous for an 'intellectual' who is not a Trade Unionist in the ordinary sense (though he may have his professional Trade Union to fight his battles) to write about Trade Union policy; for there are always Trade Union leaders lying in wait to denounce him as an irresponsible meddler if he says anything of which they disapprove.[1] But in this article I am responding to a definite request to write an article for a Trade Union journal, and I must risk being told that I have no right to interfere; for presumably I should not have been asked unless some Trade Unionists wished know what I thought.[2]

I think British Trade Unionism is in a very difficult transitional position. The more power it gets, the greater are the obstacles in the way of using that power. First, during the war, the Trade Unionist was told that he must do nothing to disturb national unity in the war effort. Then, when Labour achieved political power, he was told that he must do nothing to make things difficult for the Government; and with the Conservatives back in office, he is told both that the national economic difficulties are so great that he must do nothing to hamper the Government in coping with them and that the war danger makes it necessary for him to subordinate his claims to building up the

---

1 *Fusion*, 1952.

2 *Fusion* was published by the National Union of Sheet Metal Workers, London District.

armed strength of the West against the Soviet Union. If one asks 'When will the Trade Unions be free to use their power to press their demands to the full?' the real answer is 'Never'. There will always be something to stop them—a Labour Government, a balance of payments crisis, a Cold War (or even a Hot War)—always something.

This, indeed, is in the very nature of the case. The Trade Union movement is today so powerful that it can never afford to act without considering the effect of its action on the whole community—that is, without regard to national policy as a whole. When Labour is in power, it is not practicable for the Trade Unions to follow one policy and the Labour Government another without pulling the Government down. Whatever party is in office, it is not practicable for the Trade Unions to press wage-demands to the limit regardless of their effect on the balance of payments—or rather, their doing so can only lead to an inflation of prices that will do them no good. Even if they could improve the relative position of their own members, or some of them, by pressing their claims regardless of consequences, they could, as matters stand, do this in the main only at the expense of pensioners and other groups living on fixed money incomes. They cannot even advance wages at the expense of the very high profits that industry has been making, because the purchasing power embodied in these profits is needed for capital expenditure to maintain and improve productive resources for future use. It is no doubt infuriating to see these huge profits being made by capitalist concerns, and I hold strongly that they ought to be socialized. But even if they were they would not be available for consumption; for already the nation is spending too little on building up the capital resources on which its efficiency and our future standards of living depend.

The plain truth is that as long as we continue to live under the capitalist system, the Trade Unions will have to behave as the capitalist system requires, whatever may be the party label of the Government in power. We cannot have full employment under capitalism without high profits resulting; and until, politically, Labour is ready to put an end to capitalism, this situation cannot be changed. I am not suggesting that, even if the next Labour Government were to follow a thoroughly Socialist policy—which I do not expect—the Trade Unions would be out of the wood; for even if it took away all the money the rich spend on consumption that would not make a great deal of difference by itself to working-class standards. There cannot be any big increase in these standards without much higher production and better planned use of productive resources; and it is of no use to pretend that there can. Higher standards would necessarily mean more imports, which would have to be paid for by sending out more exports other countries want, at prices their inhabitants can afford to pay. There is no getting away from that.

Workers' Control

It is, however, not surprising that Trade Unionists are still suspicious of demands for higher output when they see enormous profits being made, or that they are still afraid, mindful of past experiences, that increased output will only lead to 'redundancy' and unemployment, as they see it beginning to do already in the textile trades. For my part, I do not believe that the high production at low cost which this country needs if it is to be able to maintain and improve standards of living can be got under capitalist conditions of employment, not only because the workers are reluctant to go all out to make more profits for capitalists, but also because the capitalist directors of business are afraid of over-production and unwilling or unable to take the steps needed to re-equip industry on a more up-to-date footing. On the other hand, I do not believe either that huge public corporations such as the Labour Government set up in a number of industries will give the workers the sense of working for themselves and the community that is needed to make them do their very best. I think we shall have to take all the big industries out of capitalist hands in order, not to transfer them to bureaucratic control but to put them under a decentralized form of management in which the workers on the spot—and not merely their distant full-time officials—will have an effective say.

This will mean a new kind of Trade Unionism, in which many more of the rank and file members will be required to play an active part. One effect of the growth of Trade Union power under the conditions of the years since 1939 has been that the Trade Unions have become much too centralized, and that Trade Unionists have come to expect everything to be done for them by their officials and national executives instead of doing things for themselves. It is not 'workers'' control, or anything like it, for the national leaders of the Trade Unions to be consulted about policy, without the local members—even the active ones—having any real say. In my view, both the Labour Party and the Trade Union leadership (partly out of fear of Communists) have become much too bureaucratically minded. I want, and mean by 'democracy', a system in which *everyone* is given the opportunity to play an active part, according to his capacities, even if only a minority takes actual advantage of the chance. I want Trade Unions which are capable of running industry, and set out to help their members to train themselves, in day-to-day action as well as by attending educational classes for the job of running it.

An Educated Membership

The leaders are apt to reply that there are not nearly enough keen or responsible Trade Unionists to take on so formidable a task. But, if there are not, one reason for the shortage is that those who might become capable are given too little encouragement. In particular, there has been almost nothing for many years past to foster the fighting spirit on which the real vigour of Trade Unionism depends; and when Trade Unionists have been urged to play a part, as in joint consultation, they have often been told to do so in a spirit of co-operation with capitalism rather than of preparing themselves to supersede it and to take over control. I do not believe that the movement is really so short of able men and women, who could become active if there were anything for them to be active about, as the centralizers among the leaders, of both the Labour Party and the Trades Union Congress seem to believe.

I do, however, agree that the Trade Union movement, as it exists today, is not equipped to become an active force in the working of a really democratic Socialist society. Such a society can neither come into being, nor exist successfully, without the active and intelligent participation of a large body of its citizens. If we want such a society, then, the Trade Unions will have to set out deliberately to equip their members for it by education and by giving them more local responsibility and power—particularly more power to shop stewards and works representatives to handle matters which directly affect the working lives of the workers they represent. If, instead of doing this, the Trade Union leaders accept centralization as a natural tendency, and do nothing to counteract its effects, Trade Unionism will continue to have power without the means of using it, and, however many million Trade Unionists there are, we shall get no nearer to real democracy. At any rate, that is how I feel; but I am far from pretending that even the best organized and most intelligent Trade Union movement would find the tasks facing it simple.

For the national emergency is real: we are in an economic jam, which has not been created, but only made worse, by our folly in carrying expenditure on armaments far beyond what we can afford without disaster, and in allowing ourselves to become subservient to America in foreign policy—so that, instead of trying to come to terms with the Soviet Union and to reopen large scale trade between East and West, we have become parties to a policy of encircling and outpowering Communism that is likely to land us in a disastrous and unnecessary world war. I say this, not as a Communist, but as a democratic Socialist who sees that our only chance of decent living lies in preserving the peace and coming to terms of live and let live with the Communist half of the world.

WHAT IS SOCIALISM?

WHAT IS SOCIALISM? THERE HAVE BEEN SO MANY NOTIONS OF IT; BUT IF THE name has any real meaning there must be some common element, however elusive it may be.[1] The word has been in frequent use for upwards of a century in both French and English: in which of the two countries it originated is still uncertain. It seems to have been used first—apart from a single earlier use in Italian in an entirely different sense—at some time in the second half of the 1820s, and to have passed quickly into fairly general use to describe certain theories or systems of social organization. 'Socialists' were the persons who advocated these theories or systems. Alternatively such persons were called 'Owenites', or 'Fourierists', or 'Saint-Simonians', or by a variety of other names derived either from the originators of particular systems or from the names these originators gave to them—for example, 'Harmonists', or 'Associationists', or 'Icarians'—this last after Cabet's projected Utopia, described in his *Voyage en Icarie* (1840). Jerome Blanqui, the economist, brother of the better-known revolutionary, Auguste Blanqui, dubbed them all 'Utopians': Karl Marx took up the word, and grouped them in the *Communist Manifesto* of 1848 as 'Utopian Socialists', by way of distinguishing their doctrines from his own 'Scientific Socialism'. Thereafter there were said to be two sorts of 'Socialism'—'Utopian' and 'Scientific'. To these was soon to be added a third kind, Libertarian or

---

1 *Political Studies*, 1953.

Anarchist, of which in their several ways Proudhon and Bakunin were the pioneers. Later still came a fourth kind, often called 'Fabian' or Evolutionary Socialism, differentiated from Marx's Scientific Socialism by its belief in what is termed 'gradualism'—the creed of most of the western Labour and Socialist parties of today. What had all these kinds of Socialism in common, to be called by the same name? The answer, in brief, is—hostility to *laissez-faire* and economic competition, and belief in some sort of collective or co-operative action as a means of improving the condition of the many poor.

The 'Utopian' Socialists whom Marx claimed to supersede were all essentially moralists. They set out, some with more and some with less regard for time and place, to prescribe the conditions needed for the establishment of the 'good society', or of 'good societies' which would enable men to escape the evils of the actual societies in which they were living. It was a common view of all of them that existing societies were corrupt and corrupting to their citizens, and that the possibility of living a good life depended on devising and establishing a right structure of human relations. Most, if not all, of them believed that in some valid sense good living was 'natural', and bad living a consequence of artificial departure from 'natural' conditions. Most, if not all, of them, while they roundly denounced the abuses of existing societies, at the same time believed in progress as 'natural', and were optimists about the future of humanity. Most, if not all, of them also believed that a great advance in the art of living was on the point of being achieved, and connected the prospect of this advance with the progress made in human knowledge. Some of them stressed the intellectual aspect of this progress; others the technological. Most of them believed that the development of science and of the techniques of production had put mankind into a position to solve once and for all the problem of poverty, by producing enough to provide the means of natural good living for the entire human race. Most of them held in addition that men tended to become more rational in action as their knowledge increased, and that the application of reason to politics was destined speedily to revolutionize human relations. Many of them identified knowledge with virtue, or at any rate held that to know the good was virtually the same thing as to act rightly. In this spirit they projected their Utopias, in the confidence that rightly adjusted social structures could not fail to induce men to behave reasonably and to co-operate in making these structures work well.

Thus the 'socialists' of the early part of the nineteenth century were moral reformers who held that the clue to moral reformation was to be sought in the reformation of the social order. They were 'Socialists', first and foremost, because they put the main stress on social arrangements as the operative causes of good and bad living, and of individual virtue or vice. They tended to regard evil conduct as a consequence less of individual sins or shortcomings than of a bad, 'unnatural' environment. Get the environment right, they said, and most men will behave decently and reasonably in their mutual affairs. They differed, indeed, to some extent concerning the process by which the change in individual behaviour would come about. Some, such as Owen and Saint-Simon, emphasized the influence of education on the formation of character, and assigned great importance to rational education as a factor in the making of the new society. Others, especially Fourier, argued that there was no need for any change in human nature, because all men's passions, including those which in existing societies led to anti-social conduct, would work for good in a society organized to fit in with men's natural propensities. But this difference, important though it was, did not prevent them from agreeing that the essential thing was not to preach virtue to individuals so much as to establish an environment in which there would be the greatest possible encouragement to men to act virtuously, because the system of expectations surrounding the individual would be such as to make virtue come easy to him, and vice difficult.

'Utopian Socialism', then, made its début as a plan for a system of social organization designed to further human happiness and well-being by the facilitating of good behaviour. All its proponents agreed that existing societies, far from doing this, gave most men strong temptations to act antisocially. They differed in the stresses they put on different aspects of the evils of society as it was; some of them denounced 'privilege' as the principal cause of social ills, others 'competition'. The former pointed out how the system of privilege for a limited group within society was inconsistent with the fundamentally equal right of all men to pursue happiness and well-being, because it involved a structure of preferential 'rights' and therewith a denial of the rights of the many in deference to the claims of the few. Some—for example Saint-Simon—also argued that it was manifestly wrong for privilege, if it were to be accorded at all, to go to the unproductive (*les oisifs*) at the expense of the productive (*les industriels*). Others, such as Owen and the 'left-Ricardian' economists who preceded Marx, stressed chiefly the evils of competition, as encouraging men to contend against men, instead of fostering habits of mutual co-operation in a common pursuit of the good life. Which of these arguments got most emphasis depended largely on the kind of society the reformers were thinking of as needing to be overthrown. Against the *ancien régime* it was natural to stress the iniquities of privilege: against the rising capitalist system the evils of competition in money-making. Wherever the stress was put, the 'Socialists' were at one in denouncing the exploitation of the real producers of wealth by the ruling classes, and in demanding that in the new society co-operation, and not mutual antagonism and conflict, should be the guiding principle of social organization.

It has sometimes been said that the 'Utopian Socialists' differed from their successors in having no notion of Socialism as a 'class-issue'. This is true only in a qualified sense. Many of them were acutely conscious of the exploitation of the working classes under the existing social order and of the unjustifiable privileges of the superior classes. Indeed, I think they all denounced this exploitation, though they did not all think of it in the same terms. Saint-Simon, for example, usually thought of the industrial employers as having a common interest with the workers against the old privileged classes of nobles, land-owners, and militarists. He recognized that in fact the employers were apt to treat the workers ill, but attributed this to their being caught up in a system based on the exploitation of *la classe la plus nombreuse et la plus pauvre,* and believed that if the privileged classes were overthrown, the technicians and administrators would act as the servants and not the masters of the people, becoming the *fonctionnaires* of the new industrial order. In order to ensure this, his followers wished to abolish inheritance of wealth and to make land and capital public property, to be entrusted to those persons who were capable of making the best use of it in the general interest. Fourier proposed to allow investors of capital a return on their investments in his projected *phalanstères* (associative communities), and did not envisage the advent of the new society as involving any struggle between capitalists and workers; but he also proposed to levy what amounted to a very stiff progressive tax on unearned incomes and contemplated that every worker would become in some measure an investing co-owner as well. Owen always expressed strong opposition to class-hatred: employers and capitalists, he said, were fellow victims with the workers of the bad, competitive system; and he called upon them to join hands with the workers in abolishing it. He was prepared to allow investors in his 'Villages of Co-operation' to receive a limited interest on their capital, but believed they would soon cease to claim it when the virtues of the new order had been proved in practice. As for the working employers, he expected them to be chosen by the workers as managers of the new co-operative establishments that were to replace capitalist enterprise. But Owen was as fully aware as any of the Socialists of the actual exploitation of the workers and of the existence of class-antagonisms in capitalist society.

Where most of the early Socialists differed from the Marxists who became the inspirers of later Socialist movements was not in being unaware of class distinctions but in resting their case on arguments of justice and human brotherhood rather than on a conception of class-power. Marx's 'Scientific' Socialism was an attempt to demonstrate the certainty of the conquest of power by the working class quite apart from any consideration of what ought to happen, in a moral sense. Of course Marx, as much as any other Socialist, believed class-exploitation, class-privilege, and class-monopoly to be morally bad, and wanted them to be swept away in the interests of human well-being. But he claimed that this was bound to occur, whether he wanted it or not, because of the inexorable movement of economic forces which were fundamentally independent of men's wills. This was his 'scientific' doctrine, resting on his

Materialist Conception of History, which altogether excluded considerations of right and wrong. Marx believed in a natural law of social evolution which involved, as men's knowledge of productive techniques advanced, a growing 'socialization' of the processes of production. This, he held, carried with it a corresponding evolution in the field of human relations, destined to result in a complete democratization of economic affairs and in the achievement of a classless society. The way in which this must come about, he held, was the way of class-conflict, because no privileged class would ever yield up its superiority except under pressure from the class or classes it had been holding in subordination. Thus the progress of society from worse to better depended, not on appeals to goodwill or reason, but on the development of the power of the subjected class that stood next below the existing class of rulers. This conception of power as the key to the social problem did not mean that there were no moral issues at stake: it did mean that the moral aspect was irrelevant from the standpoint of predicting the course of events.

Herein lay indeed a sharp contrast; for all the 'Utopians' believed that, apart from considerations of power, it was possible to affect the future by appealing to reason and conscience. Among the 'Utopians', Saint-Simon had the keenest sense of historical development and was most clearly in the succession of the great eighteenth-century philosophers of the Enlightenment. For Saint-Simon, as for Condorcet and Turgot, the course of human history was essentially a matter of the progress of the human spirit—of the growth of reason, based on the growth of human knowledge. His language came near to Marx's at times, when he was proclaiming the advent of the industrial age and its corollary in the supersession of the old privileged orders by *les industriels*. But for Saint-Simon this process of historical evolution was a progress of the human mind—of scientific knowledge, including the knowledge of man himself: it was not a 'material' power external to man's will. It may be answered by Marxists that Marx also recognized the mind of man as a force in the making of history, as a part of the 'material' power which determined the course of development. But the emphasis was entirely different. Marx stressed the course of economic evolution as a natural force independent of men's wills (though not of their advance in knowledge, which was an essential part of the 'powers of production' as he defined them); whereas Saint-Simon stressed the progress of *les lumières*—of human enlightenment—as the essential formative force, which determined the character of the productive powers. Both men were determinists: both thought they could predict the future; but the one based his prediction on a belief in a law of evolution conceived in materialist terms, and the other on a law of the evolution of the mind of man.

This difference had important consequences. Saint-Simon and his followers thought the most important thing of all was the advancement and systematization of human knowledge, and that this would necessarily lead towards a society based on high production and distributive justice. The Marxists, on the other hand, thought that the main task was that of arousing the workers to a sense of their class-power, and that this would hasten the advent of the new classless society. Saint-Simon thought men were bound, by a law of nature, to become more enlightened, and that his efforts could only hasten and make more efficient a development that was bound to occur in any case. Marx thought that the evolution of the 'powers of production' was bound to carry the proletariat to victory, but that the victory could be hastened and made more efficient by stimulating the proletariat's confidence in its historic mission.

Most of the other 'Utopians' had much less historical sense than either Saint-Simon or Marx—though there were exceptions, such as Constantin Pecqueur in France and J. F. Bray in England. Owen and Fourier, for example, both had a strong millennial tendency. Owen was apt to sweep up the entire past and present into a single heap, which he called the 'Old Immoral World' and contrasted with his 'New Society'—a society that could end human ills in a day if only men could be persuaded to establish it. Fourier, too, wrote as if all past ages up to his own had gone astray through a complete misunderstanding of human nature, which had only to be cleared up for the millennium to arrive at once. Marx was justly impatient at such unrealistic notions; and he was no less impatient at the unhistorical revolutionism of such Socialists as Blanqui, who believed that the victory of the proletariat could be achieved by a *coup de main* of a handful of determined insurrectionists, without any need for a prior development of the proletariat's own sense of power and historic mission. Marx was essentially a political realist, who fought many battles with the unhistorical revolutionists as well as with the 'Utopians'. No doubt he underestimated the time it would take for the proletariat to develop its organization and sense of power, and also the speed at which capitalism was advancing towards collapse because of its inherent 'contradictions'. But Marx, like Saint-Simon, had a keen sense of historical realism, even if his interpretations of the movement of historic forces were by no means always correct.

After 1848 the Marxist conception gradually conquered the greater part of the Socialist movement. 'Utopianism' did not disappear; but the Utopians were driven away from the centre of the political stage and found refuge, for the most part, in the various forms of Anarchism—particularly in the Anarchist Communism of Bakunin and Kropotkin. They came back—but with a significant difference—in the Syndicalist movements of France and Italy and in the Anarcho-Syndicalist movement of Spain. The difference was that, instead of working out models of perfect communities, the Syndicalists usually refused to offer any blue-prints of the future, and contented themselves with saying that when the State had been destroyed and the power of the workers established by 'direct action', the creative genius liberated by emancipation from class-oppression would speedily devise the right forms of social administration for the free communities of the new order. They accepted Marx's analysis of the problem in terms of class-power, but rejected power as the basis of the new free society which the victorious workers were to set up. They were 'Utopians' only in the sense that they believed the millennium would come in speedily when the capitalist system and its upholder, the State, had been overthrown.

The Marxist version of Socialism was fully proclaimed in 1848 in the *Communist Manifesto*; but it had little influence on the European revolutions of that year, and after their defeat Socialism went for a time almost into eclipse. In Great Britain, Chartism slowly flickered out, despite Ernest Jones's efforts to recreate it on Marxian foundations during the 1850s: Paris, which had been the great centre of Socialist ideas and movements, relapsed under Napoleon III into a quiescence partly accounted for by the dispersal in exile or prison of most of its leaders. Revival did not come, on any significant scale, till the 1860s: when it did come, Germany, rather than France, occupied for a time the leading position, with the followers of Marx and of Lassalle contending for the control of the developing working-class movement. In this contest the question of the Socialist attitude to the State came to play a vitally important part. Marx regarded the capitalist State, which in Germany, and especially in Prussia, was also the semi-feudal State of the older privileged classes, as an enemy to be fought with and overthrown. Lassalle and his followers, on the other hand, looked on the State as a mechanism that could be transformed by the establishment of manhood suffrage into an instrument of social progress: they demanded that the State should place capital at the disposal of the organized workers for the establishment of free, co-operative productive enterprises. This was no new idea: it had been urged by many Socialists in the 1830s and 1840s, and had been the central feature of Louis Blanc's policy of 'Organization of Labour'. Marx had denounced it then, as running counter to the fundamental doctrine of class-struggle; and he denounced it again when it reappeared in Germany in the 1860s. German Socialism came into being as a divided movement—the Lassallians *versus* the Marxist 'Eisenachers' led by August Bebel and Wilhelm Liebknecht—and the division persisted through the period during which Marx was attempting to rebuild on a new basis the international working-class revolutionary movement that had made its first abortive appearance in 1848.

Marx's instrument for this rebuilding was the First International—the International Working Men's Association which was founded in London in 1864. This was an amorphous body, centrally directed from London by a council made up largely of British trade unionists who sympathized with revolutions abroad without having any use for them at home, and for the rest of foreign exiles in London who were mostly prepared to accept Marx's leadership. The sections of the International which were founded in other countries, except Germany, were much less amenable to Marx's influence: the

French section was dominated by followers of Proudhon, with a minority of Blanquists and only a sprinkling of Marxists; the Belgians, under César de Paepe, had their own line which was hostile to authoritarian policies; the Swiss were divided between German, French, and Russian influences; the Italians and the Spaniards were predominantly Anarchist, and looked for leadership to Bakunin rather than to Marx. The resolutions passed at the International's early congresses were the outcome of a mixture of influences: Marx kept control of the central organization only because the British trade-union leaders, little interested in niceties of doctrine and regarding the whole affair as concerning mainly the continental working classes, gave him, up to 1871, almost a free hand. Within the International there soon developed a bitter conflict between Marxists and Anarchists, with other tendencies playing only a secondary role.

Then came the Franco-Prussian War, the collapse of Napoleon's empire, and the proclamation of the short-lived Paris Commune. The Commune was a revolutionary outbreak in which outraged patriotism combined with a working-class revolutionism that harked back to the agitations of the thirties and forties and beyond them to the Jacobinism of 1793. The Paris Marxists took part in it, but were not strong enough to have the deciding voice. Marx himself had no share in inspiring it, and knew that it could not succeed. He rallied to its defence, in the famous manifesto on *The Civil War in France,* issued in the name of the International; but he knew that it would be the International's undoing. His British trade-union supporters, intent on their own attempts at peaceable reform and shocked at the events in France, dropped off one by one; and when the Commune had been quenched in blood by Thiers it was at Marx's own instance that the headquarters of the International were transferred from a Europe now too hot to hold it to New York. There, without effective leadership and remote from the movements it was supposed to co-ordinate and control, the International expired within a few years, as it was bound to do. Marx's second attempt to put himself at the head of a great international proletarian movement had ignominiously petered out. The Bakuninists, who had been driven out before the transfer to New York, held together for a time in a rump International of their own; but they soon ceased to command a wide following outside Spain and Italy. Marxism did not, however, die after the fall of the Paris Commune: it entered speedily on a new phase, which was in effect the birth of the Social Democratic movement. The establishment of the German Empire, with a Reichstag elected on a wide popular franchise, transformed the conditions of political action in Germany and made the division of the German Socialists into two rival parties an unwarrantable barrier to electoral success, which the new franchise rendered for the first time possible. Under pressure of this electoral consideration, Lassallians and Eisenachers patched up their quarrels, and in 1875 formed at Gotha a united German Social Democratic party; and this party became the model for the establishment of new Socialist electoral parties in one continental country after another. Up to that time the franchise had almost everywhere been so restricted as to give working-class parties practically no chance of electoral success. But after the British Reform Act of 1867, the German Constitution of 1870, and the establishment in France of the Third Republic, electoral rights were extended in other countries, and it became possible to organize Socialist parties on a parliamentary basis, or rather with the contesting of parliamentary seats as one of their principal objectives. Such a policy was in practice as irreconcilable with the maintenance of Marx's attitude towards the existing State as it was with the Anarchism of Bakunin. In theory, it is no doubt possible for a working-class party to contest parliamentary elections without putting forward any projects of partial reform within the existing social and political order, and to use elections—and representatives, should any get elected on such terms—merely as means of propaganda for thoroughgoing Socialism. In practice, such a line is possible only where the executive Government is entirely irresponsible to Parliament, and there is no chance of getting valuable reforms by parliamentary means. Such conditions existed in Russia after 1905; but they did not exist after the 1870s in France or even in Germany, or over most of western Europe. In the west, the Socialists could hope to get votes only if, in addition to their long-run Socialist objectives, they put before the electors immediate programmes of reform within the existing political and economic system.

The German Social Democratic party of 1875, though it largely adopted Marxism as a theoretical creed, in effect accepted this necessity, without which no fusion with the Lassallians would have been possible. Marx, sent by his German followers an advance copy of the proposed terms of fusion, protested angrily at what he described as a betrayal of Socialist principle: his followers suppressed his long, argumentative protest, which was printed (as *Critique of the Gotha Programme*) only many years after his death. He did not make his views public, realizing that the Eisenachers would repudiate him if he did. Social Democracy was born as the outcome of a compromise of which the man generally regarded as its prophet violently disapproved.

What the Germans had done was not to repudiate Marx's doctrine of the class-struggle or his Materialist Conception of History but, while accepting these, to deny the conclusion he had drawn from them concerning the nature of the State and the appropriate political means of advancing from a capitalist to a Socialist society. They had treated his view of the State as having been rendered obsolescent by the establishment of a wide franchise, and had set out to capture the State rather than to overthrow it utterly and put a new proletarian State in its place. The full consequences of the change appeared only gradually; and in Germany they were delayed by Bismarck's Anti-Socialist law of 1878, which forced the Socialists back to underground activities. But with the repeal of this law in 1890 and the establishment of the rights of organization and propaganda, the transformation of the party went on apace. At Erfurt, in 1891, it explicitly adopted, side by side with its ultimate programme, an immediate programme of social reform. Removing the Lassallian demand for State aid in the establishment of workers' cooperatives, and redrafting the economic part of its programme in such a way as to assert its entire loyalty to Marxism, the German Social Democratic party turned, as far as the still largely autocratic constitution of Germany (and still more of Prussia) would allow it, into a constitutional party commanding a wide following concerned mainly with reform rather than with revolution. Eduard Bernstein, in his famous attempt to procure a 'revision' of the Marxist doctrine in the late 1890s, wished to make the change explicit, at the cost of openly discarding a number of Marx's more disputable doctrines ('increasing misery' of the workers, impending collapse of capitalism through its own inner 'contradictions', and the sharp division of the whole people into contending classes of exploiters and exploited). He was defeated and reprimanded; but in practice the German Social Democratic party followed more and more closely the line he had recommended to it.

The Social Democratic parties in other countries which were modelled on the German original went largely the same way. In Russia, indeed, and in Russian Poland there emerged parties which maintained the older revolutionary tradition; but this involved a split, of which the rift between Bolsheviks and Mensheviks in Russia may serve as the outstanding example. In Great Britain Hyndman's Social Democratic Federation remained too weak ever to need to make a clear choice: it was superseded as a political electoral force in the 1890s by Keir Hardie's Independent Labour party. In France the Social Democrats (Jules Guesde's *Parti Ouvrier*) constituted only one element in a Socialist political movement made up of a number of different tendencies— Blanquist, Proudhonist, Marxist, and others. The rival groups did not combine until 1905, and then only under the severe pressure of the turmoils arising out of the *affaire Dreyfus*. When they did unite, under the leadership of Jean Jaurès, their attitude to the State had much more in common with Lassalle's than with Marx's and the doctrine of outright hostility to the *bourgeois* State was sustained only by the Syndicalist *Confédération Générale du Travail,* which insisted on complete trade-union aloofness from parliamentary action. In Belgium, and also in Holland, right up to 1918 the maintenance of a narrow franchise restricted the Socialist parties to a subordinate position in the Parliaments, and thus prevented them from developing mainly as electoral parties advocating programmes of immediate reforms. They were therefore able to go on talking the language of Marxism with less inconsistency than either the Germans or the French; but in the case of Belgium the close alliance between the Labour party, the trade unions, and the co-operative societies, as equal partners in a working-class alliance, made for a conception of Socialism considerably different from that which found favour in Germany, where the political movement held the directing influence jealously in its own hands. In Italy, too, the extremely restricted franchise—up to 1913—and the economic backwardness of the country prevented the development of an effective Socialist party on the German model. Anarchism was strong in many of the country areas; and the Socialist party led by Turati was weakened by the splitting away of a Syndicalist wing, headed by the movement's leading theorist, Antonio Labriola. In Scandinavia, on the other hand, Sweden and Denmark developed parties closely modelled on the German, and these followed much the same course of development as essentially parliamentary bodies, 'revising' Marxism to fit the conditions of electoral activity.

Thus Social Democracy, which had begun as a revolutionary political movement based on a full acceptance of Marxist theory, turned under the influence of the franchise extension and the growth of parliamentary government more and more into a non-revolutionary agitation for reform and into an attempt to take over, instead of destroying, the machinery of the State. In Great Britain there was no corresponding development only because the climate of opinion among the workers was highly unfavourable to the reception of Marxian ideas. In almost all the continental countries organized religion was closely associated with political conservatism, and the working-class movements grew up in deep hostility to the churches. In Great Britain, on the other hand, nonconformist religion had a strong hold on the workers, as well as on the middle classes, and was traditionally associated with political Liberalism. Nonconformity served for a considerable time as a force causing political Labourism to develop inside the Liberal party, and served to prevent it from taking on any anti-religious character. Hyndman's Social Democratic Federation, which was anti-religious in the continental manner, came up against a blank wall when it attempted to convert to Socialism the main body of the British working class. The Independent Labour Party was able to push it aside largely because, far from setting itself against religion, it set out to harness the ethical impulses associated with religion to the Socialist cause. On such a basis there could be no acceptance of the materialist philosophy of Marxism, though, of course, some elements of the Marxist doctrine influenced Keir Hardie and his collaborators. In the hands of the Fabian Society and of the Independent Labour party and its successor, the Labour party, British Socialism grew up as a non-Marxist demand for social justice, with the Sermon on the Mount, rather than *Das Kapital* or the *Communist Manifesto,* as its ultimate court of appeal.

There was, however, a second force at work in Great Britain; and this made on the whole for the same result. The conception of the course of history as determined finally by the forces of economic development was linked by Marx to the conception of the class-struggle as involving the revolutionary displacement of one governing class by another as the economic conditions became ripe. But an economic conception of history is equally reconcilable with an evolutionary, or gradualist, conception of social development. There is nothing contrary to logic in supposing that, as economic conditions change, political and social conditions change with them gradually, and not by revolutionary upheaval. Marx had dismissed this possibility, partly because of his Hegelian way of thought and partly because he held that no governing class would ever yield up its power without fighting its hardest to retain it. As against this view the Fabians, who also held a broadly economic conception of historical evolution, argued that under conditions of extended suffrage and responsible government the electorate could use its power to extract one concession after another from the ruling class, and to claim an increasing share in political authority for any representatives it chose to elect. Thus, they argued, the existing State could by a gradual process be transformed into a 'Welfare State', and a working-class party could be carried to political power by a sequence of electoral successes. This presupposed that the old governing class would not at any point decide to fight in arms in defence of its authority; and the Fabians held that in a parliamentary State enjoying responsible government it would in practice be very difficult for the governing class at any stage to defy the constitution. In the climate of British opinion, with its long tradition of responsible government and of gradual advance towards democratic control, this view seemed to fit the situation very much better than any more revolutionary theory—indeed, the evidently unrevolutionary attitude of the working class made any other notion untenable as a basis for mass political action.

Accordingly, British Labour and German Social Democracy had arrived, by the early years of the present century, at broadly the same conclusion, though they had travelled to it by widely different roads. The conditions of parliamentary campaigning under a wide franchise had, moreover, tended in both cases to establish in the minds of the party leaders a conception of democracy very different from Marx's. By the 'democracy' Marx meant the proletariat, and no one else. He assumed that the proletariat stood for the majority; but he thought in terms, not of majorities and minorities, but of *classes* contending for power. Under a parliamentary system, however, the factor that counts is the vote of the individual elector, to whatever class he belongs. A parliamentary Socialist party cannot woo the proletariat alone: it has to get all the votes it can, from any source; and its leaders therefore think instinctively in terms not of classes but of majorities and minorities of individual voters. They are led to accept a conception of 'democracy', as meaning majority rule, which is entirely at variance with Marx's conception of it as class-rule. Thus Socialism, which in its early Marxian period had espoused the notion of the coming 'dictatorship of the proletariat', reverted later in the west of Europe, as the conditions of political action changed, to a conception much more closely akin to that of the 'Utopian' Socialists whose attitude I have discussed earlier in this essay. They were appealing, not to a single class—even if they did look to the workers for the bulk of their support—but to all persons of goodwill, and were appealing on grounds of ethics and justice, rather than as the exponents of a 'scientific' doctrine of inevitability and 'historic mission'.

Modern Communism began as a return to the older Marxist tradition. Or rather, as it began in Russia, it continued that tradition unbroken. In Russia—indeed, over most of eastern Europe—nothing had happened to throw doubt on Marx's analysis, based as it was on the conditions of the first half of the nineteenth century in the west. In Russia, what capitalist enterprise there was grossly exploited the workers, and the State, still in the hands of a feudal autocracy, stood ready to break and bludgeon, to banish, and at need to shoot down, any who rebelled. The tradition of the Socialist movement was made up of secret conspiracy, of espionage and betrayal, of revolt brutally suppressed, and, after 1905, of actual revolution. Behind the existing movement, which was sharply divided, lay a long history of doctrinal conflict—above all, of disputes between 'westernizing' Marxists and those who believed that Russia must make a native Socialism, resting on the peasant rather than on the relatively few industrial workers. Both factions were further divided—the Social Revolutionaries into a left wing with a tradition of assassination and violence and a right wing which aimed at uplifting the peasants through land reform, education, and cooperation; the 'westernizers' into a left wing which aimed straight at revolution under Socialist leadership and a right wing which held that the country must first achieve the liberal republic and pass through the successive stages of capitalist development before it could become ripe for Socialism. Right up to 1917 the Social Revolutionaries—the agrarian Socialists—greatly outnumbered the Social Democrats, Bolsheviks, and Mensheviks together; but the Social Democrats had behind them the bulk of the most cohesive group—the factory workers and miners and oilfield workers. The Bolshevik section had also the advantage of possessing the one really brilliant leader, Lenin, and the most disciplined party organization, inured to the need for cohesion by years of secret agitation.

The Social Revolutionaries had much in common with the Anarchists everywhere. They were localizers, believers in spontaneous action, distrustful of disciplined leadership and organization. As the Revolution had to face the immense difficulties of sheer disintegration due to the war, the Social Revolutionaries went down like ninepins before Bolshevik discipline and ruthless courage. So did the Mensheviks, swept aside with the weak *bourgeoisie* whom they had hoped to make the instruments of the transition through capitalism to a Socialism of the western type. The Bolsheviks remained, to reinterpret in action the Marxism of 1848, which fitted the conditions of contemporary Russia a great deal better than the Social Democracy that had replaced it in the more advanced countries of western Europe.

The Leninist Marxism which emerged during the early years of the Bolshevik regime was, in a literal sense, faithful in almost every particular—save one—to

Marx's doctrine. The one outstanding difference was that Lenin revised Marx's theory by asserting that it was possible for the proletariat, instead of first helping the *bourgeoisie* into power and then turning upon them after their victory, to take power at once and carry through the necessary process of capitalist development under proletarian control. This was Lenin's theory of 'State Capitalism', and it was definitely a departure from what Marx had held. Besides this, there was a more subtle difference. Marx had spoken of the 'dictatorship of the proletariat' as a necessary stage in the transition to a classless society. But he had never explained very clearly what he meant, except that the workers were to destroy the old State of the exploiters and set up a new one in its place. Lenin, however, made the 'dictatorship' the very cornerstone of his theory, and interpreted it as signifying in effect the dictatorship of the Communist party as the only true representative of the proletariat and the only interpreter of its historic mission. The role of the 'party', merely adumbrated in certain passages of the *Communist Manifesto*, was worked up into a complete theory of class leadership. Lenin always insisted that the party must so act as to carry the mass sentiment of the workers—including the poorer peasants—along with it: it was to 'dictate', not to the workers, but on their behalf. But the one thing led easily to the other. If the 'party' alone had a correct understanding of the processes of historical evolution and of the workers' part in them, it alone was in a position to tell the workers what to do in their own interest. According to Marx's determinist doctrine there could be only one right course, marked out by the development of the economic forces. Accordingly there had to be a central determination of party policy to ensure that this one right course should be followed. 'Democratic centralism', the laying down at the centre, after debate within the party, of a line which every party member must accept without further question, logically followed. The party became a dictatorship over the workers, and, within the party, the structure became more and more hierarchical and the determination of policy, under stress of continual danger to the régime, more and more a matter for the central leadership. Purges and convictions of 'deviationists' followed as a necessary sequel; for, when once the party leadership had decided a thing, all questioning of it came to be regarded as treason to the working class.

Most of these developments of Communist theory came only after Lenin's death. They were largely the work of Stalin, who had not, like Lenin, any understanding of western Socialism. Lenin, as an old Bolshevik, had been essentially a 'westernizer', looking to the industrial proletariat to be the principal agent for lifting Russia out of its primitive backwardness. Stalin, too, wanted to push on with industrialization, as a means of defence against western capitalism; but in his eyes the west had nothing to teach the Russians except in the technological field. In his essential ideas Stalin remained eastern; and under his influence Marxism was transformed into an oriental doctrine, untinged with any respect for the cultural, as distinct from the purely technological, achievements of the west. By a strange paradox, that very Slavophil attitude which, earlier, the Russian Social Democrats had denounced as the cardinal error of their Narodnik and Social Revolutionary rivals came back as the creed of triumphant Communism—until, presently, it had to be believed that every important scientific and technological discovery had really been due to a Russian, and that out of the west had come nothing except imperialism and exploitation.

This thoroughgoing 'revision' of Marxist doctrine was, of course, greatly fostered by western mishandling of the new Russia, both between the two world wars and after 1945. The countries of western Europe did their best between the wars to wreck the Soviet Union or to treat it as a pariah; and after 1945, when western Europe was too weak to continue along the same lines, anti-Communist hysteria took a strong hold on the United States, powerfully reinforcing the bent of Stalinism, already strong enough, towards the isolation of the Soviet peoples from contact with western movements and ideas. There were attempts after 1918 to rebuild a united Socialist International, broad enough to comprehend both Communists and western Social Democratic and Labour parties—and parallel attempts to create a comprehensive Trade Union International. On the trade union side, these efforts were resumed after 1945, with temporary apparent success. But neither between the wars nor after 1945 was there ever any real prospect of a united movement. Even in Lenin's day the ideas of the two kinds of Socialism were much too far apart; and with Stalin's advent to power the last vestige of a common outlook disappeared. The western parties and trade unions had fully accepted the policy of constitutional action, of a gradual capture of the State, and meantime of its use as an agent of social welfare, and of ballot-box democracy as the only legitimate road of advance towards a Socialist society. The Soviet party and its satellites, on the other hand, believed in the necessity of world revolution, in the impending downfall of capitalist society because of its inner contradictions, and in a one-party system which had nothing in common with the multi-party systems of the western countries. There was no bridging such gulfs.

How came it, then, that the Communists were able to find powerful working-class support in certain of the western countries—above all, in France, as well as in Italy, and, between the wars, up to the Nazi *coup*, in Germany? The answer is that, in these countries, the processes of ballot-box democracy, after carrying the Social Democrats a certain distance along the road to electoral success, showed no signs of carrying them on farther to the actual conquest of political power. Socialist propaganda and organization could win over a large minority of the population, not a majority—much less a stable majority to serve as the basis for a thorough refashioning of the economic and social system. Only in Great Britain and in Scandinavia did the Socialists reach a strong enough electoral position even to hold independent office for any length of time; and in these countries Communism remained weak. Elsewhere Socialists could only oppose, or take part in coalitions of which it was an implied condition that the basis of the social system must not be changed. A large section of the working classes accordingly gravitated towards Communism, which at least held out the hope of accomplishing by revolution, with the Soviet Union's aid, the great social transformation that seemed to be quite beyond the reach of the constitutional Socialist parties.

There were, of course, additional factors at work. In France, in Germany, and in Italy class antagonisms went very much deeper than in Great Britain or Scandinavia, or, for that matter, the United States. Germany, up to 1918, had never been a fully constitutional State; and the attempt to make it one, under the Weimar Republic, born in defeat and faced throughout with appalling difficulties, was never a success. In Italy parliamentary government had never been more than a façade, and a wide suffrage had been conceded only in 1913, just before the First World War. In both these countries Fascism, directed against Socialism and Liberalism in all their forms, engendered Communism as a counter-movement. In France, where parliamentary government had been more of a reality, the Welfare State had signally failed to develop after 1918, and the strong Syndicalist tradition of the trade unions, with its emphasis on class-war and opposition to the *bourgeois* State, was much more closely akin, despite its Anarchist element, to Communism than to western Social Democracy. Thus Russian Communism, despite its growingly oriental temper, continued to find allies in the heart of the west—allies strong enough to thwart the hopes of Social Democrats, but not to win power on their own account.

All this amounts to saying that the Socialist movement, which began as an idealistic drive for social justice and for co-operation, instead of competition, as the right foundation for human relations in the new era ushered in by the great French Revolution, has today become divided into two separate movements, resting on deeply antagonistic philosophies. This divorce was heralded by Marx, when he set out to establish a new 'Scientific Socialism' based on the concept of class-power. But western Marxism, under the conditions of political and economic development in the advanced capitalist countries during the second half of the nineteenth century, lost much of its revolutionary character, and therewith reverted more and more to ethical appeals for social justice, even while its votaries continued to recite the Marxist slogans of class-war. The revival of the older Marxism occurred, not primarily in the west, but in those parts of Europe to which Marx's diagnosis continued to apply because of their economic backwardness and of the starker conditions of class-antagonism which went with it. From these backward countries the older Marxism— with a difference due to its change of habitat—streamed back into the west between the wars as the difficulties of western capitalism multiplied, and as stalemate, or worse, overtook the leading Social Democratic parties of continental Europe. For a moment, in 1945, it looked as if, under the leadership of the victorious British Labour party, the western Social Democratic parties might be able so to rally their forces as to sweep their political antagonists, largely tainted as they were with war-time 'collaboration', from the field, and to establish in the western countries the foundations of a democratic parliamentary Socialist regime. But British Labour was neither alive enough to the possibilities nor internationally minded enough to give the required lead; and the possibility of a victorious Socialist 'Third Force' in world affairs, if it ever existed, speedily disappeared. The Social Democrats of France and Italy were reduced to a role of opposition, weakened by the desertion of most of their followers to Communism or near-Communism; and in western Germany, though stronger, they were not strong enough to win an electoral majority. It began to look as if, as a great international force, Social Democracy had shot its bolt, despite its sustained strength in Great Britain and in the Scandinavian countries.

Moreover, after the Second World War, Socialism ceased to be, as it had been previously, an essentially European movement, with no more than outposts elsewhere. The rising tide of nationalism in Asia and in the colonial territories of the European powers in other continents fitted in much more easily with Communism than with parliamentary Socialism, which was a creed devised to fit the conditions of advanced countries possessing responsible government. The Communists set out everywhere to exploit to the full the discontents of the nationalist movements, by denouncing the imperialist practices of the capitalist countries. Communism gained the day in China, and troubled the British, the French, and the Americans (in Korea) with colonial wars which dissipated their resources. Communism was a ready article for export to a great many countries for which parliamentary Socialism had no message the main body of the people could even begin to understand. Indeed, the parliamentary Socialists, forced on to the defensive, found themselves the reluctant allies of their political opponents in a reliance on American aid which involved their enlistment in a world struggle between the world's two remaining great Powers—the United States and the Soviet Union—a struggle in which the issue was primarily between capitalism and Communism, with Social Democracy as third man out.

Yet Communism, even if it be a necessary stage in the transition from capitalism to a new social order in eastern Europe, in China, and in other countries in which effective reconstruction of society can hardly begin without a revolutionary change, is manifestly inappropriate to the needs either of the United States or of the advanced countries of western Europe. These countries have far too complicated a class-structure for the simple class theory of the *Communist Manifesto* to fit their conditions, or for their peoples to want thoroughgoing revolution on a class basis as a means to change. Communism will not prevail in western Europe unless the Russians install it by sheer force in war: it cannot under any conditions prevail in the United States. The Communist *World Revolution* is not going to happen: it cannot happen in face of American immunity to its appeal. In the west, except as an outcome of war, capitalism cannot be replaced except by some form of Social Democracy; and if Social Democracy is too weak to replace it, the continuance of capitalism, however it may be modified in secondary respects, is assured for a long time to come. It shows no sign of speedy collapse under pressure of its own 'contradictions'—such as Marx, and later Lenin, expected to occur.

Socialism, then, is no longer a single movement, making in a single direction. In the west it is—as the first forms of Socialism were—fundamentally a drive towards social justice and equality, rather than a class quest for power. It can, of course, no more avoid having to think in terms of power as well as of morals than Communism, for all its insistence on the factor of power, can avoid invoking the aid of ethical appeals. The Communist needs to feel that his cause is righteous, as well as historically determined: the western Socialist needs to feel that the workers are behind him, as well as that his cause is good. Both are aiming, in a sense, at the same thing—a classless society—and both believe in collective action as the means of advancing towards it. Both regard private property in the essential instruments of production as inconsistent with the absence of class-distinctions: both in some sense want to 'socialize' men's minds by socializing their environment. But whereas the Communist seeks these ends by means of class action and regards the dictatorship of a class as a necessary step towards their attainment, the western Socialist looks to the winning of an electoral majority, however composed, and repudiates dictatorship as inconsistent with his conception of the democratic principle. Western Socialism acts on the assumption of a basic social solidarity which holds the community together: Communism denies this solidarity in any society which has not been through its social revolution and eliminated feudal and capitalist privilege. The two conceptions are related to two different kinds of society. In Great Britain, as in the United States, in Switzerland, in Scandinavia, in Canada and Australia, and to a less extent in Belgium and Holland, this underlying social solidarity is a fact based on a long historical experience. Even in France and in Germany the same tradition exists, though it is partly counteracted by other factors. But in Russia and over most of eastern Europe this solidarity has not existed in the past, and is barely intelligible to those whose thinking is based on the history of these countries. Accordingly, the conception of an overriding class loyalty, transcending national loyalty, meets with no such obstacles in eastern as in western Europe; and a Socialism that dismisses nationalism (except when it is being exploited as a means of stimulating 'anti-imperialist' revolt) as a petty *bourgeois* concept is able to make its realistic way. What has still to be seen is what will happen in the long run in those parts of the world in which Communism and nationalism are now appearing as uneasy allies.

Nationalism and the sense of social solidarity are, however, by no means necessarily the same. Nationalism can be, and often is, the creed of a group or class within a nation, rather than of the nation as a whole. Marx spoke of it as if he supposed it was always of this limited kind, because his entire philosophy involved treating every concept as in the last resort a class concept. It is of course true that in class-ridden societies the ruling classes often identify themselves with the nation; and Marx was in fact largely right about the nationalist movements of his own day—though not wholly so in relation to France, where the revolutionary tradition of national unity was strong. But there can exist, without a nationalist movement in a political sense, an attitude of social solidarity permeating a whole people, or at any rate cutting right across class-differences, in such a way as to limit very greatly the possibilities of fundamental class-conflict. Such a sentiment can exist, I think, only in societies which are either very static, so that habit suffices to hold them together, or very mobile, so that the classes they contain are continually shifting both in their nature and in respect of the individuals composing them. In the former type of society everyone has his station and knows it: in the latter, even if class is still a prominent category, status is no longer definite or unchangeable, and does not mark men off into sharply separated groups. It is in the intermediate types of society, in which there is a conflict between a static and a mobile sector, that the sense of social solidarity is least likely to be strong.

Such a conflict exists to a great extent in those economically backward countries which have been recently subjected to the impact of industrialism. As long as this impact remains mainly foreign it gives rise to forms of nationalist rejection of the foreigner which create a sentiment of union; but as soon as the forces of change come to be largely internal—through the development of native capitalism, native trade unionism, and so on—this unity tends to disappear, not being rooted in any deep social solidarity but simply in hostility to foreign influence. The Communist leaders are aware of this: they realize that, in taking sides with 'nationalism' directed against foreign influence, they are helping to create the conditions in which national unity will give place to class-conflict as the mobile elements in the societies concerned are brought into direct conflict with the static elements and as this conflict in turn is replaced, with the victory of the former, by a conflict between capitalist and worker. This is almost exactly how Marx envisaged the situation in the 1840s, except that he was then dealing mainly with a state of affairs in which there were no longer in western Europe (except in Italy) serious problems of foreign domination to be faced. There had been, however, quite recently such problems in Germany and elsewhere during the period of Napoleon's European supremacy.

Social Democratic thought cannot grapple easily with problems of this order, because it is an emanation of liberalism, based on the conditions of countries in which the static elements in the social structure have had to give way to the mobile elements—in other words, where capitalism has already subordinated the feudal elements to its own needs. Paradoxically, it is precisely in those countries in which *bourgeoisie* and *proletariat* are most free to fight each other and have least need to combine in order to fight against aristocratic privilege that these contending classes are least disposed to push their quarrel to extremes, because, far from becoming more uniform, they become more diverse and interpenetrated. But this state of affairs exists in a high degree only in a very limited number of countries; and I am afraid the conclusion has to be that the Social Democratic form of Socialism is for the present of equally limited applicability in the world. It is not applicable to countries in which a fundamental revolution—for example, in the land system—is a necessary starting-point for real social change: nor is it applicable after such a revolution until there has been time for the post-revolutionary settlement to have become stabilized and generally accepted, so that the dominance of power-considerations which is a necessary accompaniment of revolution can wear off. Only stable societies possessing a sense of solidarity can in practice give ethical factors priority over considerations of power.

This essay is an attempt to answer the question 'What is Socialism?' in terms of the present day. It contains nothing that even pretends to be a definition of Socialism, either as it exists today or in the light of its history. Socialism cannot be defined in a sentence or a paragraph because it is fundamentally not a system but a movement which has taken, and will doubtless continue to take, diverse forms both from country to country and under the influence of particular theorists and practical exponents. It can be, up to a point, described and characterized, but not defined. Thus, one essential element in it is the stress laid on the need for collective regulation of social and economic affairs, and therewith its rejection of the entire philosophy of *laissez-faire*. But Socialism is not alone in rejecting *laissez-faire*: there are plenty of 'plannists' who are among its most violent opponents. A second element is its thoroughgoing hostility to class-divisions and its aspiration towards a 'classless society'. This it shares with the Anarchists and Syndicalists, but, I think, with no one else, though there is, of course, a kind of radical individualism that is sometimes allied with it in the struggle against 'class-privilege'. Thirdly, Socialism traditionally stands for 'democracy' but democracy can be conceived of in so many different ways that the word, by itself, is not of much help. It does, however, provide the necessary clue to the deep division that exists today between Communism and the Socialism of the western countries. For Communism, the class itself is the unit in terms of which all political structures are to be assessed and accordingly democracy is the rule of a class—of the working class as the representative champion of the unprivileged. For western Socialists, on the other hand, the individual is the final repository of ethical values, and democracy involves majority rule coupled with respect for individual rights. Western Socialism, in the last analysis, is 'Utopian' rather than 'Scientific'. It is conceived of as a means to the good life for the individuals who make up human societies, and not as a destined outcome of a predetermined historical evolution that lies outside the individual's control.

THE SOCIALISM OF BRITISH LABOUR

WHEREAS IN MOST PARTS OF EUROPE, AND INDEED OF THE WORLD, THE NA-tional Socialist Parties have been built up on a basis of Marxist doctrine and have consisted of individual subscribing members, the British Labour Party has never accepted Marxism and has been throughout its existence based on Trade Union mass affiliations.[1] These two facts are of primary importance for an understanding of its attitude and policy. The British Labour Party is, ideo-logically, not Marxist but Fabian; and its policy is settled, in the last resort, not by individual adherents but by the predominant voting power of the Trade Unions which provide the bulk of its support. These Trade Unions are not, as is the case in many countries, bodies established under Socialist influence as auxiliaries to the workers' political party. On the contrary, they were well estab-lished long before the Labour Party came into being, and have been in a posi-tion to shape it continually to fit their needs. In many countries, the Socialist Party in effect made the Trade Unions: in Great Britain, it is nearer the truth to say that the Trade Unions made the Labour Party and have continued to control it, at any rate in the sense that it would be impossible for the Party to adopt any policy or programme to which the Trade Unions were opposed.

---

1   *Review of International Affairs* (Belgrade), 1953.

178 • T<small>OWARDS A</small> L<small>IBERTARIAN</small> S<small>OCIALISM</small>

To say that the Labour Party is not Marxist is by no means to say—as has been often suggested—that it lacks a philosophy or is merely opportunist. It is true that Trade Union predominance in its affairs tends to give most of its policy discussions a practical rather than a theoretical colour; but if questions of fundamental Socialist theory are but little debated at its Conferences that is mainly because there is a very large measure of agreement about them. The prevalent view among both leading Trade Unionists and party intellectuals has always been that in the conditions existing in Great Britain the correct line of advance towards Socialism is constitutional and parliamentary, and that the existing State can be transformed into an instrument for the achievement of Socialism without the need for the setting up of any new kind of State resting on the dictatorship of the proletariat. The idea that Socialism can be won only by revolutionary upheaval has been rejected in favour of 'gradualism' as the procedure called for by the conditions of British politics and public opinion. Of course, this view has been questioned again and again; but it has been at all times the view of the great majority, and of almost all the leading figures in the Party.

This attitude is explained by the entire historical background against which the Labour Party has grown to its present station. Trade Unions gained the right to organize free from police supervision and to engage in collective bargaining and strike action much earlier in Great Britain than in most countries; and the British Trade Unions began to take part in politics at a time when no British Socialist movement existed. They attached themselves to the Radical wing of the Liberal Party at a time when the Radicals were advocating an advanced social programme and were hoping to sweep the main body of Liberals along with them; and they were slow to detach themselves from the Liberals even when these hopes had been disappointed in the economic depression of the 1870s and 1880s. The Trade Unions at that time represented mainly the skilled workers: the impetus towards a break with Liberalism came mainly from the 'New Unions' of less skilled workers which entered the field, as the depression lifted, towards the end of the 1880s. The men who set out to make a Labour Party independent of Liberalism were the activists of the 'New Unionism', which began its successful course with the victories of the Gasworkers and the Dockers in 1889. These men were primarily interested in immediate demands designed to improve the economic situation of the less skilled workers. They called for a legal minimum wage, a working day of eight hours, and the recognition of the 'Right to Work'—that is, of the State's duty to find work, or failing work decent maintenance, for the unemployed. Many of the leaders were already Socialists; but it was in support of these immediate demands that they made their chief appeal to the masses to establish an independent workers' party. They were convinced that the first step was to rally the working classes and all who could be induced to take the workers' side behind a programme of demands for the establishment of a 'national minimum' of welfare and social security. Many of them believed that, in order to get these things, it would be necessary to destroy the power of the capitalists and to take the control of industry out of their hands; but most of them felt that the people would not rally behind the banner of Socialism until they had come to see in Socialism an indispensable means to the winning of the higher incomes, the increased leisure, and the economic security they felt to be theirs by right.

The first political outcome of the 'New Unionist' movement was the Independent Labour Party formed under Keir Hardie's chairmanship in 1893. This was at first planned as a federal body, to which the Trade Unions were urged to adhere; but in practice it became a society of individual Socialists working in alliance with some of the local Trades Councils, but failing to enlist the support of the national Trade Unions. Seven more years were required before the Trades Union Congress was induced to co-operate with the ILP in calling the special conference at which the Labour Representation Committee was founded; and another six years passed before the LRC became a fully constituted Labour Party. At first, only a few Trade Unions adhered to the LRC: what brought most of them in was not conversion to Socialism, or even to the programme of the 'national minimum', but a legal decision—the Taff Vale Judgment—which threatened the Trade Unions' rights of collective bargaining and strike action. The Trade Unions rallied behind the LRC in order to get this Judgment upset by new legislation securing Trade Union rights: the result was that the LRC, which had won but two seats at the General Election of 1900, won 30 in 1906, and became a fully fledged Party in the House of Commons.

Even then, however, the Party made no profession of Socialist faith, though most of its outstanding leaders called themselves Socialists. The Labour Party did not become an avowedly Socialist Party until the beginning of 1917, when it adopted a series of resolutions which became the basis for its famous policy-statement, *Labour and the New Social Order*. This statement, drafted by the Fabian leader, Sidney Webb, became the classic exposition of the policy of evolutionary, or 'gradualist', Socialism; and all subsequent Labour Party programmes have been but variations on the same theme. Whereas Marx and his followers regarded Socialism as the necessary outcome of the development of the 'powers of production', to be achieved by means of a revolutionary class struggle from which the proletariat was destined to emerge victorious, Sidney Webb, no less insistent on the historic tendency for Socialism to develop out of the evolution of economic forces, conceived of it as making its way by gradual stages through a progressive transformation of the existing State and the existing social order by constitutional democratic action and by the peaceful conversion of the majority to Socialist ways of thought. Marx felt assured that the governing classes would not give up their power except to revolutionary force:

Webb believed that, given a democratic parliamentary system and freedom of speech and democratic association, the change could be brought about by sustained agitation and constitutional action, one reform preparing the way for another, and concessions such as the minimum wage and the 'Right to Work' leading on to socialization when capitalism showed its incapacity to comply with the requirements of the 'Welfare State'.

This evolutionary kind of Socialism was mainly worked out by the Fabian Society, of which Sidney Webb was the outstanding theorist. On the continent, it is often thought of as having been mainly the work of Eduard Bernstein and the German Revisionists whose doctrines were repudiated in theory, but largely adopted in practice, by the German Social Democratic Party. In truth, however, Bernstein largely learnt his Revisionism from the British Fabians, who had formulated their essential doctrines in the 1880s. *Fabian Essays in Socialism*, in which Webb, Bernard Shaw, and a number of other Fabians collaborated, were published in 1889; and thereafter Fabian doctrine had a deep influence first on Keir Hardie's Independent Labour Party and later on the Labour Party itself. The Fabian conception of Socialism as an evolutionary force working its way by stages fitted in well with the New Unionists' insistence on setting out from a realistic programme of immediate economic and social demands; and as the Trade Unions gradually broke away from Radical Liberalism and became ready to accept Socialist objectives, the kind of Socialism that appealed to their leaders was this gradualist type, to be pursued by a combination of parliamentary action with the economic action of Trade Unions and Co-operative Societies, and to be directed to the fuller democratization of existing institutions rather than to their supersession by means of open revolution.

The Fabians, in working out their distinctive conception of Socialism, started out from an acceptance of the Utilitarian philosophy, as applied to politics by Jeremy Bentham and as developed by his follower, John Stuart Mill. Bentham had proposed as the criterion of the value of every institution, the question whether it furthered or stood in the way of 'the greatest happiness of the greatest number'. Using this test, he condemned most of the political and economic institutions of his own day, and arrived at an economic doctrine which resulted in support of *laissez-faire*, less noxious than state intervention by a State dominated by a narrow privileged class. But Bentham never upheld *laissez-faire* as a principle: he was ready to support any form of State action which he regarded as truly calculated to further the happiness of the greatest number. Mill, building on these foundations, came to advocate much more State intervention than Bentham, and advanced in his later years to a position at least sympathetic to Socialism. The Fabians, going beyond Mill, argued that the 'greatest happiness' principle provided the justification for a complete Socialist policy, and that the advance of political democracy with successive extensions of the franchise had already turned the State from being an instrument of capitalist domination into one that could be used to bring a Socialist system into being.

The Fabians were Neo-utilitarians in economics as well as politics. Rejecting the Marxist theory of value, they constructed an economic theory mainly on the foundations of the Ricardian law of rent and the doctrine of marginal utility as worked out by Stanley Jevons and Philip Wicksteed and, in Austria, by Karl Menzer. Ownership of land and capital, they held, constituted twin forms of monopoly which enabled the possessing classes to exploit the workers. Capitalist profit was in effect just as much a rent of monopoly as the rent of land; and the way to put an end to the exploitation of labour was to transfer both land and capital to some form of collective ownership. As for wages, the Fabians rejected the notion that there was any law, even under capitalism, that kept them down to subsistence level. Wages, they argued, depended on two factors—the productivity of the economy, and the pressure of the workers and their allies to get the share accruing to labour increased both by Trade Union action and by legislation to raise wages, and by Co-operative action and anti-monopoly laws to keep down the cost of living. If such pressure resulted in the fixing of wages which a particular group of capitalists was unable to pay, the branch of production affected should be taken out of their hands and transferred to public operation. Thus, the Fabians linked their advocacy of the 'Welfare State' to the policy of socialization, and allied themselves with the day-to-day struggle of the Trade Unions and Co-operatives to improve working-class conditions; but at the same time they dissociated themselves from the notion of 'increasing misery' leading to revolution and also from that of capitalism as doomed to pass, because of its inherent contradictions, into more and more severe crises leading up to its final overthrow. The Fabians accepted the idea of a capitalism still advancing and able to concede improved working conditions under pressure from a democratic electorate as well as from the Trade Unions industrially. They thought of socialization as destined to come, at any rate in Great Britain, not through violent revolution, but as an outcome of this double pressure.

It has to be borne in mind that at the time when these Fabian doctrines were formulated, and for a long while afterwards, the British economy was expanding fast, and the condition of the main body of British workers was undoubtedly improving. Moreover, capitalist crises appeared to be getting, not more, but less severe; and real advances were being made in social legislation. This tendency to improvement, subject to occasional setbacks, continued right up to 1914; and the effect of the workers' increased economic power during the First World War was seen in a fresh crop of social legislation. Then, with the onset of the post-war slump in 1921, and thereafter with the continuous depression of the British economy during the interwar period, it began to look as if the period of capitalist expansion were over, and as if the workers would be unable to improve their position further without overthrowing capitalism. These changing conditions, and the impetus to Socialist thought arising out of the Russian Revolution, produced a stimulus to Marxist ways of thinking, especially in the 1930s, after Hitler's rise to power. They did not however suffice to alter the fundamental attitude of the great majority of the Labour Party's leaders, or indeed of their followers. They did induce the Labour Party to formulate more extensive plans of socialization and to contemplate a speedier advance towards Socialism; but these plans were still made within the general conception of constitutional parliamentary action, and not of revolution. Neither the British Communists nor the other left-wing Socialists who were influenced by Marxist ideas ever came near to capturing the allegiance of the Trade Unions or to bringing the Labour Party over to a revolutionary policy.

The British people, including the British working class, is indeed so deeply imbued with the idea of parliamentary action as the main instrument for achieving social and economic advances that no group or party which rejects this conception has any chance of building up a mass following. The British workers are used to the notion of using their freedom to organize and to vote as means of improving their conditions of living; and the non-Socialist parties have so far accepted the conditions imposed by the power of the Trade Unions and of a popular electorate as to refrain, save quite exceptionally (as after the General Strike of 1926), from any fundamental challenge to the Trade Unions and from any attempt to undo more than a little of the 'welfare' legislation passed by Labour Governments. Indeed, the Conservatives have themselves, in order to win popular support, enacted a good deal of social legislation— though they have, of course, tried to do this in such a way as to throw most of the burden of paying for it on the workers, through indirect taxes and compulsory insurance contributions. The conditions of British politics render it impossible for the Conservative Party to be an out-and-out reactionary party like many of the parties which exist in continental Europe. The Conservatives are well aware that if they attempted to follow a policy of sheer reaction they would not stand a chance of holding political power. Any British party which aims at securing a parliamentary majority has to accept the basic implications of the 'Welfare State', whether it likes them or not. There are, of course, in the Conservative ranks a great many individuals and groups holding violently reactionary opinions; but the party managers dare not do more to meet their wishes than they can hope to persuade a popular electorate to accept.

Thus, the conditions of British politics are radically different from those of countries in which there is no similar tradition of parliamentary give-and-take, and in which the class struggle is more acute. The hereditary nobility and the landowning classes ceased long ago to count as a major political power; and British industrial capitalism assumed the leadership under conditions which made the relatively small employers and the shopkeepers a dominant element in the expanding electorate. The workers first took part in parliamentary politics, after the Reform Act of 1867 had given votes to the skilled craftsmen,[2] mainly as the allies of the lower middle classes against the old aristocrats and the great financiers; and the bond between the workers and the lesser bourgeoisie was powerfully reinforced by their sharing, to a large extent, a common religious outlook in hostility to the claims of the Established Church.

Indeed, the peculiar structure of British politics owes a great deal to the religious attitudes of the British people. In countries where a single Church, dominated by the ruling classes, holds a virtual monopoly, it is natural for the workers' movements to become the enemies of that Church, and therewith of all organized religion, which confronts them only as an oppressive force. But in Great Britain there has been from the seventeenth century a religious conflict between an Established Church, specially recognized by the State and supported by most aristocrats and very wealthy persons, and a number of Dissenting sects which have drawn their support from the middle and working classes. Throughout the nineteenth century these Dissenting groups provided the main basis for the support of the Liberals against the Conservatives, who were mainly supporters of the claims of the Established Church; and the struggle of the Dissenters for equal rights and social status with Churchmen was largely the reason for the close connections which grew up between the working-class leaders and the Liberal Party. A majority of the leaders of the Trade Unions and Co-operative Societies were Dissenters; and under the system of two great political parties contending for office and power it seemed natural for the workers, as they got votes, to ally themselves with the party of Dissent against the Church party, and to form a Radical wing of the Liberals rather than establish a separate party of their own. That this alliance did not continue was due partly to the failure of the Radical wing to win over the main body of the Liberal Party; but it was due also to a waning of the political activity of the Dissenters when some of their claims had been met. In the twentieth century religious Dissent rapidly ceased to be as powerful a political force as it had been before, and this relegation of religious questions to a position of less importance was a considerable factor in clearing the way for the emergence of an independent workers' party.

This new party, however, when it came, absorbed into itself much of the Dissenting ideology in which its members had grown up. Its outlook was profoundly ethical: it was by no means prepared to accept the materialism or the hostility to religion which characterized the continental Marxist parties. The British Marxists who had formed the Social Democratic Federation in the

---

2   Editor's note: This is misleading. Although male householders in the borough constituencies were enfranchised in 1867, those in counties (who included most of the miners as well as many industrial workers) waited until 1884.

1880s and had embraced the materialism of the Marxist creed found them-selves by-passed and thrust aside by the mass of working-class and other con-verts from Liberalism who founded the New Unionism and the Independent Labour Party. When the Labour Representation Committee was formed in 1900 the Social Democratic Federation, as well as the ILP and the Fabian Society, took part in the constituent conference, but seceded at once on its failure to persuade its partners to set up a party with a clear-cut Marxist pro-gramme. The SDF continued on its separate course; but it was not strong enough to win even a single seat in Parliament. After a series of vicissitudes, what was left of it became, after the First World War, the main nucleus of the Communist Party of Great Britain; but in its new guise it was hardly more successful than before in making any impact on the main body of work-ing-class opinion.

The British Labour Party, then, has its own brand of Socialism, backed by its own philosophy. It is not materialist, but idealistic; not Marxist, but essentially Utilitarian; not revolutionary, but parliamentary; not 'scientific', but essentially ethical in outlook. It believes in the possibility of advancing towards a classless society by stages, using as its instruments the legislative power of Parliament backed by the organized power of the Trade Union and Co-operative move-ments. Its first objective is the achievement of what the Webbs used to call a 'national minimum standard of civilized life' for all citizens—of what is now more often called the 'Welfare State'; and it values socialization mainly as a means towards reducing disparities of wealth and income and towards equip-ping the State with the power to assure employment and fair conditions to all. It combats educational and social inequality; but it does so in the spirit rather of diminishing class differences than of waging class war. For winning a majority of the electors to its side it needs the support, not only of the manual workers, but also of a large proportion of the 'white collar' workers and of some at any rate of the middle classes. Manual and agricultural workers together are not enough to win a parliamentary majority; for Great Britain has reached a stage of economic development at which the non-manual employees constitute an important section of the population, inextricably connected by family ties with the manual workers. Class divisions are of course most important; but they are not clear-cut and, save here and there, class feeling does not run high.

I have been attempting in this article to state, without inserting my own opinions, certain facts which seem to me indispensable for understanding the Socialism of the British Labour Party. I have not tried to say whether the po-litical attitudes of the British workers are to be admired or execrated: I have simply set out to show, as clearly as I could, what the facts of the situation are. For my own part I have always belonged to a 'left wing' of the Labour movement which has done its best to push the Labour Party and the Trade Unions towards a more aggressive anti-capitalist policy, designed to speed up the transition to Socialism. But I have not questioned the gradualism itself—only the setting of too slow a pace. There has never been any sufficient prospect of a revolutionary policy in Great Britain gaining any large body of adherents to make it worthwhile to consider such a policy seriously; and I have enough hatred of violence and of hatred itself to wish very much to believe that, in Britain at any rate, Socialism can be achieved without appealing to them as the essential means. I have never been sure about this; but I have been sure that for the time being the right way is to make the fullest use of constitutional methods for advancing towards Socialism, and I can affirm with confidence that, as a sheer matter of fact, very great advances have been made in this way. The points on which I dissent from the predominant Labour Party attitude are, first, that of the need for a more forthright attack on the maldistribution of property, and, secondly, that of a refusal to generalize from British conditions to conditions elsewhere, so as to suppose that the evolutionary policy which is right in Great Britain is necessarily right, or even possible at all, in countries with widely different social and economic structures and political and social traditions. I do not see, for example, how Yugoslavia could have advanced an inch towards Socialism without a revolution.[3]

I have discussed in this article certain underlying assumptions of the British type of Socialism. There has not been room, in a single article, to go on from this to an evaluation of the actual policies which the British Labour Party pursued during its years of office after 1945. This, if the editor gives me the opportunity, I intend to attempt in a further article. I could not attempt it without these prolegomena; for the Labour Party's present policies can be understood only in the light of the conditions under which it has grown up and won popular support, and these conditions need a good deal of explaining to readers whose national experience has been entirely different.

---

3   Editor's note: Cole was writing for a Yugoslav journal.

BRITISH LABOUR'S
ACHIEVEMENT AFTER 1945:
AN ASSESSMENT

THE PRESENT ARTICLE IS A SEQUEL TO ONE IN WHICH I ATTEMPTED TO GIVE A general count of the Socialism professed by the Labour Party in Great Britain.[1] I was dealing there with the ideas which lie behind the Labour Party's Socialism, and with the historical forces which have conditioned its growth. In this article I am setting out to describe and to assess the Labour Party's actual achievements during its years of office after its election victory of 1945 had given it a large majority of the seats in the House of Commons, though not a clear majority of all the votes cast.

In 1945 the Labour vote was approximately twelve millions, as against ten millions for the Conservatives and their immediate allies, and about two and a quarter for the independent Liberals. But under the system of constituencies each returning a single member, with the seat going to the candidate who polls the largest vote, the Labour Party, on this occasion, got 394 out of 640 seats, the Conservative bloc 215, and the independent Liberals only 12—the remainder going to splinter groups and independents of various colours. The

---

1   *Review of International Affairs* (Belgrade), 1953.

Labour Party was thus in complete control of the House of Commons, and remained so until 1950, when its strength was reduced to 315 in a House of 625, leaving it still with an overall majority, but with one which its leaders regarded as too small for carrying through any further considerable programme. On this occasion the Labour candidates polled 13,500,000 votes, the Conservatives and their allies about 100,000 fewer, and the independent Liberals well over two and a half million. Labour was thus definitely in a minority on the votes cast, though the electoral system still worked in its favour as against the Liberals. The following year a fresh General Election led to the fall of the Labour Government and the return of the Conservatives to power. On this occasion the Labour members of the House of Commons fell to 295, as against 321 for the Conservative bloc, and only 6 for the independent Liberals. The popular vote was very close—13,948,000 for Labour, and 13,724,000 for the Conservatives and their allies, with the independent Liberals polling only 730,000. It was the turn of the Conservatives to hold office with only a small majority, and of the Labour Party, back in opposition, to work out a new programme for the future.

In the light of these facts the Labour Party's achievement has to be assessed mainly in terms of what it did during its five years of office with a good majority between 1945 and 1950. From 1950 to 1951 it was attempting nothing new, though it was rounding off certain of its earlier measures, such as the nationalization of steel, which had been held up by the resistance of the House of Lords. It has, of course, to be borne in mind that in Great Britain there is still the anomaly of an hereditary Second Chamber of Peers, in which there is always an overwhelming Conservative majority. This Chamber has no control over financial measures; but it can delay any other legislation. One of the measures passed by the Labour Government in 1948 had the effect of limiting its delaying power, in effect, to a single year. The House of Lords did not in fact reject most of the Labour Government's measures; it limited itself to trying to amend them, except in the case of the Bill restricting its own powers and of that providing for the nationalization of steel. The latter, which was brought in by the Labour Government only late in its first period of office, the House of Lords was able to defer long enough prevent much from being done under it before the Conservatives came back to power and repealed it.

The achievement of the Labour Government between 1945 and 1950 needs to be studied under five main heads—social legislation (including taxation), socialization, employment policy and economic planning, international political affairs, and international economic relations. The programme on which the Labour Party fought the election of 1945 dealt fully with the first and second of these groups of problems, and to a less extent with the third, but was much vaguer about the fourth and fifth—partly because the international outlook was much the more difficult to forecast but also because much less attention had been paid to the working out of international than of domestic policies. In the first field—social legislation—a good deal of preliminary planning had been done under the coalition Government during the war, and in one part of it—education—a comprehensive Act had been passed in 1944. The Labour Government thus inherited a number of projects for which its leading members had some share of responsibility derived from their holding of offices in the coalition. In the field of socialization, on the other hand, nothing had been done under the coalition, and the Labour Party had planned its policy quite apart from other parties. On employment policy there had been a most unsatisfactory coalition pronouncement: economic planning consisted, for the time being, mainly of a continuance of wartime 'controls'. In international affairs there was an inter-party commitment to the establishment of the United Nations Organization, on the assumption that the States which had worked together during the war would continue to co-operate after the return of peace; and this commitment extended into the economic field, in connection with projects for the international regulation of currency and the promotion of international investment, and also as a result of promises made to the Americans about non-discrimination in trade policy at the time of the Atlantic Pact.

In respect of the social services, the foundations of post-war development had been laid in the celebrated Beveridge Report of 1942. Sir William (now Lord) Beveridge is (and was) a Liberal, a great figure in the academic world as a former head of the London School of Economics. He was appointed by the coalition in 1940 or 1941 to make a one-man report on the development of the social services; and he produced a document which outlined a comprehensive plan of insurance and assistance to cover unemployment, sickness, accident, and old age, including both family allowances and a national provision for disabled persons, widows and orphans, and a strong recommendation in favour of a National Health Service. The Beveridge Report became a battleground during the later years of the war, only the Labour Party being prepared to promise its complete implementation, though the Conservatives were ready to accept a good deal of it. Plans for a National Health Service drawn up under the coalition failed to satisfy the Labour Party, and were entirely recast after 1945. Children's allowances were actually introduced under the coalition; and the Labour Party, on taking office, rapidly passed into law three Acts—a National Insurance Act, a National Assistance Act, and an Industrial Injuries Act—which carried out or bettered most of the Beveridge proposals. The National Health Act followed, after a considerable struggle with the doctors, who stood out successfully against becoming salaried public servants and insisted on retaining a system of capitation fees. These Acts, together with what had been already done before 1945, established a general structure of social security, based mainly, apart from the Health Service, on payment of cash benefits and allowances to mitigate hardships arising out of loss of normal income. The payments were not large enough to prevent unemployment or disability from leaving most of the recipients a good deal worse off than when they were at work; but they did provide a subsistence income, and there were provisions for supplementary allowances in case of special need. The least satisfactory part of the scheme was that which dealt with pensions in old age; but it was also the most expensive and destined to increase rapidly in cost because of the rising expectation of life.

The provision for social security did not extend to the guarantee of a minimum wage for those in employment. But under Ernest Bevin's Wages Councils Act, passed despite a good deal of Conservative hostility during the coalition, minimum wage provision was extended to a high proportion of the worse-paid trades, and both before and after 1945 the scarcity of workers made it possible for wages to rise in these trades, so that the absence of a general legal minimum wage was not seriously felt. There was also, under legislation passed during the war, a rapid extension of paid holidays to one industry after another.

A far-reaching Education Act, as we saw, had been passed in 1944 under the coalition, with a Conservative—R. A. Butler—at the head of the Education Ministry. This Act, providing for a school-leaving age of fifteen, with universal secondary education from eleven to fifteen, and with provision for general part-time continued education up to eighteen, as well as for larger numbers to continue full-time schooling on a voluntary basis beyond fifteen, was of such a nature that the putting of it into full effect was bound to take a considerable number of years. Schools had to be built, and teachers trained before it could become a reality; and there was great pressure on the building industry for houses and other constructions as well as for schools, and also an acute shortage of building materials. Accordingly, the Labour Government could do no more than try to speed up the process of putting the Butler Act into effect, unless it had been prepared to launch an attack on the numerous private (miscalled 'public') schools outside the state system. These were schools to which well-to-do parents sent their children partly because some of them provided a very high standard of teaching—with small classes and highly qualified teachers—but also partly because they had a 'snob' appeal to parents who did not wish their children to go to the same schools as those of the working classes. There was a good deal of controversy in the Labour Party about these schools. Some wished to nationalize the good ones and shut down the rest; but the Government decided to do nothing, arguing that the time for an attack on this form of educational privilege would come only when there were enough good state schools and teachers available to meet the full need. In fact, what happened was that the insufficiency of state schools, combined with an accentuated class feeling among the middle classes, who felt their privileged educational position threatened, led to a rush of pupils into the non-state schools, despite the high fees charged and the abolition of all teaching fees in the state schools.

The advance towards educational equality was thus largely held up by the shortage of state schools and teachers, and by the reluctance of the Labour Government to attack the upper- and middle-class schools until it could make full alternative provision. There was also a big controversy over the methods to be adopted in organizing the state secondary schools under the Butler Act. Labour opinion predominantly favoured 'comprehensive' high schools, in which abler and less able children would be grouped together and alternative courses would be available in 'grammar', technical, and 'modern' subjects, to suit different bents of mind. But this policy, which was opposed by a minority on the ground that it might swamp the abler pupils and fail to educate for leadership, involved a great deal of new building to provide suitable premises; and only very slow progress has been made with it so far. Nor is the controversy by any means over: it is indeed closely bound up with the much wider issue of the Labour Party's general attitude to social equality and to the claims of the middle classes.

This brings me to the question of taxation. During the war, direct taxes on incomes had been extended to cover most adult wage-earners, and had also been very steeply graduated against the big incomes. The consequence had been a considerable narrowing of the differences of spendable income between the rich and the poor, partly counteracted by a sharp increase in indirect taxes, especially on drink and tobacco, which bear most heavily on the relatively poor. The Labour Government inherited this tax structure, and did not do a great deal to alter it. Not much more could in fact have been achieved by heavier taxation of really large incomes; and the Labour Party was not prepared to tax the middle incomes so heavily as to hit hard the middle groups of salary-earners, shopkeepers, and small employers, or the groups living on retiring pensions or savings, or on small unearned incomes. It was, in effect, not prepared to upset radically the middle income groups which make up a substantial fraction of British society, and of which not a few members had voted for it in 1945. True to its gradualist, non-revolutionary tradition, it had no wish to enforce a sudden social change which *would* throw all these groups into violent opposition, possibly of a Fascist temper.

The Labour Government did, however, continue the heavy wartime taxes on the incomes of the rich. But it did nothing either to deprive them of their property or to make an end of the huge inequalities in gross incomes before taxation. Some of its supporters deplored this attitude (I did myself), and urged the desirability of either a heavy capital levy or a sharply increased taxation of inheritance, or of both. It was pointed out that the rich, as long as they were allowed to keep their property intact, would also keep much of their economic power, and also that as long as private industry went on paying very big salaries it would be almost impossible for the nationalized industries and the public services not to do the same. These warnings were disregarded: the Labour Government contented itself with a considerable levelling of *spendable* incomes, without either reducing differences in *gross* incomes or attacking the root problem of capital ownership. It did not even attempt to nationalize the land, or to discriminate more than a little in favour of earned as against unearned incomes.

In the main, then, the Labour Government merely upheld the tax system that had developed during the war years and did not attempt to use taxation as an instrument for further economic levelling, save to the extent to which it increased the provision of social services out of taxation. The wage-earners, under these conditions, were a good deal better off relatively to other classes than they had been before the war; but the improvement was due largely to full employment and the development of the social services, and the greater part of it had occurred during the war, before the Labour Party came to exclusive power.

The second field—socialization—set the Labour Government the task of carrying out an ambitious, though limited, programme to which it had committed itself in its election appeals; and before it left office it had actually passed the whole of this programme into law. It nationalized—with compensation to the private owners—central banking, coal mines, civil aviation, railways, docks, canals, ports, road transport, electricity supply, gas supply, and the greater part of the steel industry—so that, when it left office, roughly one-fifth of the total economy was publicly owned and operated. It also carried on a number of the wartime controls of other essential industries—notably in the case of food by means of bulk purchase arrangements and rationed allocation of scarce supplies; but these 'controls' remained temporary, under wartime Acts which were renewed only for short periods. Many other wartime 'controls' were scrapped or greatly relaxed as supplies became less scarce; but some powers were retained both for the control of capital investment and of new building and for compelling private firms to export a high proportion of products which could be used to pay for necessary imports. No real attempt was made to replace the wartime 'controls' by permanent legislation giving the Government powers of regulation over private industry; even an attempt to set up Development Councils with Trade Union representation in such industries was dropped in face of the strong opposition of most of the capitalists concerned.

In the industries which were nationalized, the pattern of administration was that of a National Board or Commission for each industry, or in the case of transport for several together. These bodies were nominated by the Government, without any representation of particular interests. Their members were mostly former high administrators of private industry, or in a few cases civil servants; but each of them included at least one Trade Unionist, who had to resign his connection with his Trade Union on appointment, and became a salaried official of the nationalized service. This policy had been worked out by the Labour Party in the 1930s. Some Trade Unions objected to it, and demanded the right to choose their own representatives on the Boards; but they were overruled. Herbert Morrison was the foremost advocate in the Labour Party of the plan which was actually followed. The Railwaymen and the Post Office Workers were the principal critics: the Mineworkers, by a majority, accepted the Morrison view.

Each nationalization Act, while it put the administration of the industry in question under a nominated Board or Commission, required that body to set up, at all levels, a system of Joint Consultation with its employees and their Trade Unions. This consultative machinery was kept apart from the machinery for collective bargaining about wages and general conditions of work: it was meant to deal with questions of human relations, productivity, training for and conditions of promotion to higher jobs, and welfare services. It seems in most cases to be working tolerably well within narrow limits, without producing any outstanding results. The same can hardly be said of the Board system of administration, which has led to highly centralized control and to a feeling among many workers that there is no great difference between employment by a public body and employment by a big capitalist employer. This feeling of frustration is of course partly due to the inevitable continuance in the higher posts of most of the managers and technicians previously employed under private ownership—for who was there to replace them? Nationalization, carried through, not under revolutionary conditions, but as a measure of piecemeal reform, involved no mass disappearance of the old managers and experts, and no enforced introduction of large numbers of new men who had to make up by their enthusiasm and devotion for shortcomings of technical or managerial knowledge. It meant, for the most part, taking over the old managing personnel and, at the most, instituting new schemes of training and ladders of promotion that would gradually democratize the choice of future holders of the higher posts. Consequently, the ordinary worker was apt to be much more conscious of having still to work under the same superiors than of having acquired a new status in his industry. Only a minority consciously minded about this; but it meant that there was much less change of attitude—for example, towards productivity—than some of the nationalizers had unreasonably hoped for.

There are two distinct oppositions to 'workers' control', or 'industrial democracy', in the British Labour movement. One of these, the more powerful among the politicians, bases its hostility on insistence on control by the consumers, and regards Parliament as representing in relation to the nationalized industries the whole consuming public. As Parliament, clearly, cannot administer industry, this body of opinion favours administration either by public departments under a Minister responsible to Parliament, or by Boards working under the auspices of such Ministers, and subject to ministerial directives on matters of high policy. The other group, consisting mainly of Trade Union leaders, opposes workers' control because its effect would be either to make the Trade Unions responsible for the success of the nationalized enterprises or to undermine their authority by making it necessary to build up within each industry a distinct democratic structure for the exercise of control. Trade Union leaders are apt to fear that the acceptance of responsibility for the efficiency of the nationalized industries would result in loss of influence over their members, who demand that the Trade Unions shall act as pressure groups on their behalf, and they are also apt to fear that the delegation of power to shop stewards and work's representatives would break up collective bargaining arrangements and hand over too much authority to local leaders, who might be disposed to reject Trade Union discipline. Consequently, there has been no concerted Trade Union demand for more workers' control, and, despite fairly widespread dissatisfaction with things as they are, no alternative to the Board system has been seriously pressed. The result is that, although on the whole the nationalized industries have worked tolerably well, there has been no considerable evocation of new social incentives and no real democratization of management.

Nevertheless, the Labour Party's achievement in the field of socialization has been great. Compensation, given the principle, has been kept within reasonable limits, so as substantially to reduce the interest charges for capital; and development policies have been set on foot which should, in course of time, considerably improve productivity. Certainly the nationalized industries have worked a good deal better than they could have been expected to work under continued private ownership. There is, however, a difficulty in the way of further big advances on the lines followed between 1945 and 1950. The industries and services taken over during the Labour Government's period of office were, with the single exception of steel, eminently suitable for complete nationalization and unified control. But in most other industries there exists a multiplicity of firms, large, middle-sized and small, producing a wide variety of goods, and lending themselves much less well to unified administration. In the case of steel, the Labour Government's Act nationalized only the producers of crude steel and the firms which combined finishing processes with crude steel production, leaving in private hands the numerous finishing firms which were specialists in particular products. It seems likely that in most future schemes of nationalization this model will need to be followed, the State taking over only certain key sections of an industry, or only the bigger firms, while leaving the smaller firms still under private ownership, but subject to a considerable degree of control because they will have to procure their essential materials mainly from the nationalized sectors of the industries concerned.

The Labour Party, in considering its plans for further socialization, has been thinking to some extent along these lines. This raises a number of problems, both because where only a part of an industry is taken over there is bound to be competition between the nationalized and the private sectors, and because where a key section only is nationalized—e.g. the machinery-making section or the section supplying an essential material—it will be necessary to work out suitable techniques whereby the nationalized part of the industry will be able to exert a planning control over the rest.

These questions, however, are still mainly in the future. They hardly arose in connection with the industries nationalized between 1945 and 1951, except steel; and in the case of steel the Government fell before they had been seriously faced in practice.

The third group of matters with which the Labour Government had to deal after 1945 was that connected with employment and planning policies. At the outset, with labour scarce, much essential work waiting to be done, and a sellers' market for exports, no difficulty arose in maintaining full employment. The Government nevertheless followed a policy of encouraging investment and production by keeping down rates of interest and making bank credit plentiful. This policy had certain inflationary consequences, which led to its modification when Sir Stafford Cripps succeeded Hugh Dalton as Chancellor of the Exchequer. A moderate rise in interest rates was allowed, and spending power was held in check by taxing at a high enough rate to ensure a large budget surplus and thus restrict both consumers' spending and private investment. But this policy was not carried far enough to cause unemployment on any serious scale; and it was combined with a policy of 'wage restraint' under which the Trade Unions refrained from using the power put in their hands by full employment to press for more than moderate wage-advances. The Trade Unions' acquiescence was secured by keeping down the cost of living—or at any rate that of food—by means of subsidies; but the policy tended to break down in face of the high profits which were being made well before the Government's fall from office. These high profits were largely unavoidable where industries were left in private hands; for it was necessary to keep in operation many high-cost plants which could not be speedily replaced but were indispensable for keeping total output and employment at a high level. Trade Unionists were increasingly disposed to argue that firms making high profits could afford higher wages, even though in fact there was no surplus supply of consumers' goods on which the higher wages could have been spent, and a more rapid rise of wages would in practice have led to higher prices and to an inflation which would have reacted on the international value of the pound sterling. It was in fact necessary, under the Cripps régime, to accept a considerable devaluation of sterling in terms of the dollar—a need due partly to internal inflation, but also partly to the general world economic situation, which put a premium on dollar goods which could not be paid for by exports to the dollar area.

This brings us to the international economic policies followed by the Labour Government. In 1945 the British economy, which had been sustained by Lend-Lease during the war years in face of the loss of a large part of its export trade, found itself quite unable to balance its international accounts when Lend-Lease was abruptly withdrawn. There followed the borrowing of large sums from the United States and Canada on terms which involved a substantial sacrifice of Great Britain's freedom to pursue economic policies displeasing to the American Government. For this reason, I among others opposed the acceptance of the American Loan of 1946, though I fully realized that the lack of it would mean an immediate and serious fall in the British standard of life. I regarded it as so important that Great Britain should not become economically subject to American control and should keep its freedom to develop its own economic policy, where necessary by measures involving 'discrimination', that I preferred to face immediate hardship in the hope of building up a trading area independent of the dollar to gaining a respite by subjection to American influence. But hardly anyone then agreed with me. The leaders of the Labour Party felt it to be impossible to tell those who had voted for them that it was necessary to accept for the time a reduced standard of living and an acute shortage of goods purchaseable only with dollars. The American Loan was accepted, and speedily spent; and had it not been replaced after 1947 by Marshall Aid there would have been an acute economic crisis in Great Britain, as well as in other parts of Western Europe. At the time it was stated that Marshall Aid carried with it no political commitments; but in practice its acceptance was soon seen to involve, at any rate after the Soviet Union's rejection of the Marshall Plan, a close political tie-up with the United States.

This brings me to the question of the Labour Government's international policy in the political field. In 1945 it seemed to me, and to many others, possible to work for a close alliance of European Socialists designed to achieve the consolidation of Socialism as the ruling force in Western as well as in Eastern Europe and to establish European independence of American control. Such a policy required that the British Labour Government should take sides with the continental Socialist Parties against the capitalist parties, and in particular that it should throw all its weight into the scale in an attempt to establish a Socialist Republic in Western Germany, despite American opposition. It also involved a determined effort to rebuild close trade relations between Western and Eastern Europe, and a firm repudiation of imperialist policies all over the world, so as to create an effective alliance between Western Socialism and the colonial peoples which were struggling for national emancipation.

The Labour Government made a good beginning by accepting the complete independence of India and Burma, but it failed lamentably to take sides in Germany, or to put itself at the head of the Socialist movement in Europe. It also bungled matters very badly in Palestine, in an attempt to placate the reactionary Arab States; and it soon found itself involved in a colonial war in Malaya. Rapidly, it found itself becoming a party with the Americans, in a 'cold war' against Soviet Communism. I am not suggesting that this was entirely its fault; for Stalinist policy from 1947 onwards must bear a large part of the blame, jointly with the Americans, who unhappily coupled Marshall Aid with the 'Truman Doctrine'. But part of the harm had been done before 1947, in the failure to think out or apply any distinctively Socialist international policy in relation to Germany, or indeed to any part of Europe or of the world. The plain truth is that the Labour Government had no international policy except a reliance on the United Nations, which could not be an effective instrument unless the United States and the Soviet Union could come to terms. In these circumstances Ernest Bevin, influenced by his Foreign Office advisers and by his bitter hostility to Communism was able to do much as he pleased, and to rout his critics whenever he was challenged within the Labour Party exposing their lack of any thought-out alternative policy

I admit that such a policy was difficult to devise, or to implement even if it had been clearly conceived. Indeed I am disposed to think that from the moment when the Labour Government accepted its dependence on American aid, the power to adopt a Socialist policy was effectively forfeit. In Germany the British had to give way on one issue after another to the Americans, because the USA was meeting most of the occupation costs, and because the retention of an American army of occupation was felt to be necessary on account of British and French military weakness. An independent Socialist policy could have been followed only if Great Britain had been prepared to do without American aid and had established Socialism firmly in the British zone of occupation despite American objections.

These views were unacceptable at the time to the Labour Party leadership, which regarded them both as economically impracticable and as running counter to the 'democratic' principle that Germany must be allowed to settle the complexion of its own government without external interference, and that it would be wrong for the British Government to take sides between the Socialist Parties and their rivals in France or elsewhere. In my view, in the potentially revolutionary situation which existed in Western Europe in 1945, this is precisely what British Socialists should have done. I admit, however, that such a policy did not fit in with the essentially gradualist attitude of the Labour Party in home affairs, and that the Labour Government had no popular mandate for taking such a line. It had, indeed, on international policy hardly any mandate at all. The election of 1945 was fought and won on issues of domestic policy, with foreign affairs counting for very little in affecting the vote. This was partly because the Labour programme, as far as it dealt with international issues, was mostly platitudinous, and offered no clear lead. But it was even more because most of the Labour electors had no clear views on international matters, but were very much interested in the development of the 'Welfare State'—much more than in nationalization or in any aspect of Socialism that went beyond mere social reform.

Summing up, one has to recognize that the evolutionary, gradualist type of Socialism which has developed in Great Britain, and has never been challenged seriously by more than a small minority, necessarily makes strongly against militancy, or even any sort of Socialist action, on the international plane, as well as against domestic policies involving an appeal to 'class-war'. In domestic affairs I believe the evolutionary policy to be justified as the only policy capable of commanding any wide measure of support. But I cannot help seeing that it renders British Socialism a poor ally of the Socialist movements in countries where reaction is far more strongly entrenched and class-war much more an inescapable fact. The British Socialist is too apt to think of other countries as like his own, and of the relatively tolerant temper of British political contests as applicable to countries which have no similar traditions of parliamentary government. I do not see how this tendency is to be overcome, as long as it remains possible for a gradualist Labour Government to offer the British workers substantial instalments of social betterment without arousing counter-revolutionary opposition of a Fascist kind. There is no doubt that the Labour Government of 1945 to 1950 did pass this test, living up to its pledges and giving its supporters a considerable gain in social well-being as well as a reasonable advance in the direction of Socialist ownership and democratic planning of economic affairs. On the other hand, when in 1950 the Labour Party had to draw up a new programme, it fell down lamentably, producing only a ting of scraps and patches which failed to inspire anybody. The Party is now engaged in preparing a fresh programme on which to fight the next election; but the content of this new statement of purposes and projects is still unknown. It is due to appear quite soon; and it will then be easier to tell whether the Party exhausted its Socialist impulse during its first period of power, or is ready to go forward with a further-reaching challenge to capitalism and, therewith, towards a tougher Socialist policy in the international field.

IS THIS SOCIALISM?

Foreword

I HAD BETTER BEGIN BY EXPLAINING AS CLEARLY AS I CAN WHAT THIS PAMPHLET is, and is not, about.[1] It *is* about Socialism, by which I mean nothing less than a society without classes, and not one in which a new class structure has replaced the old. It is *not* about the policy to be followed by a Labour Government which is not seeking to establish a classless society, but only to nationalize a few more industries and add a few more pieces to the equipment of the Welfare State. I have not tried in it to argue the case for Socialism: I have taken that case for granted, and have asked only how the given Socialist objective can be achieved in a non-revolutionary way. It is not addressed to Labourites who are satisfied with the way things have been going, and, if they call themselves Socialists at all, regard Socialism only as an objective too remote to be taken account of in formulating policies for the near future. It is an attempt to indicate a way of action to those Socialists who feel a sense of frustration because Socialism means to them something radically different from the managerial Welfare State. It may well be that such persons are too few at present either to bring the Labour Party over to their point of view or, should they do so, to carry it to electoral victory. About that I do not pretend to know. I am not electioneering: I am only saying that, *if* we do wish to advance towards Socialism, these are the kind of measures we must try to persuade the electorate to accept.

---

1 *New Statesman* pamphlet, 1954.

* * *

A Socialist we used to be told, is 'one who has yearnings for the equal division of unequal earnings'. This description neatly slurred over the fact that
the inequalities the Socialists were most intent on getting rid of did not arise
out of earnings at all, but out of the possession of claims to income based on
ownership and, above all, on inherited wealth. Socialists saw the gross inequalities of income as proceeding much more from the 'rights of property' than
from differential rewards in return for unequal services. Most of them did, no
doubt, hold that the large disparities of *earned* incomes were due to a considerable extent to the existence of large *unearned* incomes, and that, if the latter
were eliminated, it would become much easier to narrow differences in earned
incomes. They denied the contention of many orthodox economists that differences in earned incomes corresponded to real differences in the value of
services rendered, and were dictated by inexorable economic laws. They held,
as against this view, that the high salaries and fees paid to professional and
managerial workers were in part a reflection of the social inequality inherent in
a social system which accepted unearned incomes based on property as legitimate and as carrying high prestige, and were in part due to the near-monopoly
of higher education by the children of the well-to-do. They wished to diminish
the inequalities of earned as well as of unearned income; but their main attack
was concentrated on the inequality due to ownership. On that ground, in the
main, they demanded the socialization of the means of production, distribution and exchange, and the elimination of the toll levied by individuals on the
social product on the score of ownership.

Incomes and Property

In practice, however, Socialists—as exemplified by the Labour Government of
1945—have attacked inequalities of *income* much more than inequalities of
property, and earned incomes almost, though not quite, as much as unearned.
True, they have nationalized a number of industries and services; but they have
compensated the owners, if not with generosity, at any rate so as to leave them
with their claims to income broadly intact. As against this, they have taken
over a structure of taxes on incomes erected to meet the emergency of war and
have used it to help finance an expansion of social services in time of peace
with very little discrimination between incomes derived from property and incomes received as a return for personal services. Admittedly, it is often difficult,
or even impossible, to draw a clear line between earned and unearned incomes
where a person gives his services to a business in which his property, or some of
it, is also invested; for in such cases there is no valid way of deciding how much
of his 'profit' comes from his invested capital and how much from his work.
But, in practice, lines are drawn, however arbitrarily, for tax purposes; and it

would have been possible to discriminate further against unearned incomes if the Labour Government had really wished to do so. It did not, because it did not really want to: in the main, it concerned itself rather with finding the money to pay for the social services and for other public outgoings in the easiest way, rather than with attacking unearned incomes as such.

Why was this? And why was it that the Labour Government made no attempt, or almost none, to attack inequalities of ownership, and contented itself with lopping off by taxation a large fraction of the really big incomes, while leaving the property that gave rise to most of them practically intact? It would certainly have surprised the Socialist pioneers very much to find a Socialist Government proceeding in this way; for they took it for granted that the advances towards Socialism would involve the abolition of the toll levied by private owners of the means of production on the current product of social labour.

Is the answer that the Labour Government of 1945 had no mandate to introduce a Socialist system, but only to carry through certain social reforms representing an advance towards the Welfare State, and to nationalize certain industries and services only on condition of *not* socializing the property rights of their previous owners? This is part of the answer; and it is reasonable to plead that the Labour Government could not have gone beyond what it did without seeking a fresh mandate. That, however, only involves recasting the question. Why, we are impelled to ask, did the Labour Party, when it put forward a programme for further advances, beyond what it had received a mandate to do in 1945, produce in succession three further programmes in which there was still virtually no attempt to attack inequality at its roots or to advance beyond mere piecemeal nationalizations to the socialization without which it was clearly impossible to set about the establishment of a classless society ?

Why Has Labour Not Attacked Inequality at its Roots?

It did not, because it did not want to—at any rate for the time being. Why then, did it not want to do what its professed Socialist faith surely required of it? Largely, no doubt, because it did not believe that a majority of the electors would be prepared to give it a mandate to do anything of the kind. The electors who returned the Labour Government of 1945 voted, for the most part, not for Socialism but for a change—and not too great a change. As far as they envisaged anything clearly, they thought of the change they wanted mainly in terms of better social services, including more equal educational opportunities, and of full employment as against a return to the depressed conditions of the 1930s. They did not for the most part think of it at all largely in terms of nationalization of industries—much less of socialization of property—though they were quite prepared to see some industries that had got into a mess taken into public ownership. They certainly did not see it as a sudden uprooting of established ways of life, either for themselves or for others.

That, indeed, was how most of the electors were bound to envisage the situation. Most people are neither Socialists nor anti-Socialists in the sense of having a thought-out view of the social and economic system they want. They have certain wants, for particular things, and certain broad preferences for one sort of society over another. But for most of them the particular wants are much more clearly present, and much more of a driving force, than the vaguer ideals they entertain; and, in a society such as ours, with its long traditions of gradual adaptation as against revolution, most voters vote on the assumption that the Government they vote for will do less than it says it intends to do, even if its declared intentions are not very extensive. Under conditions of universal suffrage, electorates do not vote for revolutions—unless the revolutions have already happened. If, in 1950 or in 1954, the Labour Party had put forward a really challenging election programme, involving a large advance in the direction of Socialism, one thing certain would have been, and would be, the loss of the ensuing General Election by the defection of the marginal voters.

In part, then, the absence of a more Socialist programme is to be attributed to the Labour Party's wish to get back to power—or at least to office. This is a very natural desire, not only because politicians naturally prefer winning to losing, but also because they honestly believe that they have a better case than their opponents. This latter belief is shared by their active supporters, and makes them also eager to win. Accordingly, if a moderate programme offers the best prospect of electoral victory, the odds are very heavily in favour of the party, as well as the politicians, preferring it to anything more drastic. If any of the latter feel qualms about it not being socialistic enough, they can always tell themselves that they must not run too far ahead of popular opinion, and that it will at any rate help to prepare the way for something further reaching later on.

Does the Labour Party Want Socialism?

But is this the whole explanation? I feel sure that it is not. I feel sure that many politicians who are professed Socialists, and not a few of their active supporters, have lost the simple faith in Socialism with which most of them began—and which, up to a point, they still hold to with part of their minds—and have come to entertain doubts whether the attempt to establish Socialism does not involve too great risks for the game to be worth the candle. Quite serious and even cogent reasons can be advanced in support of this doubt. They are very often not openly admitted, but haunt the backs of people's minds and are half-repressed. Let us try to drag some of them into daylight.

More Nationalization?

First—to take one which lies quite near the surface—nationalization, in the form of public management of industries and services, does not look quite so enticing as it did now that we have had some of it and can see how it works out in our society as it is. It is not so easy as it was to contemplate with ecstasy, or even with equanimity, the prospect of all or most of the means of production, etc. being nationalized, if that is to mean their administration by a series of Public Boards on the model of the Coal Board, the Transport Commission, and the BEA (British European Airways). We may, or may not, approve of these bodies; whether or no, it is not very easy to look forward to their extension to cover most branches of production, nor is it easy to see what alternative Socialists have to offer. So we fall to disputing about how much of industry we still need to nationalize after all, in order to infuse *enough* Socialism—if it is Socialism—into the economic system; and, in doing that, we soon find ourselves a long way off the old formula of socialization—or even nationalization—of 'the means of production, distribution and exchange'.

Social Equality?

Secondly—to go a good deal deeper—equality, or even near-equality, does not look quite so simply desirable an objective as it used to do. The Labour Government thought it saw good reasons for paying the administrators and managers it needed for the nationalized enterprises as good salaries as they would have got under private ownership, or as those holding analogous positions in capitalist industry were continuing to get. It also thought there were good reasons for not paying those of its own supporters whom it appointed to such positions less than it paid to persons taken over from capitalist industry. It therefore, on what appeared to be valid grounds, created a new Labour aristocracy of officials in the public service, and in doing so had at any rate some influence in causing such bodies as Trade Unions to increase the salaries of officials who were *not* so transferred. In effect, it sanctioned degrees of inequality of earned incomes which would have horrified the Socialist pioneers. It did this the more easily and with fewer doubts because there was proceeding at the same time so considerable an uplifting of standards at the bottom of the social scale and because so many workers in positions of superior vantage had actually become able to earn good middle-class incomes that it seemed natural for those who were higher in the scale of incomes earned by honest work to move up too. So, no doubt, it was; but that cannot alter the fact that the consequence was to undermine the old belief in a much nearer approach to economic equality, and to make it very much more difficult to launch any attack on middle-class, or even upper middle-class, incomes in general.

More State Power?

Thirdly—and here we come nearest of all to the bone—the experience of one kind of totalitarian rule under Hitler and of another kind of totalitarianism under Stalin unavoidably put into the minds of reasonable persons a fear of placing too much power into the State's hands, even if the State professed to be Socialist. The workings of universal suffrage under totalitarian conditions did not encourage the continuance of the faith that, where 'the people' had the right to vote—all nominally on equal terms and with the secrecy of the ballot guaranteed—democratic government would necessarily follow as a result. Democracy came to be thought of less exclusively in terms of electoral rights and more in terms of personal freedom—of speech and writing and association—and with this went a greater preparedness to take account of the claims of minorities and of groups within the larger society. This reacted on, and interacted with, the new look of nationalized enterprise. It began to be seen that the government of an industry by a National Board could not be simply identified with its government by 'the people', and that there was a real problem of finding out how to control the controllers.

In Great Britain, this fear of putting too much power into the State's hands has hardly come, as yet, to be more than an uneasiness. We are in no present danger of losing our rights of free speech or association, or of passing under the control of a one-party State machine. But we cannot quite avoid asking ourselves whether our present immunity in this respect may not have something to do with the fact that what we have been engaged in setting up has been, not Socialism, but only a partial embodiment, within our limited opportunities, of the Welfare State.

Socialism and the Welfare State

Of course Socialism involves the Welfare State: that is implied in the old slogan 'From each according to his capacities, to each according to his needs'. It has always been one of the essential Socialist objectives to put an end to poverty and to ensure that in the distribution of incomes the children, the aged and the incapacitated are not pushed aside by the predatory or the strong. To the extent of our success in advancing towards this we have been doing what every Socialist must wish to do. But the Welfare State is, all the same, not Socialism: in the form in which we have been attempting to move towards it in recent years it is at most only socialistic—if even that. For what we have been doing is not to put people on an equal footing, but only to lessen the extremes of inequality by redistributing grossly unequal incomes through taxation; and even this redistribution has quite largely taken the form of making the poor pay for one another's basic needs. No doubt, the taxation levied on large incomes has been severe: no doubt, it would have been quite impossible to develop even such social services as we have developed without putting the major part of the cost on the workers and the middle classes, for the simple reason that the total income of the rich, even had it been possible to take it all, would not have been nearly enough. Nevertheless, we need only use the evidence of our senses to assure ourselves that the rich are still among us and that the class structure of our society remains, if not intact, very much in being.

What is Happening to the Class-Structure?

What has happened, stated in the broadest terms, appears to be something like this:

(i) *THE BOTTOM DOGS*

At the bottom of the scale, sheer hunger and malnutrition have been greatly diminished. Nobody need starve: nobody, in the last resort, need go without the absolute minimum needs of life. I know that many old age pensioners are having a raw deal, and that the conditions are still heavily weighted against large families; but it will hardly be denied that, in comparison with 1939 or any earlier date, there has been a great improvement in the position of both these groups, especially when the supplementary payments from the Assistance Board are taken into account. Those who suffer sheer want today for absolute lack of means are fewer by far than they used to be. In spite of this, the 'bottom dogs' remain: there is still a stratum that lives under conditions of want and maladjustment. But this stratum owes its inferior position today less to the lack of social legislation designed to meet general needs than to a failure to devise special means of dealing with special cases. The 'submerged tenth', which is today much less than a tenth, presents a long-run problem which is not so much one of further redistribution through taxation as of devising, by education and training, improved ways of equipping for useful activity those who have something mentally or physically wrong with them, but are not incapable of earning their livings and looking after themselves if we help them to discover how.

(ii) *THE UNSKILLED WORKERS*

At the next level, that of ordinary unskilled labour, the improvement in economic conditions has been immense. This stratum has benefited most by full employment, both in its ability to command a better wage and in the increased regularity of employment. These factors have been much more important for it than the development of the social services, though that of course has counted too—especially sickness benefit and the supplementary help given through the Assistance Board, and also children's allowances, despite their inadequacy. Many of the families belonging to this stratum are, no doubt, still rather bad at spending their money; and many of them are hampered by very bad housing. But there can be no doubt that this is the part of society that is benefiting most from what has been accomplished, and will continue to benefit if full employment holds. We must not, however, forget that it is also the group that would be flung back most disastrously were full employment to disappear—though even so its lot would be better than in the past because of the better social services on which it would be able to fall back, if it can be assumed that these services could and would be maintained intact in face of a slump.

(iii) *THE SEMI-SKILLED WORKERS AND THE WHITE-COLLAR BRIGADE*

At the next higher level, we come to the main body, not of highly skilled workers, but of the semi-skilled in manual jobs and to the corresponding groups of non-manual workers, such as shop assistants and the lower grades in clerical employment. These groups include a rather high proportion of women workers who are not heads of households and are in many cases living in households in which there is also a male earner—a father or a husband. Such earners—men as well as women—have also benefited greatly from full employment, as well as from the growth of the social services. On the other hand, there are in this stratum a good many heads of households, especially those with young families, who have benefited much less because they are in time-working jobs for which wages have risen less than the average. This applies particularly to some of the non-manual groups, and also particularly to those who are engaged in employments that do not produce profits—such as the public services. But side by side with these relatively unfortunate groups there are others, especially piece-workers on repetitive work in flourishing industries, whose earnings have risen by much more than the average; and for such workers the gain has been large. Economically, they have risen to parity, if not beyond parity, with large bodies of skilled manual and non-manual workers who used to have both higher incomes and higher social prestige.

(iv) *THE HIGHLY SKILLED AND THE LESSER PROFESSIONS*

Fourthly, we come to the definitely skilled manual workers and, on a broad level with them, to the higher grades of clerical and distributive workers and to such large bodies of professional workers as draughtsmen, teachers, nurses, and professional auxiliaries of many other kinds. In comparison with most of those in the groups lower down the scale, this stratum has fared rather badly. The manual workers included in it have benefited much more than most of the non-manual workers from full employment, and also more, I think, from the extension of the social services. But wage differentials between skilled and less skilled manual workers have been reduced, except for a smallish minority which has been enabled by special bonuses and allowances, or by high piecework payments, to earn very good money indeed—mainly because certain kinds of highly skilled labour have been seriously scarce, so that employers have gone out of their way to retain its services. These small privileged groups have risen notably in the economic scale, whereas the highly skilled non-manual workers, except those who have been promoted to managerial positions, have lost ground—especially those in non-profit-making salaried employment that allows no scope for extra earnings. On the whole, skilled manual workers have gained more than salaried employees; and among skilled manual workers there has appeared an increasing differentiation between those who have been able to secure special treatment and those who have found the margin of difference between their wages and those of the less skilled considerably reduced. But even the manual groups to which this last condition applies have in many cases reaped great gains through full employment.

(v) *THE LESSER BOURGEOIS CLASSES*

Partly on a parity with the fourth stratum, partly rising above it, and partly below it comes the large mass of shopkeepers and independent jobbing small masters in such trades as building repairs and decoration. About these it is difficult to generalize. Many small traders complain of cut margins; but I think it is undoubted that in general their position has been improved by quicker and more assured turnover resulting from full employment and from scarcities of goods, which have reduced dead and idle stocks. Some traders have undoubtedly done remarkably well—even apart from the smallish minority of black marketeers, who have had the time of their lives. The independent jobbers have also done well in most cases, because of full employment. In general, the relative social and economic position of these groups has not greatly changed: if anything they have done better than the average—certainly better than the salaried minor professionals or the less fortunate groups among the skilled manual workers.

(vi) *THE HIGHER PROFESSIONS AND THE MANAGERS*

This brings us to the higher professional groups, including the higher ranges of the public services and of teaching and academic research, the doctors, dentists, and other medical groups of comparable status, the practising barristers and solicitors, the middle ranges of business management, including the higher technicians, and the owners of businesses having a comparable status. The net incomes of all these groups have of course been considerably cut into by high taxation; but the gross incomes on which these taxes fall have moved very differently for different groups within this broad stratum of society—the part of the upper middle class which works for its living and gets its payment in salaries or in professional fees. Here again, the fixed salary earners in occupations which do not result in profits have fared worst—except the medical groups, which have done remarkably well for themselves by effective and obstinate bargaining. The managerial grades have, on the whole, done better than the professionals, at any rate in the more flourishing industries under private ownership: elsewhere, they have not done so well, but a good deal better than most of the *salaried* professionals. Owners of smallish or middle-sized businesses have mostly flourished, because full employment and shortage of capital for investment in displacing obsolete plant have made profits easy to earn—though they are now in many trades less easy than they were a few years ago. As long as new capital goods remain scarce and demand high, profits will remain high too; and small businesses as well as large will reap the benefit of an unexpectedly long life for their plant.

(vii) *THE TOP GRADES*

At the highest level among earned incomes we come to those of the topmost managers and administrators; and these are not only the best placed for supplementing their incomes by means of expense allowances but also the most likely to be able to eke them out with capital gains. Only a thin line separates them from the big entrepreneurs who draw not salaries but dividends as their main source of income. Whoever has suffered as a consequence of high taxation, they among the wealthier groups have suffered least; and they have been reinforced by the highly paid chief executives of nationalized industries, whose rewards help to cast a halo round theirs.

(viii) *THE FARMERS*

There remains one group that calls for separate mention, not as the highest, but as ranking undoubtedly among those which have most improved their position. Farmers, large and small alike, have had a big lift as a result of the measures adopted to increase the home output of food. They are in fine feather, whether they have been 'feather-bedded' or not.

Summarizing these broad generalizations, we can safely say that most 'bottom dogs', most unskilled workers, some semi-skilled workers, a minority of skilled workers, most shopkeepers and jobbing builders, most doctors and dentists, most of the higher business executives, most private employers, and nearly all farmers are both absolutely and relatively a good deal better off than they or their predecessors were before 1939; that some semi-skilled and most skilled manual workers, most blackcoats in clerical and distributive jobs and in public employments, and most professional workers in non-profit making occupations are at any rate relatively worse-off; and that it is impossible to generalize about the middle grades of managerial and technical employees. This makes up a general picture of income redistribution, as a consequence of full employment and taxation combined, embodying highly significant changes, but certainly not anything that can be regarded as carrying us far in the direction of a Socialist society. The picture needs of course to be completed by bringing in those social groups which depend on unearned incomes. To these we can now turn.

(ix) *THE SMALL AND MIDDLE INVESTORS*

The small investors, who hold a high proportion of fixed interest securities and preference shares, have definitely lost ground. This affects particularly retired persons, including those living on pensions and insurances. It affects also the non-employed members of rich families, and also those who derive middle-class incomes partly from work and partly from property. Indeed, those in this group who depend on fixed salaries *plus* small investments have been hit in both capacities. In general, the sections of the middle classes who do not work for a living have lost a great deal of ground. Landlords of small house-property have been badly affected by rent controls, though some of them have profited by the continued occupation of dwellings that ought to have been pulled down long ago, had it been practicable to replace them.

(x) *THE BIG CAPITAL-OWNERS*

The bigger investors, most of whom are in a better position to go in search of capital gains through speculation or change of investments, and who tend to hold more ordinary shares than bonds or preference shares, have fared much better; and those of them who own urban land and non-residential buildings (or premises not subject to rent control) have also done well. Agricultural landlords, where they have been in a position to revise rents, have been able to skim off a share in the farmers' gains.

These conclusions about what has been happening to unearned incomes are not very comforting from the standpoint of those who would like to believe that we have been advancing towards Socialism by easy, equitable stages. They may not be prepared to spend much sympathy on the declining sections of the *rentier* middle class; but it is hardly socialistic to weight the scales in favour of the richer capitalist as against the poorer.

Achievements of the Welfare State

The gains achieved through full employment and the Welfare State are beyond doubt considerable in terms of the reduction in the amount of sheer suffering and enfeeblement of human quality by privation. So far, they are a great good. They depend, however, at least as much on full employment as on the expansion of the social services, and are precarious to the extent to which there is a danger of severe unemployment coming back. Moreover, these gains have been secured at the expense of a narrowing of the differentials awarded for most, though not for all, kinds of superior manual skill, and *may* be reacting on the future supply of skilled workers by making it less worthwhile to learn a skilled trade. The supply of new recruits for the non-manual occupations which have declined in relative earning capacity is for the most part less likely to be affected because our educational system has a strong bias in favour of such occupations and because some of them are more attractive in themselves, and may still carry higher prestige, than better-paid manual jobs.

Are We Advancing towards a Classless Society?

What does all this indicate in respect of the class-structure of the society towards which we have been moving? Certainly not that we are advancing towards a classless society. Except at the very bottom of the scale—the numbers in which have been reduced—there has been a diminution of economic and social inequality between skilled and less skilled manual workers, and between manual workers and 'black coats'. But there is also a tendency for a new grade, or even class, of highly paid super-skilled manual workers to develop and to increase its distance from the main body. These are not Stakhanovites; for many of them are time-workers or setters-up rather than operators of machines, and even where they are piece-workers their exploits are not announced in the newspapers or rewarded with public decorations. But they constitute a new and growing labour aristocracy, with money to burn because they are only now adjusting their living standards to their increased earnings. They are still, however, in this country only a small group, not at all comparable with the much bigger labour aristocracy that has grown up in the United States. Nor is there at present any sign of a wish on their part to dissociate themselves as a group from the groups lower down in the economic hierarchy.

More widespread for the present is the economic assimilation between the large body of fairly skilled, but not super-skilled, manual workers and the main body of 'black coats': so that these too are being merged economically and to a considerable extent socially as well into a single stratum. A step above them socially, and sometimes but not always economically, the lesser professional groups and the general run of technicians constitute, together with the middling tradesmen, an intermediate stratum—a *petite bourgeoisie* which, far from dying out, is more than holding its own in relative numbers. With it go a large part of the farmers and many small employers, such as garage keepers, jobbing builders, wireless dealers, and electrical contractors: so that this stratum includes groups of widely divergent fortunes and interests. It is linked on the one hand to the major professions and on the other to the group of middling profit-makers and industrial executives. A part of it has been losing, and a part gaining ground: it has no common social outlook or political allegiance, though the greater proportion tends to be politically Conservative, with some tendency to swing over when things go badly wrong.

The Rich Remain

Above all these strata the rich remain. But they have considerably changed their composition. Riches and aristocracy still go together in the case of a limited group of old families which have large holdings of urban or industrial land or have used the accumulations of the past from land to become great investors in business. To these must be added the aristocracy of banking and commerce which has bought or married its way into the 'upper classes' in the traditional sense of the term. But side by side with these, and as rich or richer, are those who have made great fortunes in business too recently to be counted among the 'idle rich'; and this group of new wealth, including now many high-level business administrators who draw large salaries and have risen by personal exertions from the middle or lower grades, forms a larger proportion than ever before of those who can afford to live at a luxury level and to hobnob, without much feeling of inferiority, with their American opposite numbers.

Is the Welfare State a Step towards Socialism?

Such a society as this is definitely not Socialist; and I cannot feel that it is even on the way to becoming Socialist. It is, of course, much less aristocratic than the society it is displacing: in terms of social origins the top classes of today are a very mixed lot. Oxford and Cambridge are no longer gentlemen's preserves to anything like the same extent as they used to be; a much lower proportion of top Civil Servants and of the successful members of the higher professions come from a small group of gentlemen's schools; and on the boards of directors of the great business concerns there are to be found a large number of self-made men who have risen, if not from the ranks, at all events from quite low beginnings. Our society has become a good deal more open than it used to be, in the sense that the old distinction between 'gentlemen' and 'not gentlemen' has largely broken down. A 'player' can not only captain England, or his county, at cricket: he can also captain the Nuffield Organization or Unilever—or, of course, the BEA. But on the whole the new recruits to both grammar schools and universities tend to come much more from the poorer sections of the middle classes than from the families of manual workers—and to come hardly at all from the less skilled sections of the manual working class. No doubt, some children of manual workers get their higher education rather through technical schools and colleges than through grammar schools and universities; and account has to be taken of this in estimating the effects of educational development on the class structure. But in this case too the children of the unskilled workers are largely left out.

What we are getting in practice appears to be a society in which the field of recruitment for the superior positions is being considerably widened, so as to give those who can get as far as the higher ranges of grammar or technical education an improved chance of rising further even if their parents cannot afford to help them. But at the same time we are putting an increasingly difficult barrier between those who do get so far and those who do not; and this is still in the main a class barrier, though it has been moved further down the social scale. Moreover, among those who surmount this barrier only a small proportion can actually move up to positions of affluence and power; and those who do achieve this become assimilated to the new mixed upper class, take over its ways and spending habits, and with it constitute a new oligarchy of high executives which falls heir to the old gentlemanly prerogative of ordering its inferiors about.

If this is a correct picture, the question that arises is whether a society of this sort is on the road to Socialism. The question is whether it does not, as a hard matter of fact, offer the prospect of even greater resistance to Socialism than the society it has displaced. In other words, is the Welfare State, in the form in which it has been developed so far, a step on the road to Socialism, or a step in quite different direction—that is, a step, not towards a classless society, but rather towards a new stratification that is likely to persist and to become more marked?

The situation outlined in the preceding paragraph is of course only a new version of a very old dilemma. In France the peasants, when they had got the land and destroyed the old feudal privileges, turned promptly into a conservative class and became a bulwark against Socialism. They might easily have done the same in Russia had not the Bolsheviks first stamped hard on the kulaks and then collectivized the villages. In our society, the opening of higher education to wider class groups (but by no means to all, regardless of class), combined with full employment and greater social security, may well be creating barriers in the way of Socialism rather than helping its advance, especially if a child's whole chance of rising to the higher social and economic levels is to depend on the results of a single test, applied at an age when the nature of the home environment is bound to be of great influence in determining these results. This kind of test looks like leading to a new class structure which will on the one hand cut the working class into two—those with a chance of rising further and those without—and will on the other animate the upper of these two segments with a desire to protect itself against the lower, and also permeate it with a belief in the virtue of personal advancement and in the values of an acquisitive society. In short, is it towards Socialism we are tending, or towards an anglicized version of the American conception of democracy? Is our goal the classless society, or only the so-called open society which is in fact still closed to a majority of the people?

The Future

What will happen to our society will evidently depend on the conditions to which it has to adapt its ways of life and on its responses to these conditions.

The days are over when Great Britain's position in the world was so commanding that other peoples had to adapt their ways to ours, and the internal trends of British development furnished, broadly speaking, a sufficient basis for predicting the future, at any rate for some distance ahead. As things now are, we cannot rely, as a nation, on getting nationally better off as we improve our productive techniques, no matter what may be the impact on us of external forces. We are caught up in a world economic process in which we are no longer the leaders, but only one people among many—and by no means the most powerful.

The Economic Outlook—First Hypothesis

Obviously one great determinant of our social future will be what happens to employment and to the national income. The real national income of Great Britain, as matters now stand, depends mainly on three factors—the productivity of British industry and agriculture, the readiness of other countries to receive British exports, and the terms of trade—that is, the rates of exchange between exported and imported goods. I do not include the level of employment as a fourth determinant, because it is mainly, though not exclusively, determined by the other three. Full employment could no doubt be undermined by ill-considered financial policies even if the other factors were all favourable; but this is rather unlikely to happen, though it could happen if the British Government were foolish enough to yield to American pressure for convertibility of sterling into dollars. Leaving that danger aside, the three factors I have mentioned are the main ones. They are, of course, to some extent interdependent. The more productive our industries are, the better will be our chances of selling our exports over whatever barriers may be set up against them and the less favourable will be the terms of trade we shall need. The fewer barriers we meet with against our exports, the more we shall be able to take advantage of the economies of large-scale production, and the better we shall be able to afford to have the terms of trade turned against us. The more favourable the terms of trade are, the less we shall be hampered by the need to restrict imports in ways that damage production and the less will be the real cost of the imported materials which constitute a substantial fraction of the value of the goods we export. On the other hand, favourable terms of trade for us mean unfavourable terms for those of our customers from whom we import, and thus reduce their purchasing power.

If all these factors act favourably, there is no reason why our real material income should not increase in future at an average rate as high as that of the post-war years, or why we should experience any difficulty in maintaining full employment. If that happens, the existing trends are likely to continue unless we deliberately take action to alter them. We shall be able to carry through fairly rapidly those further developments of the Welfare State—for example, in the field of education—to which we are already committed, and also to rectify the grievances of such groups as old age pensioners by improving social service benefits. Real wages will be able to rise, even if but slowly. Profits will remain high, and perhaps go still higher; and investment will be able to increase including something for overseas investment, especially in Commonwealth countries. But all this, which rests on the most favourable hypothesis that can possibly be entertained, will not of itself bring us an inch nearer Socialism, and may even carry us away from it by strengthening the tendencies towards class differentiation on the new basis and making a majority of the electorate prefer going on as they are to embarking on any risky adventures, in social and economic change.

Second Hypothesis

Having taken the most favourable hypothesis, let us now take the least. If productivity stagnates, if foreign markets are obstructed by fresh barriers or reduced by unwillingness or inability to buy, and if the terms of trade turn against us, it will become impossible to maintain full employment and necessary to reduce real wages and possibly social service benefits in order to cut down consumption of imported foodstuffs and materials to what we can afford to buy with our restricted exports. Such a situation, highly unfavourable though it would be to Trade Union bargaining, would almost certainly benefit Labour politically—unless the Labour Party had the misfortune to be already in office when it set in. It would engender mass discontent, not only among the workers but also in the middle groups, and might clear the way for a considerable move towards Socialism if the Labour Party were minded and prepared to attempt such a move.

The economic catastrophe envisaged in the preceding paragraph is, however, unlikely to occur in any such complete form. If foreign markets for our exports were seriously reduced by a world slump, the effect would almost certainly be to turn the terms of trade for what exports were left in our favour and not against us. Even so, the situation would be difficult enough, and the maintenance of full employment would hardly be possible. With fewer jobs than workers looking for them, the bargaining power of the Trade Unions would be weakened, especially for the workers in the export trades and for the less skilled workers in general. Real wages would slip back: the cost of the social services would rise sharply; and we should soon feel how inadequate a protection they give when the buttress of full employment is removed. The effect of such a situation, though less drastically than in the more pessimistic hypothesis of the preceding paragraph, would be a growth of social discontent which would create a stronger *working-class* demand for a more socialistic programme, but might fail to swing the intermediate groups, or enough of them, over to supporting it. In that event, we might easily get a Labour Government more like that of 1929 than that of 1945, impotently plastering the distress, but quite unable to make up its mind to attempt a drastic cure, or perhaps failing to carry a majority of the electors with it even if it did make the attempt.

Remedies: The Abolition of Large Inherited Fortunes

This is a depressing view; but what else can we fairly expect? Hardly anybody is at present seriously trying to make converts for Socialism, or for anything more than further advances, as occasion allows, towards the Welfare State. Indeed, no one has even attempted to think out how Socialism can be compatible with the tendencies which the Welfare State accentuates and promotes, though clearly it must be made compatible with those tendencies if we are to progress towards it via increasing instalments of social welfare.

The first question that arises here is that of the extent to which Socialism is to be regarded as compatible with economic inequality in its various forms. I think it is clearly incompatible with any social system that allows great fortunes, or even moderate fortunes *that have been inherited once,* to be transmitted at death. I see no reason why it should be regarded as inadmissible for a person to pass on to his wife or children, or perhaps to other near relatives, moderate sums which he has accumulated by saving in his own lifetime, or of course to transmit in moderation personal possessions which are not of a capital kind; and I see every reason why it should remain possible for security of tenure, subject to good use and payment of rent, to be granted to the families of farmers or householders from one generation to the next. But beyond these reasonable limits I think Socialists are bound to stand for doing away with inheritance, because *they cannot recognize any able-bodied person's right to live in idleness on the labour of others or to claim on account of inherited wealth a much bigger income than he can earn by his own exertions.* Accordingly I believe that not merely higher death duties but positive abolition of the right of inheritance beyond fairly modest limits should take a high place among Labour's next steps towards its declared Socialist objective. The transition could, if it were thought fit, be eased by allowing limited additional annuities to be paid for a single further life; but beyond the permitted sums generally applicable, the capital should pass to the public, subject to such transitional charges as might be allowed.

This is, of course, a very longstanding Socialist demand. It goes back to the followers of Saint-Simon in the 1820s, if not even further; and those Socialists who have not explicitly made it have passed it over only because they have merged it in wider demands for the complete expropriation of the sources of unearned income. In a social revolution such expropriation may be possible;

but for us, who are seeking a way of advance towards Socialism by constitutional methods, it is clearly out of the question. Piecemeal nationalization involves compensation, and does not solve the problem of eliminating the claims of ownership. In such a situation, these claims can be dealt with only in two ways—by levies on the capital assets of the living, or by narrowing the right to acquire wealth by inheritance. I am not ruling out the first of these methods, especially if the second proves to be too slow; but surely the second is the better, because it involves much less dislocation of established expectations and fits in best with the widespread feeling that, as far as possible, the members of each new generation should start fair, without preventible handicaps or advantages. No doubt, in the minds of many people, there is also a sentiment that a parent ought to be allowed to provide for his widow and his children; and in our class-divided, unequal society this sentiment is natural enough. Let us then concede to it, as long as serious economic inequalities remain in being, the testator's right to leave to his widow or children his house or farm, up to a maximum value, or an equivalent capital sum, but beyond that, not property, but only annuities equivalent to a proportion of what he is worth at death. Under this arrangement all property above the permitted maximum would become at once public property, and the annual charge upon it would be wiped out at the close of a single further life.

A New Way of Socialization

Such taxation of inheritance would, of course, mean that the State would have to be prepared to take over the actual property of those dying with considerable fortunes and not money payments supposed to represent their value. For it would create a situation in which there would be far too few buyers for the estates passing at death to be sold to new private owners. It would therefore mean that the Government would be continually acquiring ownership both of shares and bonds of all sorts and of other forms of property, such as houses, landed estates, and private businesses. Nationalization, or rather Socialization, would thus advance by a new route, even if no further industries were taken over by the methods hitherto adopted. The State would become, to an ever-increasing extent, part proprietor of a host of productive businesses, and the holder of mortgage charges on many estates and non-company businesses remaining in private hands. It could use the powers it would thus acquire to appoint its own directors to joint stock enterprises and to foreclose on concerns which failed to meet their obligations. For a time, it would find itself the partner of profit-making business men, and engaging in profit-making enterprises. But I can see no valid objection to this, if it is merely a stage in the process of acquiring total, or majority, ownership of the businesses in question; and I can see the positive advantage that it would not involve the creation of more top-heavy centralized administrations of the type of the Coal Board and the Transport Commission. Of course it would be necessary for the directors whom the Government would appoint to such businesses, not only to play an active part in their operation in the public interest, but also to work together, through some sort of collective body including all the state directors within an industry, and to follow a collective policy laid down by the Government's planning agencies. It would be necessary to train men specially for these tasks, in order to ensure well informed intervention in the affairs of the businesses concerned; and *the long-run effect would be to establish socialized production over a wide field without setting up giant organizations in forms of enterprise better suited to relatively small-scale, and within limits competitive, operation.*

The Problem of Large Earned Incomes

The restriction of inheritance would of itself do nothing to lessen inequalities of earned income, though it would do a good deal towards levelling those who receive large incomes partly from work as managers or members of the higher professions and partly from ownership of property. In the main, excessive disparities of earned incomes would have to be tackled by other methods. *As the Government now meets a large part of the cost of higher education and professional training, it is no longer reasonable for the incomes of those who have received this help to be calculated at rates meant to pay back the expenses of their professional preparation.* Nor should there be any need to pay in business occupations the very large salaries which are based largely on a comparison with what is received by capitalist employers in the form of profit. It is, however, much easier to state the case for bringing down the higher earned incomes to a reasonable level than to find effective methods of setting about it. One thing that could be done would be to impose much stricter control on the granting of expense allowances, or even to abolish them altogether save in very exceptional cases. What more will be needed, will depend partly on what happens to the cost of living. If this continues to move gradually upward, the desired result can be secured by a simple refusal to allow the higher salaries to be increased as prices rise, and at the same time by using the influence of public directors to prevent excessive payments in directors' fees and emoluments. If, however, the cost of living falls or remains stationary, stronger measures will be called for; but these can be held over for the time being, in order to see how prices go, on condition that steps are taken to prevent further rises being given to those who are already getting too much.

As for the middle incomes, no special action seems to be called for, except a steady policy of reducing trading margins so as to squeeze out the inefficient as fast as they can be replaced by more efficient producing or trading firms— which should become fully practicable if the level of new investment is made high enough to keep pace with technical progress.

Wage Problems

Wage incomes and the lower ranges of salary incomes raise more complex problems. It is fully consistent with Socialist principles to allow whatever differentials turn out to be needed to procure adequate recruitment for the more skilled kinds of work, and also to offer whatever piecework or similar incentives turn out to be necessary in order to secure high output. Nobody, however, can believe that the existing wage structure complies with these requirements, or is anything other than a confusion due partly to the varying fortunes of the tug-of-war between employers and Trade Unions and partly to sheer accident or tradition. In a Socialist society, it will clearly not be possible to continue to allow wage rates to be settled by a large number of uncoordinated bargains, influenced largely by the degree of shelter or exposure of particular industries to outside competition, or to the expansion or contraction in the demand for their products. There will have to be both some general way of determining how large an aggregate of wage-payments the economy is able to afford, and, broadly, how what is deemed to be available shall be divided among the various claimants. It would be premature today, while non-wage incomes remain uncontrolled and while the greater part of industry is still under capitalist operation for profit, to introduce any national wages policy under which a body of highly placed officials would have the right to fix wages as they might think fit. But, as we advance further towards a Socialist society, the planning of wages will become indispensable, if only because wages and prices are inevitably linked together and it will be as a rule a matter of choosing between higher wages and higher prices, with the balance of advantage shifting in favour of lower prices as the toll levied by unproductive consumers is reduced by the erosion of incomes derived from ownership.

Towards Social Equality

Class structure is a matter, not only of incomes, but also of culture and of social prestige. I regard it as a great calamity that Labour Governments have allowed themselves to fall into the evil habit of conferring titles both on persons who are barely distinguishable from those ennobled by their political opponents and—worse still—on persons who are supposed to share with them in the Socialist faith. In the case of peerages, this practice is defended on the ground that, as long as the House of Lords exists as a legislative chamber, Labour has to be represented in it; but no such excuse can be put forward for the growing practice of authorizing Trade Union and Co-operative leaders to stick 'Sir' in front of their names. As for peerages, surely the correct course is to abolish the House of Lords at the earliest possible moment, and in the meantime, to make do with those who have been ennobled already to assist it in winding up its affairs. I cannot help saying that it fills me with sheer disgust to see Labour leaders accepting titles for no conceivable purpose except that of denying their alleged faith in social equality—I mean those who become 'Sirs', or join the peerage without being specially needed to represent the Government in the Upper Chamber. *I cannot conceive how any Socialist can defend this kind of social snobbery, which does immense harm to the Socialist cause by compromising the Labour Party with the unclean thing and spreading cynicism about the sincerity and disinterestedness of those who lead it.*

In the educational field, Labour is to be congratulated on the good fight it is putting up in many places for the Comprehensive School; for educational equality is a vital part of social equality, and as long as we allow snob schools to continue we shall have a steady stream of snobs coming out of them. Parity of esteem is impossible between schools most of whose pupils leave at fifteen and schools where most stay up to eighteen and a substantial proportion then go on to College or University. It is even impossible between the Modern School and those Grammar Schools many of whose pupils leave at sixteen or at most seventeen. There used to be an undeniable case for parents who objected to sending their children to schools where they would not only get an inferior education, but also pick up bad manners and ways of speech, and perhaps diseases too, from the children of the slums. But that case has largely disappeared, thanks to the great improvement in the economic condition of the less skilled workers. A residue is left, but must be dealt with by special measures and not by perpetuating the 'two nations' policy of nineteenth-century schooling. Of course, in order to make the Comprehensive School workable as a general practice, we shall have to improve the quality of teaching, as well as to do a great deal of new building and equipment. These things will take time: there is no danger whatsoever of our going ahead with them too fast. They must be given a high priority because, even so, they are bound to take so long in the doing.

We must, however, be careful to ensure both that our Comprehensive Schools do not keep back the quicker and cleverer children—whose brains and skill our society needs—and that we get in them a proper attention to the training of manual as well as intellectual capacities. I do not mean only technical education designed to prepare pupils for particular occupations, even in a broad way. I mean also that everybody—boys and girls alike—ought to come out of school with a reasonable capability for doing ordinary manual jobs about the house and garden and with an adequate acquaintance with the household arts; and I mean too that there ought to be the fullest opportunity for each individual to follow his particular bent in the use of his hands as well as in more literary or cultural pursuits. We have suffered badly in Great Britain from an unnatural divorce between literary and technical education, not only at the higher levels but at the elementary levels as well. In order to correct this, we need in every type of school teachers who know how to use both their heads and their hands and can teach their pupils to do things as well as to learn about them in the abstract. A society of social equals, as distinct from one of masters aided by servants to do the dirty work, needs an all-round training in the art of looking after itself, without calling in a professional 'workman' to do simple repairs or just letting things go to ruin for lack of aptitude for putting them right.

The Supply of Ability

Some people say that a more equal society is impossible, or will lead to disaster, because there are too few able persons to run it. They argue, for example, that the increased numbers in higher education have already involved a fall in average quality. I believe this to be nonsense: I do not profess to know whether the supply of real first-raters can be greatly increased by improving our educational system; but I feel no doubt that the supply of good second-raters can be, and that more good second-raters are what we chiefly need to do the jobs which the advance towards a fair deal for everybody will require us to fill. No doubt, it would be nice to double our supply of first-raters; but a limited number can go a long way if they have good seconds-in-command at call.

The Ageing and the Handicapped

This educational side of Socialist policy is becoming more and more important now that we are already well on the way towards solving the purely economic part of the problem of the 'bottom dogs'. Hardly less important are two other problems which we are much less near to solving—that of the residue of physically or mentally handicapped persons, and that of the increasing average age of the population. Slowly, we are learning that, given the right methods, a great deal can be done to retrieve the mentally handicapped and enable them to take a useful place in society; and to help the physically handicapped to overcome their disabilities; but we have still a long way to go in these matters, which are of vital importance in the making of a society bent on diminishing social inequalities to the fullest possible extent. The other matter is that of adapting our economic arrangements so as to make it easy for old people who can no longer do a full week's work at the occupations in which they have been engaged either to continue in part-time employment or to find openings for alternative work within their capacities and desires. This problem is of the same order as that of making better provision for the rehabilitation of the partially disabled and for their employment as far as possible on a self-supporting basis. These matters are all important not only because an ageing society cannot afford not to make full use of every person capable of doing a useful job, but also because work, for those who are capable of it, affords much better prospects of happy living than enforced idleness and enables the aged and the handicapped to play a much more equal role in the life of the community.

I should like to see the Labour Party taking up this group of problems and giving it a high place in its programme. It is not a simple matter of welfare legislation: it involves ensuring that industry shall be so organized as to make room for the work of the groups concerned and to devise special arrangements for them, wherever these are needed, in ways that will isolate them as little as possible from other workers, and will emphasize their capacities rather than their disabilities. What is needed is to put as many as possible of them into employment, not in segregated groups, but as the colleagues of ordinary workers; and this involves making arrangements with the Trade Unions as well as compelling employers to provide the necessary openings. Above all, it involves doing all that can be done to help the partially disabled and the ageing to develop and maintain their productive capacities at the highest practicable level.

Industrial Democracy

I come now to the major problem of industrial democracy. Given full employment, Trade Unions are in a powerful bargaining position, because employers cannot afford to lose the services of even moderately efficient workers. *Full employment has been chiefly responsible for the great changes that have come about in factory relations and in industrial discipline as a whole.* The foreman can no longer play the tyrant as easily as he could in the past; and the higher management has to mind its P's and Q's when Trade Union susceptibilities are in question. In some industries, including those which have been nationalized, there have been considerable developments of joint consultation in the workplaces as well as at higher levels; and Trade Union bargaining has spread to many trades in which it was previously almost non-existent. So far, so good; but *neither Trade Union bargaining nor joint consultation makes the worker a responsible partner in industry,* or necessarily gives the individual a sense that it is up to him to render of his best and to think of himself as a member of a team co-operating in the performance of an essentially social task. He cannot, indeed, be expected to have this sense of responsibility where businesses are still being carried on for the profit of absentee shareholders, or where the management still behaves as a caste of superiors issuing orders to inferiors to whom it recognizes no democratic responsibility. Exceptionally, a few managers or employers do contrive, by virtue of sheer personality, to establish really friendly and co-operative relationships; but most managements are incapable of achieving this and will continue to be so as long as they represent a business structure in the control of which the workers have no share. This applies even to the nationalized industries, in which the controlling boards are far too remote from the actual workers to give them any sense of participation—and would remain so even if the Trade Unions were allowed to appoint members to sit on them in a formally representative capacity.

In the past, in a society explicitly based on inequality, it was for the workers to obey orders and for the representatives of their 'masters' to give them. Obedience was enforced partly by custom, partly by inducements such as higher earnings for greater efforts, and partly—and to no small extent—by fear of the sack or of being 'stood off' for offending the authorities, or in extreme cases of being blacklisted as well as sacked. Nowadays, these fears have become much less potent, though they still exist. Piecework incentives and other monetary inducements still retain their power, but have been to some extent weakened by the introduction of guaranteed minimum rates and by the diminished danger of getting dismissed for not producing enough. The greatest change of all, however, has been in the lessened prestige of those who give the orders and the sense of increased power to question them among those to whom they are given. The consequence is a relaxation of discipline which is bound, for the time being, to react adversely on output. This is partly to the good, where it prevents slave-driving or feverish self-driving under the influence of fear; but it is also to the bad, where it conduces to irresponsibility or to a refusal to co-operate in team work. I am not suggesting that, in most industries, average output has fallen; on the contrary, it has been going up despite a small reduction in average hours of work. But the increases have been due mainly, if not entirely, to greater mechanization and improved working arrangements rather than to higher effort or better co-operation.

If we mean to constitute a really democratic society, permeated by the spirit of social equality, we shall have to find ways of replacing the old incentives of fear and habit with new inducements more consistent with the recognition of equal human rights. In large enterprises I do not think this can be done as long as they continue to be conducted for private profit: in small ones it *sometimes* can, where the human relations are good. Social ownership will not of itself put matters right, as the experience both of the nationalized industries and of Co-operative employment abundantly shows. *Social ownership is only half the battle: the other half is real participation by the workers in control—not only at the top, but at every level from the work-group upwards.* By participation I do not mean merely consultation: I mean *real control.* This is necessary, not only for the sake of its effects in making the workers more conscious of their responsibility for high productivity, on which the standard of living must depend, but also because it is impossible to have a really democratic society if most of the members have to spend most of their lives at work under essentially undemocratic conditions. What a man is at his work he will tend to be also in his pleasure and in his activities as a citizen. Industrial democracy is therefore an indispensable part of social democracy—that is, of Socialism.

Productivity and the Standard of Living

That the possibility of maintaining a satisfactory standard of living and adequate social services to protect the individual against the contingencies of life depends on high output should be self-evident; for even an absolutely equal distribution of incomes, after making due allowance for the portion of the current product that must be set aside for replacing worn-out capital goods and for new investment, would have only a small effect on the standard of living of the majority of households.[2] In the past, it was possible for social reformers to advocate that social services should be financed by taxes on the wealthy and higher wages paid, at least in part, at the expense of profits. Today, in view of what has been already accomplished, what can still be done in these ways is narrowly limited; for though profits are high a large part of them is not available for consumption but is needed for investment in capital goods in order to keep our industries efficient and responsive to changing demands. It does not of course follow that the sums needed for this purpose should be allowed to be appropriated by private persons merely because they own the assets of the businesses by which these profits are made. Indeed, as socialization of business assets proceeds, this form of appropriation will progressively disappear. But public ownership of such profits will not render them available for consumption when they are needed for investment; and for as far ahead as we can see the need for investment is likely to remain high, both because we have big arrears to overtake and because the pace of technical change is likely to continue to be rapid.

Improved standards of living must therefore come mainly out of higher production. Indeed, unless we keep up a high rate of investment we shall not be able to maintain even the standards of living we possess now; for in face of intensified competition in the international market in which we have to sell our exports and buy our imports we shall need at the least to keep pace with the rise of productivity in the countries which are our chief competitors—notably Germany, Japan, and the United States. Great Britain has lost the favoured position in the world market that it used to enjoy when, aided by cheap and abundant supplies of coal—which was then the key material—it profited by being first in the field in the Industrial Revolution and was able to stimulate demand for its export both by its imperial position and by having a large surplus of capital for investment overseas. Nowadays, competition in efficiency takes place on more equal terms between the leading countries; and the ability to supply capital for overseas has passed mainly to the United States—for a country can in effect export capital only if there remains a surplus

2   By equal distribution I here mean of course equal as between adults, with smaller allocations for juvenile earners and with proper dependents' allowances for children and young persons not at work.

on its balance of payments after paying for imports and such other current charges as it has to meet.

Great Britain, therefore, has to depend on increasing productivity for improving, and even for maintaining, present standards of living. This means that the working classes can no longer afford to regard high productivity and low costs of production as exclusively the employers' business, and their own role as simply that of extracting as high wages and as good conditions as they can from their employers, and of demanding, by political action, improved social services to be financed mainly by taxing the rich. It is to their own interest—indeed, it is of vital importance to them as a class—that the national product shall be as large as possible. This means both that they need to use their political power to insist on proper organization and planning of industry, and also that they need to use their industrial power to bring about better organization of productive processes and factory relations, so as to eliminate the inefficiencies that necessarily arise when managements and workers are pulling in opposite directions.

Responsibility and the Worker

This brings us back to the question how far it is psychologically possible or socially desirable for the workers and their organizations to accept any sort of responsibility for the efficiency of profit-making industry. Psychologically, any such notion encounters very strong resistance, both rational and irrational. 'Why should I work harder, or produce more', says the Socialist workman, 'in order to swell my capitalist employers' profits?' That is the rational objection; and with it, over a much wider field, goes the non-rational resistance to a change of traditional attitudes which rest on the long experience of exploitation to which the workers as a class have been subjected. Socially, too, there are powerful arguments against collaboration, because it is liable not only to destroy the fighting spirit of the Trade Unions but also to break up class solidarity and put in its place a loyalty to the particular firm which unscrupulous employers can use as a means of undermining Trade Union influence.

The Conditions of Responsibility

These arguments are so strong as to be conclusive against collaboration, save under certain indispensable conditions. The workers as a class cannot properly be invited to collaborate on any terms which envisage an indefinite continuance of the toll levied on their labour by profit-making employers or shareholders, or the continued private appropriation of that part of their product which is needed to finance new investment. They need to be assured that the toll levied on labour by the claims of ownership will be brought to an end as speedily as possible and that immediately a beginning will be made with the transfer of profits needed for investment to public ownership.

We have seen already how, by means of the abolition of large inheritances, the ownership of existing capital assets could be transferred to the public by stages not too prolonged. Side by side with this gradual transfer, the State could begin at once to assume public ownership of that part of profits—or of a part of the part—that is needed for new investment. This could be done by (a) *statutory limitation of dividends*—that is, of the part of profits that can be paid out to shareholders as incomes; (b) *statutory allocation of a share in profits to a capital fund which would become at once public property* and, if invested in the business, would carry shareholding rights to be exercised by public nominees. The public would thus acquire holdings of capital in what are now private enterprises by a double process—through the lapsing of shares to it at the owners' deaths and through the new shares to be created out of profits placed to reserve. By rapid stages private ownership of joint stock enterprises would be extinguished: they would become public property, and the State would be free to make what arrangements it might think best for their future conduct. It could, for example, sell or lease some of them to the Consumers' Co-operative Movement, convert others into Producers' Co-operative Societies, and arrange for others to continue as publicly-owned joint-stock companies. It could amalgamate businesses into larger concerns where this seemed likely to increase efficiency; but it would be under no necessity to set up huge organizations except where the technical conditions required them. *The outcome would be a highly varied and flexible system of socialized ownership and control, which would not preclude leaving as many small enterprises as might be considered desirable to continue under private ownership and control, subject to due provisions to ensure good working conditions and compliance with planning requirements.*

Given a clearly defined Socialist programme of this sort, I do not see why the workers should not be prepared to collaborate with the dying capitalist under the control of a Socialist Government pledged to carry it through to the end. There remains, however, the obvious difficulty that under our political system no Government can be sure of remaining in office for more than five years, and that accordingly the carrying out of the programme might be broken off short by the return of the Conservatives to power after an election victory. To be sure, this difficulty applies to every attempt to advance towards Socialism by non-revolutionary means: *it is part of the price we pay for preferring parliamentary government to dictatorship under a one-party system.* There is no doubt that most people in Great Britain do prefer parliamentary government, and the Socialist who wishes to see his ideas carried out has to proceed on that assumption. This, I agree, makes it much more difficult than it would be if continued office could be assured to persuade the workers to modify their traditional attitudes: indeed, they cannot fairly be asked to modify them in any way that would reduce their ability to resume their fighting posture in face of any attempt by a Conservative Government to undo the achievements of its predecessor. This means that any collaboration that can be advocated under present conditions must be carefully safeguarded so as to preserve, and where possible to increase, Trade Union power.

Towards Real Workers' Control

This I believe to be entirely practicable, provided that the policy receives the full backing of a sympathetic Labour Government—but not otherwise. What it involves is, first, that the Trade Unions shall set out deliberately to *extend the area of collective bargaining* to include much that employers still regard as belonging to the sphere of managerial functions and therefore outside Trade Union competence, and secondly, that they shall use this extension to *transfer to the workers, under Trade Union supervision, certain of the functions of workshop discipline and organization* that are at present in the hands of foremen and supervisors appointed by the employers to order the workers about. Under this second head I have in mind the replacement of foremen by elected supervisors chosen by the workers themselves from among properly qualified candidates and the substitution, in suitable cases, of collective contracts under which groups of workers will undertake to carry through a particular job, or series of jobs, at a collective price, making their own arrangements for the organization of the work and sharing the proceeds in accordance with rules drawn up by the Trade Unions to which they belong.

The effect of these changes, would be to throw upon the workers responsibilities which they would exercise, not jointly with nominees of their employers, but by themselves, under arrangements negotiated by their Trade Unions with the employers and their associations. The transfer of functions to the workers, far from undermining their collective power, would add to it, and would provide the foundation for extending their authority into further fields. Such arrangements could, and should, operate both in nationalized industries and in those remaining in private ownership or in transition from private to public ownership. *They would constitute the reality of workers' control where the putting of a few Trade Union nominees on National Boards would give only the appearance of it.* Indeed, I feel sure that Trade Union representation on National Boards can be desirable only after a measure of real workers' control has been established in this more real form—if even then.[3]

---

3 For a fuller discussion of this issue see my recent book, *An Introduction to Trade Unionism* (1953).

The Danger of Stabilizing Inequality

I have written this pamphlet in the belief that since 1950 Labour's official leadership has shown clear signs of not knowing how to make a further advance towards Socialism and perhaps even of not much wanting to. Certainly some Labour Party leaders, notably Herbert Morrison, have made no bones about saying that what is needed now is a pause for consolidating what has been set on foot rather than a venture into new projects. I do not agree with this view, partly because I do not believe there is any satisfactory halting place between a mainly capitalist and a mainly Socialist economy, but also because I am afraid that *the effect of what has been done, if we halt at the point we have reached, will be to establish a new class system rather than to clear the road for a further advance towards a classless society.* We are in danger of coming to regard large salaries, titles for Trade Union and Co-operative leaders, and the control of industry and the workers by highly paid administrators imposed from above, not as necessary evils of transition, but as right and proper elements in the new society we are attempting to create. We are in danger of accepting 'reasonable' profits and the maintenance of capitalist operation as legitimate for the major part of industry, provided only that the Government holds certain very broad powers of planning and control—powers which, under such a system, it is very difficult to use effectively in any matter upon which the capitalists are not prepared to play ball. We are in danger of failing to carry through the major reorganization and large investment programme which many of our industries need because capitalist insistence on profit-taking, which provokes workers' insistence on higher wages, does not leave enough resources for capital development or make it possible to guide investment into the right channels.

Our Socialism badly needs, I think, a new look, based on a fresh angle of vision. I can sum up what I have been trying to say very briefly in the following propositions.

A Summing Up

We need

1. *a forthright attack on economic inequality based on the ownership of capital.* The best approach to this is by the abolition of inheritance beyond certain fixed limits, subject to such transitional alleviations as may seem to be desirable.
2. *a no less forthright attack on social inequality.* This involves abandoning the practice of handing out titles on any account; abolishing the House of Lords; and ceasing to create a new class of very highly paid administrators in the nationalized services.
3. *a real attempt to diffuse economic responsibility*, especially by extending

range of collective bargaining and by transferring managerial functions at the workplace level to groups of workers acting under rules established by Trade Union bargaining.

4. *a rapid advance towards greater educational equality*, especially through Comprehensive Schools and greater attention to technical and manual education for those whose bents lie that way.

5. *greater attention to means of enabling elderly people to remain at work, and disabled or handicapped people to receive better rehabilitation, education and training*, both in order to increase production and thus raise living standards, and because such measures will increase happiness.

6. *limitation of dividends and compulsory allocation of part of profits to new capital which will become the property of the public, and not of the shareholders.*

7. *extension of public ownership and control of industry not only by further measures nationalizing entire industries or concerns but by the progressive taking over of shares and direction through inheritance taxation and the creation of public shareholdings out of profits.*

Socialism—or What Else?

There will, I am sure, be many objectors to the new programme outlined in this pamphlet. Some who regard themselves as Socialists will object to it on the ground that it is bad electioneering. To them I answer that I do not care if it is—for the time being, I am a Socialist and a believer that Socialism means, above all else, a classless society. I am not in the least interested in helping the Labour Party to win a majority in Parliament unless it means to use its majority for advancing as fast as is practicable towards such a society. I do not expect a majority of the electorate to agree at present with what I have said, for the simple reason that it differs from what they have been used to hearing. For the same reason I do not expect a majority even of the active leaders of the Labour Party to agree; for it is not what they have become used to saying. For a long time now, many of them have given up talking Socialism and have been talking instead about nationalization and the Welfare State. They have now, thanks to the enterprise of the Labour Government between 1945 and 1950, got nearly as far as they can go along these lines, until they set about doing two other things as well—smashing the class system by a direct attack on property rights, and putting real responsibility into the hands of ordinary people.

It took a considerable time and a great deal of apparently fruitless effort to get the working-class movement solidly behind the programme which the Labour Government carried through between 1945 and 1950. It will take a great deal of effort to get similar support for a new programme that will carry us on towards Socialism. Therefore, the sooner we begin on this essential task of education and propaganda, the less long shall we have to wait for its results.

The alternative is to rest content with what has been achieved, and to give up trying to establish a Socialist society. That, I fear, is what many who continue to call themselves Socialists are really minded to do, sheltering their apostasy behind the assertion that the majority of the electors could not be induced to vote for it. But what is the use of winning an election, except as a means to an end? To win an election without a policy is the surest way of losing the next, and of spreading dismay and disillusionment among one's supporters. If the end is no longer Socialism, but something else—what else? If it is still Socialism, let us tell the electors frankly how we propose to advance towards it.

NOTE. I have not discussed Labour's international policy. If I did, I should need to say far more about it than I could compress within the limits of a single pamphlet covering home policy as well. I propose to deal with the all-important international aspects of Socialism in a second pamphlet.[4]

---

4   Editor's note: That pamphlet was never written.

WHAT NEXT? ANARCHISTS OR BUREAUCRATS?

IT OFTEN AMUSES ME THAT I HAVE BEEN ACTIVELY CONNECTED WITH THE Fabian Society for so large a part of my life, and that I am today its President.[1] For I have never been, and am not, a Fabian by instinct. I do not like 'lingering ways', or waiting patiently for 'the right moment'; and, although I learnt to like the Webbs as well as to respect them, my conception of the essential qualities of a Socialist society has always been very different from theirs. How then did it come about that I joined the Fabian Society during my first week as an undergraduate at Oxford—being then already a member of the ILP—that I sat on its Executive until, in exasperation, I flung the dust of the Society from my feet, and that, having once made this escape, I came back to it and, when I found it again past praying for, instead of making a final exit, joined forces with a number of others to found a new society in its image, to usurp its name, and in the fulness of time to take it over and endow it with a new lease of life—which I hope is not yet turning into a second second childhood?

All this happened because, though I did not like the Fabian attitude, I did admire and believe in the Fabian method. I felt very strongly indeed that British Socialism needed an organization of intelligent people who were in a

---

1 *Fabian Journal*, 1954. (This issue celebrated the Society's 70th anniversary.)

position to stand, with at any rate part of their minds, away from the immediate expediencies of party politics and from the acceptance of ready made gospels, and to treat Socialism as a serious intellectual problem, which deserved to be studied in the objectively scholarly way that is sometimes abusively called 'academic', and yet to be studied not in a spirit of aloofness or rejection of practical responsibility, but so as to make the Socialist scholar a practical planner as well. The standards set by the Society in these respects were high; and I believed that the great influence it had been able to exert had been due mainly to this fact. I wanted to see that tradition continued; and the will to maintain it kept on bringing me back to Fabianism despite my strong disagreement with a great deal in the stamp of doctrine which had been imposed on it mainly by Sidney Webb.

Anarchists and Bureaucrats

In the days when I joined, in 1908, the Fabian Society emphatically had a doctrine, though not a dogma. It was ardently collectivist, though not dogmatic about the precise form which the collective organization of the affairs of society was to take. The Webbs, in those days, used to be fond of saying that everyone who was active in politics was either an 'A' or a 'B'—an anarchist or a bureaucrat—and that they were 'B's'; and I think no one who knew the Fabian Society of that time could be in any doubt that it was collectively on the side of the 'B's', even if there were some few dissident 'A's' among its members. Beatrice Webb told me, very early in my Fabian career, that I was an 'A'; and I gladly accepted the label. And yet I could not get the Fabianism out of my system, because I wanted to use the methods that the 'B's' had made their own, and to put them at the 'A's' service, and could find no agency except the Fabian Society through which this could be done.

Checking the Planners

But I wanted, not only to see done for the 'A's' what the Webbs had been doing so successfully for the 'B's', but also, if not to turn the 'B's' into 'A's'—which is impossible—at any rate to persuade the 'B's' that the 'A's' were not quite such fools as they thought them. I did not want to capture the Fabian Society for the 'A's' and to send the 'B's' packing, but to induce 'A's' and 'B's' to sit down together and see whether they could come to terms. I wanted this, because it was clear that the Labour movement would come to grief if it became disunited, and that unity was possible, in the long run, only on the basis of a Socialist attitude that incorporated both 'A' and 'B' elements. I was therefore content to work in the Society with any Socialist who was sincerely trying to think in a spirit of loyalty to the Labour movement as a force united much more than divided in aims and ready to recognize how many different sorts of people will need to find the means to happiness in a Socialist world. With all this, I had always the sense—I have it now—of being a natural *minoritaire*; for, at any rate among middle-class British intellectuals past student age, the 'B's' far outnumber the 'A's', and the 'A's' have always an uphill task in asserting their part of the essentials of the Socialist way of life. Intellectualism, planning, and B-ness tend to go together; and it is obviously much easier to make plans if you begin by assuming that people will agree to be planned for. I too, being an intellectual and having a tidy mind, am a planner; but I happen not to be a 'B' because I have a deeply rooted dislike of obedience, which makes me want always to plan for the diffusion of initiative and responsibility rather than for mass indoctrination or unquestioning submissiveness to the better judgment of the expert planner.

I have tried, throughout my connection with the Fabian Society, to uphold the cause of the 'A's'—the weaker party—and to establish in the Society a balance between A-ness and B-ness corresponding to the balance that I believe exists in the whole community for which we are setting out to bring into being a Socialist way of life. But I know I have failed. The Fabian Society has always been, and remains today, preponderantly 'B'. In the past, this has not stood in the way of its influence: indeed, it has been able to influence the course of events and the development of Labour and Socialist policy all the more easily because of its B-ness. The 'B's' have been the type best able to find out the line of least resistance in the advance towards the Welfare State, in the promotion of state enterprise, and in the attack on anti-social vested interests. They have been the right people to undertake the main tasks of social planning, as long as it has been a matter mainly of pressing for the assurance of a national minimum standard of life, of devising schemes of redistributive taxation, and of attacking private monopolies with proposals for unification under public ownership. But—and here I come to the essential point of this article—are they the right people to discover how to make the new social order they have partly succeeded in setting up *work* when it has been established?

The answer to the question, What is wrong with Socialism today? is, I feel sure, that it has reached a point at which the real problem is to find the right spurs to action in making social democracy work, whereas the 'B's' who dominate it cannot solve this problem, or even understand its nature, without paying much more attention to the 'A's' than they have found it necessary to pay in the past. I do not believe the Fabian Society will keep up its recruitment among young, clever people—who are indispensable for its tasks—unless it can address itself with all the vitality it possesses to this problem. I am not referring only to my own King Charles's head of workers' control, though that is part of it. Surely exactly the same problem is facing the Colonial Bureau which, after doing the excellent work to which Rita Hinden refers in her article[2], has gone stale precisely because it does not know how to tackle the issues that arise in making colonial self-government work in terms of the human beings who will have to work it. The same thing is true when one turns to the international aspect of Socialism, which is now quite plainly a matter much less of devising better machinery for international action than of arousing an imaginative response to international problems by giving many more people a positive role in relation to them. Everywhere the great task that lies ahead of us is that of passing beyond the Welfare State, in which people get given things, to the kind of society in which they find satisfaction in doing things for themselves and one another and this means that we have to be considering most of all how to reconcile the flatness of large-scale, centrally controlled organization with the provision of inducements to creative effort. But this is precisely what the 'B's' are temperamentally unfitted to do by themselves: only the 'A's', held in check by the 'B's', can do it in any effective way. It will certainly not be done by drawing up plans, on the familiar lines for nationalizing more industries, or providing more social services, or improving the tax structure, or planning investment, or getting the balance of payments straight, necessary though all these aspects of Socialist policy may be. Nor will it be done by vague exhortations to return to the spirit of Keir Hardie or Blatchford, or by erecting the gospel of 'practical Christianity' into a substitute for serious thinking.

Is Our Socialism What People Want?

What, then? I think we have to begin over again, by asking ourselves certain fundamental questions about human beings in the machine age, and not shrinking back if the first answers we get are rather appalling to us. For example, if we come to the conclusion that the present setback to democratic Socialism, not only in Great Britain, but all over Western Europe, is not a mere swing of the electoral pendulum, but arises out of the fact that the kind of Socialism that is being offered is not what most people, or even most workers, are really keen about, what are we to do next? Go on offering them more of the same medicine? Or ask ourselves whether, practically, democratic Socialism does mean simply the Welfare State plus creeping nationalization, or means a society in which people do really manage their own affairs, and is unworkable unless they can be induced to want to manage their own affairs for themselves.

If I am right about this, it means quite big changes in the day-to-day work of the Fabian Society. For in relation to these new tasks we have not nearly reached the stage at which it is profitable to ask a series of experts to write a

---

2   Editor's note: 'The Fabian Society and the Colonies', an article in same number of the *Fabian Journal*.

series of pamphlets setting out projects, as we have asked them to do in relation to the problems of the past. In this new field there are no experts: they will arrive only when they have found out by an immense amount of discussion what are the real problems that need solving and how to set about finding the right answers. That was to a great extent the situation in which the founding fathers of the Society were in its early days; and, as Margaret Cole points out in her contribution to this issue, in those days they were few enough to meet and talk, and did meet and talk, again and again in order to find out what they wanted to say to the rest of the world, and what they needed to know in order to say it well. But today, though Fabians still meet and talk in the local Societies, there is no common talking shop for the whole Society, and for the most part nothing comes out of the talk because it has no common direction.

Our Talking Shop

I think we have to get back to the conception of the Fabian Society as a talking shop, and to try to make it again the place where the best and frankest Socialist talking is done. We cannot, of course, do this in the old way: there are too many of us, and some of us have too many other things to do. But I believe we should (a) publish fewer pamphlets of the present types until we are surer we have something new to say; (b) circulate among our members and local Societies many more discussion drafts dealing with fundamental questions of Socialism, and not be afraid of ventilating in them extremely unorthodox opinions; (c) try to get our local Societies, or as many of them as will join in, discussing the same problems, and sending their conclusions, and still more their problems, for the national Society to try to sort out and work further upon; (d) start again one or more circles for regular meeting and discussion among our more active members in London, in the hope of recreating some sort of Fabian *camaraderie* in the pursuit of Socialist truth; and (e) in connection with these new orientations, ask each member of the Executive to undertake a quite new responsibility for getting into personal touch with, say, a dozen at present inactive members, finding out what their interests are, and whether they can be drawn in to take an active part in some aspects of the Society's work—and to go on doing this until every member has been paid the compliment of a personal approach.

It may be felt that, in celebrating the Society's seventieth birthday, its President was in duty bound to say some nice things about it. I have no bouquets to offer—not because I fail to value the Society (or I should not be its President) but because I am so greatly in fear of the whole cause of democratic Socialism being lost through failure to find an effective substitute for the righteous indignation that has been its main driving force hitherto—but grows inevitably weaker as it succeeds in taking the fine edge off social injustice—or to face candidly the problem of making the new society work without the old incentives of greed and fear. There is no other agency in sight to take the place of the Fabian Society in tackling these tasks. Politicians, *qua* politicians, cannot think: Trade Unionists and Co-operators, *qua* Trade Unionists and Co-operators, cannot get outside their immediate corporative problems. Save for a natural genius here and there, who may come out of any class or schooling, only intellectuals can think, because only they are trained for the job. Often, they think very foolishly, when they fail to appreciate the needs and wishes of ordinary people; but unless they do think, the thinking simply does not get done. The Fabian Society is, or should be, British Socialism's thinking machine. I wish it would think, for the time being, more about first principles, and less about detailed plans, which can be got right only when the ends are clear.

SOCIALISM
AND THE WELFARE STATE

Many of us have been saying to ourselves, these latter days, reflecting on what has happened since 1945, 'The Welfare State is not Socialism: it is only a way of redistributing *some* income without interfering with the causes of its maldistribution'; and 'Nationalization is not Socialism: it is only a change from one form of wage-slavery to another form'.[1] Yet, if neither nationalization nor the Welfare State is Socialism, what is?

Socialism, as I have always understood it, means a classless society of comrades and, in the world as whole, a friendly league of such societies. This implies an economic system under which the distribution of incomes is got broadly right in the first instance, and does not need to be put right by complicated and wasteful methods of redistribution through taxation and private benevolence. It implies, too, the conduct of society's essential affairs, including production, on a basis of partnership and widely diffused responsibility that is altogether at variance with the relation embodied in the wage-contract—with what Carlyle and Ruskin used to denounce as the shame of the 'cash-nexus'. Socialist nationalization would mean a system of real workers' participation in management, such as the Yugoslavs are now attempting to apply, and the

---

1   *New Statesman*, 1955.

Histadrut in Israel has actually applied. Socialist social services would mean a pooling of resources to meet the risks and inevitabilities of sickness, accident and old age—not mere State subsidies to schemes of insurance based mainly on regressive tax contributions from the poorer classes.

In effect, both the Welfare State and nationalization, as they exist at present, far from breaking away from the class system, rest on its acceptance and seek only to render conditions under it more tolerable. In nationalized industry the worker is 'consulted', but he has no power or responsibility save that which he gets from his trade union as an outside pressure group; and in the social services he remains subject to a measure of class inferiority. His contribution, and even his direct taxes, are collected from him by his employer—a method which Hilaire Belloc used to speak of as an evident hallmark of the 'Servile State'!

In effect, those of us who say that the Welfare State and nationalization are not Socialism are entirely in the right. But it does not at all follow that there is anything positively wrong about them on this account. I can hardly find patience to answer those—and I meet quite a number of them—who refuse to admit that the position of the working classes has improved as a consequence of the advance of the social services, and indeed of nationalization too—to say nothing of the higher taxation imposed on the larger incomes. It is a matter of plain fact that incomes—real, spendable incomes—have been redistributed to the advantage of the poorer groups and especially of the less skilled workers, and also that the existence of full employment has done away, for the time being, with one of the most important sources of working-class insecurity. Nor is it really arguable that the workers in the nationalized industries have not benefited by the change—above all, in the coal mines, but in the transport and public utility services as well. The State is not an ideal employer; but in terms of material conditions it cannot afford to be a bad one, by current standards, for it is exposed in this matter to greater pressure of opinion than can be brought to bear on capitalist business.

These are real and substantial achievements, which it is folly to deny or to minimize on the grounds that they 'are not Socialism'. They are *not* Socialism; but it would be sheer stupidity to throw them away, or not to take every possible step to pursue and to develop their advantages. This remains true whether or not it is in the long run possible for them to be pursued within the structure of capitalism. I have been taken to task for saying that I see no sign of capitalism nearing the point of final crisis at which it is destined to break down and dissolve. If I am right in not regarding the fall of capitalism as necessarily imminent, it is obviously desirable to do what can be done to improve the position of the workers under it by hurrying on as far as possible with the development of the Welfare State. But even if I am wrong, and capitalism is heading for an early collapse, the better off the workers are when the crisis comes, the stronger will they be for facing it and for advancing to the creation of a new society.

I am impelled to make this point because some Socialists have been speaking or writing as if my urging the need to establish a new movement for World Socialism meant that I was trying to draw men away from the everyday political struggle on the ground that it is not directed to the establishment of Socialism. On the contrary, I wish to urge every Socialist to be active in that struggle, but believe that activity will be more powerful and better directed if those who engage in it have a vision which extends beyond the immediate parliamentary possibilities in both time and space. I hold that the clue to getting a better Labour Party and Labour programme is to be found in the impregnation of the party's active workers with a sense of vision to transform society fundamentally, and not merely to lessen its abuses; and that in the world today this sense of vision can be assured only on an internationalist appeal. I do not believe in 'Socialism in One Country'; on the contrary, I feel sure that those who seek this merely internal Socialism will find it turning, even if they succeed, into something terribly different from what they sought. Twentieth-century Socialism must be an affair of establishing the conditions for human decency and social equality in all countries, and for men and women of every colour and creed.

I want a world crusade for Socialism in order to emphasize the essentially international character of the Socialist faith—not to distract men and women from the struggle in their several countries, but to give them added energy and enthusiasm which they can transmit to others. For this reason, I try to stand aloof from quarrels within the Labour movement when they appear to turn on purely internal issues—not because I have no views on these issues, but because they seem to me to be secondary and to threaten the solidarity of the workers' movement for no sufficiently good reason. If we are to quarrel, let it be about the things that really matter; but about these we are least likely to quarrel because, in the main, our ultimate objectives are the same. We—that is, all Socialists— would like to see a classless society in a classless world of brothers. We differ only about the immediate importance we attach to working positively for such an objective, and about the amount of consideration to be given to it in everyday propaganda. The Socialists of old, before Socialism had become a party-political force, did carry on their propaganda in this spirit and were much more intent on making Socialists than on winning doubtful votes. They knew that every real convert to Socialism was worth, through the influence he could exert on others, quite a number of votes. But today propaganda for Socialism has become submerged in propaganda for the next steps in social reform; whereas the two should go together, each reinforcing the other. This cannot be, as long as the convinced Socialists have no effective means of meeting together, either in one country or internationally, except through parties whose first preoccupation is necessarily with getting votes rather than with arousing Socialist sentiment and enthusiasm for Socialism as a world-wide cause.

We who take this view will, however, get ourselves into bad trouble if we allow ourselves to be seduced by our zeal for Socialism into decrying the Welfare State. All round us is evidence that in spite of the perilous condition of world affairs there is more happiness and much less unhappiness in the world than ever before. In our own country there are many fewer undernourished and wretched people; and in the countries where standards of life are still appallingly low, there is more hope and more conscious struggle for improvement. So let us not belittle what the Labour Party here, or the Communists in Russia, have done, or dwell overmuch on the imperfections and defacements that have accompanied their achievements. On balance, they have done immense good, on both sides of the 'iron curtain'. What matters is what is to be done next, and how we can work together internationally in advancing beyond nationalization and the Welfare State to the free society and the free world of our legitimate and practicable aspirations.

REFLECTIONS ON DEMOCRATIC CENTRALISM

WHAT IS 'DEMOCRATIC CENTRALISM'?[1] I HAVE RECENTLY READ A DEFINITION OF it, or rather of the term 'centralism' as applied to a political party, as meaning '(i) that minorities shall accept the decision of majorities, and (ii) that lower party organs shall accept the decision of higher party organs.' These two requirements, I am told, appear in the rules of the British Communist Party. If this were all, I imagine most of us would be ready to accept the label of 'centralists'; but clearly it is not all. One wants to know what are the majorities and minorities in question—majorities and minorities of what precisely? And one also wants to know what are the 'higher' and 'lower' party organs; for this is not a matter on which agreement can be taken as a matter of course.

Does majority in this connection mean majority of all the members of the party, ascertained by referendum or ballot vote? If so, it has to be admitted that by no means all issues can be settled in this way. Some are too technical for mass voting to be appropriate: in other cases there is no time, or no opportunity, to take a ballot vote. Even if major questions of principle are settled as far as possible by referendum, some other agency has to be used for taking the secondary decisions. There has to be an *executive* body able to do this;

---

1 *Reasoner*, November 1956.

but an Executive, even if it is democratically chosen, is not a 'majority', and its decisions are not majority decisions which all members can be required to obey on that ground. In practice, questions of principle are more often decided at a Congress or by delegates or representatives than by referendum; but a Congress, however democratically chosen, does not constitute a majority, or even necessarily express the majority's will.

After all, then, it cannot be simply that minorities are required to accept the decision of majorities. It turns out that what is meant is that, except in case of referendum, majorities are being required to accept the decisions of minorities that are deemed to represent them (Congresses) or to have some special authority to prescribe a correct line of conduct (Executive Committees). It is clearly reasonable to give representative Congresses a large power to decide on matters of principle or high policy where the use of the referendum is felt to be inappropriate, or where it cannot be used; but it is a very different matter to endow an Executive, which cannot be representative in anything like the same degree, power to issue orders to the majority—in effect, to almost everybody concerned—even if the Executive is limited to acting in what it holds to be in accordance with Congress decisions. For one thing, there will inevitably be many issues on which Congress has not given judgement; and, for another, even when it has there may be wide differences of opinion concerning the right way of applying such judgements to particular cases or situations, above all in a situation that is not static, but subject to rapid development.

Thus, the first real and substantial point that arises in relation to the claims of centralists is this. How much power is the *Executive* to be given to issue orders binding the members and branches or regional organizations? If the Executive is given virtually complete power in this respect, subject only to obeying decisions of Congress, this amounts to a very great subjection of the majority to the Executive—that is, to a very small minority deemed to be in some sense its representative. Clearly, in any party organization, the Executive must be given considerable powers, and must be able to rely on its orders being for the most part carried out by the members. But must a branch or regional body always obey the Executive, whatever it orders and even if it regards the Executive as acting in violation of Congress decisions? Or should there be limits, in addition to those involved in Congress decisions, on what the Executive can order? For example, should the Executive (or only the Congress) have the right to expel, or to suspend, a member or branch accused of 'subversive' practices or opinions? Should the Executive have a right to lay down a 'party line', and to require all members to confirm to it, and to switch the line when and as it thinks fit?

In the case of Communist Parties there is a further problem. Under the Constitution of the Comintern (now defunct) each national Party was required to regard itself as a branch or section of the Comintern and to accept the orders, not only of an International Congress, but also of the Executive Committee of the Comintern (ECCI). Thus the international *Executive* was treated as 'higher' than even the *Congress* of a national Communist Party. It may be said that, since the dissolution of the Comintern, this situation has ceased to exist; but how far was the place of the ECCI taken in practice by the central organs of the Communist Party of the Soviet Union? It seems clear that well before Stalin became a dictator—indeed, while Lenin was still active—the principle that an international *Executive* was 'higher' than a national Party *Congress* was laid down as an essential principle of centralism. This was indeed largely what centralism meant when the term first came into widespread use.

The conception of 'higher' and 'lower' party organs is not simple. A national Executive is obviously higher than a local Executive; but is it 'higher' than a regional Congress, or even than a widely attended branch meeting?

So far, I have been dealing only with the term 'centralism', and not with the qualifying adjective, 'democratic'. What does 'democratic' mean, in this context? Clearly, it must mean that the persons who, as Congress delegates or Executive members, lay down policies and issue orders are chosen by the members so as to represent their views. Does this mean that all such persons ought to represent the views of a majority of the entire membership, or is it consistent with some of them representing local or sectional majorities whose views are not those of a majority of the whole Party? If the former, it seems to exclude all real debate either on the Executive or in Congress itself, and to involve that both should be 'monolithic' bodies so chosen that no minority spokesman can secure election to them. This would exclude all forms of election to represent particular localities or groups, and would imply that the majority view was known already before the elections took place. In the case of Congress delegates it would involve empowering the Executive to decide who should get elected, by excluding all candidates standing for 'deviationist' views; and, up to a point, this does seem to have occurred, though not by any means completely. In the case of Executive members, it would seem to involve election not by rank-and-file nomination or by mass vote, but by a Congress already sufficiently hand-picked in the way described.

Is this 'democratic', even if it does result in a Congress and an Executive that represent the view of a majority? Or does 'democracy' require some recognition of the rights of minorities? My conception of democracy does include such a recognition, which I regard as inconsistent with the conception of centralism that has so far been accepted, at any rate in most cases, by the Communist Parties. For, if minority views (including those of local or sectional majorities) are not to be represented, real free discussion is made impossible, and in practice too much power is put in the hands of those who represent the majority at a particular time, not only in conducting party affairs without regard for minority views, but also to perpetuate their power after they have ceased really to represent the majority view. *New* views, including adaptations of policy to meet changing circumstances and opportunities, are bound in most cases to be at the outset minority views; and to prevent such views from being expressed and taken notice of is to condemn a party to utter dependence on the personal qualities and the adaptability to new situations of those who represented the majority when they were chosen, under conditions which make it difficult for them to change their minds—for were they not chosen to carry out a determined monolithic policy? Free discussion is indispensable for the discovery of new truths or working hypotheses; and the monolithic conception of leadership is therefore wholly unscientific, as well as contrary to any constructive conception of democracy.

'Democratic centralism' could mean, and was presumably meant at least in part by its originators to mean, something widely different from 'monolithicity'. It could mean that throughout the party, the fullest opportunity was given for free discussion in framing and reframing policies, but that when, after such discussion, a definite decision had been reached by the Party as a whole, such decisions (until revised) should be binding on all its members. This, I think, could be called 'democratic' only if the power to make such binding decisions was reserved exclusively for Congresses so elected as to give thorough scope for the representation of minority views and to exclude all central pressure designed to influence the electors. It is not 'democratic' for an Executive to be allowed to take such binding decisions, or even for a Congress that is not freely elected in such a way to ensure due representation of minority views.

There remains a further question. Even when these conditions of 'democracy' have been satisfied, is a Party Congress entitled to lay down decisions binding as orders on all the individual members of the Party? I think not. Clearly, such a Congress must have the right, in the last resort, to expel an individual, or a group, that it considers to be acting seriously against the Party's interest and well-being. But it should invoke such power only in the very last resort, and never merely because of what may be merely temporary disagreements on tactics, or even on fundamental policies, except after every possible attempt to work with the dissentients, or allow them to go their own way, as long as their actions do not threaten actually to disrupt the Party, as distinct from causing trouble or inconvenience to the persons actually in control of its affairs for the time being. The other side of this is that the individual member must never be called upon to *act* in support of any policy to which he objects on grounds of morality (conscience), though he may, in certain circumstances of this order, be strongly urged *not to act* against such a policy, except by using his right as a member to agitate for getting it changed—and to join with fellow members in any such agitation; for to deny this right to act with others is to deny the right to agitate to any real purpose. It is a fundamental moral principle that no man should be required to act against his conscience, either by condoning for reasons of party expediency things of which he morally disapproves or by being made to do things which revolt his sense of justice or fair dealing.

This degree of respect for the rights of the individual is indispensable among Socialists, in whatever sort of society they are living. For any other attitude involves sacrificing the individual's rights, not to those of his class, but to the conception of class rights held by a particular body of persons who find themselves for the first time in command of the party machine.

Really free discussion, such as the continual discovery of new truths or working hypotheses requires, is not possible unless it exists at every level of party organization, and cannot work democratically unless policies are allowed to find their way upwards and outwards from the smaller—local or sectional—groups to the higher levels. It is not *democratic* centralism when policy is allowed to emerge only from the centre, even if *some* criticism of the central proposal is thereafter allowed before final and binding decision are arrived at. In practice, the more control an Executive is allowed to have over the framing of policy, to the exclusion of the smaller groups, the less democratic the process is—above all, if the Executive is so constituted as to exclude, or nearly exclude, representation of minority views.

Where Parties, like the Bolsheviks in Tsarist Russia, have to operate under conditions of police persecution and cannot meet and discuss freely at all levels, it is made impossible for them to work in thoroughly democratic ways and, especially in revolutionary situations, there may be no alternative to the adoption of undemocratic centralist methods. But the recognition of this necessity provides no reason for regarding as desirable in themselves methods which inevitably involve great dangers of the Party falling into the hands of a dominant clique or of a masterful individual intent on enlarging his own power.

WILLIAM MORRIS AS A
SOCIALIST

I BECAME A SOCIALIST MORE THAN FIFTY YEARS AGO WHEN I READ *NEWS FROM Nowhere* as a schoolboy and realized quite suddenly that William Morris had shown me the vision of a society in which it would be a fine and fortunate experience to live.[1] Needless to say, I have not lived in such a society, or in any even remotely like it; but I count myself not the less fortunate to have been shown that vision; and I can truthfully say that from the day when I first read *News from Nowhere* my Socialist convictions have remained firmly fixed. I went on to read *A Dream of John Ball* and many more of Morris's writings, and to enjoy many of his works of art and craftsmanship, from tapestries, cretonnes and wallpapers, to finely printed books; and in all of them I found the quality that strongly appealed to me and gave me a deeper devotion to Morris as a person than I have ever felt for any other whom I have not met face to face. This quality is, I think, best summed up in the words Morris put into the mouth of the hedge-priest, John Ball, when he said that 'Fellowship is heaven, and lack of fellowship is hell'—a deep, pervading sense that all men should live together as brothers, not contending one against another for sordid advantages, but uniting their strength to make the best of the world as their common

---

1   Lecture given to the William Morris Society, 1957.

living-place, conserving and developing its beauty and sharing its fruits and not needing to be troubled with politics or to be badgered about by persons set in authority over them.

I was of course aware, even from the first, that *News from Nowhere* had to be taken as a personal vision of a good society and not as a prophecy of what could come about in my own day or indeed ever, in any complete achievement of mankind. It presented an ideal to work for, or towards; and an ideal was what I wanted, and still continue to want. Morris himself, in his review of Edward Bellamy's *Looking Backward*, emphasized this very point—that any utopia worth wanting must be the expression of a personal preference and valuation of human goods, rather than a forecast of the future made on the basis of a purely objective study of the forces actually at work. Morris doubtless believed that a sort of Socialism not wholly at variance with his ideals was germinating in the world as a product of certain historical forces that had been described above all others by Karl Marx. He said so in the book he wrote in collaboration with Ernest Belfort Bax on *Socialism: Its Growth and Outcome*. But he worked for Socialism, not because it was historically destined to come, but because he deemed it to be good and worth working for. He was an idealist who did not share Marx's dislike of subjective valuations and saw nothing amiss in endeavouring to picture the shape of the new society he was attempting to bring to birth.

Morris, however, was like Marx in that he saw this new society, not as a continuation of tendencies that were already at work in the capitalist societies of his own day, but as the sequel to a sharp break with these societies and with the values that chiefly found expression under their influence. Thus, whereas the Webbs, like Bernstein in Germany, thought of Socialism as something that would emerge out of Capitalism in the course of social and economic evolution by gradual stages—reform being added to reform in a progressive series that would, step by step, transform the one into the other—Morris, like Marx, envisaged rather a sudden, catastrophic revolution that would displace Capitalism once and for all from power, and would thus set the workers free to remodel the collective institutions of society on radically new foundations. Even more than Marx—indeed, much more—he was distrustful of every sort of reformism; and the break to which he looked forward was even sharper than the Revolution as envisaged by Marx, and was unaccompanied by any transitional stage of proletarian dictatorship during which the workers, organized as a class, would exercise supreme authority for the purpose of bringing a fully Socialist society gradually into being. Hating authoritarian government and control, by whomsoever exercised, Morris envisaged the Revolution, as he described it in the early chapters of *News from Nowhere*, as leading straight to the institution of a classless society set free from governmental coercion and able to shape its course directly in accordance with the needs of the free spirit of man. He was able to do this because he thought of most men as naturally disposed to behave in friendly, co-operative ways, and as perverted from their real natures by the evil institutions to which they were subject under Capitalism: so that almost all that was needed to make them their own masters and to induce them to put their mastery to good use was release from the capitalist incubus: whereas Marx, without saying much about the prospective character of the coming society—except that under it men would 'make their own history'—anticipated a transitional period during which the means of production associated with Capitalism would undergo rapid development under proletarian control. Indeed, Marx's orthodox Social Democratic successors, such as Kautsky, laid great stress on the development under socialist control of more and more concentrated large-scale methods of production, and looked on the growth of larger and larger capitalist combinations as preparing the way for a Socialism that would take them over and apply their productive powers to a rapid improvement of material standards of living. The Marxists had a high contempt for the small-scale producer—craftsman, artisan, or peasant—as an obsolescent type, which it was the task of Socialism to liquidate in the interests of higher output resting on the most advanced and highly concentrated machine-techniques. Morris, on the other hand, though he said that there would have to be more machinery before there could be less, took this as a sign that things would have to get worse before they could get better, and regarded it as the mission of Socialism, not to maximize output by the adoption of mass-production methods, but to put an end to those mechanized processes which resulted in the substitution of 'useless toil' for 'useful work' and thus robbed the labourer of an essential part of his birthright—joy in the labour of his hands.

This conception of joy in labour—of production as a source of joy or pleasure to the maker as well as to the user—was indeed a fundamental part of Morris's Socialist faith. He could not conceive of men enjoying happiness, unless they were able to enjoy their work as well as their leisure. He considered that, as things were, a great deal of the labour of man was given over to making useless things—things it could give no pleasure to use any more than to make. His heart was set, not on increasing the volume of goods produced, regardless of their power to yield real satisfaction, but rather on improving the quality—above all, the artistic quality—of everyday goods, from houses to the commonest materials used in them and to the smallest objects of personal possession. He believed there would be no difficulty in making more than enough of such things for everyone to have as much of them as he would want, as soon as the incubus of an exploiting class could be lifted from the people and they were set free to arrange the powers of production for their common advantage. For he believed that, as soon as the class system was done away with, most men would cease to wish to pile up possessions or luxuries for their private enjoyment and would turn to simple ways of living that would dispense with a great mass of artificial needs created by the unnatural exigencies of the capitalist way of living. Men would then, he felt sure, rapidly amend their tastes and would demand that whatever they needed should be good of its kind and also, as workers, that whatever they made should give them pleasure in the making. In a society so minded, there could easily be enough for all without any coercion upon the producer to labour hard at making things under unpleasant and unnatural conditions. Indeed, in *News from Nowhere*, he pictured his citizens as complaining that work was becoming unduly scarce and as seeking voluntarily for the chance of it without any expectation of receiving any remuneration for it. You will remember that in 'Nowhere' there was no longer any buying and selling, or any payment for work of any kind. The work that was done got done for the pleasure of doing it, and for no other reason: and no difficulty was met with in producing under these conditions fully as much as the citizens demanded without being called on to pay anything for it.

In these days we are much more alive than Morris ever was to the prevalence in the world of a condition of primary poverty that clearly cannot be done away with simply by abolishing capitalist exploitation—and could not be, even if the fullest practical use were to be made of all the techniques of mass production known to modern man. It is impossible for us, thinking, as we have to do, on a worldwide scale, and faced with the intense population pressures that exist most of all in the less developed countries, to regard the problem of producing enough as having been solved, even if men were content to live much more simply than the citizens of 'Nowhere' appeared to be living. We can hardly avoid seeing that Morris's solution of the problem of production was unduly simple, or from recognizing that it would need much more than the abolition of Capitalism to diffuse over all mankind a tolerable material standard of living such as Morris postulated. I do not think the reader is ever told how many people there were in 'Nowhere'—which was clearly meant to be England, or perhaps Great Britain—after the great change. But the reader can hardly help getting the impression that there were many fewer than there are now—or how did they contrive to produce enough food to meet their needs? Nor is it easy to accept the view that, set free from class exploitation, most people so easily turned their backs on the desire to add to their material possessions, or lost their tastes for gadgets that could be produced in sufficient numbers only by resort to the mass-production methods that Morris so heartily disliked. Morris often lamented that, as a manufacturer of goods of high quality and artistic value, he was forced to serve only the wealthy or at least the well-to-do. He appeared to believe that, given Socialism, most people would value and want the kinds of things he knew how to make by methods into which mass production did not enter at all. But would Socialism of itself turn most people into good judges of fine craftsmanship and artistic excellence;

and, if it did, how much hard labour would be called for to meet their requirements? I fear that, however reluctantly, we must dismiss this element in Morris's Socialist Utopia as something past hoping for in any near future, or perhaps ever, and must reconcile ourselves to the view that, over a large part of the field, mass production will have to be continued for a long time to come if mankind is to escape from the curse of primary poverty. Indeed, even if we were to leave most of the world out of account—as today we cannot—and were to consider only the needs and demands of the British people, it is clear enough that these can be met only with all the aid that can be given us by developing large-scale production to the utmost, while diverting it as much as we can to supplying real wants on a basis of greatly diminished inequality between man and man.

This, I suppose, is obvious; but let us beware of allowing the argument to carry us too far. Even if we admit that, for as far ahead as we can see, there will be a shortage in the world of consumer goods to satisfy everybody's actual wants, it does not follow that the right course is to subordinate everything else to the quest for higher output, regardless of the conditions under which this output has to be made. Morris was laying stress on a thoroughly valid point when he insisted that men could not be happy as long as they were condemned for most of their lives to kinds of toil that were irksome to them, so that things got produced only under the compulsion of the need to earn a living, and work had to be regarded as an evil, valuable *solely* for its service in satisfying the consumers' wants. He was right in insisting that the 'disutility' of such labour ought to be set against the 'utility' of the goods produced by reason of it, and that, measured by this double standard, a substantial part of the current output of industry was not, in hard fact, worthwhile. He was right in asserting that men ought not to be coerced into working under conditions that made them unhappy unless they really preferred a larger supply of goods, made available at such cost, to a smaller supply produced under more favourable conditions, and in saying that under Capitalism no such choice was open to the great majority. It did not, however, follow that men, if they were free to choose, would abandon mass production in order to recover the joy in really satisfying forms of work, no matter what the cost might be in reduced total output. It did follow that everything possible should be done to reduce the irksomeness of routine labour, both by improving the conditions and environment of work and by dispensing with goods that were not greatly wanted and were especially unpleasant to make. This, however, leaves open the road to greater mechanization by the use of techniques which eliminate or greatly reduce the burden of irksome production, as well as to the substitution of craft products for those of mass production involving a large amount of routine repetitive employment. In effect, what is now called 'automation', as well as craftsmanship, can have its place in lessening the burden of unpleasant toil.

Nor can it be taken for granted that the labour of mass production is always unpleasant or irksome. There is undoubtedly a real joy to be got from the designing and management of large-scale machines, though not, I think—or at any rate but seldom—from the routine operation of them. What has been most displeasing in mass production up to the present time has been, on the one hand, its tendency to widen the gulf between the technologists and other experts who preside over its working, and the mass of routine operators on whom they exert a largely unchallengeable control, and, on the other hand, the plain fact that these latter have been subject to exploitation for capitalist profit and have been treated as mere adjuncts to the machine instead of being regarded as men and women with as good a claim as anyone else to have a say in deciding the conditions under which they are to work. The wrong human relation that this structure of industry has involved is often called, nowadays, the 'Managerial Revolution': the other aspect, that of exploitation for profit, is characteristic of the capitalist system as a whole. Socialism would do away with the second of these, but not necessarily with the first, for public ownership and operation of industry are not in themselves inconsistent with a sharp division between controllers and controlled.

In Morris's eyes it was fully as important that the common man should not be subject to the control of a vast administrative or managerial machine as that he should not be exploited for private profit. He knew that it would be impossible for him to do good work or to be anything except deeply unhappy in working within such a machine; and it was with him an instinct to credit other men with feelings like his own. He wanted small-scale production, not because he was an individualist, but because he believed in co-operation, but was unable to conceive of real co-operation except on the basis of small, face to-face groups. Regarding architecture as the highest of the applied arts, he could not mean by this that men could not be happy co-operating in a great enterprise requiring the labour of many hands; but he insisted that they could do so fruitfully and happily only if each of them could have as his own, either individually or in common with a few companions, a clearly defined task, to be executed well or ill and to stand as evidence of a definite creative achievement. Given this apportionment of tasks, large bodies of men could work together happily in pursuit of a common purpose which each man, through his special contribution, could make his own. He could, however, do this only on condition that the task assigned to him was not merely the routine execution of the architect's plan, but allowed scope for a creative achievement of his own. In Morris's view the supreme sin of modern architecture had been that it had divorced the routine executant from the artist-designer, and had thus destroyed the opportunity for the craftsman to employ his creative impulses, converting what should have been joyous creative effort into merely mechanical toil and, in the process, depriving the detailed work of all real meaning.

In what he said and wrote on this theme Morris was of course largely echoing what he had learnt from Ruskin, whose chapter from *The Stones of Venice* on 'Gothic Architecture' he rejoiced in reprinting at his Kelmscott Press. But his doctrine of craftsmanship was none the worse because Ruskin was his master in declaring it; and what Ruskin had written in particular relation to architecture Morris came to apply over a much wider field. As a believer in human fellowship resting on a recognition of basic equality between man and man, he deplored the general tendency in the modern world to divorce the executant from the designer or planner as disastrous both for the arts and for the dignity of common labour, and looked forward to a society in which such divisions of status would no longer exist and every worker in an enterprise would be reckoned and treated as a creative partner. He did not of course mean to deny the existence of functional differences between architect and craftsman or between manager or technologist and manual worker; but he insisted that the former ought to understand the practice of the operations they directed, and that the latter should be given the largest practicable freedom in carrying out their work under the general directives imposed by the master plan.

This has always appeared to me to be a vitally important element in Morris's thought, not only about the arts, but also about the world's work as a whole. Clearly it runs counter to very strong tendencies operating in the modern world both in the arts and in industry as it becomes more and more affected by complex scientific techniques. It should, however, be observed that, whereas in Marx's day the predominant tendency was towards the substitution of unskilled repetitive machine operation for skilled craftsmanship, today the growth of automation seems likely to lead to a progressive elimination of such purely repetitive labour and towards a need for more skilled and responsible co-operation of the labour needed for watching the operation of complex automatic machines. It is still too soon to say how rapidly automation will develop, or what effects it will have on the demand for labour in terms of either quality or quantity; but clearly the tendency is likely to be in the direction of reducing the relative amount of mainly repetitive work, and of increasing the relative demand for more highly qualified workers. This may render possible before long a substantial further reduction in the length of the working day, and may accentuate the tendency for the proportion of the total labour force employed in direct production to fall. There are evidently serious dangers of redundancy leading to a decline in the bargaining power of the Trade Unions affected should automation proceed faster than arrangements for absorbing into other employments the workers displaced by it. But it is far from certain that this will occur, whereas it seems clear that the case will be strengthened for giving the workers whose services continue to be needed a greater participation in settling the conditions that affect their working lives and a larger responsibility and freedom in their work itself.

Morris, of course, could not foresee these developments. It appeared to him that the way to re-establish the worker's freedom was to emancipate him from his subjection to capitalist profit-making and to restore conditions under which the demand for craft products would revive and quality would be preferred to quantity in the consumers' judgments of value or utility. Not that he wished to abolish factory production altogether. There is a tract of his—*A Factory as it Might Be*—in which he contrasts the sordid character and surroundings of the typical factory of his own day with his vision of a factory well laid out in beautiful surroundings and not crowded into a narrow city space—a factory in which work could be carried on under healthy and pleasant conditions and the workers employed in it could live in pleasant dwellings in close touch with unspoilt country. Since he wrote a good many factories have in fact been built, if not according to his prescriptions, at any rate in such ways as greatly to diminish both the sordidness of the working conditions and the squalor of the housing provided for their workers. But too many of the older sort remain; and even of the newer factories too many are so thoroughly built round as to lose their contact with the countryside and to add to the size of the great towns in which they come to be engulfed. We have been getting, not the decentralization of towns and factories that Morris desired, but only a suburbanization which, though much better than what preceded it, raises serious social problems of its own.

I must now, however, turn from this aspect of Morris's Socialism to a wider consideration of his general attitude to politics and economics after he had come to see in Socialism the only hope of setting the world's affairs to rights. A good many of those who have written about Morris have been primarily interested in his artistic work and have been disposed to lament that instead of giving his whole mind to it he allowed himself, much against his personal inclinations, to be drawn into the toil of Socialist propaganda, for which he was not well fitted, and to be subjected to the uncomradely bickerings of a pack of disgruntled and ungrateful fellow Socialists whose conduct made him thoroughly unhappy and ended by reducing him almost to sheer despair. I agree that Morris was bad at street-corner speaking and that even in indoor Socialist meetings his audiences often failed to understand or appreciate what he was trying to say. I agree that he was unfortunate in many of his colleagues both in the Social Democratic Federation and in the Socialist League and that in the latter, while it was being captured by the Anarchists, he was shabbily and exasperatingly treated. I agree that Morris carried his sense of the obligations involved in his conversion to Socialism to quixotic lengths and that his refusal to claim any special privileges for himself as an artist with his own work to do led him, in face of the paucity of available workers in the Socialist cause, to take excessive burdens on himself, and to allow himself to be exploited by the 'comrades' beyond what they had any right to demand. But I do not at all agree that Morris should have been exempted, as an artist of world reputation, from taking his Socialism very seriously or from working hard for the cause he had made his own. I honour him for his behaviour, even if it meant that he accepted obligations that were both outside his competence and beyond his physical strength. The Socialist League was admittedly of no great account as a force for Socialism; but Morris's personal work for it contributed to the cause of Socialism something of which the influence extended far beyond the League and inspired many others by his example—among them, men as different as Robert Blatchford and Bernard Shaw, who both paid generous tribute to his personality and influence.

What were the essential characteristics of the Socialist gospel as it appeared to William Morris? In one aspect, Morris's Socialism was fundamentally Marxist. Marx's theoretical economics, indeed, made little appeal to him: he was not an economist and did not do his thinking in terms of economic theory—either Marx's or anyone else's. But the historical chapters of *Das Kapital* did appeal to him very strongly, and he fully accepted Marx's view of history as a sequence of class struggles that would end with the victory and emancipation of the workers as the last exploited class. He believed in a coming social revolution in which the workers would make an end of the system of class exploitation and would institute a classless society in which men would become free to shape their collective institutions on a basis of friendly, democratic co-operation in the pursuit of happiness. Morris thought of this coming society in terms, by no means of a powerful, centralized dictatorship of the workers as a class, but of a decentralized structure of free co-operation of man with man, with a minimum of authoritarian government control, the need for which he expected progressively to fade away with the liquidation of the old order and, as men learnt to work together, with little or no coercion for the furtherance of their common ends. In his day, the idea that Marxism involved, even as an instrument of transition, anything in the nature of a centralized proletarian dictatorship was not at all widely entertained. Such a notion became a part of Marxism only with Lenin, though it had been foreshadowed earlier by Blanqui and his followers and there were a few passages in Marx's own writings that could be interpreted as supporting it. Morris, I think, was never called upon to pronounce on this issue, because it was never raised. But I cannot doubt that, had he been, he would have reacted most strongly against the conception of 'democratic centralism' that came to be a cardinal doctrine of modern Communism. When Morris, in his well-known lecture to the Fabian Society on *Communism*, used the word 'Communism' he clearly meant by it something much more closely akin to the Anarchist-Communism of Kropotkin, with its insistence on the autonomy of the small neighbourhood group, than to the authoritarian structure of one-party control that was built up in the Soviet Union, chiefly by Stalin after Lenin's death, though Lenin laid the foundations for it by his insistence on the dominant role of the Communist Party.

Morris, when he spoke of Communism, used the word in its older sense, to indicate a society in which there was no buying and selling, either of human labour or of ordinary consumer goods, but each citizen rendered service according to his capacity and received goods and services freely according to his needs. He expressed, in his acceptance of Communism in this sense as his ideal, his hatred of the entire commercial system and his hankering after a society untroubled by pecuniary considerations, in which men would give their service freely to their fellow-men and would be moderate in their demands on the labour of others. This was the accepted ideal of the theorists of Anarchism as well as of many Utopian Socialists. But Morris was not an Anarchist. He fell foul of the Anarchists who formed a group in the Socialist League and were able to dominate it in the days of its decline; not because he held their ideal to be wrong, but because he disapproved of their methods and tactics at a time when what was called 'Anarchism of the Deed'—resort to bomb-throwing and other forms of violence by way of protest against the injustice of contemporary society—was coming very much into fashion and was causing sharp differences of opinion among the Anarchists themselves, many of whom were deeply shocked by it. Morris had no sympathy at all with this sort of Anarchism, which he regarded as criminal folly; but he did sympathize strongly with the Anarchists in their dislike of the State as a coercive class agency and in their insistence that free social institutions could rest only on a foundation of autonomous local face-to-face groups. He shared too their deep distrust of parliamentary institutions and their hostility to reformist parliamentary action. The alleged democracy of the parliamentary system of representation seemed to him essentially a sham, which served to pervert those who took part in it and to divert men's minds from the social revolution he believed to be necessary. The few Labour men who sat in Parliament as Liberals seemed to him to be wasting their time, and to have allowed themselves to become prisoners of the existing order; and he was convinced that no candidate who presented himself as an out-and-out Socialist stood any chance of getting elected, or could do so until, by propaganda and education outside Parliament, the Socialists had won over the main body of the workers to their views. For the time being at any rate, what mattered was that the work of propaganda and education should be carried on unfettered by the confusions involved in appealing for electoral support to a predominantly anti-Socialist electorate. He wanted the propagandists and educators to go the whole Socialist hog; and he felt that whoever diluted the Socialist message in order to win votes was doing much more harm than good. He therefore opposed parliamentary action, at any rate for the time being, and he also, I think, believed that when the main body of the workers had been won for Socialism they would find much better ways than that of parliamentarianism for introducing a Socialist way of life. The Socialist message, once he had accepted it himself, appeared to him—as it does to me—so simply convincing that he could not but believe that it had only to be stated often and plainly enough to be sure of carrying conviction to the majority of the people—indeed, to all who were not blinded by self-interest. Years of continuous propaganda for Socialism and of experience of the personal short-comings of many with whom he had to work dimmed this assurance during the last few years of his life, but never quite extinguished it. He remained certain in his mind that the only way to get Socialism was by persuading more and more of the people—above all, of the workers—to believe in it; and he continued to envisage the 'great change' he believed to be on its way in terms not of a gradual accumulation of piecemeal reforms but of a sudden upheaval that would cause men to turn their backs on the evil past and to set to work manfully constructing a radically new society.

In effect, Morris was a revolutionary Socialist who believed in the power of ideas and of ideals to transform the world. He credited other men with the fine qualities of disinterested energy that were present in him, just as he credited them with the potentiality of a feeling for the beautiful not less compelling than his own. He recognized, indeed, that the conditions of Capitalism de-graded both the tastes and the morals of its victims, causing them to prefer the 'cheap and nasty' to the beautiful and to lower their moral standards under the exigencies of money-grubbing in a world dominated by capitalist exploitation. But he deemed both these degradations to be products of Capitalism, contrary to man's essential nature and therefore certain speedily to disappear when the capitalist incubus was lifted from their necks. Love of beauty and decency of conduct were in his view both natural to man, and would re-exert their power over men as soon as they were set free to shape their own destinies. This was the faith in which he believed; and it was an old faith, which had gone to the making of the great French Revolution a century earlier and had been an im-portant element in Utopian Socialist thought from the days of Robert Owen and even of Babeuf.

There are, no doubt, many who will regard this utopian element in Morris's Socialism as a weakness. Out-and-out Marxists will treat it as an example of 'petit-bourgeois prejudice', and will contrast with it the Marxian view of Socialism as a product of historical necessity. For my part, I agree with Morris in seeing no inconsistency between the two views. Socialism may be on its way as a scientifically predictable stage in the process of historical evolution; but, even so, why should anyone put himself out to work for it unless he also believes it to be good and that his work can make some difference in helping to bring it about. The fact—if it be a fact—that Socialism is destined to come does not make it good unless we believe that whatever is destined to happen must be good. The only valid reason for working for a cause is that one wishes to bring to pass what it stands for, as something good and worth the effort. I myself do not believe either that only good things happen or that the coming of Socialism can be demonstrated with scientific certainty; but if I did hold the latter belief I should still, before stirring a finger for the 'cause', need to assure myself that I held Socialism to be worth working for and so, of course, would anyone else, whatever pretences to the contrary his mistrust of moralizing might induce him to make.

I very much enjoyed reading my friend, Edward Thompson's, recent full-scale biography of William Morris, which seemed to me in most respects an excellent piece of work—above all, in the great attention it paid to Morris as a Socialist and to the part he played in the Socialist movement. Thompson's book had, however, one serious weakness, apart from being cluttered at certain points with too much detail. Its author was legitimately eager to clear Morris of the charge so often made—often indeed with approval—of having been merely a sentimental Socialist—an artist sentimentally misled into an inappropriate application of his essentially aesthetic ideas. Thompson was concerned to show that Morris threw himself wholeheartedly into the Socialist movement of his day and understood thoroughly what he was doing. So far, I agree; but Thompson allowed himself to be misled into making Morris out to be, not only a Marxist—which up to a point he was—but also one who would have been in full sympathy, had he been living now, with the Communist interpretation of Marxism—one-party dictatorship, so-called 'democratic centralism', and all; and this, I feel sure, rests on a misconception of Morris's fundamental attitude. It was entirely contrary to the spirit of Morris's thought and feeling to endorse any policy that must involve regarding men in the mass as mere units in a social class, or the concentration of immense power in the hands of a few men claiming to be inspired representatives of a class, and its vanguard, and entitled as such to ride roughshod over the claims of individual men to be treated as ends as well as means, or to repudiate the very notion of rights as extending to men who were regarded as 'class enemies'. Morris, whatever his shortcomings as a thinker, had a deep sense of the right of the common man to be treated as important in himself and to be given freedom to shape his own conditions of living in common with his fellows on a scale not too large to afford him a real chance of managing his own affairs. He saw with exceptional clarity that most men could not have this chance as long as, through the greater part of their lives, they were condemned to work under orders at routine jobs in which they could find neither creative satisfaction nor any recognition that they were men and not merely parts of an inhuman productive machine they had no share in directing. He saw that the existence of such conditions in most men's daily work was bound to react adversely on their leisure and on their entire way of living, unfitting them to be either good, responsible citizens or happy and satisfied in their private lives. As remedies for this denial of humanity he proposed two things—the abolition of capitalist exploitation and the restoration to the common man of the joy in creative labour which mass production had taken away from him and of which he found convincing evidence in the quality of the everyday products of more primitive peoples and in the supreme achievements of medieval architecture and decorative art. He may have been mistaken—I think he was—in supposing that mankind could afford to turn its back on modern technology and to go back to handicraft as the means of meeting the everyday needs of its vast consuming public. But he was not wrong, but eminently right, in seeing that society could not be in health as long as it condemned most of its members to lives of irksome drudgery, made tolerable only by the pecuniary rewards attached to it. If we are to reject Morris's plea for a return to handicraft as the means of restoring the creative quality of everyday labour, we have to seek alternative ways of making work a source of pleasure instead of an evil that has to be endured in order to provide mankind with the means of living. To a person such as I am, who has always been able to do work he has enjoyed doing and would be miserable unless he could, this problem of joy in work appears absolutely fundamental to the achievement of the good life. Moreover, like Morris, I refuse to believe that other men are so different from myself as not to suffer deeply from spending their lives in tasks in which they find no pleasure, and I refuse to contemplate working for any kind of society that does not put high among its objectives the restoration to man, at a level much higher than that of the primitive peoples, of a chance to engage, in friendly co-operation with others, in satisfying forms of creative work. This is not the place for me to embark on any explanation of the means by which I believe modern societies can set about achieving this purpose without sacrificing the essential benefits of large-scale production. It is, however, pertinent to record that in thus defining an important part of the Socialist goal, the two Socialists to whom my debt is greatest are, first, William Morris and after him Fourier, who made man's pleasure in creative labour the cornerstone of his system.

SOCIALISM AND SOCIAL DEMOCRACY

Socialism, as conceived by all true socialists, is not simply an economic or political system, but fundamentally a way of life.[1] Its most deeply rooted idea is that of social equality involving not so much absolute equality of incomes (indeed it may not involve this at all) as basic equality of status—that is to say, a society without economic or social classes or other artificial barriers in the way of free and equal intercourse among all its members. Socialism involves a society in which friendships, marriages, and other personal and private contacts can be made at will, subject only to such barriers as it is beyond the power of organized society to remove. Evidently, under Socialism as under any other system, individuals will differ one from another very greatly both in personal tastes and interests and in the various kinds of ability—intellectual, technological, artistic, and so on. Some will excel others in capacities serviceable to the community, and some will positively disserve it, the more the abler they are. It cannot be any part of Socialism to eliminate inequalities of these kinds, though it can be to encourage the full development of valuable and to discourage that of anti-social behaviour. It must, however, be a most important part of the Socialist task to provide as far as possible for all a common basis

---

1 Unpublished typescript, n.d.

of knowledge and culture that will lessen the obstacles to free and equal intercourse in such a way as to remove the existing gulf between persons widely separated by differences of class, or wealth, or education.

In order to achieve this, Socialists must clearly stand for certain far-reaching economic and social changes. Though absolute equality of incomes may not be necessary, or even desirable, because of the need to preserve some monetary incentives to effort, differences of monetary reward must be small enough to prevent them from setting up barriers to easy intercourse on equal terms between those who are engaged in higher and in lower forms of work or service. This is fully possible because in a society in which income differences are small, small differences in monetary rewards can be as effective in stimulating effort as much bigger differences in a society where the range of incomes is very wide. As long as scarcity remains an inescapable part of the human condition—and that means, for the world as a whole, for as far ahead as it is profitable to look at present—the main need is to raise the basic standards of living and to expend on allowing a minority to enjoy higher standards only what must be so spent in order to maintain and increase production and to elicit other kinds of useful service. Socialism is entirely inconsistent with the continued existence of rich men; for the co-existence of riches and poverty renders the basic equality I have spoken of quite unattainable. Socialism is further inconsistent with the continuance of unearned incomes except those accorded by society to citizens who are unable to earn enough to sustain a tolerable standard by their own efforts—that is, the children, the aged, and the mentally or physically disabled. It therefore excludes both the inheritance of more than quite small amounts of money or property and the receipt of private incomes derived from rent or profits or interest unaccompanied by useful work. It does not, on the other hand, exclude modest incomes accruing to small farmers or shopkeepers or working craftsmen or professionals, where these incomes involve no exploitation of hired labour. How far such incomes will survive will depend on the forms or organization adopted for the conduct of such activities under Socialism: and this is a matter not of absolute principle but of convenience and is likely to vary from one society to another. In these fields, however, as well as in others, it will be necessary for a Socialist society to confine economic inequalities within narrow limits, in order to prevent the continuance or recrudescence of class distinctions.

The narrowing of income differences, however, is only one aspect of the social equality which Socialists have, as a matter of principle, to seek and to maintain. The elimination of artificial differences in education is no less important. I do not mean that in a Socialist society every individual should get either the same amount or beyond certain limits the same kind of formal education; but I do mean that for all, or rather nearly all, the earlier stages of schooling should take place in common schools, irrespective both of the pupils' individual abilities and of the parents' means and wills. So large a part of the educational process takes place outside school—mainly in the home—that a common school system by itself cannot establish educational equality. It can, nevertheless, make a substantial contribution and do a great deal, over generations, towards narrowing the differences of home environment, or at any rate establishing in this respect a much higher minimum standard. The common school does not, of course, mean that teachers are to disregard differences of bent or ability among children. The purpose is not to treat all alike, regardless of such things, but to ensure that, as far as possible, all mix together in school on socially equal terms and enter into possession of a common basic culture, however their abilities and interests may vary from child to child. One great advantage of the common school is that it makes possible varied provision for different interests and capacities without therewith dividing the children off into separate groups held apart by school snobbery, and that it prevents certain schools from becoming segregated places of preparation for more prestigeful jobs and for living in accordance with an exclusive code of behaviour.

This need for the common school arises not only in primary education but fully as much at the secondary and higher stages. For the present it is impracticable, even in most of the advanced countries, to put the minimum age for ending full-time schooling higher than sixteen, mainly for lack of enough competent teachers. But sixteen should be the irreducible minimum, and the aim should be to raise it by stages to eighteen, while perhaps allowing between sixteen and eighteen, in instances where a good case can be made out in the child's interest, some time to be spent out of school in approved courses of training on the job. What is supremely important, from a Socialist standpoint is that, during the secondary and higher stages of schooling there should be the same social mixing irrespective of ability or of parental means or status, of all children except that relatively small minority whom it is clearly necessary on the grounds of physical or mental abnormality to provide for in some kind of a special school.

I do not regard this basic equalitarianism as preventing some young persons from remaining at school to a higher age than others, on grounds of special ability or of the need for longer preparation for some sorts of jobs than for others. It would be palpably absurd to suggest that all children should, after staying at school up to seventeen or eighteen, go on to a University or College for a further three or more years. To suggest this would not only quite destroy University and College standards but also mean subjecting a great many young people to an educational process to which they are altogether unsuited, and which many of them would dislike and resent. In a Socialist society, as much as in any other, there will be jobs calling for many different levels, as well as kinds, of educational qualification and attainment; and one purpose of any educational system is bound to be the turning out of young people in roughly the right proportions for filling these various jobs. Not of course the sole purpose; for the most fundamental purpose of all is to turn out men and women capable both of being good citizens and of living satisfactory and rounded lives of their own in ways compatible with the general well-being. No society, however, can afford to ignore the vocational aspect of education, or not to adapt its provision to changing vocational needs: nor can any society, in the interests of equality, afford not to give more and higher education to those who will be needed to perform the more exacting tasks in the planning and execution of economic and social affairs as well as in the fields of learning and culture. A democratic society, no less than other kinds, needs leaders and pioneers: the difference is that it tries to draw upon all useful talent, irrespective of social background, and to prevent its leaders from becoming isolated from the rest of the people as a privileged group or caste.

I have stressed the importance of basic equality in formal education at both the primary and the secondary stage; but it is hardly less important to do all that can be done to make it easy for those who have entered on gainful occupations to continue in their education in adult life either to equip themselves for more exacting jobs or to improve their capacity for citizenship or the quality of their personal lives. Adult education ranks for Socialists not as a relatively unimportant amenity, but as an essential service for wide groups of men and women who can find in it the means to more satisfactory living: and the higher the general standard of education becomes the more demand for it there is likely to be, both as a vocational and as a general civic service. It is an essential part of democracy, and therefore of Socialism, that society shall be so organized as to draw as many as possible of the citizens into active participation in its affairs, not only in politics and in local government or in economic matters, but also over the immense field of private life, where group activity is needed for the successful pursuit of the art of living. A democratic society is one in which power and responsibility, and therewith active participation, are widely diffused at every level, in such a way as to give everyone the best possible chance to be active and influential in whatever kinds of group action best suit his bent. Though it is undeniable that some men and women are, in general terms, much cleverer and possessed of much more initiative than others, it is also the case that there are many not easily transferable kinds of special ability, resting on natural endowment and specialized interest. And it is no less important, in a democracy, to provide ample scope for these specific abilities than to make the most of more all-round superiorities of capacity.

To a limited extent, social participation comes of itself and depends on the capacity of the people for organizing their own affairs without needing help or support from the state or from any official body. This, however, is true only to a very limited extent, even in the most advanced societies. In order to be able to engage in social activities, people must have places where they can meet in reasonably convenient conditions—playing fields, clubrooms, halls that can be hired at not undue cost for meetings and entertainments, libraries and reading rooms, and so on. They need help in forming and maintaining dramatic and musical societies, and in cultivating the arts of neighbourliness. In the poorer areas sheer poverty is a formidable obstacle to social activity, which even in its simpler forms costs money which most peasants and low-paid workers cannot afford; and to leave these things entirely in the hands of commercial providers is apt to mean that little or nothing is done to meet the needs of a larger part of the people—above all of the elderly and of those who are out of tune with the tastes of the majority. Not only are the poorer quarters of our towns singularly ill-provided with meeting-places, playing fields, and open spaces, and with every kind of social amenity designed to foster good neighborhood and free co-operative activity: it is also, alas the case that in building new suburbs and housing estates we have too often erected mere aggregations of dwellings, with little or no provision for sociable activities extending beyond the individual household. Moreover, in Great Britain at any rate, though something has been done to provide village halls in many of the more populous villages, there remain a large majority of villages devoid of any social centre except the church or chapel and the public house; and in many of the smaller villages the closing of the local school has not only removed one possible, though usually inconvenient, meeting place, but has also deprived the small community of a key figure in the collective social life—the local school teacher. This closing may have made for higher educational efficiency, and have saved expenditure on replacing obsolete buildings; but it has also been a factor in lowering the vitality of community life in the small centres affected by it. Such matters, far from being of minor importance, deeply affect the quality of living in both town and country.

There is indeed nothing more essential to the making of a truly democratic Socialist community then the taking of effective steps to counteract the tendencies towards centralization and bureaucracy that manifest themselves in all big organizations and are greatly aggravated in the world of today both by international tensions and by the recent developments of scientific technology. States that are engaged in an arms race cannot avoid accumulating centralized power into their hands; and the centralization of power inevitably means bureaucracy, whether the bureaucrats are soldiers or civilians. At the same time the vast scale on which the key operations of mass production need to be carried on and the ever increasing domination of these processes by advanced scientific techniques intelligible only to specialists make for the centralization of economic power in the hands of a few men who are at the head of huge, and often, monopolistic business structures and, because of their key position in determining the course of investment, become in effect a second Government with which the political Government can on no account afford to quarrel.

This centralization of industrial power is found in privately and in publicly owned industries alike. There is not much difference in this respect between the National Coal Board or the Central Electricity Authority in Great Britain, or the Renault administration in France, and such giants of private enterprise as Imperial Chemical Industries or the British Motor Corporation, or the great coal or steel enterprises in the continental Coal and Steel 'Community'—except that the nationalized enterprises are less free to operate or to establish business connections outside the national frontiers. Attempts have been made to allow the workers a sort of consultative participation in matters of industrial policy through 'joint consultation' in Great Britain and in France through the compulsory institution of *comités d'entreprise*. But such methods, though they may have their advantages, do nothing to confer on the workers any real share in management or control. Under conditions of full employment organized workers have no doubt a considerable power to refuse to do what management tells them when its commands run counter to established trade union or workshop practice. But this power is entirely negative; it sets up tensions which there is no way of resolving save by a trial of strength. Joint consultation can, I agree, work well within limits where both sides are determined to do their best to make it work, and above all where management takes care to consult the workers before reaching a decision that affects them, and not when it has already decided what it wants to do. But such real consultation becomes much more difficult where the projects which effect working conditions are the outcome of some major plan worked out by a management at the highest technological level, so that one part of them cannot be modified to meet workers' objections without upsetting the whole intricately interrelated plan. In such cases it is exceedingly difficult to make joint consolidation a reality, or to prevent the small band of high technologists from becoming the effective arbiters of the working conditions of the whole enterprise.

This is a very serious matter; for democracy cannot effectively exist in industry unless it can be applied, first and foremost, on a small scale, in the actual workshops where the pinch is directly felt. It may be possible to build up on foundations of workshop democracy a superstructure of democratic participation at higher levels. What is quite impossible is to establish this higher level democracy without these foundations—for example, by consultation between employers' associations and trade unions at national or regional levels or by the appointment of trade union directors to the boards of big industrial concerns—as in the German form of *Mitbestimmung*. In the one case, the trade union negotiators are too remote from the workers they are deemed to represent to be able to understand all the varied grievances arising out of particular workshop situations; in the other, the trade union director necessarily becomes involved in an insoluble conflict of loyalties—to the trade union and its members and to the firm as a business unit. To the extent to which automation develops, involving remote control of productive operations by electronic methods, the obstacles in the way of effective co-determination of working conditions at the factory or workshop level seem likely to become still more formidable.

These and other considerations, such as the alleged absence of any desire for participation in managerial responsibility on the part of the majority of rank and file workers, have led many who regard themselves as Socialists to dismiss for the demand for 'industrial democracy' as impracticable, and to insist that the true road to democratic responsibility lies through the subjection of the high management to effective parliamentary control. Parliament, it is said, should be regarded as presenting the whole people in their capacity as consumers; and the boards and commissions to which the administration of nationalized enterprises has been entrusted should be made more thoroughly responsible to Parliament as well as to the Ministers of the public departments to which they are at present loosely attached. The Communists, from a different approach, arrive at a very similar conclusion, asserting that 'workers' control' means control by the entire working class and not by any section of it and that centralized planning under the authority of the workers' State constitutes the essential reality of democracy in its application to industrial affairs.

In my view, both these opinions entirely destroy the possibility of real democracy. I am in favour of Parliament and of the Government taking a much more effective part in the direction of industrial policy in the nationalized industries than it is doing today in either Britain or France. But, in the first place, it is sheerly impossible for Parliament to exercise effective control over the nationalized industries in respect of the host of detailed matters that affect the well-being and satisfaction of the workers, and secondly, government departments could do this only by duplication at immense cost, and to the accompaniment of endless friction of the technical and administrative apparatus of these industries, which would thus come to have two rival managements getting continually into each other's way. Competent technicians and administrators are not so plentiful that any country can afford to use their services so wastefully; nor would the institutionalization of friction be likely to lend to efficient work. If close and detailed government control is wanted, the only way to bring it about is to abolish the boards and commissions which have been set up to administer the nationalized industries and to put their management fairly and squarely in the hands of the Civil Service, subject only to the usual, not very effective, ministerial control. This, however, is precisely the system which boards and commissions were designed to avoid; for not so long ago it seemed to be generally agreed that civil service methods were quite unsuitable for the conduct of regular business operations. Moreover, even if this method were adopted, the problem of bringing the industries in question under effective control by *Parliament* would be no nearer solution. Parliament has neither the time nor the experience needed for such a purpose; and a Parliament that did possess these capacities would be quite unsuited for its other and certainly no less important tasks.

It is indeed very necessary to ensure, even in the 'mixed' systems of public and private enterprise that prevail today, effective control of the major policies of nationalized industries especially in the fields of investment and pricing, by representatives of the whole people; and this need would evidently be greater still in a Socialist society. This, however, has not a great deal to do with the kinds of participation in management that are of most interest to the workers as directly affecting the conditions under which their work is done. The matters of most concern to the rank-and-file worker are those which alter the nature of his job, the tools he is given to work with, the allocation of tasks, and the discipline under which the work has to be done—and also, of course, the conditions of engagement and dismissal, or 'standing off', and of production and retirement, the arrangements for learning and apprenticeship, and the amenities or lack of amenities provided. It makes an immense difference to the rank-and-file worker what sort of person his foreman or superior is and how the higher management encourages its foremen or superiors to behave; how good, and how fair, the prospects of promotion are; what safeguards exist against unreasonable dismissal or favouritism in 'standing off' or in the allocation of tasks; how well and considerately arrangements for training are made; with what companions a man or woman is grouped for squad work, or where jobs need to be passed on from shift to shift; and so on, through a host of matters that are very largely particular to a single factory, or workshop, or department, and can be dealt with only on the spot, by direct relations which it is impracticable for the most part to regulate by nationwide or even by district bargaining between employers' associations and trade unions, or even by written agreements between trade unions and particular firms.

These are the basic issues relating to what, in Great Britain, is commonly called 'workers' control'. (I am aware that, in French, the word *controle* has a substantially different meaning.) They are predominantly small-scale issues, even in the largest establishments; and they are largely matters of the social atmosphere prevailing in particular establishments. A great many of the small unofficial strikes that have occurred in recent years, at any rate in Great Britain, have arisen out of the friction over this type of thing, and have been difficult to settle because the matter has been, at bottom, one of bad or unimaginative personal relations. A worker spends so large a part of his waking life in the place of employment that whatever occurs during the hours of his work is bound to react powerfully on his general outlook. If the work atmosphere is one of hostility and of disclaiming all responsibility for giving of his best in the collective effort, how can it be expected that this attitude will not in a great number of cases, be carried over into other parts of men's lives, so as to incline them to be worse citizens, worse husbands or parents, and more wary and mistrustful in their everyday personal intercourse? I am not suggesting that everyone is affected in these ways; but I feel sure that a great many are, and that it is foolish to expect an atmosphere of ill-temper and irresponsibility at work to go, in general, with the atmosphere of friendliness, co-operation, and acceptance of mutual responsibility which a democratic Socialist society requires. No doubt, the bad atmosphere that exists in many places of work is partly due to the class opposition that is inherent in capitalism; but it is undeniable that it is also much affected by the specific behaviour of managers, supervisors, and rank-and-file workers in particular establishments, and that public operation of industry is not necessarily a cure.

The conclusion I have drawn for many years—and still draw to-day—is that the delegation of as many small-scale managerial and supervisory tasks as possible to the workers themselves is not a concession to be made grudgingly in response to working-class pressure, but an imperative need of Socialism. I do not see how the work of a Socialist society is to get properly done unless the main body of those who do it can be got into a mood of feeling personal responsibility for doing it well. A Socialist society could not, even if it would, coerce its workers, or any considerable proportion of them, into working harder or better than they felt like working of their accord. Even capitalist society is finding very great difficulty in doing this under conditions of full employment, which have caused the 'sack' to lose most of its terrors; and the longer full employment lasts the more will the workers feel independent of any external coercion to produce more or better than they feel an impulse to do. A Socialist society, if it is to be a democracy, will have to master the art of diffusing a keen sense of responsibility for good work among the main body of the workers; and I can imagine no way of doing this except by placing real responsibility in the workers' hands and positively encouraging them to 'run their own show' on a co-operative footing. This, as I see it, involves accepting their right to work under supervisors, not imposed on them from above, but of their own choosing, and to be given the greatest possible scope for determining, in their workplace groups, the rules and arrangements under which their work is to be done, including, wherever practicable, choice of immediate workmates. I do not indeed suggest that all supervisors should be chosen simply by election by those whose work they are to supervise. I recognize the need to limit the choice to adequately qualified candidates; but subject to that, I do hold that in a Socialist society the moral rule should be for foreman and supervisors to be chosen by those who will have to work under them and to be regarded as members of the working group rather than as 'bosses' men' imposed on the group by the higher management. I believe such a change could have a profound effect on the atmosphere of workplace relations and could do a great deal towards developing an attitude of personal and group responsibility for doing the job well.

When I am told that most workers feel no desire for this responsibility I am neither surprised nor disposed to deny the fact. Desire for responsibility comes to most men and women, not of itself, but as a response to inspiring leadership; and under a system which has steadily repulsed every proposal to delegate responsible powers to the workers it would be most surprising if the desire for it were widely felt. It is the positive task of Socialist leadership to arouse this desire; but this cannot be done as long as so many leading Socialists are too distrustful of the workers to be ready to help towards putting the reality of power into their hands.

I have written at some length about the question of industrial democracy because I remain convinced that it is a key question and that the man who rejects the principle of democracy as inapplicable to the workers in his work, even if he calls himself a Socialist, is no democrat in any real sense of the word. As long as industry is run by a hierarchy from above, penetrating tight until the conditions of the ordinary workers' daily tasks, it will be foolish to look for a society permeated in all its activities by the democratic spirit. He who is a slave or a rebel in his daily working life will be also, in enough cases to affect the working of society, a slave, a rebel, or a tyrant in his conduct as a citizen and as a man. Democracy, as the stamp on a social system, cannot exist in one aspect of life if it is persistently denied in another.

Similarly, outside the economic field, democracy needs for its maintenance the greatest possible encouragement for its leaders to free associative activity in every part of the social body—encouragement and positive help to form and carry on associations, clubs and informal groups of friends and neighbours for doing in common whatever it is harmlessly pleasant or socially useful to do by such means. And, just as the most important aspect of industrial democracy is concerned with the small-scale doings of the particular workplace, so, in these other fields, what matters most is every opportunity to act together at the neighbourhood level, and the superstructure cannot be soundly built except on strong foundations at the primary points of personal contact. The great consumers' Co-operative movement, though to-day it has to face many problems which drive it in the direction of centralized organization and control, owes its vitality mainly to having been built up in the first instance, on essentially local foundations, and has steadily lost the loyalty of its members as the societies have become too big for personal contacts to count as they used to. The same could be said of many other organizations, which have lost the personal touch as their membership has expanded without adequate measure being taken to preserve the vitality of those basic units. The same disease has notably affected political parties, especially in Great Britain, where two distinct factors have been at work to strengthen bureaucratic centralization and to undermine the vitality of local groups. One of these is the increasing extent to which modern constituencies have come, in the pursuit of numerical near equality, to stand not for real local communities but for more fractional parts of an entire country, with their boundaries altered again and again on account of relative population changes. This type of constituency, the result of a misguided search for numerical equivalence of voters, in practice favours the 'carpet-bagger' against the real representative of local community opinion, and destroys an essential quality of real parliamentary representation—for whom, or what, is the real 'carpet-bagger' really supposed to represent, unless it be the central caucus of his party? Secondly, the growing intensity of national party conflict and the close balance of the leading parties have been responsible for the practical elimination of the 'independent' and for a severe tightening up of central party discipline that has made the MP an exponent much less of his own or of his constituents' opinions than of an official party line. This curse of centralized party rule has also penetrated deeply into local government so that local government elections are now fought much more on national than on local issues and the local councillor comes to represent increasingly, not his constituents, but the distant party office which directed his campaign.

Centralization, except in relation to matters which imperatively require uniform treatment over large areas, is always the foe of democracy, and should be the foe of Socialism. But, alas, many who call themselves Socialists are actually strong supporters of centralization and even look to Socialists to carry it further still. This was always a characteristic of German Social Democracy, with its Marxist tendency to identify the trend towards Socialism with ever increasing unification of the control of the means of production and its dislike of the libertarian Socialism of Proudhon and Bakunin, of Kropotkin and of William Morris, and of that considerable Belgian theorist, César de Paepe. Communism has inherited this tendency to worship hugeness, and leave out of account the fact that men get no bigger as the size of the implements they need to control increases; so that so-called 'mass democracy' becomes very difficult to distinguish from the tyranny of things over men, who become the instruments of the vast, inhuman structure which they themselves have set up. Even if democracy meant only the reduction of all men to a common insignificance, democracy could not flourish under such a regime; for in practice the few small men who are elevated to the task of controlling these juggernauts become inflated into tyrants whose power grossly exceed their capacities and who are at present busily leading mankind to the very brink of disaster.

Yet one must not, in reaction against the evils of the contemporary world, lean too far backwards against the largely unavoidable growth of centralization, bureaucracy and large-scale forms of economic and social action. It is immensely desirable to increase production in order to get rid of the shortages which oppress both body and mind; and there are many valuable activities which can be organized only on a vast scale if their products are to be made available to the common run of men. It is illegitimate to oppose these activities on the ground that they are difficult to carry on democratically, for to do so involves attempting to deny men and women many things that they have every right to want and to demand. The most we can properly do is to resolve that, as far as we can influence the course of events, no activity shall be organized on a larger scale than technical considerations clearly require and that every advance of centralization shall be accompanied by all practical measures for offsetting its human effects by creating special instruments to check the abuse of centralized power and to promote co-operative defence among those who are exposed to its effects. We cannot afford to forego large-scale organization; but the larger it has to be, the more must control and administration be shared by it with smaller groupings, endowed with real, though limited, powers and the more must the experts who administer it be trained and encouraged to consider the human as well as the technical consequence of their acts and be made subject to checks imposed by the concerted action of those who are subject to their commands. In this respect all social activity is interdependent; a victory or a defeat for democratic freedom in one field becomes a victory or defeat in another that may seem quite remote from the first.

We must, however, be always on our guard to make sure that the freedoms we set ourselves to uphold and extend are democratic freedoms. It is all too easy, in the name of freedom, to rally to the defence of freedoms that are meant substantially, to apply only to the privileged few. The defence of democratic freedom should not involve any of us in defending freedoms which are in fact freedoms, not of men as men, but of the purse. I do not dispute that democratic tolerance requires a large measure of freedom for individuals and for groups to run counter to the behaviour that it would be most convenient to make universal, or general, in the interests of unified planning. It is of the very nature of democratic planning to be much less tidy and complete than centralized planning from above can be made to appear, at any rate on paper. But the price of untidiness and non-conformism is well worth paying to a considerable amount, wherever it can be shown to be, not bolstering up privilege under the pretext of *laissez-faire*, but making it easier for unprivileged persons and groups to stand out against the planners' wish—maybe well-intentioned—to order them about. This is largely a matter of the social atmosphere as a whole and of the diffusion of social prestige among the people. A society divided into conflicting classes is all too apt to give weight to human grievances and aspirations proportionate to the prestige of the complainants rather than to the nature and strength of their case. Socialism is designed to get rid of those forms of differential prestige that arise out of class distinctions and to narrow even those which are based on differences dependent upon occupational status and function. To achieve this elimination and narrowing is an essential element in the making of a democratic Socialist society. I have tried to indicate some of the ways in which it is possible to set about these tasks; but I am well aware of the strength of the forces making the other way and anticipate no easy victory. The harder the task, however, the more we ought to try, if the Socialism we stand for is more than the victory of centralized bureaucracy over private capitalist exploitation, and if our ideas of Socialism extend not only to political control but also to the development of democratic participation in every field of social action, and above all at the neighbourhood level that fits in best with our diminutive human statures.

HOW FAR MUST WE
CENTRALIZE?

It is an assumption running through all Marxist writings—and through most of the books of other economists as well—that advancing techniques of production mean larger and larger-scale production, and therewith an increasing aggregation of the industrial proletariat into bigger and bigger agglomerations of human beings.[1] This was indeed a model characteristic of industrialism when Marx formulated his theory; and, as he also assumed that Socialism would take over and develop further the highest technical accomplishments of capitalism, it seemed to him to follow that the growth in the scale of production was helping to make the world ready for Socialism, and that Socialism would involve an increasing concentration of the labour force in large establishments. It was also assumed that agriculture, in order to become highly productive and to apply really modern techniques, would have to be removed from the hands of peasant households cultivating on a family basis and somehow collectivized, either in State farms employing rural labourers in large numbers or in peasant collectives supported by State-provided tractor stations as well as by State or Co-operative credit. Moreover, in industry small-scale artisan production, Co-operative as well as individual, was looked down

---

1 Unpublished typescript, c. 1958.

on as obsolescent and as destined to disappear as the inability of the artisans to compete with the big mechanized factories became more and more manifest.

These views were largely correct as simple descriptions of the trend of capitalist production in the nineteenth and early twentieth centuries, at any rate in the industrial field. It is true, that, even in industry, small-scale production showed itself a good deal more resilient and persistent than Marx had expected it to be, and that it continually found new scope for its activities in newly developing branches or production, in supplying components for the great firms, and in meeting market demands for a variety of luxury products. Nevertheless, in each advanced country each successive study or census showed an increasing proportion of workers concentrated in the bigger establishments and also a tendency for these to get bigger still in terms of the numbers employed in them—even apart from the evident tendency for the scale of business organization and coordinated financial control to outrun the scale of production by bringing a number of establishments under common control.

Can we, however, take it for granted that these tendencies are still operative in the second half of the twentieth century? I, for one, do not think so, even if they still persist quite strongly. I argue that the scale of production—and, even more, that of unified financial control—continues to increase, and that till quite recently the aggregation of workers into larger and larger establishments has, on the whole, been increasing with it, despite the arrival of some large establishments—for example, flour-mills—in which mechanization has been carried so far that only small bodies of workers are employed. But, in general, the growth in the size of the big labour units has been due to the multiplication of repetitive, routine jobs, at most semi-skilled; and if a large proportion of these jobs are taken over by automatic machines the most potent factor making for the aggregation of workers in large establishments would cease to operate. The establishments might nonetheless be large and employ larger and larger means of capital; but instead of hosts of machine-minders they might employ only much smaller numbers of workers, each carrying a larger measure of responsibility and being called on for a more exacting display of skill. To bring this about is of course precisely the characteristic of what is called 'automation'; and, rash as it would be to prophesy how rapid the speed of automation is likely to be, no one, I think, doubts that it will spread widely, in the long run at least. As this spread occurs, the mass-employment establishment with its thousands of routine workers is likely to be superseded by the automatic establishment employing a relatively small labour force: so that the establishments employing most workers will no longer be those with the highest total output, but rather those in which the scale of output is not large enough to cover the high capital costs of automation.

It is true that there has been as yet little sign of this actually coming about. In the country which has been expanding output in the heavy industries at the fastest rate—the Soviet Union—the biggest concerns are still those which also employ most workers. But this may be, at any rate in part, because in the Soviet Union capital is still a scarcer factor than labour: so that it is easier to expand production by employing more workers than by installing complicated and expensive labour-saving devices. These, indeed, have found more favour in the United States, whose capital is more plentiful than workers, and high wages provide a strong incentive for economy in the use of labour. But, even if the Soviet Union is at present still deterred from automation by its high capital cost, it is surely unlikely that this state of affairs will continue indefinitely. Indeed, the immense spread in the Soviet Union of technical and technological education strongly suggests an impending shift of emphasis to the techniques characteristic of the most advanced sectors in the capitalist world.

If and as this shift comes about, either in the Soviet Union or elsewhere, under Socialism or under capitalism, it is likely to be accompanied by a change in the structure and mental attitude of the working-class movement. In the present phase of working-class organization, one sees largely reflected the growth of mass organization aggregating a growing proportion of the workers into large groups subject to a common discipline and reacting to this discipline in numerous ways. The temper and atmosphere in a factory or other workplace employing thousands of men and women is usually very different from that of a small establishment employing a few dozens, or even a few hundreds. It is not necessarily more militant, though I think it tends to be so; but it reflects a more habitual acceptance of common leadership, and favours the growth either of inclusive industrial unions or of the enormous general unions which have developed so rapidly in this country. In doing so, it strengthens the full-time trade union officers, and makes for [missing word[2]] activity on the part of their rank-and-file members.

If this structure were now to change, and a high proportion of their routine workers were replaced by automatic devices, clearly the atmosphere of the establishment affected would change too. The workers who remained in them would be, to an increasing extent, technicians possessing a special competence and training in tasks of machine supervision and control, and playing each a much more distinctive part in the running of the establishment than was played by the [missing word] machine-minding labour force. Of course, if the change came suddenly, there would be a vast displacement of workers who would be unable to find alternative jobs, and the effects on trade union bargaining power would be disastrous. But I think we can be reasonably sure that automation will not come in like that—if only because of its very high capital costs; and if it comes more gradually there will be time for the trade unions to adapt themselves and for the displaced workers to be trained for alternative

---

2 Compare p. 28 above.

jobs and reabsorbed. It should, however, be borne in mind that the pace at which automation can spread economically depends very greatly on the rate of expansion in the demand for consumers' goods and on the standardization of this demand: so that any attempts to cut wages because of labour redundancy would in itself tend to slow down the process of automation by depressing consumers' demand. Indeed, today in Great Britain the Government's attempts to compress the total volume of demand—spending plus investment—is having just this effect by slowing up the process of mechanization as well as by holding down wages.

My present concern, however, is not with the Government's mistaken economic policy, but with the working-class movement. Theorists, whether of the Communist or of the Social Democratic varieties, have alike accepted the assumption that the most advanced techniques—and accordingly those most appropriate to Socialism—involve not only a continued increase in the scale of production, but also workplaces employing even larger aggregations of routine workers. The most notable writers who have stood out against the acceptance of this trend have been not Socialists, but Anarchists such as Kropotkin and original thinkers such as Gandhi. To Kropotkin, writing before automation had become technically possible, it appeared that the spread of electric power would give a new opportunity to the small workshop and could bring about the decentralization of industry; while Gandhi envisaged the economic development of India largely in terms of relatively small production units resting on village production. These, I know, are unpopular authorities to quote to present-day Socialists; but may they not prove to have been prophetic? Were they not, in any event, right in seeing the mass-industrial establishment not as a blessing and a real advance of the human spirit, but rather as a means of evolving man to a mass-discipline which could add to the [missing word] of the labour-process, and thus make for unhappiness in work?

At any rate, I am suggesting that Socialists have been a good deal too ready to take it for granted that growing aggregation of workers into large groups is a necessary condition of high productivity and a necessary concomitant of technological progress. I at least should feel a good deal happier if this assumption were less readily made and if more emphasis were put on the quality of work rather than on its scale or the size of the labour force brought together by it. For to [missing word] the future on larger and larger aggregations of routine operatives and to regard such aggregations as preparing us for Socialism does not hold out, to me at least, the prospect of a Socialism under which men would be happy or making the best use of their creative qualities.

SOCIALISM, CENTRALIST OR LIBERTARIAN?

To MY MIND, THERE HAVE ALWAYS BEEN TWO FUNDAMENTAL CLEAVAGES IN Socialist thought—the cleavage between revolutionaries and reformists, and the cleavage between centralizers and federalists.[1] But much more attention is nowadays paid to the first of these than to the second, partly no doubt because the second line of division is less clear and varies a good deal from country to country, and partly because the second is all too apt to be dismissed as a quarrel between Socialists and Anarchists or Anarcho-Syndicalists, who were turned out from the Second International and then from the Third, and have been excluded by revolutionists and reformists alike. It is true that, in recent years, there has been a good deal of talk about 'decentralization', first of all in Yugoslavia and more recently in the Soviet Union as well; but 'decentralization' and federalism are essentially different ideas. Broadly speaking, decentralization, at any rate in the Soviet Union, is only a matter of local or regional freedom and initiative in administrative matters, rather than in the control of high policy, whereas federalism involves an insistence on local control as primary, and on the federal co-ordination of affairs over larger areas, so as to leave the final authority in the hands of local agencies directly responsive to

---

1   *ISSS Information*, 1959.

popular opinion. Bakunin's hostility to the State rested on regarding it as essentially a coercive and authoritative organ of government, set over and against the people, and on his insistence that the only legitimate basis of cooperative or communal effort was a locality small enough to be permeated by the spirit of local fellowship and solidarity; whereas Marxists, defining the State as essentially an organ of class-coercion and maintaining that it was destined to wither away in a classless society, at the same time insisted on the need to capture and remake it for the purpose of the transition, rather than to abolish it prematurely as an instrument of Socialist construction. This holds good both for Social Democrats and for Communists, though the former aimed at capturing and adapting the existing State, whereas the latter insisted on destroying the bourgeois State and replacing it by a workers' state embodying the principle of proletarian dictatorship. Moreover, both—but especially the Communists—laid emphasis on the growing internationalism of economic affairs, as requiring a more than sectional unity of the working class for taking over the control of them.

Indeed, both right-wing and left-wing Marxists have always been strong supporters of centralized authority, and deeply hostile to all notions that involve breaking it up. Long ago, Social Democrats were arguing—as Kautsky, for example, did repeatedly—that the process of capitalist unification of businesses into large trusts and combines was preparing the way for Socialism as a unified structure of economic control and welcoming large-scale enterprise as a necessary prerequisite of Socialism. Marxists always had a peculiarly strong dislike of the peasant, because of the small-scale characteristic of peasant agriculture, and insisted that the large industrialized farm was greatly superior to it. Indeed, they again and again prophesied the impending disappearance of the peasant because of his inability to compete with large-scale farming, and received with displeasure and even incredulity statistical evidence of the persistence of peasant holdings. In the Soviet Union the collectivization of farm holdings was regarded as a great and essential step in the direction of Socialism both because large-scale farming was believed to be more productive, as making possible the mechanization of farm processes and the application of higher techniques and because collectivization would help to socialize the minds of the peasantry by weaning them from individual to collective habits of mind and by assimilating them to the industrial proletariat. According to the Marxian doctrine, Socialism involves the application of the most advanced techniques to every branch of production; for otherwise the high output needed to put an end to the scramble for the means of good living cannot be brought to an end. Large-scale production is assumed to mean more efficient production, and its full application to involve still greater concentration of control, up to the co-ordinated planning of whole economies on a national, and even on a supra-national, scale.

Thus Marxists—Social Democrats equally with Communists—have always been unifiers, and have regarded the building of Socialism as bound up with the extension of mass-production techniques. As capitalism has, in any case, tended to bring about an ever-increasing scale of both production and marketing, this has meant that Marxian Socialists have been, to a considerable extent, working with rather than against the grain of capitalism, in a technological sense, and have regarded as 'ripest' for socialization those industries and services which, under capitalism, have already become concentrated in few hands. They have also gone beyond what has been achieved under capitalist auspices by advocating fully planned economies, resting on unified planning of output and marketing in all branches of production.

Against this concentrationist tendency of Marxism there have always been ranged tendencies to insist on the importance of the small unit as offering a greatly superior chance for real democracy. This tendency has been manifested in a number of movements which have rejected the concentrationist aspect of Marxism without necessarily rejecting its other aspects. In Bakunin the form taken was insistence on the fundamental importance of the local community group, as embodying a natural solidarity essentially different from the artificial solidarity of larger groupings. In Proudhon the same tendency took the form of insistence on the key importance of a social basis of 'free contract', backed up by a system of 'gratuitous credit', as the means of ensuring for the small producer the full fruit of his personal or family labour. In Pelloutier's version of the Syndicalist utopia and in other variants of Anarcho-Syndicalism the stress on the natural solidarity of the local Commune re-emerged, but with greater stress on the specialized occupational groups comprising the Commune and accordingly with more emphasis on the role of the *syndicats*—the local trade unions—in the structure of the coming society. The Guild Socialists and the Industrial Unionists in America dissolved the extreme localism of Anarcho-Syndicalism by assuming that functional democracy could be realized on a larger, national scale; but they too—or at any rate the Guild Socialists—aimed at a practical diffusion of authority as a means of preventing undue concentration of power in a single instrument, however conceived. They were Pluralists, in opposition to the monolithic tendencies which seemed to them to be inherent in the Marxism of both Communists and Social Democrats; and they found themselves in conflict with both variants of Marxism because they wished to diffuse social power and responsibility instead of concentrating them in the hands of an omni-competent State, whatever its nature. On these grounds, they were dismissed by the Marxists of both camps as 'petit bourgeois ideologues', putting forward notions inconsistent with the Marxists' insistence on the pre-eminence of class and class unity in the struggle for Socialism.

Yet the libertarian Socialists certainly did not regard themselves as unfaithful to the conceptions of class-struggle and class-unity. Both Bakunin and

Proudhon wrote eloquently, in their several ways, about working-class solidarity; and the doctrines of class-war took a prominent place in the expositions of the Syndicalists in France and Italy and in American Industrial Unionism. The Guild Socialists, too, made their appeal to the class of producers and sought to build up the new society on a foundation of working-class solidarity. What marked all these off from the Marxists was a tendency to insist that the working class was not an undifferentiated mass, to be progressively unified in terms of class under the leadership of an industrial proletariat engaged in large-scale industry, but rather a greatly diversified body of persons having common basic interests which would find concerted expression through their own organizations, so that the control of society as a whole would express their unity in difference rather than their simple unity. This difference comes out very clearly in controversies over the control of industry. Thus, while Social Democrats argue for ultimate control by consumers—that is, by all, in their normal capacity as consumers—and Communists reject, in the name of working-class unity, projects of sectional control in industries by those engaged in them—Syndicalists and Guild Socialists urge the need for control to be broken up, so as to be brought more nearly home to bodies of workers employed in a common industry or enterprise, while recognizing the need for co-ordination between industries and enterprises in terms of an agreed common objective.

It is because I agree fundamentally with the last of those views that I have never regarded myself as a Marxist. It has always appeared to me that to treat either the whole body of consumers—or working-class consumers—or the entire industrial proletariat as constituting in essence a single unified mass is inconsistent with real democracy because masses so large and amorphous are incapable of acting together except under a top leadership which is bound to substitute its own control for the control of the mass it is supposed to lead. In other words, so-called 'mass democracy' inevitably leads to bureaucracy and bureaucratic control in which the individual is unable to make his voice heard in shaping of policy. The worst example of this tendency in practice is the so-called 'democratic centralism' of the Soviet Union, under which the democracy fatally disappears, and what is left is only the centralism of a party leadership able to ride roughshod over the main mass, and more and more inclined to outlaw as 'fractionalism' every attempt of persons and groups outside the recognized leadership to think for themselves and seek to influence policy. Men are not so constituted that they can extend the scale of their operations indefinitely without forfeiting the power of controlling them. The place where the shoe pinches most, in everyday affairs, is the place where a group of fellow workers are engaged in a common enterprise of a specific kind; and if men are deprived of the opportunity to regulate their common affairs at this modest level they are incapable of exerting any real control over the conduct of greater affairs, which are often past their understanding and technical competence.

Ordinarily, in the conduct of associations which are supposed to be under the members' control, the need is recognized for splitting up the larger aggregation into branches or groups, to which are assigned at any rate some powers of self-determination and control. Even the Communist Parties have their local branches and cells, to which certain limited powers, as well as functions, are assigned. But it makes a vast difference how powers are actually distributed between the centre and the lesser units of an organization. Thus policies and proposals can either be habitually passed down from the centre for local or group endorsement or can be passed up from the lesser units for central consideration—or, of course, there can be a two-way process providing for both methods of policy making. What seems to me beyond question is that, where the initiative rests mainly or exclusively with the centre, real democracy vanishes and is replaced by a totalitarian form of control. Even if the central body is in a better position than any branch or section can be for envisaging the total result of any proposed line of action, this does not justify it in imposing its will on the lesser groups, or in monopolizing the flow of relevant information so as to deprive the lesser groups of effective access to proposals coming up from below, or advocated by a dissident section of opinion. This cannot be secured unless a diversity of views is placed before the whole body of members, or unless the holders of divergent opinions are free to engage in propaganda for them without being accused of 'deviation' or worse. The alternative, under which one set of opinions is passed from the centre and the effective expression of other views is suppressed, or severely limited, is 'centralism' no doubt, but not democratic centralism, which could be at most an enforcement of unity in action after full and free discussions of alternative lines of policy.

I am not saying, be it observed, that it is *never* right to suppress expressions of opinion. I agree that, especially in revolutionary situations, such suppression can rightfully occur, and is fully consistent with the spirit of democracy. But suppression should be directed only against opinions which are clearly hostile to democracy, and dangerous to it; and it should never be used to enforce conformity in any matter in which conformity is less than essential in the pursuance of democratic ends. There may be, in *some* circumstances, *some* matters on which conformity is truly indispensable; but they are surely few, and the occasions for them exceptional. It is all too easy for a well-entrenched bureaucracy to suppose that exact compliance with its opinions, in word and deed, is a *sine qua non*: most of all, when the bureaucracy has convinced itself that there is but one correct view, of which it is the rightful interpreter. But it is a mere mockery to call a system whereby such conformity is enforced democratic. Indeed, the only argument by which such a claim can be plausibly defended is that a class is so far removed in character from the individuals comprising it that will is an attribute, not of individuals, but of classes, and that to each class in society there corresponds a single, unified class-will. Opinions, of course, will in fact differ; but, in this view, the divergent opinions of individuals or of groups are mere utopianism or sectarianism, sharply distinguished from the collective will and doctrine belonging to the class as a whole. This collective doctrine is regarded as something in the possession of the bureaucrats as class-leaders; and even if they begin by seeking to act as interpreters of this class will, it is all too easy for them to slip over into mistaking their own will and interest for that of the class and thus ceasing to be interpreters and becoming dictators instead—dictators on behalf, no longer of the class, but of themselves. Nor is it unlikely that, having taken this step, they will follow it up with another by assigning to one man—the most powerful and authoritative among them—the task of proclaiming the collective will, provided that he constitutes himself the protector of their special interests as a bureaucracy.

This is clearly what took place in the Soviet Union in Stalin's later days, and had begun to happen from the moment when Stalin had cleared the rivals from his path and consolidated his ascendency over the Soviet Union bureaucracy of party officials. That this was so was implicitly, and in fact explicitly, recognized in Khruschev's furious attack on Stalin in 1956; but that attack stopped short at denunciation of the 'cult of personality' and did not go beyond recalling the Soviet Union to centralism of a more collective type, in which the tasks of leadership were shared among the members of a dominant group without any repudiation of centralism as such. It is true that the ending of Stalin's personal autocracy was a considerable gain; but is the dictatorship of a caucus really any more democratic than that of an individual? During the past years there has been, undoubtedly, some relaxation of the extreme rigidity of Stalin's reign of terror and also some attempt to apply measures of administrative decentralization; but, after a short period of relatively unfettered discussion, a halt was speedily called to the freer expression of divergent opinions, and the decentralization appears rather to have been devoted to strengthening the regional and local bureaucrats than to putting any real power into the hands of the main body of party members, who are still called upon to follow without question the policy leadership given them. I do not deny that there has been some relaxation of the discipline exercised in the name of the party over the individual citizens; but nothing, I think, has been done to touch the essentially bureaucratic conception of party leadership.

More has been done, no doubt, in Yugoslavia, especially during the period of acute tension between it and the Soviet Union. The decentralization of functions into the hands of Workers' Councils and People's Committees—the latter being the new organs of local government—has involved a real diminution in the functions and powers of the centre, and has given both the rank-and-file workers and the general body of citizen-producers an increased influence in economic matters. But one cannot help wondering how far this has gone in practice, or questioning whether there has been any corresponding diminution of authoritarian control in political matters. I, for one, simply do not know how in practice functions are divided between Workers' Councils, Managing Boards, and the individual establishment directors, or between all these and the superior planning and controlling authorities; and it is almost impossible to arrive, by study of the published documents, at any conclusive judgment on the matter. It seems, however, clear that, whatever decentralization of control may have been achieved in the economic field, politically the party oligarchy remains firmly entrenched.

However that may be—a question on which I feel compelled to defer judgment—the essential issue of one-party rule remains. The issue of free discussion and democratic participation is clearly bound up with that of 'one-party' rule. Now, the notion that there can be but a single party authorized to rule is based on the idea of class unity. There can be, it is said, but one dominant class, placing its impress on all essential social institutions; and therefore there can be but a single party, embodying the collective will of the dominant class. If differences of opinion exist in fact within the dominant class, this can be only because some individuals or groups are in error about the collective class interest and therefore put forward what are in fact sectarian points of view, and must accordingly be suppressed in order to prevent them from misrepresenting the class. Such dissidents cannot constitute a real party, because they do not represent a class: they are mere sectarians, seeking to substitute their individual or sectional opinions for the will of the class. There is no wrong, it is argued, in suppressing them, because, however much support they may elicit, they represent no real social force.

The plausibility of this argument rests on the double assumption that there is a single rightful class doctrine and that those who in fact control the party machine are in full possession of it. But surely either of these views may be mistaken. It is by no means self-evident that to the question, 'What is the class interest in such and such a matter?', there is only one possible correct answer. Surely there may be cases in which there is something to be said for and against two or more ways of dealing with the particular problem, and the pros and cons may be fairly evenly balanced. If so, the answer, wherever possible, should surely be sought in full discussion of the alternatives over the evident possible field, without the balance being tilted by any monopolization of the argument by the advocates of one solution as against another. Secondly, even where there is only one legitimate answer, the bureaucracy may be mistaken in supposing that it is in full possession of this answer, and that accordingly no discussion is called for. To maintain this is in effect to throw over democracy in favour of authoritarian bureaucracy; for the application of democratic methods might possibly record that the bureaucrats are in truth the sectarians advancing as class truth what is no more in reality than sectarian bureaucratic interest.

Finally, one either believes in democracy, or disbelieves in it, whether the democracy in question is that of a class or of the whole people. The essence of democracy, in either case, is the real and effective participation of all those concerned in the process of decision-making, from the stages in which the decision to be taken begins to be debated up to the point at which it is finally taken. In theory, the Communist philosophy accepts this, with the added corollary that the decision, when taken, becomes universally binding, even upon those who have thrown their weight against it while it was under debate. But in practice this cannot happen if decisions are made at the centre without prior and widely diffused debate, and critics are allowed no opportunity of expressing and organizing dissident opinions.

It is, moreover, a most dangerous error to suppose that uniform decisions are necessary on most questions. Even if there has to be a broad general framework of accepted doctrine, there is every reason for limiting it to as few matters as possible, and for encouraging diversity of experiment in other matters—for example, against subjecting the Ukraine or Arctic Russia to more than a very limited basic uniformity of institutions. I am, of course, aware that the Soviet Union is in form a federation, and that each Republic within it has its own partly autonomous institutions, whose range of competence has been to some extent widened recently. But with this must be considered the fact that the entire Soviet Union has a single Communist Party and that this party has largely taken over the functions of central government and substituted itself for the Soviets as the essential organ of guaranteed power. Indeed, the process of substitution goes still further; for the Communist Party of the Soviet Union, acting in these days directly and not, as previously, through a Comintern which it despotically controlled, claims the right to dictate policy to the Communist Parties in other countries and to ensure the compliance of their policies—and of their leaders—with its own. This would be much less harmful if the Communist Party of the Soviet Union was internally a democratic party, in which decisions were arrived at by free discussion among the whole body of members; but, as things are, it means that the controlling Russian bureaucracy dictates not only to critics of the Soviet Union but to a considerable extent to Communists throughout the world—subject of course to the possibility of those parties feeling strong enough—as in the case of China—to stand out against such dictation, or—as in the case of Poland—being driven to do so by the force of opinion pressing on them from within a country.

I do not wish, in this article, to enter in the dispute between those who conceive of democracy in terms of entire populations, irrespective of class, and those who think in terms of class democracy and claim the right to exclude from it those who are regarded as class enemies. Even if the latter view is preferred, and only class opinion needs to be taken into account, I claim that all such opinion ought to be counted, and not exclusively that of a particular 'vanguard' within the class. Even if a narrower view is taken, and consideration is given only to opinion within a class party, it must still extend to all sections of the party, and not exclusively to a 'vanguard' within the 'vanguard' composed of the party leadership alone. It must, moreover, take full account of both local and sectional variations of such opinion, and must refrain from imposing on the whole party an inflexible orthodoxy save in a very few matters in relation to which uniformity is really indispensable. Lenin himself was a highly authoritarian thinker, who did not mince his words in denouncing dissidents; but he did at any rate insist on a considerable amount of free party discussion and showed no vindictiveness in pursuing his critics, unless he felt them to have gone over irretrievably into the hostile camp—which he was, no doubt, in certain cases, too prone to do. I think Trotsky was right in holding that Lenin would have been horrified by the degeneration of party democracy that had taken place even before his death, and that advanced so swiftly after his removal, converting the dictatorship of the party as the vanguard of the proletariat into a dictatorship of officials over the party, over the proletariat, and over the whole Soviet Union and the Communist Parties outside it.

The contrast between the two conceptions of Socialism, centralist and federal, has, however, nothing to do with this degeneration. The Communist conception is, quite apart from it, definitely centralist, with the emphasis on unity and unification over large areas and on the advanced proletariat engaged in large-scale industry as the constructive force in the making of Socialism. The entire conception of the Federalists, of a society built up on the natural comradeship of the neighbourhood among small groups of fellow workers, is utterly alien to the spirit either of Communism or of Social Democracy, which alike envisage Socialism as a higher stage of economic development resting on the most advanced techniques of large-scale production. As against this, Peter Kropotkin used to argue that large-scale production was by no means necessarily the most efficient, and that in particular the advent of electrical power could provide the opportunity for a scattering of industrial operations over country districts and for a return to small-scale production using the most advanced techniques and thus defeating the mass producers at their own game. Admittedly, there is not yet much sign of this in the advanced countries; but we are at any rate beginning to see that it is highly relevant to the problems of such countries as India, where manpower is superabundant and capital very scarce in relation to it; and I think it may also be highly relevant to areas such as Southern Italy, in which somewhat similar situations exist, and also to the problems of peasant economics in many countries. Proletarian Socialism, finding its support among the workers in big, mechanized establishments, has always been instinctively unfriendly to peasants, even when it has sought to use them as allies, because it has regarded peasant agriculture as an obsolescent method of production; whereas it may not be so, given both full use of co-operative methods in purchasing, marketing, and the supply of credit and also full access to electrical power and modern machinery for its day-to-day operations.

Similarly, ever since Marx predicted the impending disappearance of the 'artisans', the craftsmen engaged in small-scale production, who, he held, were destined to be flung down into the rocks of the proletariat, proletarian Socialists have been scornful of these artisans and have refused to recognize them as full proletarians in their own right. They have been regarded rather as petit bourgeois, or at any rate as sharing in the petit bourgeois attitude to social questions. Yet it is undoubtedly true that the artisans have contributed largely to the development of Socialist ideas—especially to those forms of Socialism in which a high value is put on personal and small group liberties and to the wide diffusion of power and responsibility in a free Socialist society. From the days of the Paris artisans and of the Swiss watchmakers of the Jura Federation, the artisans have been among the foremost advocates of a libertarian Socialism hostile to the mass Socialism of the Marxists, and have contracted many battles with them. Until quite recently, despite the persistence of relatively small-scale enterprise, such libertarians have appeared to be working against the grain of technological development, which has fostered the growth of mass production and concentrated a growing proportion of the workers in large establishments for the performance, in the main, of repetitive machine-tending operations. But today the trend seems much less certain. Mass production will no doubt continue to involve more and more branches of production; but will it continue to involve the aggregation of great masses of relatively unskilled labour? Broadly, the trend has been hitherto towards such aggregation; but the tendency now seems to be to get rid of much of the machine-tending labour, which is to be replaced by automatic devices calling out for much less numerous bodies of relatively skilled supervisors. So, even if the establishments continue to grow larger, it no longer follows that the labour force will grow larger with them. We may be facing a situation in which, at any rate in the most advanced countries, a much larger mass of capital will be needed to set each productive worker to work and such workers will come to be actually employed in considerably smaller groups, especially where the most advanced techniques are introduced. If this comes about, will there not be a return to a situation more closely akin to that of artisan production, with each individual playing again a more responsible part in the work? I remember that the first of the great Anarchist philosophers, William Godwin, in his dislike of the tendency towards mass production, looked forward to a day when the most advanced instruments would be operated by single workers, with the aid of great reserves of mechanical power. This at any rate looks much less unlikely today than it did while technical progress was turning the aggregation of workers into bigger and bigger productive groups, while undermining for most of them the distinctiveness of their individual operations and reducing each of them to a mere unit in a larger and larger mass. Marxism as a centralist doctrine grew up while this tendency was everywhere gaining force in the advanced countries: we may be on the eve of a period during which it will be revised, not in respect of the scale of the operations themselves, but in that of the type of employment involved.

If this is the case, may we not expect it to be accompanied by a change in the nature of Socialist ideas—by a reversion to stress upon the smaller human unit and to the distinctiveness of its contribution, and therewith to a reassertion of the claims to participate effectively in control by these relatively small groups of distinctive contributors to productive service? I think so; and I think I see already signs of it in a revival of the demand for 'workers' control' exercised by workers on the job in their several establishments as against control by the entire working class envisaged as an undifferentiated mass of human labour. I am not suggesting that there is not a need for control in both forms, or that those employed in a particular establishment can claim a right to operate it as they please, without regard for wider social needs. What I am suggesting is that if all, or nearly all, the emphasis is put on collective control by the whole mass, and none, or hardly any, on diffused control on the particular job, the vital question of personal and small-group liberty is in danger of being overlooked, and what is likely to result is a formal mass democracy which will degenerate in fact into bureaucracy. I am indeed suggesting that precisely this degeneration has tended to come about in the operation of industries both under Communism and under Social Democracy, which have both made the mistake of confusing high technical development with the aggregation of the producers into larger and more homogenous masses of routine workers.

I do not, of course, profess to know how far or fast automation will advance, either in the most advanced areas of production or elsewhere. But Socialists, who profess to stand for something superior in its productive efficiency to even the most advanced capitalism, are clearly called upon to think ahead of the trends of capitalist production and should be on their guard against basing their plans on an assumption that the trends of the past will be continued indefinitely, or they may find themselves laying plans for carrying further trends which are already becoming technically obsolete.

I feel no doubt that, in the case under discussion, a reversal of past trends is ardently to be desired by Socialists who value the quality of life as well as the mass of commodities made available to the whole body of consumers. As long as sheer poverty exists in the world, it is impossible for Socialists not to be in favour of increased production; for Socialist aspirations cannot be fully realized while there is still a scramble for scarce means of living. But it is surely much to be desired that the highest practicable production shall come to be consistent with the liberation of mankind from the sheer burden of uninteresting repetitive routine labour and that the mass of mankind shall come to enjoy both greater leisure and more interesting employment, which they will be more and more able to regard, not as unavoidable drudgery, but as an opportunity for creative self-expression. To be sure, if automation brings about under capitalism a sharp decline in the demand for labour it will become a still more urgent task to achieve its supervision by an economic system based on a fairer allocation of the fruits of productive effort, as the only way of averting a relapse into large-scale unemployment. But no one, except some capitalists and sheer reactionaries, wants to re-establish a permanent 'reserve of labour' in order to keep the employed workers from asserting their claims; and Socialists need anticipate no difficulty in meeting a fall in the demand for labour on account of automation by reduction of the working day to a required extent. What I want to see is steady pressure from the trade unions for such reduction, accompanied by increasing claims for a share in control 'on the job' and by measures designed to prevent the sacking of workers alleged to be redundant without the offer of suitable alternative jobs and, where needed, adequate training for them.

In short, I hope and believe that the time is coming when the libertarian tendencies in Socialism will be enabled to reassert themselves with growing strength, and when the bureaucratic tendencies will be correspondingly weakened. I am not a Syndicalist; but I believe none the less that Syndicalism had hold of an important element of the truth which has been grossly underrated by the politicians of Communism and of Social Democracy alike, as shown in the Marxian emphasis on the virtues of large-scale production and in the belief that it involves the progressive disappearance of individuality from the productive process and the increasing resolution of the working class into an undifferentiated mass of what Marx called 'abstract human labour'. As against this, I believe that the individual and the small working group count for a great deal in terms of sheer productive efficiency and also in determining the satisfying quality of work, which occupies necessarily so large a part of the lives of men—even if it can come to occupy them less as the curse of poverty is progressively conquered by technological improvement. Socialists, far from being able to ignore the importance of productive techniques must always endeavour to be well ahead of the capitalists in interpreting them; and my suggestion is that, for the most part, they are no longer interpreting them aright.

INDEX

Broadley, Rosamund, 28
Building Guilds (Germany), 117. *See also*
　Guild Socialism
bureaucracy: and centralism, 282, 283–85;
　Cole on, 18–19, 20, 22–23, 26; and
　Fabianism, 232–34; and public owner-
　ship, 70; and socialism, 79, 117, 265;
　and syndicalism, 115; and trade unions,
　153
Burma, 102, 104, 196
Burns, John, 110
Butler Act (1944), 190–91
Butler, R.A., 190

Cabet, Étienne, 155
Canada, 172, 196
capitalism: and automation, 289–90; and
　centralism, 25; and class stratification,
　73; and communism, 102–3, 171; and
　democracy, 62–63, 124; and direct
　action, 110–11; and education, 132,
　145; and Fabianism, 180, 181; and fear,
　incentive of, 76–77; and full employ-
　ment, 269; and international affairs,
　104; Lenin on, 168; and Marxism, 93,
　94, 109, 160–61, 170, 172, 248–50;
　Morris on, 248–50, 251, 257; and
　nationalization, 99; and new unionism,
　179; and production, 153, 275–76;
　in Russia, 167, 169; and social dem-
　ocracy, 172, 174, 280; and socialism,
　92–93, 105, 115–16, 125, 126, 128,
　227, 280–81; and socialization, 66; and
　trade unions, 152; in United States, 86;
　and utopian socialism, 157–58; and
　war, 111–12, 181–82; Webb on, 13;
　and Welfare State, 238
Carlyle, Thomas, 237
Carpenter, L.P., 12
Central Electricity Board, 21, 83, 99, 266
centralism and centralization: and bureau-
　cracy, 22, 265–66; Cole on, 24, 26;
　and democracy, 270–73; democratic,
　118, 168, 241–45, 255, 258, 267,
　282–83; and libertarianism, 279–90;
　and Marxism, 118, 168; and socialism,

24, 25, 265, 271, 275–78, 279–90; and
　Soviet Union, 127; and trade unions,
　20, 153, 154
A Century of Co-operation (Cole), 20
Chamberlain, Joseph, 138
Chaos and Order in Industry (Cole), 7
Chapelier, law of (France, 1791), 34
character, 129, 133–34, 143, 156–57
Chartism, 135, 161
Chesterton, G.K., 10
China, 103, 127, 128, 171, 286
Christianity, 134–35. *See also* religion
Churchill Coalition, 101
Civil War (USA), 86
Clarion, 91
Clay, Sir Henry, 18
class: and communism, 85–86, 171–72;
　and democracy, 166; and education,
　129–30, 133, 138, 140–41, 142,
　147–49, 190–91, 219; and incomes,
　217–18; and international affairs, 170;
　and Labour Party, 9, 101, 184; and
　libertarianism, 281–82; and liberty vs.
　order, 81–82, 83, 87; and Marxism,
　159–60; and nationalism, 173; and
　one-party rule, 285; and parliamentary
　action, 182; and religion, 183; and so-
　cialism, 73, 85–86, 111–12, 172, 174,
　205–9, 210–11; and taxation, 191; and
　titles of prestige, 218–19; and utopian
　socialism, 157–58; and Welfare State,
　205, 211–12, 238
coercion, 12, 16, 17, 133, 248, 250, 255,
　269, 280
Cold War, 102, 197
Cole, G.D.H.: and anarchism, 16–17,
　24, 27; on centralism, democratic,
　241–45; on centralization, 24, 275–78,
　279–90; death of, 28; on democracy,
　7–8, 19–20, 61–67, 64, 67, 261–73;
　on education, 129–50; election ad-
　dress, 69–71; on Fabianism, 231–36;
　and Guild Socialism, 5, 13–14, 25;
　and ILP, 11–12; on labour movement,
　British, 89–106; and Labour Party, 12,
　18; on Labour Party, 177–85, 187–98;

libertarianism of, 18; on liberty vs. order, 81–88; life and education of, 5–7; on loyalties, 47–59; on Morris, 247–59; on nationalization, 21–22; and New Left, 22–23; publications and work of, 7, 9–10, 11, 15, 17, 23–24, 27–29; on socialism, 11, 73–79, 107–28, 155–75, 199–229, 261–73; socialism of, 3–4, 6, 11, 12–13, 18, 23, 25, 26–27, 70, 90–92, 184–85; on socialization, 12, 21; on social obligations, conflicting, 31–46; theoretical influences, 8, 24–25, 27; on trade unions, 151–54; Webb on, 14–15; on Welfare State, 22n46, 23, 237–40

Cole, Margaret, 9–10, 16, 18, 29, 235

collaboration, 224, 226. See also workers' control

collective bargaining, 94, 178, 179, 193, 194, 226, 228. See also trade unions

collectivism, 14, 95, 139, 232, 280. See also centralism and centralization

colonialism, 171, 196–97

common ownership. See ownership, public

communism: and centralism, 258, 280, 281–82, 283, 287, 289; and Cole, 26, 74; and democracy, 286; and education, 140, 146; future prospects of, 171–72; in Germany, 118; and Guild Socialism, 117; and hugeness, 271; international context, 103–4, 120–24, 126–28, 154, 169–70; and Labour Party, 97–98, 100–101, 197; and liberty, 81–82, 83, 85; Morris on, 255–56; and nationalism, 173; in Russia, 167, 169; and socialism, 11, 102, 127, 171, 172, 174; and workers' control, 267

Communist Manifesto (Marx and Engels), 112, 122, 155, 161, 171

Communist Party of Great Britain, 10, 100, 140, 184, 241, 242–43

Communist Party of the Soviet Union, 95, 123–24, 168, 255, 286

community, 19–20, 31–32, 35, 41, 51, 172, 270–71, 281

comprehensive schools, 142, 144, 146–47, 149, 191, 219, 228, 263. See also education

Condorcet, Marquis de, 159

Confédération Générale du Travail (CGT), 110–11

conformity, 86, 165, 283. See also centralism and centralization

congresses, 242–44

Connolly, James, 116

Conservative Party (Great Britain): and Beveridge Report, 189; and Labour Party, 96, 98, 99, 114, 187–88; and nationalization, 83; and religion, 183; and socialism, 182; and trade unions, 151

consultation, joint, 21, 76, 154, 193, 221, 222, 266

co-operative movements: and centralization, 270; and Cole, 19, 20, 23; and Fabianism, 180, 181; and inheritance, 225; international, 164; and Owen, 133–34, 143, 158; and religion, 183; and socialism, 75, 146, 156; and titles of prestige, 218, 227

craftsmanship, 249–54, 259, 275–76, 288

Cripps, Stafford, 100, 195

Crosland, Tony, 27

culture, 143, 148. See also education

curriculum, 136, 137–38, 141, 143, 144, 149. See also education

Czechoslovakia, 102, 103

Dalton, Hugh, 195

decentralization, 10, 25, 279, 284–85. See also centralism and centralization

Dedijer, Vladimir, 3–4

de Jouvenel, Bertrand, 19

De Leon, Daniel, 114

democracy: and centralism, 24, 243–44, 270–73, 282–83, 285–87, 289; Cole on, 19–20, 61–67; and education, 144; functional, 7–8, 13, 26, 44, 74, 281; industrial, 11, 21, 43, 193, 221–22, 266–70; and liberty, 204; and localism, 281; meaning of, 124, 153, 285–86; and parliament, 267; and socialism, 61–62, 74, 125, 166–67, 169, 261–73;

70, 99, 192; and parliamentarianism, 9, 95, 178, 182, 184, 198; reorganization of (1918), 96–97; and socialism, 97, 101–2, 126, 170, 177–85, 197–99, 202, 227–28, 238; and titles of prestige, 218–19; and trade unions, 100, 107, 151–53, 177–78, 182, 184, 192–94, 203; and world wars, 101, 118, 119
Labour Representation Committee (LRC), 113–14, 179, 184
Labour Unrest, 93–94
Labriola, Antonio, 165
Lancaster, Joseph, 134
land, 70, 158, 167, 181, 192, 209, 211. See also inherited wealth
Lansbury, George, 100
Lansbury's Labour Weekly, 98
Larkin. James, 116
Laski, Harold, 3, 29
Lassalle, Ferdinand, 161, 163–64, 164
leadership, 78, 147–48, 244, 264, 270
Lenin and Leninism: and Bolshevism, 167–68; and communism, 140; and Marxism, 255; and social democracy vs. communism, 122, 125, 169, 172, 287; and socialism, 112–13, 119
liberalism: and communism, 170; and Labour Party, 93, 97, 99, 184; and personal liberty, 87; and religion, nonconformist, 165; and social democracy, 174; and socialism, 138; and trade unions, 178, 180
Liberal Party (Great Britain): and Labour Party, 90, 92, 96, 114–15, 187–88; and religion, nonconformist, 165, 183; and socialism, 138; and trade unions, 113, 178
libertarianism: and American politics, 86, 87; and centralism, 24, 271, 279–90; and Cole, 16, 18, 25, 70; and Guild Socialism, 95, 139; and Labour Party, 9, 99; and production, 288; and socialism, 27, 155–56
liberty, personal, 73, 77, 78, 81–88, 204
Liebknecht, Karl, 118
Liebknecht, Wilhelm, 161

Litvinov, Maxim, 123
Lloyd George, David, 92, 95, 97, 115, 119
Local and Regional Government (Cole), 20
localism, 281, 287. *See also* centralism and centralization
Locke, John, 35, 48
London Passenger Transport Board, 21, 83
Longuet, Jean, 118
Looking Backward (Bellamy), 248
Lovett, William, 135
Lowenfeld, Margaret, 28
loyalties, 47–59
Luxemburg, Rosa, 112–13, 118

MacDonald, Ramsay, 12, 37, 95, 96, 97, 98–99, 118
MacDougall, William, 50
MacIver, R.M., 52
Maeztu, Ramiro de, 5
Maitland, F.W., 8, 52
Malaya, 197
Mann, Tom, 94
Mansbridge, Albert, 132
Marshall Aid, 196, 197
Martin, Kingsley, 10
Marx and Marxism: and Bolshevism, 112, 121; and capitalism, 93, 94, 109, 160–61, 170, 172, 248–50; and centralism, 118, 280–81, 282, 288–89; and Cole, 24, 48; and democracy, 124–25, 166; and dictatorship of proletariat, 166, 168, 248, 255, 280; and education, 129–31, 132–33, 135, 139, 140; and Fabianism, 181; and gradualism, 166; international context, 170; and Labour Party, 165, 177, 178, 182; and loyalties, conflicting, 58; and Morris, 248, 255, 257, 258; and nationalism, 173; and Paris Commune, 162; and production, 275, 276, 280, 288, 290; and religion, 183; in Russia, 167–69; and Social Democrats, 108, 112, 163–65; and socialism, 170, 179; and socialism, scientific, 155–56, 158–61
materialism, 128, 159, 163, 165, 183–84
Maurice, F.D., 134

4; and religion, 183; and social democracy, 266; and socialism, 113–14, 116, 127, 162, 214; and Syndicalism, 164; Tawney on, 9; and wage restraint, 195; and workers' control, 116, 153, 194, 221–22, 224, 226, 228
Trotsky, Leon, 122, 287
Turati, Filippo,165
Turgot, Jacques, 159

unemployment, 12, 82, 98, 99, 125, 178, 190, 195
United Nations, 189, 197
United States: and communism, 128, 169, 171–72; and exports and imports, 223–24; and industrial unionism, 115–16, 117; and international affairs, 102–3, 104, 128, 141, 154; and Labour Party, 196, 197; and personal liberty, 86, 87–88; production in, 277; and socialism, 76, 102–3, 127, 171, 172; and trade unions, 126; and unemployment, 82
utilitarianism, 138, 180–81, 184
utopian socialism, 90, 130, 155–57, 159–61, 166, 175, 256, 257

Veblen, Thorstein, 48
vocation, 143, 146, 148, 264. *See also* education
Die Vorausetzungen des Sozialismus (Bernstein), 109. *See also* gradualism
Voyage en Icarie (Cabet), 155
Vrooman, Walter, 132

wages, 181, 190, 195, 206–7, 214, 218, 237, 278
Wallas, Graham, 50, 53, 53n2
Ward, Colin, 3–4, 28
Webb, Beatrice: and anarchists vs. bureaucrats, 23, 232; and Cole, 13, 14, 27; collectivism of, 139; and Guild Socialism, 95; and socialism, 248; on Soviet communism, 123–24, 127; and Welfare State, 184
Webb, Sidney: Cole on, 27; collectivism of, 139; and education, 137–38; and

Fabianism, 232; and Guild Socialism, 95; and Labour Party, 97, 113, 119; and socialism, 179–80, 248; on Soviet communism, 123–24, 127; and Welfare State, 184
Welfare State: achievements of, 209–10; and bureaucracy, 233, 234; and Cole, 22n46; Fabians on, 181; in France, 170; future of, 214; and gradualism, 166; and Labour Party, 104, 125, 182, 184, 201, 228; and Social Democrats, 122; and socialism, 23, 126–28, 180, 199, 204, 211–12, 215, 237–40
Wells, H.G., 14, 149
Whitman, Walt, 49
Wicksteed, Philip, 181
will, general, 31–35, 37–39, 42, 44–46, 48–53, 59
Wilson, Harold, 3, 28
workers' control: and centralism, 289; and Cole, 21, 23; difficulties of, 267–69; and Guild Socialism, 11, 13, 94–96, 117; and labour movement, 193–94; and Labour Party, 99; and Russian Revolution, 95–96; and socialism, 228; and syndicalism, 7; and trade unions, 116, 153, 194, 221–22, 224, 226, 228
Workers' Educational Association (WEA), 10, 91, 131–33, 136
working-class movements: and automation, 277–78; and British socialism, 178–79; and education, 132, 136; international context, 111, 120–21; and Labour Party, 228; and religion, 165; and socialism, 161, 163, 238
The World of Labour (Cole), 7
World War I, 9, 26, 86, 90, 95, 113, 118–19, 181
World War II, 19, 70, 82, 86, 101, 169, 189
Wright, Tony (Anthony W.), 25, 29

Yugoslavia, 127, 185, 237, 279, 284

AK PRESS is small, in terms of staff and resources, but we also manage to be one of the world's most productive anarchist publishing houses. We publish close to twenty books every year, and distribute thousands of other titles published by like-minded independent presses and projects from around the globe. We're entirely worker run and democratically managed. We operate without a corporate structure—no boss, no managers, no bullshit.

The **FRIENDS OF AK PRESS** program is a way you can directly contribute to the continued existence of AK Press, and ensure that we're able to keep publishing books like this one! Friends pay $25 a month directly into our publishing account ($30 for Canada, $35 for international), and receive a copy of every book AK Press publishes for the duration of their membership! Friends also receive a discount on anything they order from our website or buy at a table: 50% on AK titles, and 30% on everything else. We have a Friends of AK ebook program as well: $15 a month gets you an electronic copy of every book we publish for the duration of your membership. *You can even sponsor a very discounted membership for someone in prison.*

Email **friendsofak@akpress.org** for more info, or visit the website: **https://www.akpress.org/friends.html**.

There are always great book projects in the works—so sign up now to become a Friend of AK Press, and let the presses roll!